Fundamentals of Sentencing Theory

Essays in Honour of Andrew von Hirsch

Edited by

ANDREW ASHWORTH
MARTIN WASIK

CLARENDON PRESS · OXFORD
1998

Oxford University Press, Great Clarendon Street, Oxford OX2 6DP
Oxford New York
Athens Auckland Bangkok Bogota Bombay Buenos Aires
Calcutta Cape Town Dar es Salaam Delhi Florence Hong Kong Istanbul
Karachi Kuala Lumpur Madras Madrid Melbourne Mexico City
Nairobi Paris Singapore Taipei Tokyo Toronto Warsaw
and associated companies in
Berlin Ibadan

Oxford is a registered trade mark of Oxford University Press

Published in the United States
by Oxford University Press Inc., New York

British Library Cataloguing in Publication Data
Data available

Library of Congress Cataloging in Publication Data
Data available

ISBN 0–19–826256–6

1 3 5 7 9 10 8 6 4 2

Typeset by Jayvee, Trivandrum, India
Printed in Great Britain
on acid-free paper by
Biddles Ltd., Guildford and King's Lynn

Contents

Part III: Relating Theory to Contemporary Punishment Practice

Notes on Contributors

ANDREW ASHWORTH is Vinerian Professor of English Law, University of Oxford

ANTHONY BOTTOMS is Wolfson Professor of Criminology and Director of the Institute of Criminology, University of Cambridge

R. A. DUFF is Professor of Philosophy at the University of Stirling

JOHN GARDNER is Reader in Legal Philosophy, King's College London

DAVID GARLAND is Professor at New York University

BARBARA A. HUDSON is Professor of Criminology and Penology, University of Northumbria

DOUGLAS A. HUSAK is Professor of Philosophy, Rutgers University

NILS JAREBORG is Professor of Criminal Law, Uppsala University

JOHN KLEINIG is Professor of Philosophy at John Jay College, New York

NEIL MacCORMICK is Regius Professor of Public Law, University of Edinburgh

ELAINE PLAYER is Reader in Criminology and Criminal Justice, King's College London

MARTIN WASIK is Professor of Law, University of Manchester

LUCIA ZEDNER is Fellow and Tutor in Law, Corpus Christi College, University of Oxford

General Editor's Introduction

This is the second volume in the series to take the form of a themed set of essays. Its contributors endeavour to carry forward the debate on a number of fundamental issues in sentencing theory, from the role of the State and of victims through to the approach to young offenders and the problem of discriminatory sentencing, thus retaining a close link with contemporary issues in sentencing policy and practice. This collection has been put together in honour of Andrew von Hirsch, who has played and continues to play a leading role in the revival and reorientation of sentencing theory, and whose monograph *Censure and Sanctions* is a prominent title in this series.

Andrew Ashworth

Editors' Introduction

Our purpose in presenting this collection of essays is to celebrate the influence of Andrew von Hirsch on contemporary sentencing theory by stimulating further exploration of fundamental issues by leading scholars whose work is in broad sympathy with his approach.

In 1976 Andrew von Hirsch's book *Doing Justice* quickly became the leading exposition of the 'just deserts' approach to sentencing. In the two decades since then, von Hirsch has developed, reconsidered and refined desert theory both at a philosophical level and in terms of practical sentencing policy. In two further books, *Past or Future Crimes* (1985) and *Censure and Sanctions* (1993), and in a whole host of articles, he has re-examined the justifications for taking account of previous convictions in sentencing,[1] has elaborated the distinction between ordinal and cardinal proportionality,[2] has re-worked the foundations of desert theory so as to discard the 'unfair advantage' rationale in favour of justifications for censure and hard treatment,[3] has attempted (with Nils Jareborg) to develop a scheme of ordinal proportionality for victimizing crimes,[4] has demonstrated (with Martin Wasik and Judith Greene) how non-custodial penalties can be made compatible with desert theory,[5] and so forth. There have also been significant contributions to criminal law theory, but we focus here on sentencing.

Andrew von Hirsch has also been influential in the development of sentencing policy. He has advised several of the sentencing commissions in the USA, although he has never identified himself with the sentencing guideline movement as such. Instead, his chief concerns are proportionate sentencing and parsimony in penalty levels. His writings on the Swedish sentencing reforms of 1988[6] helped to cement his influence over policy in England and Wales, and the Home Office's White Paper of 1990 bears out this and the influence of his work on non-custodial sanctions.[7] The Criminal Justice Act 1991 is the clearest endorsement of the general principle of proportionality, in terms of selecting both the form and the duration of sentence. Under the Act, sentencers are required to justify their sentence in terms of the relative seriousness of the offence—is the offence 'serious

---

[1] e.g. 'Desert and Previous Convictions in Sentencing', (1981) 65 *Minnesota L. R.* 591, and 'Criminal Record Rides Again', (1991) 10 *Criminal Justice Ethics* 55.

[2] e.g. 'Equality, "Anisonomy" and Justice', (1984) 82 *Michigan L. R.* 1093.

[3] See 'Proportionality in the Philosophy of Punishment', in M. Tonry (ed.), *Crime and Justice: an Annual Review* (1992), p. 55.

[4] 'Gauging Criminal Harm: a Living-Standard Analysis', (1991) 11 *Oxford J.L.S.* 1.

[5] 'Punishment in the Community and the Principles of Desert', (1989) 21 *Rutgers L.J.* 595.

[6] See 'Principles for Choosing Sanctions: Sweden's Proposed Sentencing Statute', (1987) 13 *New England Journal on Criminal and Civil Confinement* 2; 'Guiding Principles for Sentencing: the Proposed Swedish Law', [1987] *Crim.L.R.* 746; and (with Nils Jareborg) 'Sweden's Sentencing Statute Enacted', [1989] *Crim.L.R.* 275.

[7] Home Office, *Crime, Justice and Protecting the Public* (1990).

enough' for a community sentence, or is it 'so serious' that only a custodial sentence can be justified? The only significant exception to this was the power of sentencers to pass 'longer than normal' sentences on the basis of public protection from those convicted of violent or sexual crimes. Legislative changes since the 1991 Act have watered down a number of its key provisions. In particular, the introduction of a statutory scheme of unit fines was regrettably abandoned only a few months after its implementation; and section 29 of the Act (on the relevance of previous convictions to offence seriousness) was also repealed in 1993 and replaced by a more loosely-worded provision.[8] Many sentencers were hostile to the 1991 Act and, predictably perhaps, the Court of Appeal has failed to fulfil the role, assigned to it in the White Paper, of developing comprehensive offence guidelines around the basic philosophy of the Act. Instead, the Court has chosen to assert the continuing importance of deterrence when fixing sentence levels and, in a series of decisions, has set the custody threshold at a level almost certainly lower than it had been before the Act.[9] Unsurprisingly, an initial downturn in the prison population soon after the implementation of the 1991 Act has given way to a rapid escalation in the use of imprisonment to unprecedented levels.

The penological climate in England in the 1990s has been one of increasing punitiveness. Although it has sometimes been suggested that the 'just deserts' philosophy has simply been hijacked by the political right, the tide of 'law and order' policies developed through the mid-1990s has been swept onward not by considerations of proportionality but by the increasing use of incarceration for social protection and deterrence, epitomized by the former Home Secretary's frequent assertion that 'prison works'. There has been no great difference between the two major political parties in respect of penal policy: politicians from both sides have been striving to outdo one another in the rhetoric of being 'tough on crime', and in doing so they have probably contributed (with the media) to 'talking up' the use of imprisonment. The Criminal Justice and Public Order Act 1994 increased the courts' powers to give custodial sentences to young offenders, in particular extending the power to impose long-term detention on juveniles as young as 10. By contrast with the philosophy of the 1991 Act, both major political parties have stressed the need for sharply escalating sentences for repeat offenders, sometimes termed 'progression in sentencing'. The Crime (Sentences) Act 1997, a central part of the Conservative Government's policy which was passed with minimal opposition from Labour, introduces one mandatory minimum sentence (subject to a finding of 'exceptional circumstances') and two presumptive minimum sentences for a range of repeat serious offenders. The Labour Government has implemented two of the three minimum sentence provisions, and appears to have held back on minimum sentences for third-time burglars for

---

[8] cf. M. Wasik and A. von Hirsch, 'Section 29 Revised: Previous Convictions in Sentencing', [1994] *Crim.LR* 409.

[9] See A. Ashworth and A. von Hirsch, 'Recognising Elephants: the Problem of the Custody Threshold', [1997] *Crim.LR* 187.

lack of prison places rather than on any ground of principle. Throughout this period of greater repression, Andrew von Hirsch has continued to deploy his principled approach in arguing against such escalation of punishments.

THE ESSAYS

The contributions to this volume seek to carry forward sentencing theory, building on the enrichment of theory which Andrew von Hirsch's work has inspired. The volume presents eleven essays, grouped loosely into three sections. In the first section come three essays on the moral, political, and constitutional foundations of the power to punish. Neil MacCormick and David Garland explore, in the manner of a dialogue, the basis of the right to punish. They recognize the argument that civil society requires, if only for the pragmatic reason of preserving a degree of order, that powers to adjudicate and to punish should not be put into the hands of the victims of crime. MacCormick develops this into an argument for the State to assume these functions, whereas in his part of the dialogue Garland suggests that there may be other groups in society which have a strong claim to exercise these functions. While liberal theorists have focused on principles for restraining the excesses of (State) power, they provide little in the way of guidance on the development of criminal justice policies and agencies which draw other social groupings into the structure of authority.

From a different point of view, John Gardner also addresses the question of the roles of the State and the victim in sentencing. He examines punishment's function of displacing private retaliation, and goes on to analyse the roles of proportionality and due process at the sentencing stage. Linking the philosophical with the political, Gardner points to the danger to social stability of embracing populist approaches to sentencing. He concludes that, although greater attention ought to be given to support and services for victims of crime, it is wrong in principle to allow victims to have determinative power over sentencing.

The third essay, by Anthony Bottoms, both concludes the first part of the book and points the way to the second. Bottoms sets out to propose refinements of proportionate sentencing theory by re-examining the notion of fairness in several of its manifestations. The centrepiece of his argument is that the justification for State punishment must lay greater emphasis on establishing the legitimacy of the criminal justice system. Hand in hand with this goes a need to attend to the symbolic aspects of sentencing, especially in terms of the communication of censure. Bottoms focuses on five 'puzzles' in Andrew von Hirsch's desert theory. The first concerns the problem of matching a penalty scale to a scale of offence-seriousness. The second raises the question of proportionality of sentence and multiple offences, also discussed by Jareborg (see below). The third puzzle concerns the nature and place of the probation order. The fourth goes down to the basic structure of desert theory, reconsidering the roles of censure and prevention. And the fifth takes that discussion into the realms of practical sentencing policies and choices. Through his proposed reconceptualization of these questions, Bottoms argues, proportionality theory would be both more secure in its social and philosophical foundations and better able to link closely with daily penal practice on a range of issues.

The essays in the second part of the book are concerned with the application of sentencing theory in particular problem situations. The first of these is Martin Wasik's contribution on the offender-victim relationship, and its relevance to crime-seriousness. He argues that while the susceptibility of the particular victim to the crime is normally a matter of detailed aggravation or mitigation of sentence, and need not form part of general desert theory, there are certain important distinctions to be made among victims as a class. Desert theory ought to address cases such as the specially targeted victim, the vulnerable victim, and victims who may be said to have contributed to the offence through their own fault. He concludes that these are cases in which the offender-victim relationship impinges significantly on assessments of harm and culpability, and so they should receive greater attention in the translation of desert principles into sentencing practice.

Next, the neglected and awkward topic of sentencing for multiple offences is tackled by Nils Jareborg. How can principles of proportionality accommodate the sentencing of an offender for several offences? After a review of practices and their supposed justifications in three European countries, Jareborg explores the interaction between ordinal proportionality and the principle of parsimony in punishment, arguing that in respect of multiple offences the principle of parsimony should have the upper hand.

Antony Duff examines the complex and controversial justifications for the long-term incapacitation of offenders whose records display a pattern of persistent offending in violent or sexual crime. After an analysis of what is entailed by the concept of criminal dangerousness, showing that dangerousness is an assessment of an offender's present condition rather than merely a prediction of future conduct, he argues that it may be possible to reconcile the demands of retributive justice with those of crime prevention in a very limited class of cases. While maintaining that existing 'three strikes' laws are far too loose in their application, Duff draws an analogy with licensing and disqualification provisions to argue that a small number of dangerous and persistent offenders display such utter and continuing disregard for community values that there is a presumptive justification for their permanent exclusion from that community.

Lucia Zedner enquires into a sphere of sentencing which has often tended to be treated as separate and as calling for a different set of principles—young offenders. It is one thing to establish the non-responsibility of the very young; it is quite another to decide how the State should respond to offences committed in the years of transition between childhood and 'full' adulthood. Approaches based on a welfare ideology or on 'justice' are subjected to critical scrutiny, as is the contemporary call for increased parental liability for the offences of their offspring. Zedner concludes with a plea for a more sensitive and more differentiated approach to the problem of responding to young people's offending, an approach which might focus more on community involvement than on the State as such.

Douglas Husak confronts another pressing but relatively neglected problem of punishment theory: how to deal with offences of possessing drugs in the context of a proportional sentencing system. Placing his discussion in the context of contemporary American penal policy and the 'war on drugs', he shows that current sentencing levels for offences of drug possession cannot be justified on desert grounds. Husak analyses, and rejects, several possible arguments based upon harm and culpability offered by those who advocate high sentencing tariffs as a response to the drug problem. His conclusion is that the principle of proportionality may be invoked to show either that possession of drugs is not such a serious offence after all, or that the penalization of drug possession may be an unwarranted use of the criminal sanction in the first place.

The essays in the third section turn to some problems of relating justificatory theories to the realities of contemporary State punishment, in its actual form and in its social setting. Barbara Hudson focuses attention on the differential sentencing of women, and analyses the research evidence on discriminatory sentencing of offenders from ethnic minority groups. She unravels the various issues of principle raised by the sentencing of offenders from each of these groups. In particular, she constructs a poverty-based argument which points to recognition of economic duress as an important factor in sentencing, which would have practical implications for both black and female defendants. Her argument is for greater sensitivity to differences of situation among offenders, within a desert framework of sentencing.

Andrew Ashworth and Elaine Player also argue for greater sensitivity to differences of situation, but their focus is upon the interaction between prison conditions and sentencing policy. Ought a sentencing system to take account of prison conditions and variations in their harshness? Ought it to make allowances for the harsher impact of prison conditions on certain offenders? Their answers, broadly speaking, are that account should be taken and allowances made, for reasons of fairness. It is recognized that this proposal raises issues about the relationship between proportionality and equality of impact as fundamental principles of sentencing, and also about the pragmatic limits which should be placed on the complexity of sentencing calculations.

In the final essay in the volume John Kleinig looks into the issue of harsh treatment in prison conditions from another point of view. He asks what ethical considerations should determine or limit this harshness, and offers a structure of principles for assessing the appropriate hardness of hard treatment. He considers the standard of 'cruel and unusual punishment' and the extent to which incarceration can properly be regarded as 'inhumane' and 'degrading', but goes on to argue that prison policy should move beyond the avoidance of such practices to the fostering of appropriate social goals. He concludes that current prison environments commonly fail to achieve even basic humanitarian standards.

RE-ASSESSING THE FUNDAMENTALS

One of Andrew von Hirsch's great achievements has been to strengthen the connections between penal theory and penal practice. The contributors to this volume endeavour to point to directions in which this important task might be taken further. The essays are, of course, selective and not comprehensive: there is, for example, little discussion of the limitations on the role of sentencing as part of criminal justice and as an element in the machinery of social control, and there is no attempt to examine all the forms of sentence currently in use. But there are several major themes which emerge from the essays, and we draw three of them together here.

The first theme signals the necessary complexity of a working theory of sentencing. This is not to deny the value of general theories in the philosophy of punishment. The point is rather to indicate ways in which such general theories need to be developed, or supplemented, if they are to link fruitfully with the practicalities of sentencing. In this sense, theory must be responsive to the range of issues which a modern sentencing system has to confront—not merely the different criminal records of offenders, a topic which has attracted considerable attention, but also the problems of dealing with multiple offenders, young offenders, dangerous offenders, and mentally disordered offenders. Some of the essays suggest that central concepts of desert theory, such as harm and culpability, may need to be refined further in order to take account, for example, of offenders who target victims, of the harm caused to particularly vulnerable victims, and of questions about the culpability of young offenders and their parents. To attempt to apply a single general theory to the whole range of practical sentencing issues may result in a certain forcing and stretching: it is unlikely that a general theory, even if worked out in Benthamite detail, can supply guidance on all these issues without drawing upon other principles with other sources of justification. Re-casting the 'general justifying aim' may have its own merits, as Bottoms argues, but many of the other essays suggest that there are distinct principles of fairness and social justice which may need to be drawn into the circle.

These reflections lead into a second theme: how a sentencing theory should deal with questions of equality and difference raised by sentencing in the context of contemporary social values. These questions are perhaps most obvious in relation to sex differences and to ethnic minorities, but they are also raised by the varying impact which a given sentence may have on different offenders, and by the sentencing of young offenders. Is it sufficient to invoke the principle of equality before the law, or a principle of equal impact? Or are there persuasive arguments for going further—for example, by developing an approach to sentencing which attempts to compensate for the social or other disadvantages of certain groups, and yet to ensure that there is no clandestine or unintended increase in the severity of the resulting sanctions?

Thus to explore the social context of sentencing leads to the third theme: how is sentencing linked to the social and political structure and, in particular, by what authority and in whose name are sentences imposed? In recent times, and in the essays presented here, reconsideration of these questions has been prompted by increasing concern for victims of crime. The possible answers lead in various directions, and the claims of some form of community tribunal or family group conference must be considered (see Zedner, and MacCormick and Garland). The related issue of legitimacy, raised by Bottoms, also has several implications, including the compliance of penal measures such as imprisonment with basic humanitarian standards (see Kleinig, and Ashworth and Player). The question of who should be regarded as the addressees of sentencing also arises in this context: if censure is an essential element in sentencing, and granted the importance of ensuring that it is appropriately communicated, how can we preserve the essential message, and its close connection with proportionality, if other principles (such as equality of impact) are to have a determinative effect on sentencing?

Finally, in dedicating this collection of essays to Andrew von Hirsch, we record our admiration for the pathbreaking work that he has done and continues to do in the field of criminal justice and sentencing policy. The contributors to this volume all responded with great enthusiasm to the invitation to be involved in the project. We have been fortunate indeed to have Andrew as a colleague and friend.

Part I

Foundations of the Power to Punish

1

Sovereign States and Vengeful Victims: The Problem of the Right to Punish

NEIL MacCORMICK AND DAVID GARLAND*

'Revenge,' said Bacon, 'is a kind of wild justice'.[1] Is justice then no more than revenge tamed? Or, to put the question less figuratively, how does and should the criminal justice process relate to the sense of injury or grievance felt by those who are in one form or another victims of criminal misconduct? In what interest and for whose sake is punishment imposed by the State on convicted criminals? Is public justice to be considered as something set apart from the vindication of private right, or is it simply one form of process that human beings have devised for protecting the rights each of them has as an individual? These questions have a sharp contemporary point in view of the prominence given by the media nowadays both to the injuries suffered by victims, and to the demands of victims and their families for punishment stiff enough to assuage the sense of grievance or resentment they actually feel. No doubt this demand of victims for satisfaction is locally attuned to the penal conventions of a country's culture. In the USA only the death penalty will do, in the United Kingdom nothing less than life imprisonment, in the Netherlands, the victim demands a long sentence of 10 years . . . But amidst such local variations, the questions posed here have a resonance throughout 'Western' societies of the late twentieth century.

1. CRIMINAL JUSTICE AND PRIVATE REVENGE

In public rhetoric, in the media, and sometimes even in parliaments, judges and magistrates (or, in the USA, jurors) come under criticism for excessively lenient sentencing judged from the standpoint of the severity of a victim's suffering. The

---

* In this chapter, which is structured as a dialogue around an essay by Neil MacCormick, with an interpolated commentary by David Garland, Neil MacCormick's text is printed in roman typeface and David Garland's is in italics.

[1] Francis Bacon, 'Of Revenge', in J. Spedding, R. L. Ellis and D. D. Heath (eds.) *The Works of Francis Bacon* (New York: Garrett Press, 1968) vol. VII.

idea of permitting the individual victim to have a say in sentencing—which is what is being proposed by some parts of the victims movement, and is already present, at least indirectly, in the practice of providing victim impact statements to the court or to the prosecutor—opens up all sorts of problems about subject-ively experienced harms, as opposed to foreseeable and culpable injury.

Does it then capture something true and important about crime and punish-ment, or is it only a sign of troubled times when we read of the families of murder victims outside courthouses in Texas or California praying for the death penalty to be imposed by a jury on the murderer, or protesting in Scotland or England against leniency for criminals or the release on licence of lifers? The families of the 'Moors murders' victims have been and remain implacable in their demand for the incarceration of Myra Hindley for her whole natural life, and they are heeded by newspaper editors and Home Secretaries. Often the same media which portray the domestic situation straightforwardly in such cases report as something wild, strange, and exotic the proceedings of courts in, for example, Saudi Arabia, where in a case of premeditated murder the Shari'a law requires a sentence of death by beheading unless the victim's heirs seek clemency and accept money compensa-tion instead of calling for the full rigours of the law to be carried out. Is this the strange, even barbarous, practice of a culture set apart from us, a fragment of what we may be inclined to regard as an archaic world, or is it rather a variation upon more familiar themes? How does it compare, for example, with the judg-ment for damages awarded against O. J. Simpson to his late wife's family, in the context of their having been disappointed of a guilty verdict in the murder trial?

The historical record certainly suggests that the questions posed here have, in practice, been answered differently in different times and places. It may indeed be the case that there is something quite contemporary about the new (or rather renewed) prominence given to the victim's voice, and what this suggests is that the modern western division between 'public justice' and 'private right' is currently being redrawn, in minor but significant ways. The modern system of crime con-trol—centred upon a State-run criminal justice system which claims a monopoly of punitive powers and an authority to exercise these 'in the public interest'—seems to be unravelling in important respects. In particular, operational defin-itions of the 'public interest' seem to be changing. Whereas it was once accepted that this interest could be authoritatively defined from on high by criminal justice agencies—the police, the prosecution, the courts—a new, more dialogic, rela-tionship is now being forged between particular private interests and the collect-ive public interest, between individual and State, customer and provider.

The story of how this has come about is very interesting. At the most general level, it seems to be one aspect of a large-scale and widespread modernizing process. Contemporary public organizations, which enjoy the stability and legit-imacy conferred by the achievements of bureaucratic rationality, tend to become 'post-bureaucratic' in significant respects. With the help of new information technology, and recipes borrowed from the private sector, they become capable of more flexible, customized, responses to particularized demands, and of course, in the context of consumer society and functional democracy they find themselves under pressure to behave in precisely this manner. The attitude of (increasingly individualized) citizens to public institutions becomes more assertive, more demanding, and increasingly modelled upon the relation between customers and commercial organizations. The success of the 'welfare State', the growth of the middle class, and the spread of consumer capitalism mean that individuals have high expectations and individualized demands. It becomes increasingly difficult for public agencies to treat individuals en masse as undifferentiated 'cases' to be administered in standard ways that suit the organization. A more responsive, flexible, customer-oriented service is expected—the client's voice must be heard.

It therefore becomes increasingly unacceptable for 'the public interest', or even the routine practices of an organization affecting members of the public, to be determined from above, without consultation, without stakeholder involvement, without consumer research. The re-emergence of the victim as a distinct 'interest', as a voice to be listened to in criminal justice deliberations, is in part a consequence of this general trend—a trend which began to assert itself in the 1960s, at the height of a long post-War period of affluence, when the achievements of the welfare State began to be taken for granted and subjected to consumerist criticism. It is a shift in the balance of power between organizations and the individuals that they 'represent', and a remaking of 'the State' in a more responsive, accountable form.

But the revival of the victim's voice is also a consequence of a more specific set of developments that are peculiar to criminal justice. The penal policies that prevailed for most of the twentieth century denied much importance to the vindication of victim's rights or the expression of public resentment. The penal-welfare orthodoxies that dominated in the post-War years proposed a form of utilitarian justice that emphasized a non-punitive, correctional, response to offending. The victim's voice was silenced, the expression of vindictive sentiment became taboo (at least among criminal justice officials and liberal élites), and attention focused upon the individual offender and his or her prospects for reform. Current developments amount to a backlash against these, now discredited, policies. According to the now dominant political analysis, penal-welfarism and its criminal justice specialists failed to protect the public, and may even have facilitated the massive rise in crime rates that occurred in the decades during which these liberal policies prevailed. Social workers and correctional experts are increasingly discredited. They don't have the answers, aren't in touch with what the people want, and can't be trusted to manage the risks and dangers that criminals embody. The victim's interests are now to take priority over the offender's. The protection of the public is more important than the rights of offenders or their prospects for reform (as witness, for example, the new laws on notifying the community about the whereabouts of sex-offenders, or proposed restrictions on the availability of parole, home leave from prisons, and the like). The utilitarianism of correctional justice is increasingly replaced by a more expressive, punitive justice, and its ambitious, civilized aims are increasingly displaced by more a basic anxiety about safeguarding the public.

The rapid expansion of the private security industry that has occurred since the 1960s, and the increasing resort to crime prevention routines and technologies on the part of citizens, are, like the rise of expressive, punitive, populism and the obsession with protecting the public, responses to the perceived failure of the criminal justice State. These private responses are perhaps a more practical, adaptive reaction. Certainly they are less concerned with symbols and the venting of anger and resentment, and more concerned with effective measures for protecting property and providing security. The expansion of this private, civil society response to crime—led by the commercial sector, spreading to the general public and now recognized as necessary by the criminal justice authorities—has begun to undermine the monopoly claims of the criminal justice State and to downgrade the 'public' response to crime. The division between 'public justice' and 'private right' is being quietly redrawn. Punishment and crime control are increasingly sponsored by citizens in their various aggregations rather than being the exclusive preserve of a corporate State which authoritatively represents these citizens. The image of the State as a rational moral agent, dispassionately dispensing justice in the name of everyone, looks increasingly hard to sustain in the face of high levels of individuation and moral diversity.

Perhaps more important than the historical explanation of this change are the ethical and political issues raised by this new balance of interests. We have yet to develop the kind of criminal justice ethics that will allow us to deal in an informed and judicious way with victims' interests and with privatized crime control.[2] The jurisprudential inventiveness that developed the ideas and apparatus of the rule of law as a means of domesticating State power now faces a new and more complex challenge.

This is indeed a task of great importance, and the present dialogue may contribute a little to the process of rethinking criminal justice ethics, even if in part it involves a re-reading of old books with fresh eyes. The urgency of the need is made visible by the way in which many politicians espouse 'law and order' themes in fairly raw terms as part of their electoral programme, and thus respond to, or give a lead to, the public sense of concern that malefactors do not get off too lightly, when their evil-doing causes such palpable suffering.

2. POPULAR JUSTICE

The punitive populism of today's politicians marks a 'return of the repressed'— the revival of explicit expressions of punitiveness after a period in which these

---

[2] A workshop on Situational Crime Prevention in Context, organized by Andrew von Hirsch at Cambridge in December of 1996, addressed itself to ethical and jurisprudential issues of this kind. A publication of the proceedings in the form of an edited collection is planned.

had been marked as taboo in the official discourse of civilized society. After a half century in which the word 'punishment' never appeared in the titles of statutes and government reports, it suddenly reappears on the covers of White Papers and Acts of Parliament from the late 1980s onwards while, in the same period, politicians increasingly resort to the rhetoric of condemnation and punishment.[3] Nor is this merely rhetoric without practical effects. Sentencers feel the weight of public opinion and victims' demands, as represented by politicians and the press, and have tended to respond by imprisoning more offenders and increasing average prison sentences.[4]

The question of whether politicians 'respond' or 'give a lead' to public concern about crime is an important one. Critics of punitiveness often suggest that the phenomenon has very shallow roots, attributing it to short-term 'political tactics' and sensationalist 'media scares'. They imply that the majority of people are not, in fact, deeply invested in these policies and that it is a false image of the public that is invoked and misrepresented by manipulative political rhetoric. If real people are outraged about crime it is largely because of the incitement and arousal occasioned by exposure to law and order rhetoric. But this view gives too much credence to the magical powers of ideology, and forgets that punitive discourses and policies are popular and persuasive only in specific historical settings. Law and order politics played little part in British electoral competitions until the 1970s (or in the USA before the mid 1960s). The appeal of such politics today has its roots in the culture and everyday life of the population and not merely the guile of populist politicians. There is nowadays a reservoir of public concern and resentment from which politicians draw support for punitive policies—a reservoir fed by the daily irritation and expense of having to take precautions against trivial crime, as well as by the more troubling anxieties provoked by the images of evil and dangerous criminals which the press and television bring into every living room.

It is worth noting, however, that the expression of resentment and the demand for retribution are often re-phrased in political discourse as a matter of providing public protection against dangerous criminals. Even the most populist politicians share a certain wariness about advocating unvarnished punitive justice. There seems to be a tacit acknowledgement of the need to defer to more instrumental considerations, and perhaps to the concerns of criminal justice professionals.[5] Finally, one might remark that the relationship of victims and their organizations to these punitive policies is a complex one. Many supporters of victims' rights are

---

[3] See, for example, *Punishment, Custody and the Community* 1988; John Major's proposal that we should 'Condemn more and understand less', Tony Blair's slogan: 'tough on crime, tough on the causes of crime', etc.

[4] On this see 'Sentencing and the Climate of Opinion' by Andrew Ashworth and Michael Hough, [1996] *Crim.LR* 776–87.

[5] A vivid example is the 'prison works' rhetoric of the mid 1990s. This slogan, which represented the resort to mass imprisonment as a utilitarian means of crime reduction, was the respectable gloss used to represent a policy which was unmistakably punitive in its original formulation and political resonance.

embarrassed to find themselves associated with retributive policies, though it seems undeniable that the social roots of the two phenomena are closely intertwined.

One serious problem to which these tendencies in thought and public rhetoric give rise concerns the 'Rule of Law'. The danger is that in responding to individual, or, all the more, to popular, indignation, the State and its officials will depart from the objective justice required of them, swayed by the momentary subjectivity of the mob.

But the secular changes already noted suggest that it is increasingly difficult for officials to represent their practice as approximating to 'objective justice'—since that idea depended upon a tight set of conventional agreements shared by a governing and largely unaccountable élite.[6] The rise of the citizen-consumer, the discrediting of the system's experts, and the extension of democratic controls makes this less likely, particularly in pluralistic societies. Criminal justice is deeply politicized and increasingly hard to represent as 'objective' or absolute.

Even so, basic civil rights require that punishment be restricted by the twin requirements that there may be no sentence of punishment without an express crime charged and proven (*nulla poena sine crimine*) and that there must be an explicit law enacted in advance that prohibits the crime in question (*nullum crimen sine lege*).[7] The issue for a criminal court is simply whether there has been a breach of criminal law proven as charged, and what penalty is then appropriate within the discretion conferred by law. In such a process, the victim's role is as witness, not as adviser upon sentencing policy, far less upon individualized sentencing discretion in particular sentencing decisions. The *Rechtsstaat* as a State that lives under law and respects fundamental rights must be a State that stands apart from any undue attention to the resentment of criminals.

3. Ideas of Public Justice

With this in mind, we pick up our opening question, that concerning the relationship of public justice to private revenge. Allowing that there have been profound societal changes affecting attitudes to these matters, how shall we conceptualize State punishment now? Does the State, when it exacts punishment after due process of law, vindicate its own right, or simply stand in for the citizen who has been wronged? Is it the 'Queen's Peace' really that is breached by crime, or is this simply an archaic ideological form of words that glosses the public appropriation of private quarrels? Should we reconceptualize criminal law as

---

[6] See Bankowski and Mungham, *Images of Law* (London: Routledge & Kegan Paul, 1976).

[7] *One should recall that these basic civil rights, so central to liberal conceptions of justice, were modified at the margins of the criminal justice system by the penal-welfarism that prevailed for much of the twentieth century. This was especially true in juvenile justice institutions and in respect of the coercive powers of prison officials and parole boards.*

lying in the ownership of citizens aggregatively, rather than in their State corporately? If so, the traditional separation of public from private law, and allocation of criminal law to 'public', will need substantial reconsideration.

The de facto situation has changed with the changing character of the State's legimation claims, though the language of the law has been slow to express this. The democratization of the State has coincided with the historical shift from the notion of the law as the will of the sovereign to the law as the embodiment of the democratically expressed will of the people. The contemporary demand that the State respond to the expressed interests of particular citizens is a phenomenon of the democratized State. Anachronistic terms such as 'the Queens' Peace' or 'law and order' tend to obscure this.

In some ways, this process of democratization represents a fulfilment of earlier programmes associated with the liberal tradition, albeit it remains controversial whether republicans, communitarians or socialists have a better title to claim democracy as their project, not that of the liberals. The liberal tradition (which is not, of course, the only current to be found in criminal justice—though it has been the dominant one) has certainly and distinctively insisted on strict regard for the Rule of Law, and particularly for the *nulla poena sine lege* principle with all its implications. From its beginnings, or indeed in its precursors, this is laid down most firmly. So there might seem to be a special problem in accommodating current moves toward reconceptualizing criminal law with liberal principles.

Surprisingly, this appears not to be the case. For what we have characterized as a reconceptualization of the point of criminal law and punishment is itself to be found implicit in the argument of one of the most celebrated foundational texts for liberal political philosophy, John Locke's *Second Treatise of Civil Government*. There, Locke shows how humans in a state of nature would enjoy, in the celebrated phrase, rights to 'life, liberty, and estate'.[8]

'The state of Nature hath a law of Nature to govern it, which obliges every one, and reason . . . is that law'.[9] Since reason shows us that we are created beings, we have to acknowledge that we are put into the world for the creator's purposes, not our own. It follows that no one can rightfully take the life of another unprovoked, and that each must be able to use the fruits of nature so as to procure personal and familial survival. Hence we are free beings. But whoever in the use of that freedom mixes labour with natural goods has then the right to retain and use them, provided enough and as good is left for others in the exercise of their liberty. To take away the fruits of one's labour is equivalent to taking away the free use of the ingenuity and strength whereby they were gathered or made, and hence is an offence against the law of nature and reason. Rights to life and liberty in this understanding necessarily entail also rights to property ('estate').[10] The adoption of precious metals as media of exchange facilitates trade and makes possible the

---

[8] See John Locke, *Two Treatises of Civil Government* (Everyman's Library, London: J. M. Dent & Sons, 1924) pp. 118–24.

[9] Locke, ch. 2 para. 6, pp. 119–290.   [10] See Locke, pp. 119–21 and 129–41 (ch. 5).

legitimate accumulation of capital (since hoarded gold does not go to waste like hoarded food) at the same time as it opens the way to free wage-labour, since the liberty that cannot be taken by another can be freely sold in the form of a contract of service or for services.[11]

Why then do humans seek civil government at all? Locke's answer, of course, is the precariousness of the state of nature. Having rights is not the same as having them respected. Each is vulnerable to the wrongful invasion of his or her rights by another. And what can then be done? Only private retaliation by oneself against one's wrongdoer, perhaps assisted by one's friends (but what if the wrongdoer has friends as well?). In a state of nature, each is of necessity a judge in her or his own cause. And having judged, and concluded that punishment is appropriate to the case, one has to be one's own enforcement agency as well. But none will trust others to act fairly in their own cause, nor will acknowledge as just a punishment privately exacted on this basis. So the original (alleged) wrongdoer, smarting under perceivedly unjust and right-invasive punishment, in turn sets up to judge of this wrong, and to determine upon a condign punishment therefor, and to exact it. Feud and vendetta are the inevitable result. The problem about the state of nature is not that humans lack rights in it, but that they necessarily have one right too many, in that they are possessed of this 'executive power of the law of nature', the right to punish for breaches of their own rights.[12]

All this enables us to infer or construct the terms necessary for the compact that will establish civil government. What each must agree (or be deemed to have agreed) to transfer to the corporate community, is this 'executive power of the law of nature',[13] the power to judge cases of alleged wrongdoing, and to determine and exact appropriate forms of compensation and/or punishment for breaches where these are established through fair and objective inquiry and proof.

Government so established is established not to create, but to uphold, the fundamental rights to life, liberty, and estate. Government that itself invades these rights is government in breach of its foundational trust, and may rightfully be overthrown.[14] Since, however, there are obscurities and differences of opinion about the exact content or proper statement of rights, and there is obvious need to regulate matters ancillary to upholding them, government is properly possessed of a legislative power for 'clearing and condescending upon the law of nature', as Locke's Scottish contemporary Stair put it.[15] That power, however, ought to be vested in the hands of an agency separate from those who exercise the State's powers of adjudication. So, although the State as punisher is essentially stepping into shoes vacated by citizens as they sign up to the social contract, the conditions upon which it legitimately exercises the power of punishment transferred to it are precisely those of the 'Rule of Law'. The *Rechtsstaat*, it turns out,

---

[11] Locke, pp. 139–41.   [12] Locke, pp. 159–60.   [13] Locke, p. 160.
[14] Locke, pp. 165–6.
[15] See James, Viscount Stair, *The Institutions of the Law of Scotland*, 2nd edn. (ed. D. M. Walker) (Edinburgh: Edinburgh University Press, 1981) I.1.16.

is a 'Right-state' in a double sense: it exists to protect primary natural rights of every citizen, but in doing so by exercising the power to punish, it has to respect the due process rights of those upon whom it acts.

This should not be overstated. Locke is concerned to justify and limit the State's power to punish, and is thus to be seen as the theorist of the stable, secure commercial society. Hobbes is the thinker whose vision seems most relevant in situations where 'law and order' is perceived to be breaking down. Some of the excesses of contemporary culture seem to be linked to the perception that the State has failed to deliver security to its citizens, and that social order is increasingly precarious. The relative pacification of society secured by the modern nation State was one of the key conditions for the 'civilizing' of our social institutions.[16] Our reversion to more punitive and primitive forms of justice are certainly linked to (though not caused by) the high rates of crime and insecurity that have plagued societies such as the United Kingdom and the USA in recent decades—in effect, a 'de-pacification' of the social landscape. Where criminal justice fails to provide citizens with a satisfactory level of security and confidence, one frequently sees the re-emergence of vigilantism.

Granted the contrast between Locke and Hobbes, one can nevertheless see how in situations where Locke's theses apply tolerably well, it is possible to derive from the Lockean materials a radically privatized conception of the State and its power to punish. Robert Nozick has notoriously done that very thing in *Anarchy, State, and Utopia*.[17] From essentially Lockean premises, Nozick derives a conception of a legitimate minimal State (legitimate because minimal) out of the kind of private 'protective association' (the private security industry writ large!) that could emerge by free bargaining among individuals with Lockean rights and the wish to keep them secure.

Even if one rejects a radically privatized form of justice, where that means an individualized or commercialized system, one may nevertheless question the right of the State to enjoy, as if by its very nature, a virtual monopoly in this area. A State monopoly (i.e. an arrangement in which the criminal justice agencies of the State have primary and exclusive responsibility for preventing and processing complaints about crime) is very unlikely to be effective in relation to crime control in contemporary social conditions. Historically, it has worked only where it has been supported by a very active civil society with highly developed routines of social control and mutual restraint. It is preferable to see the responsibility to prevent crime and to deliver security—not at all the same thing as the power to punish—being shared with intermediate associations: with local authorities, businesses, chambers of commerce, communities, neighbourhood organizations,

---

[16] On this, see Norbert Elias, *The Civilizing Process*, vol. 1, 'The History of Mannera', (Oxford: Blackwell, 1978), vol. 2, 'State Formation and Civilization, (Oxford: Blackwell, 1982) and D. Garland, *Punishment and Modern Society* (Oxford: Clarendon Press, 1990).

[17] Oxford and New York, 1974.

voluntary associations and so forth. One of the problems of the liberal tradition is that it tends to think in terms of the State and the individual, thus excluding the intermediate zone where most social activity and group life actually takes place.

These are important points, and ought to be taken as a reminder that the right to freedom of association, strongly endorsed by liberals, has not led to full enough attention to the rights of, and functions exercised by, associations and social organizations of the kind mentioned. Nozick is by no means the worst offender here, for he has quite a lot to say of the role of non-State associations of various kinds. But even allowing for that, there remain, from the viewpoint of concern about the character of the criminal process, at least two objections to the case Nozick puts. Most fundamentally, the rights asserted are simply arbitrary. In Nozick, indeed, they are merely assumed. In Locke, they are argued for, but the argument postulates a deity with presumed purposes for humankind. And the presumed purposes turn out to be the ones that legitimate the rights that are derived. They as well answer the question 'What would God have to be like for commercial society to be justified?' as the question 'What rights do we have, assuming that we are the creatures of a rational and benign creator?'

Secondly, it is highly questionable whether the public powers that they would justify, even when we make the relevant arbitrary assumption, include as such the power to punish. Reparation is not punishment, and the argument that says that one whose rights are infringed has the right to take proportional reparation points rather toward a system of private law with enforceable remedies for breach of rights, essentially aimed at compensation, at restoration of the *status quo ante* in favour of the party who suffered the infringement. That is different from crime and punishment.

4. The Resurgence of Reparation

This is true. But one should notice that the State's response to criminal offending of a minor kind is increasingly phrased in terms of reparation and compensation—and fines (which are often regarded as a charge on illegal activity, rather than a truly penal sanction) are by far the most frequently used sanction in criminal cases. Reparation orders were introduced early in the life of the Labour Government after the election of May 1997, community service orders account for a growing proportion of dispositions made in criminal cases, and there is an increasingly extensive resort to statutory fines, fiscal fines, and fixed penalties of one sort or another, all of which have something of the character of restitutive measures. Compensation is also one of the chief demands of victims, whether paid directly by the offender, or else from the tax-funded Criminal Injuries Compensation Board. Durkheim argues, in his account of penal evolution, that modern societies will increasingly shift away from penal, repressive responses to crime towards restitutive, civil, compensatory measures.[18] *He is half-right about this. The tendency towards restitutive or 'civil' justice is today accompanied by a resurgence of expressive, punitive justice. The explanation of this contradictory state of affairs is a pressing problem for the sociology of punishment, but it seems likely that the answer lies in a series of social and cultural adaptations prompted by high levels of crime. The massive frequency with which the criminal law is nowadays breached encourages an administrative tendency to manage crime by defining deviance down, rendering it mundane, and managing it in cost-effective ways that reserve the most punitive (and usually most expensive and time-consuming) responses for crimes that are considered particularly serious—crimes of violence, of sexual assault, of abuse, for example, for which compensation and insurance are viewed as insufficient or inappropriate. But the normality of high rates of crime also lends itself to a sense of frustration and insecurity on the part of the public. The credibility of the authorities is not enhanced by a merely restitutive, managerial approach to crime, nor does this approach reassure those citizens who fear that social order is breaking down, and that criminals go unpunished. In consequence, a criminal justice system that makes extensive use of low-key, low-cost, restitutive responses to offending will come under pressure to use much more expressive, more punitive measures in response to those crimes that do excite public emotion. A State that is perceived to be failing in the fight against crime may find some political advantage in resorting to highly publicized displays of its punitive resolve, without actually dismantling the restitutive practices that make up the standard response to the mass of offending behaviour. Highly visible rituals of punitive justice can thus co-exist with widespread practices of restitution, and may tend to expand in the face of criticisms about the system's effectiveness and credibility.*

In any event, there is a real difference here. Differentiating punitive from reparative responses to untoward acts is not a point that rests on a mere 'definitional stop'. What is in question is not to give (or presuppose) stipulative definitions of punishment and of reparation, but rather to focus attention on two distinct kinds of response to human conduct. Sometimes, I am primarily concerned with what you do because of its impact on me. I want to get you to treat me better, or to restore something to me, because that is how things ought to be for me. Other times, I am concerned with what you do because of the value or disvalue I ascribe to your doing thus and so. Then I want to praise or blame, approve or reprove. Or perhaps I am in a position to, and think it right to, intervene yet more forcefully than by mere reproof in a case of ill-doing. Then what I do is punish.

This seems persuasive, but perhaps the point is expressed too exclusively in the style of 'methodological individualism'. Individuals do indeed respond to each other as stated, but this interaction occurs in a social context and involves implicit or explicit reference to collective values. In any such interaction,

---

[18] E. Durkheim 'Two Laws of Penal Evolution' in S. Lukes and A. Scull (eds.) *Durkheim and the Law* (Oxford: Blackwell, 1983).

collective sentiments and arrangements are at stake, and these entities have a special status and power on account of their collective character—a status and power that shape the responses of the interacting individuals as well as those of the onlookers. The figure of 'the social'—or more prosaically, the relation of the individual to the group—is central to this phenomenon.

This correction is entirely just, and the distinction drawn is indeed to be understood in those terms. Nevertheless, to invite each person, or each reader, to reflect on differences in the way he or she responds to others' conduct in a context of commonly understood social values, is one way of drawing attention to the social reality of the distinction. By contrast with so-called 'reparation', which looks at conduct in the light of the detriment it causes another and seeks to make good the damage, punishment (both as here explained and as it is popularly understood) looks at conduct in its character as misconduct, and responds to it by some adverse intervention aimed at the miscreant just because of the misdeed committed. Of course, misdeeds often infringe victims' rights, and both reparation and punishment may then be in order or even called for. But an account of the rights people have to 'life, liberty, and estate', while it answers the question how we can justify exacting reparation, does not answer the question what business one adult person has administering reproof or punishment to another. Moreover, it may divert attention from the many situations in which that which is considered wrongful and punishable simply infringes an important common value but does not injure any specific individual particularly.

If one thinks in terms of the social interests at stake—which is how individuals are thinking when they think morally—then the question is not 'what right does any one individual have to punish' but rather, who is the authoritative representative of 'the social' or the group? The answer to this question depends upon the nature and composition of the group. It is possible to imagine social arrangements—the frontier society of the nineteenth century American West for example—in which individuals are entitled and expected to enforce the law for themselves. The standard answer in modern Western societies is, of course, the legal institutions of the State, although punitive powers are also delegated to other group authorities, in schools, families and professional associations.

Nevertheless, there is reason to delay over the thought that it is (principally) 'adults' who are punished by the criminal process. Does this not merit special attention? The punishment of children when they behave naughtily or badly seems intuitively easier to justify than the punishment of adults by adults. Morally and socially, adults, anyway parents, grandparents, uncles and aunts, schoolteachers and the like, have an authority over children that is commonly taken to justify their having recourse to punishment (though it is controversial nowadays how much if any physical infliction of pain they should use in this). And the common justification is the need to bring children up to be decent and responsible members of the community, both for their own sake as moral beings and for the sake of the others in the community they will discommode if they grow up to be bad citizens, selfish, wilful, and irresponsible. According to widely held social values, it is a mark of good parenting or of good educating that children and young persons under their tutelage develop their inherent moral faculties and learn how to behave themselves decently and responsibly towards others, and develop self-command and an awareness of the intrinsic, not merely instrumental, value of living with a lively conscience, but an easy one.

This account of the legitimacy of punishment in the context of child-rearing and education is persuasive. But notice that what is being discussed here is corrective discipline and the sanctions necessary to it. It is not, and is even in contrast with, retributive punishment. The pattern of sanctioning involved, the aims of the institution, its guiding conception of purpose, even the methods of sanctioning that are most appropriate, are somewhat different in the two cases.

We ought to reflect carefully how deep or essential the differences are. For it has become a commonplace in discussions of punishment to treat the panoply of the criminal law, with formal accusations, pre-announced laws, trial by due process of law, formal sentence, and enforced execution of the sentence, as the paradigm for punishment, while every other instance of 'punishment' is seen as counting only to whatever degree it appears analogical with the paradigm case. But this may surely be doubted. For there is a kind of natural authority of parents, and more generally of concerned adults, over children, and although this is often abused, or in the case of the feckless or irresponsible never truly possessed, it is not always abused and not all forfeit authority by their own incapacity for it.

In what sense is this authority 'natural'? Perhaps 'natural' in the sense of universally recognized, growing out of the conditions of human group life, etc. But of course the precise forms of that authority, and the extent to which it is shared with other organizations, vary greatly from culture to culture.

It is natural indeed in that sense, but the circumstances of human maturation from childhood do seem to contain elements that are common across cultures, for all the foreground elements of cultural variability. There may here be one core element of what has been called a 'minimum content of natural law'.[19] For it is readily arguable that, where authority is not abused or forfeited, the impossibility for children to develop their moral and other capacities without nurture, care, and sound education is itself the very thing that justifies ascribing such authority to parents and others *in loco parentis*.

From this point of view, the problem case is not the punishment of naughty children by reasonable parents or schoolteachers. It is the punishment of adults by the State. What moral authority does the State have, or the legislators the citizens elect and the judges the executive appoints (with, perhaps, advice and consent of the legislature)? What would allow us to repose in the State the kind of

---

[19] H. L. A. Hart, *The Concept of Law* (Oxford: Clarendon Press, 1961) ch. 9.

authority that we find it necessary, albeit sometimes and in some cases problematic, to acknowledge parents and teachers having in respect of their juvenile charges? The healthy suspicion towards public authorities that the tradition of Locke and Nozick encourages is a suspicion that would seem to magnify our doubts about all this. So far from justifying public punishments to secure private rights, this picture of civil society would leave us hard-pressed to justify it at all. Is there then perhaps a fresh start or a new way out?

This argument for the 'naturalness' of the family's right to punish the child is really an argument for the authority of the group over the individual. It is assumed that the family is the particular group in which such authority should reside, and the argument draws upon the long-established (though by no means unquestioned) legitimacy of that institution. The same structure of argument could, in principle, give other institutions or associations the power to punish their members. The issue is, which groups and institutions are to be privileged in this way? And again, the choice is not simply between the state and private individuals.

It would be damaging indeed if the family is simply here assumed as a natural institution. The point intended is the less provocative one that human beings are born particularly defenceless and undergo a phase of maturation that seems protracted by contrast with other mammals. During this period the tutelage of some socially recognized set or community of adults is apparently a necessary condition for the successful development of social and moral competence. If, however, we assume that social and moral competence entail the acquisition of the status of an autonomous moral agent, which is a key idea at least for most liberals, the authority that earlier has this 'natural' justification does become problematic, and it may well be beyond the resources of Lockean theories to get out of this thicket.

A different guiding influence is perhaps needed. Where one progenitor of modern liberalism leads us into darkness, another may light a fresh torch. Let us abandon the rationalism of Locke awhile and turn to the moral sentimentalism of Adam Smith. Smith's moral theory is a theory of sentiment rationalized, a theory in which a crucial part is played by observation of the human capability for 'sympathy' in the eighteenth century philosophers' usage of the term, perhaps better captured today by the term 'empathy'. This sympathy is the capacity to enter into the feelings of another, to feel as she/he feels, albeit in a more muted way.[20] As I see you spill hot water over your leg, I wince and feel in my leg something as you in yours, but I do not have the real pain caused to you by the burn on your skin.

Now suppose a more complex case. It was not you who spilt water on your leg, but Adam who angrily splashed the contents of a boiling kettle at you in the course of a quarrel that I observed (or heard of later). Your feelings in this case are more complex than in the first. You have the same agonizing burn on your leg, but you are aware of having it because of what Adam did to you, did deliberately,

---

[20] A. Smith, *A Theory of Moral Sentiments* (eds. D. D. Raphael and A. L. Macfie) (Oxford: Clarendon Press, 1976), pp. 9, 12–13, 21–2, 31, 51–2, 83–5.

as it appears to you. Then you do not merely suffer pain, you resent the pain you suffer. These pangs of resentment include a wish to retaliate, to hurt the one who hurt you. Observe, this raw sentiment is not a demand for reparation, for (say) some payment to assuage pain, and further payment to cover the cost of medical treatment and pain-relieving embrocations. It is a rawer and more immediate response of wishing to hurt the hurter. Smith thinks of this 'resentment' as a very fundamental element in our psychology, and introspection, self-observation, and the general experience of everyday life seem to lend support to his view.[21]

Turn next to the observer. The sympathy is now more complex, as is the emotional state of the victim. I do not merely feel for you in your scalded pain; I feel with you in your anger towards Adam for doing this to you. Still, I can maintain a degree of detachment. I can ponder the question if Adam really meant to scald you with water from the kettle or did it by careless accident while gesticulating in the course of the quarrel. If so, I may be ready to share your anger with him over his carelessness with a notoriously dangerous thing, but no longer would I be able to share with you the resentment that encourages you to seek to return a deliberate hurt for the hurt deliberately inflicted. For in truth no hurt was *deliberately* inflicted. If indeed I have the capacity to enter by sympathy into your feelings in this case, then necessarily the same capacity applies with respect to Adam. If he did commit a careless splashing of hot water, he will be feeling a measure of regret and remorse, and if you attack him verbally or physically for a deliberate assault (where in truth no deliberate assault took place) this will hurt him, and he will have something to resent, too. Depending on whether or not I believe his account, I will on reflection either enter into your resentment, or not, either enter or reject Adam's counter-resentment of your response to him.

Again, the point is made in terms that are perhaps unnecessarily individualistic. People can and do feel outraged and resentful about crimes that do not injure a particular, sentient individual in ways that we can literally feel. Some American citizens feel outraged when the American flag is burned. Others feel equally outraged when this expression of political dissent is criminalized. Members of the British public feel righteous indignation and anger when it is proved that Ministers entrusted with public duties and accorded the status of 'right honourable' are found to have lied to Parliament for the sake of their selfish interest. Here again the point taken above about the involvement of 'the social' is relevant. There is a sacredness about group values that includes, but is not limited to, our mutual regard for other individuals. In this respect, Durkheim's account seems to offer better guidance than that of Smith.

It is certainly true that in his earlier *Theory of Moral Sentiments* Smith gives a somewhat individualistic and psychologistic account of his point; at least he can be read in this sense. But in the later *Lectures on Jurisprudence*[22] we see that he

[21] Smith, *Theory* pp. 34–8.
[22] A. Smith, *Lectures on Jurisprudence*, (eds. R. L. Meek, D. D. Raphael, P. G. Stein) (Oxford: Clarendon Press, 1978).

thought it possible and indeed necessary to locate the ideal spectator in a defined social context so that in its developed form the theory is one of social-moral sentiments.[23] Whether this is a move that can be successfully made within the overall framework presupposed by Smith is a point to ponder (but not to explore here). Presuming the possibility of a favourable answer on this point, such a Smithian approach invites us to generalize from the actual observer to an impartial spectator who would have no greater pre-involvement with one person than another. Then it invites us to go a further step and contemplate a spectator who, unlike any of us in reality, would be ideally well informed about the true state of people's intentions and motives. To imagine such an ideal spectator is to provide oneself with an intellectual tool for self-critical reflection on one's actual raw sentiments whether as agent or as actual sympathetic observer. Moral sentiments are raw sentiments reformed by critical reflection on a rational ideal. The process of critical reflection, indeed, transforms sentiment into judgement.

Criminal justice procedures are intended to turn hot vengeance into cool, impartial justice. They aim to interpose rationality, reflection, circumspection, balance, and collective group interests as a brake upon the unrestrained expression of individual emotions. To quote Bacon's aphorism in full 'Revenge is a kind of wild justice, which the more man's nature runs to, the more ought law to weed it out'. But if these procedures are to function satisfactorily, they must permit the (controlled) expression of emotion as well as rational procedures of fact-finding and judgement. Hence the ritual, the symbolism, the discourse of condemnation and anathematization, the public pronouncement of sentence, and the widespread attention that are still brought to bear for the most serious crimes.

The judgement, in some cases, may well be that an ill-doer's conduct is such as to arouse grave and justified resentment on the victim's part. If, not in blind rage, but in a measured and careful way, the victim were to deliver a reasonably calculated retaliation upon the wrongdoer, the third party judgement, both ideally and really, might be that this was justified, leaving the now-punished wrongdoer with no residue of justified resentment back at the original victim in her or his fresh guise as righteous punisher of an evil-doer. Obviously enough, however, this is a highly idealized conception.[24] We can figure or perhaps even recall cases of this kind in our own experience. Literature offers good instances, too. The extra-legal ruination of Dominick Medina in John Buchan's *The Three Hostages* could stand example here. But in truth, the justice that can sometimes be represented by personalized revenge is usually all too wild a justice, and the process of exacting it a standing threat to public peace.

Isn't the usurpation of group authority by the individual victim a problem, even when he or she acts in a reasonable way?

But the point is that the individual cannot usurp the group's position, for the individual needs in effect to acknowledge the group in order to be capable of having

---

[23] See, e.g., *Lectures* pp. 87–9.   [24] See Smith, *Theory* p. 218.

a standard of the individually reasonable. And indeed this position has to agree with that of Locke in holding that human beings would be rash to leave the task of responding adequately to injurious wrongdoing solely in the hands of its victims as individuals or voluntary associations of individuals. This would be a recipe for escalating feud and vendetta. This, however, is not because we can erect an 'executive power of the law of nature' on the back of a scheme of private rights to life, liberty, and estate. It is because the natural tendency of humans to resentment and retaliation of hurts suffered in the course of interpersonal interactions can indeed be transformed into justified punishment. But the circumstances of this being safely achieved almost always require the institutionalization of agencies of impartial judgement. We need not imagine these to be the product of some articulate social contract. The history of their evolution is complex and exhibits many false starts and untimely collapses, many trajectories and varieties of institutional form.

Imperfect as public agencies of State always are, corrupt as they frequently can be, they are better capable of approximating the rational ideal of the impartial spectator-cum-judge in the large scale and impersonal transactions of industrial and post-industrial societies than unregulated individualistic retaliation could possibly be.

Yes, but note that there is not an exclusive alternative between State agencies and unregulated individual retaliation. Might not one think in more pluralistic terms? Is it not possible that some of the responsibilities of crime control—and perhaps even aspects of the power to punish—might be devolved to authorities intermediate between the State and the individual?

In this sense, the State's legal ordering, albeit always to be held under jealous scrutiny, can actually come to represent a serious exemplar toward, though no substitute for, the moral judgement of the autonomous moral agent that each human being aspires to be.

The argument suggested has been of the style of Smith rather than expressly in his terms. It needs to be further acknowledged that Smith in his *Lectures on Jurisprudence* uses similar argumentative materials to construct an understanding of private law rights and remedies, as those we have appropriated for the discussion of punishment. Whether they work as serviceably in that context as they appear to do for the present purpose is a question beyond this chapter's scope. But the idea that there are basic rights worthy of protection through different legal mechanisms, and that these have a less arbitrary explanation than Locke's, is intrinsically important for the project of establishing a liberal or post-liberal account of the legitimate power of punishment exercised by the State, and the limits within which the power remains legitimate. There is force in the insight that the criminal law has at its heart the protection of persons and their legitimate interests, [*but not only 'persons', the protection of social institutions, ways of life, the social as variously defined* . . .] and that in taking these seriously the State both makes unnecessary and makes unjustified resort to personal retaliation and vigilante tactics.[25] The State that fails to handle this fails in one of the fundamental functions of the fair and effective government that government by consent must always be, fairness and effectiveness being among the conditions of reasonable consent. [*Our own, modern State would seem to have failed to some extent, and to be currently subject to the consequences of failure.*]

In this sense, indeed, the liberal State is intrinsically and not accidentally a State that has and uses the power to punish, and that in using it creates the conditions of social peace.

5. SOVEREIGN STATES AND THE POWER TO PUNISH

Perhaps the lesson of the twentieth century is that the State, by itself, is incapable of creating social peace and guaranteeing 'law and order'. Perhaps one of the great mistakes of the modern period has been the assumption that crime control can be achieved by means of specialist State agencies which monopolize the field and drive out other forms of social control. The various forces that are currently reconfiguring the public/private divide (forces which include the rise of private security, the development of community policing, the revival of the crime control responsibilities of civil society, and the victims movement) are adaptations to that failure, as is (more regressively) the new brand of penal policy that stresses expressive punishment and public protection.

The power is a dangerous power, because it can be tyrannically exercised, and because the conditions of its existence (relatively centralized police agencies, etc.) are conditions that can be exploited by those with ambitions towards tyranny. It is interesting to note that the most effective protection against the tendency to tyranny yet devised, certainly when we consider the issue in a West European perspective, has been the growth of international and supranational arrangements such as those represented by the institutions of the European Union and the Council of Europe, through the European Convention on Human Rights and the Human Rights Court and Commission. The taming of the power to punish that justified the erection of the sovereign State has turned out to require a considerable elision of that sovereignty. Whether the post-sovereign State can over the longer run be effective in combating crime to the degree sufficient to continue to merit the consent of citizens is one of the test-questions of our times.

Perhaps the test-question for our time is: 'Can we succeed in building crime-control institutions and nurturing forms of social control that are not part of the central State apparatus, but which are aspects of the everyday life and routines of civil society in its various aspects?' Liberalism is a necessary counter to the

---

[25] This concern of the criminal justice system to protect offenders and suspected offenders against private retaliation is what Nigel Walker refers to as 'Montero's aim', after the Spanish criminologist who emphasized it. See N. Walker, *Sentencing in a Rational Society* (Cambridge, Ma. and London: Harvard University Press, 1980).

authoritarian tendencies of such organizations, but it lacks the resources to give positive inspiration in developing them.

This last point enables the present authors to conclude on a common note. It is interesting to discover that within the liberal tradition even at its foundations there are materials that are helpful for reflection on crises that have arisen out of the failures of practical liberal and post-liberal programmes of crime control and social welfare. It is worth taking seriously the arguments that are helpful, though it may be contestable how helpful they are. In any event, it will require rather more original thought to take the argument beyond this point. In a volume presented to Andrew von Hirsch, it is a pleasure to acknowledge the special contributions he and his frequent collaborator Nils Jareborg have made to that task.

2

Crime: in Proportion and in Perspective

JOHN GARDNER*

1. THE DISPLACEMENT FUNCTION

What is the criminal law for? Most explanations nowadays focus exclusively on the activities of criminal offenders. The criminal law exists to deter or incapacitate potential criminal offenders, say, or to give actual criminal offenders their just deserts. In all this we seem to have lost sight of the origins of the criminal law as a response to the activities of *victims*, together with their families, associates and supporters. The blood feud, the vendetta, the duel, the revenge, the lynching: for the elimination of these modes of retaliation, more than anything else, the criminal law as we know it today came into existence.[1] It is important to bring this point back into focus, not least because one common assumption of contemporary writing about punishment, including criminal punishment, is that its justifiability is closely connected with the justifiability of our retaliating (tit-for-tat, or otherwise) against those who wrong us.[2] The spirit of the criminal law is, on this assumption, fundamentally in continuity with the spirit of the vendetta. To my mind, however, the opposite relation holds with much greater force. The justifiability of criminal punishment, and criminal law in general, is closely connected to the *un*justifiability of our retaliating against those who wrong us. That people are inclined to retaliate against those who wrong them, often with good excuse but rarely with adequate justification, creates a rational pressure for social practices which tend to take the heat out of the situation and remove some of the temptation to retaliate, eliminating in the process some of the basis for

* School of Law, King's College London. I am grateful to participants in a staff seminar at the University of Nottingham, and particularly to Paul Roberts, for putting this chapter through its initial paces. Later drafts benefited from Stephen Shute's generous help and advice.

[1] For those who accept that ancient criminal law had this *raison d'être* but who doubt whether it has done much to shape criminal law 'as we know it today', I commend J. Horder, 'The Duel and the English Law of Homicide', (1992) 12 *Oxford Journal of Legal Studies*, 419.

[2] For instance: P. F. Strawson, 'Freedom and Resentment', (1962) 48 *Proceedings of the British Academy*, 187; J. M. Finnis, 'Punishment and Pedagogy', (1967) 5 *The Oxford Review*, 83; J. G. Murphy and J. Hampton, *Forgiveness and Mercy* (Cambridge, 1988); M. S. Moore, 'The Moral Worth of Retribution' in F. Schoeman (ed.), *Responsibility, Character, and the Emotions* (Cambridge, 1987).

excusing those who do so. In the modern world, the criminal law has become the most ubiquitous, sophisticated, and influential repository of such practices. Indeed, it seems to me, this displacement function of the criminal law always was and remains today one of the central pillars of its justification.

This is not to deny the justificatory importance of the criminal law's many other functions, several of which obviously do focus on the activities of offenders. As students of criminal law we have all been brought up on the idea that the various arguments for having such an institution are rivals, each of which takes the wind out of the others' sails. We must, therefore, decide whether we are retributivists, or rehabilitationists, or preventionists, or reintegrationists, or whatever else may be the penological flavour of the month. If we insist on an intellectual 'pick and mix', we are told, we can maybe get away with allocating different arguments strictly to different stages of the justification, e.g. deterrence to the purpose of criminal law in general and retribution to the justification of its punitive responses in individual cases.[3] Still, we must make sure the rival arguments are kept strictly in their separate logical spaces, or else, according to received wisdom, they tend to use up their force in clashes with each other.[4] To my way of thinking, however, this supposed rivalry among justifications for criminal law and its punitive responses is illusory. The criminal law (even when its responses are non-punitive) habitually wreaks such havoc in people's lives, and its punitive side is such an extraordinary abomination, that it patently needs all the justificatory help it can get. If we believe it should remain a fixture in our legal and political system, we cannot afford to dispense with or disdain any of the various things, however modest and localized, which can be said in its favour.[5] Each must be called upon to make whatever justificatory contribution it is capable of making. If and to the extent that the criminal law deters wrongdoing, that is one thing to be said in its favour. If and to the extent that it leads wrong-doers to confront and repent their wrongs, then that counts in its favour too; likewise the power of the criminal law, such as it is, to bring people with mental health problems into contact with those who can treat their conditions, to settle and maintain the internal standards of success for social practices such as marriage and share-dealing, and to stand up for those who cannot stand up for themselves. Even apparently

---

[3] The classic version of such a structured hybrid justification is H. L. A. Hart, 'Prolegomenon to the Principles of Punishment' reprinted in his *Punishment and Responsibility* (1968). A different variation is to be found in A. von Hirsch, *Censure and Sanctions* (1993).

[4] For more or less frank expressions of this anxiety, see N. Lacey, *State Punishment: Political Principles and Community Values* (1988), p. 46 *et seq.*, esp. at 52; P. H. Robinson, 'Hybrid Principles for the Distribution of Criminal Sanctions', (1987) 82 *Northwestern University Law Review*, 19, esp. at 31–4; N. D. Walker, *Why Punish?* (1991), 135–6; R. A. Duff, 'Penal Communications: Recent Work in the Philosophy of Punishment', (1996) 20 *Crime and Justice*, 1 at 8. More theoretically, puritanical critics go further, and argue that mixing different arguments for the justification of punishment is doomed irrespective of attempts to keep them in separate logical spaces: e.g. J. Morison, 'Hart's Excuses: Problems with a Compromise Theory of Punishment' in P. Leith and P. Ingram (eds.), *The Jurisprudence of Orthodoxy* (1988); A. Norrie, *Law, Ideology and Punishment* (1991), pp. 125–35.

[5] Contrast the position recommended by A. G. N. Flew in 'The Justification of Punishment' in H. B. Acton (ed.), *The Philosophy of Punishment* (1969), where the justification of punishment is held to be 'overdetermined' by the many reasons which count in favour of punishment.

trivial factors such as the role of the criminal law in validating and invalidating people's household insurance claims must be given their due weight. All of these considerations, and many others besides, add up to give the institution whatever justification it may have, and to the extent that any of them lapse or fail, the case for abolition of the criminal law comes a step closer to victory.

It is true, of course, that sometimes the considerations conflict, i.e. in some cases some of the considerations which support the criminal law's existence point to its reacting in one way while others point to its reacting in a dramatically different way, or not reacting at all. Sometimes it is even the case that considerations which partly support the criminal law's existence turn against it, and partly support its eradication. The only general thing that can be said of such conflict cases is that they reinforce still further the need for the criminal law to muster whatever considerations it can in its own defence, since by their nature these cases pit additional arguments against whatever course the law adopts for itself. So the existence of such cases strengthens, rather than weakens, my main point. It is also true that different arguments contribute to justifying different aspects or parts of the criminal law to greater or lesser extents. Considerations of deterrence do not support the criminalization of activities which cannot effectively be deterred by criminalization, and considerations of rehabilitation do not support the criminal conviction of people who cannot effectively be rehabilitated. In similar vein, the criminal law's function of displacing retaliation by or on behalf of victims does not support the criminalization of victimless wrongs, or of wrongs whose victims do not offer or inspire retaliatory responses. Criminalizing these wrongs will fall to be justified on an accumulation of other grounds, or else not at all. That still leaves the displacement function, however, as a central pillar of the criminal law's justification. By describing it as a central pillar I mean only that some core parts of the edifice of the modern criminal law cannot properly remain standing, in spite of the existence of other valid supporting arguments, in the absence of the law's continuing ability to pre-empt reprisals against wrong-doers. In this chapter, accordingly, I want to sketch some of the major and (I believe) escalating difficulties of principle and practice faced by the modern criminal law in attempting to fulfil this displacement function and keep the heart of its edifice intact.

2. HUMANITY AND JUSTICE

To continue fulfilling its displacement function satisfactorily has always been a grave challenge for the criminal law, because by the nature of the endeavour there is very little margin for error. On the one hand, the criminal law's medicine must be strong enough to control the toxins of bitterness and resentment which course through the veins of those who are wronged, or else the urge to retaliate in kind will persist unchecked. On pain of losing a central pillar of its justification, therefore, the criminal law cannot afford to downplay too much its punitive ingredient, the suffering or deprivation which it can deliberately inflict on the offender

in response to the wrong. In the end, particularly in the absence of genuine con-
trition from the offender, that deliberate infliction of suffering or deprivation
may be all the law can deliver to bring the victim towards what the psychother-
apists now call 'closure', the time when she can put the wrong behind her, finally
laying to rest her retaliatory urge. On the other hand, the law's medicine against
that same retaliatory urge cannot be allowed to become worse than the affliction
it exists to control. It must stop short of institutionalizing the various forms of
hastiness, cruelty, intemperance, impatience, vindictiveness, self-righteousness,
fanaticism, fickleness, intolerance, prejudice, and gullibility that the unchecked
desire to retaliate tends to bring with it. On pain of sacrificing a central pillar of
its justification, therefore, the criminal law cannot simply act as the proxy retaliator any more than it can simply dilute its punitive side to the point where it is
incapable of pacifying would-be retaliators.

As if this perennial predicament were not difficult enough for the criminal law,
two further rational constraints upon the modern State have only served to compound the problem as we face it today. The first is the modern State's powerful
duty of humanity towards each of its subjects. To avoid surrendering the whole
basis of its authority—as the servant of its people—the modern State in all of
its manifestations is bound to treat each of those over whom it exercises that
authority as a thinking, feeling human being rather than, for instance, an entry
on a computer, a commodity to be traded, a beast to be tamed, a social problem,
an evil spirit, a pariah, or an untouchable. The anonymous bureaucratic machinery of the modern State which came into existence to honour this duty is also,
notoriously, the main contemporary cause of its violation. It is a depressingly
short step from stopping thinking of someone as a serf to starting thinking of
them as a statistic. But even if the pitfalls of bureaucratization are avoided, the
practice of punishing criminal offenders inevitably calls the State's humane
record into question, because of the element of deliberately inflicted suffering or
deprivation which punishment by definition imports. Such an infliction of suffering or deprivation by the State cannot be justified solely on the ground that worse
suffering or deprivation will be avoided as a result, even if the suffering which will
be avoided as a result is suffering that would otherwise be deliberately inflicted on
that very same person by other people's reprisals against her. The State's duty of
humanity to each person has an agent-relative aspect, i.e. it emphasizes the State's
own inhumanity towards a person and not just the sum total of inhumanity
towards her which occurs within the State's jurisdiction or under its gaze.[6]

---

[6] I cannot offer a proper defence of this claim here. For those who are interested, the basis of such
a defence lies in the fact that the moral duties under discussion in this section occupy the lower level of
a two-level approach to moral reasoning. They summarize and organize certain ultimate moral
considerations, but are not ultimate moral considerations themselves. Therefore they tend already to
display some sensitivity to the limits of our possible compliance with ultimate moral considerations.
One familiar indication of this is to be found in the philosophical myth that 'ought implies can'. It is a
somewhat perplexing myth. Nobody denies, I think, that one can have *reason* to do what one cannot
do. Otherwise where is the rationality in frustration? But many say that one cannot have a duty to do
the very same thing, i.e. that there cannot be a *mandatory* reason to do the impossible. That seems to
me to be a mistaken view, but it is an understandable extrapolation from a wide range of cases in which

This means that, other things being equal, the State's proper response to the fact that a wrong-doer is faced with the threat of retaliation is to protect the wrong-doer rather than to punish her, even if, thanks to the ruthlessness and cunning of the would-be retaliators, punishing her promises to be more effective in reducing her overall suffering.[7]

For punishment to be a morally acceptable alternative to protection, the State has to assure itself not only that the measure of punishment controls retaliation while stopping short of becoming a mere institutionalization of the retaliator's excesses, but also that the act of punishment affirms, rather than denies, the punished person's status as a thinking, feeling human being. That is not impossible. Many familiar features of modern criminal law, including some important substantive doctrines of the general part as well as many procedural, evidential, and sentencing standards, reflect the State's successive efforts to meet this condition. Together these features are supposed to ensure that trial and punishment for a criminal offence affirms the moral agency and moral responsibility of the offender, and in the process (since moral agency and moral responsibility represent a significant part of what it is to be a human being) affirms the offender's humanity.[8] For the reasons just outlined, I regard the constancy of this affirmation as a *sine qua non* of the criminal law's legitimacy. In saying this I am not retreating from my earlier claim that the function of displacing reprisals against wrong-doers is a central pillar of the criminal law's justification. I am only adding the complication that, for better or worse, this function cannot always be legitimately performed by the criminal law.

That point is reinforced when we move from the State's duty of humanity to its parallel, and no less important, duty of justice. Questions of justice, unlike questions of humanity, are questions about how people are to be treated *relative to one another*. Some contemporary political philosophers imagine that all questions dealt with by the institutions of the modern State should be dealt with, first and foremost, as questions of justice. 'Justice' as John Rawls put it, 'is the first virtue of social institutions'.[9] The basic thought behind this view is the sound

---

what people cannot do is already taken into account in shaping their moral duties, because of the sheer pointlessness of their having a moral duty to do what they cannot do. This means that the level of moral duty can be sensitive, as the level of ultimate moral concern is not, to the limits of our ability to comply. And since I cannot lead your life for you, my possible compliance with agent-neutral considerations based on the value of your goals and projects is limited. This lends an agent-relative dimension to my duties when your goals and projects are implicated in them. That holds for the State's duties as well. It means that the State, like other agents, is morally bound to have a low-level focus on its own moral compliance, systematically but not corruptly concealing morality's higher-level agent-neutrality.

[7] That might include e.g. providing a safe house, or taking criminal libel proceedings against those who make public accusations in a way which will incite reprisal. The demand for protection applies *a fortiori* to those who did wrong but who were acquitted at law, where reprisals not only threaten the wrong-doer but also challenge the law's own authority to deal with the wrong.

[8] I have discussed some aspects of the substantive criminal law which contribute to this aim in 'On the General Part of the Criminal Law', in R. A. Duff (ed.), *Philosophy and the Criminal Law* (1998).

[9] J. Rawls, *A Theory of Justice* (1971), p. 3. Rawls' slogan can bear various interpretations apart from the rather literal one I have adopted in the text. On one very different interpretation, Rawls was only saying that justice is the *last resort* of social institutions, i.e. when all else fails social institutions

liberal one that under modern conditions the State should keep its distance from its people, leaving them free to make their own mistakes. Casting all questions for the State in terms of justice is one possible way to ensure this distance because, as the old adage goes, justice is blind. To do its relativizing work, justice must isolate criteria (although not necessarily the same criteria in every context) for differentiating among those who come before it. And to give these criteria of differentiation some rational purchase, they must be implemented against a background of assumed, but often entirely fictitious, uniformity. The just person, if you like, refuses to take sides in order to take sides; she artificially blinds herself to some qualities of people and aspects of their lives in order to be able to make something of the other differences between them. Rawls memorably conveyed the idea when he spoke of 'the veil of ignorance' behind which just policies are conceived.[10] Now, as many of Rawls' critics have demonstrated, it is very doubtful whether cultivating this kind of artificial blindness to some of our qualities and some aspects of our lives is the proper way for the modern State as a whole to keep its distance from us. It leads to the wrong kind of distance, a remote and sometimes callous disinterest in people's well-being, which the State cannot legitimately, or even (some say) intelligibly, maintain across the board.[11] On the other hand, there is very good reason to think that at least one set of institutions belonging to the modern State, viz. the courts of law, should normally keep their distance from us in precisely this way. Courts are law-applying institutions, and it is in the nature of modern law, with its 'Rule of Law' aspiration to apply more or less uniformly to all of those who are subject to it, that questions of how people are to be treated relative to one another always come to the fore at the point of its application. If we pursue this line of thinking, which of course calls for much more detailed elaboration, justice does turn out to be the first virtue of the courts even though not of other official bodies. The courts' primary business becomes, as the law itself puts it, 'the administration of justice'.

In the criminal law context, where (if the Rule of Law is being followed) the substantive law is relatively clear and certain, the most obvious everyday impact of the court's role as administrator of justice is in the procedural and evidential conduct of the trial—in determining, for example, the probative relevance and prejudicial effect of certain background information about offenders and witnesses, or the acceptability of certain modes of examination-in-chief and cross-examination. In these matters the court's first priority is to specify the density of its own veil of ignorance, the scope of its own blindness, the limits of forensic cognizance.[12] And it must do the very same thing once again at the sentencing stage

should at the very least be just. See J. Waldron, 'When Justice Replaces Affection', (1988) 11 *Harvard Journal of Law and Public Policy*, 625.

[10]   *A Theory of Justice* (1971), 136 *et seq.*

[11]   Both the conceptual and the moral objections are represented in M. Sandel, *Liberalism and the Limits of Justice* (1982), 24–8 and 135–47. Likewise, with a strikingly different twist, in J. Raz, *The Morality of Freedom* (1986), 110–33 and 369 *et seq.*

[12]   Isn't there a basic problem with letting an institution decide what it shall take notice of? Doesn't it have to know what it should not know in order to know whether it should know it? True enough.

of the trial where the law, rightly attempting to adjust for the inevitable rigidity and coarseness of its own relatively clear offence-definitions, typically leaves the court's options more open. Of course, in approaching these sentencing options, the court cannot ignore the State's duty of humanity, in the fulfilment of which the State's law-applying institutions must also do their bit. This is a duty which also has implications for sentencing. In the name of humanity, there must always be space for something like a plea in mitigation to bring out the offender's fuller range of qualities, the wider story of his life, some of which was necessarily hidden behind the 'veil of ignorance' during the earlier parts of the trial. But we may well ask: what is it, exactly, that falls to be mitigated when a plea in mitigation is presented to the court? If I am right so far, what falls to be mitigated is none other than the sentence which is, in the court's opinion, required by justice. Identifying a just sentence is thus the proper starting-point. A court which begins from some other starting-point, some other *prima facie* position, is a court which fails to observe its primary, and indeed one may be tempted to say definitive, duty.

Again, nothing in this proposal detracts from my original claim that the control of reprisal is a central pillar of the criminal law's justification. The proposal merely introduces a further troublesome complication. The complication is that, while the control of reprisal forms a key part of the argument for having criminal law and its punitive responses in the first place, those who must implement the criminal law and its punitive responses cannot legitimately make the control of reprisal part of *their* argument for doing so.[13] Displacement of retaliation is a reason for punishment which cannot be one of the judge's reasons for punishing. Judges cannot begin their reasoning at the sentencing stage by asking: What sentence would mollify the victim and his sympathizers? Instead they should always begin by asking: What sentence would be just? I should stress that I am not assuming at the outset that these two questions are unconnected. At this stage I mean to leave open the possibility that, for example, victims and their supporters might want nothing more than the very justice which it is the court's role to dispense, so that doing justice will reliably serve that ulterior purpose. My only point is that the courts should not share in this ulterior purpose themselves; they should insist on thinking in terms of justice irrespective of whether doing so serves the further purpose of pacifying retaliators. For the criminal court, justice is an end, and that remains true even if, for the criminal justice system as a whole, justice is at best a means. In this respect, the criminal court in a modern State is a

That is why, in trial by indictment, the *voir dire* exists to separate the function of determining what will be hidden by the veil of ignorance from the function of deliberating about guilt and innocence behind the veil of ignorance. This double-insulation against unwitting prejudice provides a major part of the case for retaining a right to jury trial whenever serious criminal charges are laid. On the question of a criminal charge's seriousness, see sections 3 and 4 below.

[13] This helps us to see why as theorists we should not fear the multiplicity of considerations which add up to justify the practice of criminal punishment. As administrators of justice judges are heavily restricted in their access to many of these considerations, and thus do not have to face all the conflicts among them in their raw form. I have discussed this in greater depth in 'The Purity and Priority of Private Law', (1996) 46 *University of Toronto Law Journal*, 459.

classic bureaucratic institution. It has certain *functions* which cannot figure in its *mission*, and which therefore cannot directly animate its actions.

It is not surprising that this distinctively bureaucratic aspect of courts, and especially criminal courts, has been a cause for much complaint, particularly among victims of crime and their sympathizers, who accuse the courts of leaving them out in the cold, being out of touch with their concerns, stealing their cases away from them, etc. I already mentioned the challenge of maintaining a humane bureaucracy, and maintaining humanity towards victims is an aspect of that challenge to which I will return at the very end of this chapter. But in the context of the criminal law, the pre-eminence of the court's duty of justice creates a prior difficulty, which this discussion was designed to highlight, and aspects of which will occupy our attention over the next few pages. As I explained before, in ful-filling its displacement function the criminal law must always walk a fine line between failing to pacify would-be retaliators and simply institutionalizing their excesses. What we have just added is that under modern conditions an extended section of this fine line, the section which passes through the domain of the courts, must be walked wearing justice's blindfold. What hope can we have for the criminal law's fulfilment of its displacement function under these conditions?

3. THE PROPORTIONALITY PRINCIPLE

In exploring this question, I want to focus attention on one particular principle of justice which is of profound moral importance for the criminal courts in their sentencing decisions, namely the principle that the punishment, if any, should be in proportion to the crime. I choose this principle not only because of its moral importance (to the explanation of which I will return presently) but also because so many people apparently read it as a principle which focuses on how the offender is to be treated relative to her victim or victims, and thus see it as a straightforward way of having the retaliatory impulses of victims systematically reflected in the administration of justice. To my mind, this victim-oriented read-ing is a serious misreading of the proportionality principle. The State's duty of justice, like the State's duty of humanity, has an important agent-relative aspect. The relativities with which the modern courts must principally contend under the rubric of justice are relativities between the State's treatment of different peo-ple, not relativities between how the State treats someone and how that someone treated someone else.[14] Therefore the question of proportionality in sentencing which concerns a modern criminal court is primarily the question of whether this offender's sentence stands to his crime as other offenders' sentences stood to their crimes. This means that the proportionality principle does not in itself specify or even calibrate the scale of punishments which the State may implement, but sim-ply indicates how different people's punishments (or to be exact their *prima facie*

---

[14] See n. 6 above.

punishments before any mitigating factors are brought to bear) should stand *vis-à-vis* one another on that scale.[15]

It does not automatically follow from this, however, that the victim's predicament or perspective cannot properly be introduced into the court's deliberations under the heading of proportionality. According to the proportionality principle, the sentence in a criminal case should be proportionate to *the crime*. If the court can point to features of the crime committed in the case at hand which make it more or less grave than other comparable crimes that have been dealt with by the courts, then the proportionality principle plainly points to a corresponding adjustment of the *prima facie* sentence. It means that everything turns on the applicable conception of 'the crime' and the specification of its axes of gravity. Now it may be thought that the law itself sets these parameters, so that the matter is simply a technical legal one. Crime, some will say, is a purely legal category, and a crime is none other than an action or activity which meets the conditions set by law for criminal conviction.[16] Thus 'the crime' referred to in the principle of proportionality can be none other than the crime as legally defined. It would follow that whether the victim's predicament or perspective is relevant under the heading of proportionality would depend only on whether the legal definition of the crime made specific mention of it. A crime defined in terms of the suffering or loss inflicted upon its victim would leave space for, even perhaps require, the degree of that suffering or loss to be brought to bear on the sentence under the proportionality principle, thus giving some aspects of the victim's predicament or perspective a role in the court's deliberations under the heading of justice. But a crime without such a definitional feature would naturally leave no such space and offer no such role to victim-centred considerations.

In fact, the problem is much more complicated than this. It is true that crimes are, in one ('institutional') sense, just activities which meet the conditions for criminal conviction. But criminal conviction is an all-or-nothing business. Questions of gravity can certainly be a relevant factor, on occasions, in determining which of a number of related crimes the accused should be convicted of, e.g. whether he is a murderer or a manslaughterer, a robber or a thief, etc. But for any *single* criminal offence considered by the jury or magistrate the ultimate answer can only be guilty or not guilty; gravity is neither here nor there.[17] What is more, where the rule of law is properly observed, criminal offences are defined so as to

---

[15] Thus I am going to be writing about what von Hirsch calls 'ordinal proportionality' rather than 'cardinal proportionality': von Hirsch, *Censure and Sanctions* (1993), 18–19. As it happens I also believe in a principle of cardinal proportionality, but it has a very different foundation and applies to the legislative business of setting sentencing maxima rather than to the sentencing stage of criminal trials. It is also worth mentioning that both cardinal and ordinal principles of proportionality need to be applied with the State's duty of humanity in mind, since this forbids cruel or brutalizing punishments even when these would be proportionate. None of this affects the substance of my argument.

[16] G. Williams, 'The Definition of Crime', [1955] *Current Legal Problems* 107.

[17] It is true that the Scots allow for 'not proven' as a *tertium quid*, but of course it still has nought to do with the gravity of the crime. The American solution of 'first degree' and 'second degree' crimes may look at first like another counter-example, but all it does in reality is multiply the number of separate crimes to which the 'all or nothing' guilty/not guilty decision must be applied.

facilitate exactly this kind of 'all or nothing' decision-making. Rape, in England, is sexual intercourse without consent undertaken in the knowledge of, or reckless as to, the lack of consent. Grey areas and borderline cases of consent, sexual intercourse, knowledge, and recklessness have all been, so far as possible, defined out.[18] There is nothing in the definition of rape, apart perhaps from the difference between the knowing rapist and the reckless one,[19] that could conceivably afford a sentencing judge any significant axis of gravity. So does the proportionality principle, by itself, prescribe the same sentence for all knowing rapists, irrespective of their brutality, treachery, bigotry, cowardliness, arrogance, and malice? This challenge cannot be avoided by observing that most crimes do harbour some residual questions of degree in their definitions—that grievous bodily harm is more grievous in some cases than in others, that some acts of dishonesty are more dishonest than others, etc. That is not the point. The point is that, where the rule of law is observed, individual criminal offences are not defined in law so as to retain a topography of gravity for the sentencing stage, but rather so as to flatten that topography, so far as possible, for the all-or-nothing purposes of conviction and acquittal. There is no reason to think that a definition crafted primarily for one purpose, viz. that of flattening the rational variation between different cases of the same wrong, should be regarded as authoritatively determining the scope of the court's veil of ignorance when its job turns, at the sentencing stage, from eliminating such rational variation to highlighting it. There is no reason to assume that the court will find all, or any, of the relevant variables still inscribed on the face of the crime's definition.

It follows that, for the purpose of the principle that the sentence should be in proportion to the crime, we need to go beyond a purely institutional conception of the crime. I do not mean to write off all institutional circumscriptions. It seems to me to be a sound rule of thumb, for example, that evidence which was inadmissible in the trial on grounds of its irrelevance to the charge before the court should not be taken into account when the gravity of the crime is being assessed for the purposes of proportionate sentencing. That an act of dangerous driving caused death should be treated as irrelevant to the gravity of the crime if the crime charged is dangerous driving rather than causing death by dangerous driving. No doubt this is bound to frustrate victims of crime and their sympathizers who may have little patience with the due process principle that people should only be tried for the crimes with which they are charged and sentenced for the crimes which were proved against them at trial—recall that the predictability of such impatience was among the factors which justified the State in monopolizing retaliatory force to begin with. But be that as it may, the due process principle *itself*

---

[18] *Olugboja* (1981) 73 Cr App Rep 344 and *Linekar* [1995] 2 Cr App Rep 49 illustrate the law's attempts to turn certain grey areas between consent and non-consent into brighter lines. *Kaitamaki* [1985] AC 147 does the same with respect to 'sexual intercourse'. The *mens rea* elements were hotly debated in the early 1980s, but the debate was simply between two different ways of artificially stripping grey areas from the concept of recklessness, the broader contrived definition in *Pigg* [1982] 2 All ER 591 giving way to the narrower one in *Satnam S* (1983) 78 Crim App Rep 149.

[19] cf. *Bashir* (1982) 77 Cr App Rep 327.

requires that we go beyond a merely institutional conception of the crime. To implement the principle of due process, just as to implement the principle of proportionality in sentencing, we need some grasp not only of the crime's legal definition but equally of what counts as the *substance* or the *gist* or the *point* of the crime as legally defined—and that is an unavoidably evaluative, non-positivistic issue.[20]

Here, for example, are a couple of classic due process questions. Apart from the charge spelt out in the indictment or summons, were there other lesser offences with which the accused was also implicitly being charged, which did not need to be spelt out? And when does the defendant's previous wrong-doing pass the 'similar fact' test, so that evidence of it is relevant for the purposes of proving the offence charged on the present indictment? Lawyers have often struggled to answer these questions in institutional terms, by pointing to features of crimes which figure in the positive legal definitions.[21] But that, as we should all have realized by now, was always a false hope. One cannot apply or even adequately understand these questions without developing what we may like to call the moral map of the crime, highlighting evaluative significances which may be missing from the law's pared down definition. Thus even if, as I suggested, the principle of proportionality in sentencing does usefully borrow some institutional circumscriptions from the due process principle, that ultimately just reiterates rather than eliminates the fundamentally evaluative, non-positivistic question of what counts as 'the crime' for the purposes of assessing the proportionate *prima facie* sentence. One still needs a moral map of the crime, and the question remains, after all this, of whether the predicament or perspective of the victim can figure anywhere on that map.

4. PERSPECTIVES ON CRIME

One significant strand of the literature on criminal law and criminal justice proceeds from the thought that many, if not all, crimes are covered by one and the same moral map. This is the map of the offender's *blameworthiness* or *culpability*. Following this map leads to a specific interpretation of the principle of proportionality, according to which making the sentence proportionate to the crime means making the sentence proportionate to the offender's blameworthiness or culpability in committing the crime.[22] Let's call this the 'blameworthiness

---

[20] This is not a criticism of legal positivism. Legal positivists hold that validity of a law turns on its sources rather than its merits. That does not prevent them from holding that legal reasoning reflects on the merits as well as the sources of laws, since there is no reason to suppose that legal reasoning is only reasoning about legal validity. See J. Raz, 'On the Autonomy of Legal Reasoning', (1993) 6 *Ratio Juris*, 1.

[21] See *Novac* (1977) 65 Cr App Rep 107 and *Barrington* [1981] 1 All ER 1132 to see how the issue arises in relation to the similar fact doctrine; concerning counts in an indictment, the issue is well-illustrated in the leading case of *Wilson* [1984] 1 AC 242.

[22] A random selection: H. Gross, 'Culpability and Desert', in R. A. Duff and N. Simmonds (eds.), *Philosophy and the Criminal Law* (ARSP Beiheft 19, 1984), p. 59; C. L. Ten, *Crime, Guilt, and*

interpretation' of the proportionality principle. In the minds of many adherents as well as many critics, the proportionality principle in its blameworthiness interpretation systematically excludes victim-centred considerations from the proper scope of the court's *prima facie* sentencing deliberations. The pivotal thought behind this is that a person's blameworthiness in acting as she did is a function of how things seemed to her at the time of her action.[23] It may of course be a more or less complex function. On some accounts of the function, blameworthiness increases or decreases according to how much of the evil of her action the agent appreciated. For others, it is a question of how much the agent should have appreciated, given the various other things she knew at the time. Either way, the crucial manoeuvre so far as blameworthiness is concerned is supposedly to look at the situation *ex ante*, from the perspective of the perpetrator. But that perspective, it is often claimed or assumed, is fundamentally at odds with the perspective of the victim, who looks at the wrong *ex post* and is interested not so much in how things may have seemed to the perpetrator, but rather in how things actually occurred or turned out.[24] On this view the victim and those who sympathize with him are aggrieved first and foremost because of what he suffered or lost at the perpetrator's hands, whether or not the perpetrator appreciated or could have appreciated the full extent of this loss or suffering at the time of acting. If that is so, then the conception of the crime which lies at the heart of the proportionality principle on its blameworthiness interpretation is not the victim's conception. In fact it is diametrically opposed to the victim's conception. If anything, the proportionality principle in this interpretation seems to oblige courts systematically to *compound* the frustration of victims and their sympathizers, and hence to *aggravate* their retaliatory instinct, by insisting on seeing things the offender's way and hence (through the already aggrieved eyes of victims and their sympathizers) doggedly taking the offender's side in the whole conflict. Thus, on this

Punishment (1987), p. 155 *et seq*; A. Ashworth, 'Taking the Consequences' in S. Shute, J. Gardner, and J. Horder (eds.), *Action and Value in Criminal Law* (1994), p. 107 at pp. 116–20. Von Hirsch also makes culpability the only axis of crime-seriousness when he introduces the proportionality principle on p. 15 of *Censure and Sanctions*. But contrast the more complex 'harm-plus-culpability' standard used for proportionality on p. 29 of the same volume, and elsewhere in von Hirsch's work, e.g. in his *Past or Future Crimes* (1985), p. 64 *et seq*. See further n. 30 below.

[23] Among diverse writers who allocate blameworthiness on these terms we find D. Parfit, *Reasons and Persons* (1986), pp. 24–5; S. Sverdlik, 'Crime and Moral Luck', (1988) 25 *American Philosophical Quarterly*, 79; R. Swinburne, *Responsibility and Atonement* (1989), pp. 34–5. D. Husak and A. von Hirsch, 'Culpability and Mistake of Law' in *Action and Value in Criminal Law* (1994); Ashworth, 'Belief, Intent and Criminal Liability' in J. Eekelaar and J. Bell (eds.), *Oxford Essays in Jurisprudence: Third Series* (1987), p. 1 at p. 7.

[24] Talk of the 'victim perspective' and the 'perpetrator perspective' on wrong-doing will be familiar to those conversant with the literature on anti-discrimination law. See A. D. Freeman, 'Legitimizing Racial Discrimination Through Antidiscrimination Law: A Critical Review of Supreme Court Doctrine', (1978) 62 *Minnesota Law Review*, 1049. The version of the distinction relied upon here is slightly less ambitious than Freeman's, although the two are closely related. The distinction I am speaking of figures prominently in Sverdlik, 'Crime and Moral Luck' (n. 23 above) and in A. Ashworth, 'Punishment and Compensation: Victims, Offenders and the State', (1986) 6 *Oxford Journal of Legal Studies*, 86 at e.g. 96. cf. also J. Coleman, 'Crimes, Kickers and Transaction Structures' in J. R. Pennock and J. W. Chapman (eds.), *Criminal Justice* (Nomos XXVII, 1985), p. 313 on the contrasting 'economic' and 'moral' perspectives of tort law and criminal law.

view of the matter, fidelity to the proportionality principle scarcely militates in favour of the sentencing process making a systematic positive contribution to the fulfilment of the criminal law's displacement function.

There is, however, a great deal of confusion in this line of thinking. I can only scratch the surface of a few of the problems here. The problems start with a failure to spell out what blameworthiness or culpability *is*, which leads to an over-simplification of the principles on which it is incurred. Blameworthiness has a four-part formula. To be blameworthy, one must (a) have done something wrong and (b) have been responsible for doing it, while lacking (c) justification and (d) excuse for having done it. Each of elements (a), (b), (c) and (d) can undoubtedly be sensitive, to some extent and in some respects and on some occasions, to how things seemed to the blameworthy person at the time of her action. Elements (c) and (d) in fact incorporate an across-the-board partial sensitivity to the *ex ante* perspective of the perpetrator. Take element (c) first. An action is *justifiable* if the reasons in favour of it are not defeated by the reasons against; but it is *justified* only if the agent acts for one or more of those undefeated reasons.[25] It follows that a purported justification based on considerations unknown to and unsuspected by the agent at the time of the action is no justification at all. Thus justification always does depend, in part, on how things seemed to the agent at the time of the action. Conversely, justification also depends, in part, on how things actually were. No matter how things seemed to the agent, if the reason for which she acted was not in fact an undefeated one then she can have no justification. If she fails the test of justification on this score, the agent must retreat to element (d), the excuse element, to resist the allegation of blameworthiness. Here we find an additional sensitivity to the *ex ante* perspective of the perpetrator: here the agent can rely on what she mistakenly *took* to be undefeated reasons for her action, provided only that she was justified in her mistake. But again this last proviso shows that even excuses are not entirely insensitive to how things actually were; for whether the agent was excused by her mistakes depends on whether her mistakes were justified, and that in turn depends, like any justification, on whether there really were undefeated reasons for her to see the world as she did.[26] So in both elements (c) and (d) we have questions which focus on how things seemed to the agent *as well as* questions which focus on how things really were. Justification and excuse have some across-the-board agent-perspectival dimensions, but are neither of them a pure function of how things seemed to the agent at the time of the action.

Things get more complicated still when we add elements (a) and (b) to the stew. It is tempting to think that wrong action is the mirror image of right or justified action, so that, adapting from the account of right or justified action just outlined, whether one's action is wrong depends on whether the reasons in favour of performing it were defeated by the reasons against and whether one

---

[25] I have defended this account of justification in 'Justifications and Reasons' in A. P. Simester and A. T. H. Smith (eds.), *Harm and Culpability* (1996), p. 103.

[26] Ibid, at pp. 118–22.

acted for one of the latter reasons. Thus obviously no action could be wrong if the agent had no inkling of anything that made it wrong. But right and wrong are in fact dramatically asymmetrical. There are many more ways of doing the wrong thing than there are of doing the right thing. In particular, there is no general sensitivity of wrong-doing to the reasons for which one acted. It is perfectly true that some wrongs, e.g. deceit and betrayal, cannot be committed without certain knowledge or belief on the part of the person who commits them, and others, such as torture and extortion, require a certain intention. But this is not true of all wrongs. One may do wrong by breaking a promise or neglecting one's children quite irrespective of what one knew or had reason to know, and *a fortiori* quite irrespective of why one did it. The same holds true, I believe, of killing people or wounding them, damaging their property, poisoning them, and countless other wrongs which are of enduring importance for the criminal law. It is wrong to kill people or wound them, and one may kill someone or wound them by playing with intriguing buttons or switches which were none of one's proper concern, quite irrespective of whether one knew or had grounds to know the true awfulness of what one was doing. If one's *ex ante* perspective is to be relevant to one's blameworthiness in respect of such killings or woundings, on this view, it must be relevant by virtue of some other element of blameworthiness, such as the justification or excuse element. To be sure, it may also be relevant to one's responsibility, element (b) of the blameworthiness equation. But again its relevance here can only be occasional and limited. To deny that one was a responsible agent one must not only deny that one knew what one was doing, but also point to some underlying explanation such as psychotic delusion, infancy, or (on some views of the phenomenon) hypnosis which puts one temporarily or permanently out of reach of reason so that normal rational standards of justification and excuse do not apply to one. This is a very limited (and decidedly 'bottom of the barrel') opening for one's ignorance to affect one's blameworthiness. So again there is nothing here to make blameworthiness, in general, into a function of how things seemed to the agent at the time of his or her action. In fact, the influence of elements (a) and (b) in the blameworthiness equation fragments and complicates the conditions of blameworthiness even further, so that very few things can be said, in general, about the balance of agent-perspectival and non-agent-perspectival factors which will bear on the net blameworthiness of the agent.

Whatever one may think about the details of this elaboration of the conditions of blameworthiness, it draws attention to one crucial point which is far too easily overlooked. The crucial point is that there is no such thing as blameworthiness at large, or blameworthiness *tout court*. Our blameworthiness is necessarily our blameworthiness in respect of some specific action or activity we engaged in, such as killing, wounding, deceiving, betraying, torturing, or breaking a promise.[27]

---

[27] While we are blameworthy only in respect of actions, we are *to blame* in respect of consequences. To be to blame for a given consequence, we must be *responsible for* that consequence. Doesn't this complicate element (b) of my blameworthiness equation, which spoke only of responsibility for *actions* and therefore (you may say) swept under the carpet the further agent-perspectival

And whether and to what extent our blameworthiness is a function of how things seemed to us at the time of our action depends in very large measure on *which* action or activity we are supposed to be blameworthy in respect of, since different agent-perspectival conditions for blameworthiness evidently come into play for different actions and activities. Now there are those who try to make the determination of which action or activity we engaged in *itself* a function of the way things seemed to us at the time when we acted. Their response to my example of the person who kills unwittingly by playing with intriguing buttons and switches is to deny that it involves a killing, not just because killing in particular is held to be, like deceit, an action with some definitive knowledge requirement, but rather because the scope of agency is always, so to speak, in the eyes of the agent. Fundamentally, we do only whatever we take ourselves to be doing.[28] Personally, I find this a deeply counter-intuitive account of human agency.[29] But more importantly for present purposes, if this account of human agency is accepted, it makes a mockery of the process of determining blameworthiness which I outlined in the previous paragraph. We cannot ask, as I asked in the last paragraph, whether the killer was a responsible agent when he killed, or whether he had any justifications or excuses for doing it. For on this account of human agency *there was no killing*. The most the agent did was press buttons, or fiddle with things that didn't concern him. Having no possible inkling of the death-dealing aspect of what he was doing, he didn't kill anyone. All the hard work which the piecemeal doses of subjectivity in the separate elements of blameworthiness were supposed to do is thus pre-empted by a massive and all-consuming injection of subjectivity in the doctrine of human agency to which it is applied. We are not deprived of our (admittedly controversial and seriously under-specified) answer to the question of whether the button-presser was a blameworthy killer. *We are summarily deprived of the question itself.*

If we rescue the question, as I am sure we should, by jettisoning the extremely restrictive account of human agency which put it out of bounds, we can instantly see that the juxtaposition with which this section began was grievously exaggerated. There is no automatic and comprehensive opposition between assessing the

conditions of responsibility for consequences? The answer is no. Whether we are responsible for consequences is already taken into account in element (a) of the blameworthiness equation. In the relevant sense, we are responsible for those consequences which contribute constitutively to the wrongness of our doing as we do. We are *to blame* for those consequences, accordingly, when that condition is met and elements (b), (c) and (d) of blameworthiness are also present. There is thus no further question, on top of those already anticipated in my blameworthiness equation, of whether our responsibility or blame extends to a particular unforeseen or unforeseeable consequence of our actions. Much effort in moral and legal philosophy has been wasted thanks to the mistaken assumption that one has two bites at the cherry: first one can deny that one was blameworthy in respect of the action and then one can deny, separately, that the blameworthiness extended to a given consequence of the action. In fact the correct answer to the first question necessarily settles the second.

[28] cf. Elizabeth Anscombe's misleading remark in *Intention*, 2nd edn. (1963), p. 53: 'What happens must be given by observation; but . . . my knowledge of what I do is not by observation'. Ashworth's 'Taking the Consequences' is an example of a work which rigorously implements the highly subjectivized account of agency which this remark may be taken to support.

[29] I also believe it is incoherent: see 'On the General Part of the Criminal Law', n. 8 above.

gravity of a crime in terms of the offender's blameworthiness and assessing the gravity of a crime according to the way it impacts upon its victim. That is because, to assess the offender's blameworthiness we must begin by asking 'blameworthiness in respect of which action?' and this requires us to interrogate our account of human agency. Since on any plausible account of human agency there can be actions which are, like killing and wounding, defined at least partly in terms of their actual impact upon other people independently of the way things seemed *ex ante* to the perpetrator, it follows that an inquiry into the perpetrator's blameworthiness cannot be made independent of this impact. In fact, if we were to examine more thoroughly the so-called 'victim perspective' with which we started, I think we would find that the link between the blameworthiness of an offender and what irks the victim or her sympathizers is even more intimate than this last remark suggests. I believe it is the action of killing or wounding, complete with (but not limited to) the death or wound it involves, that normally aggrieves victims and their sympathizers and sparks their retaliation. Thus the starting-point of the blameworthiness inquiry—the action which was wrongful—is also the normal trigger for retaliatory responses on behalf of the victim. Of course there may be differences of perception and emphasis. It is true, for example, that *excuses* tend to be looked upon less generously by victims and their supporters than their importance for blameworthiness would indicate. Victims and their supporters may also have trouble with some justifications where their interests were not among the main reasons in favour of the justified action, and they may be more doubtful than the court might be, especially under the influence of psychiatric testimony, about a wrong-doer's supposed lack of responsibility. This means that the blameworthiness inquiry could certainly drive some wedges between the court's proportionality-driven thinking on matters of *prima facie* sentencing and the demands of victims and their supporters. But one only drives wedges between surfaces which are in their original tendency attached to one another. On my account that is exactly the situation with the offender's blameworthiness and the victim's grievance. It follows that there is no fundamental opposition of perspectives, no chasm of understanding, dividing the blameworthiness interpretation of the proportionality principle from the demands of those whose retaliation must be displaced if the criminal law is to fulfil its displacement function.

Here I am talking as if the blameworthiness interpretation of the proportionality principle came out basically unscathed from the process of correcting the analysis of blameworthiness which went into it. But of course it did not. What we have discovered in the process of explaining the concept and conditions of blameworthiness is that it makes no sense to prescribe, simply, that the sentence in a criminal trial should be in proportion to the offender's blameworthiness in committing the crime. For that prescription falls into the trap of presenting blameworthiness as an independent quantity, something that one can have more or less of *tout court*. Now that we have brought to mind the important point that blameworthiness is always blameworthiness in respect of some action, the blameworthiness interpretation in its original form should be replaced by a sharper ('modified blameworthiness') interpretation of the proportionality principle according to which the sentence should be in proportion to the offender's wrongful action, adjusted for his blameworthiness in respect of it.[30] This reinterpretation, with the slightly more complex moral map of a crime it implies, makes several important advances over the simpler blameworthiness interpretation it replaces. Let me mention just two of them here.

First, the modified blameworthiness interpretation helps to bring out what *justifies* the proportionality principle, and lends it the moral importance in the courtroom that I so confidently spoke of earlier. Although a principle of justice, the proportionality principle also contributes directly and powerfully to the court's compliance with the State's duty of humanity, and it takes much of its moral force from that contribution. As already mentioned, the State's duty of humanity requires it to affirm the moral agency and moral responsibility of those whom it punishes. The proportionality principle in its modified blameworthiness interpretation puts both the offender's agency and her responsibility centre stage. To ask about the offender's blameworthiness is to emphasize her responsibility. That is not only because element (b) of the blameworthiness equation is the element of responsibility. It is also because questions of justification and excuse—elements (c) and (d)—are applicable only to responsible agents, so that applying standards of justification and excuse to people is an assertion of their responsibility. But on top of that the modified blameworthiness interpretation brings out the importance of questions about the offender's agency which are not highlighted in the simple blameworthiness interpretation. It reminds us that treating someone as an agent is of importance quite apart from treating them as responsible. Even someone who is not responsible for their actions is an agent, and should still be treated as one. True, the duty of humanity as I expressed it goes further, and demands that offenders be treated as *moral* agents and as *morally* responsible. This arguably introduces further complications which point to a need for some further modification of the modified blameworthiness interpretation. Nevertheless the complications do not alter the main point, which is that by punishing people in proportion to their crimes, where those crimes are mapped according to the actions which made them wrongful adjusted for the offender's blameworthiness in respect of them, the court contributes decisively to the affirmation of the offender's humanity which is a *sine qua non* of the legitimacy of any modern State punishment. But remember that this is a function of the modern State's special duty of humanity towards its people, which comes of its claim to

---

[30] Compare this with von Hirsch's more complex version of the proportionality principle, mentioned in n. 22 above, which requires the crime to be in proportion to blameworthiness-plus-harm. Von Hirsch's principle comes close to mine in several ways, but still seems to leave blameworthiness as a free floating quantity. It may be said that it does not float free because it is now attached to a harm. But harms cannot be blameworthy. Only *doing* harm can be blameworthy. If von Hirsch's principle is that the sentence should be in proportion to the harm-doing adjusted for the harm-doer's blameworthiness in respect of it, then the only thing which divides us is that I refuse to reduce all wrongdoing to harm-doing. This has consequences: see n. 32 below.

authority and its associated role as servant of its people. Those of us who stake no similar claim to authority and have no similar role in other people's lives are not covered by the same strict humanitarian duty towards them.[31] Thus the strictness of the court's attention to questions of moral agency and moral responsibility need not, rationally, be mirrored in all interpersonal transactions between wrong-doers and people they wronged, or supporters, or even onlookers. That is one important reason why the victim of a crime and his or her sympathizers may sometimes *quite properly* (i.e. independently of their various impatiences, hastinesses, prejudices, etc.) have less time for the niceties of blameworthiness than the court is morally required to have.

Secondly, the modified blameworthiness interpretation has the advantage that it alerts us to the *limitations* of the proportionality principle as a principle of justice for scaling criminal sentences. The principle's usefulness depends first on the court's ability to discern what is supposed to be the wrongful action in the crime, and then the court's ability to compare this action with other actions, before it can even start to settle degrees of blameworthiness as between them. This may not always be possible. Some pairs of wrongful actions are incommensurable. It means that the proportionality scale will not always be perfectly transitive.[32] The adjustments for differential blameworthiness required by the modified blameworthiness interpretation of the proportionality principle can only take effect within the transitive parts of the scale. It may be possible to compare a less blameworthy robbery with a more blameworthy theft. But it will not necessarily be possible, even in principle, to assess a more blameworthy theft alongside, say, a more blameworthy assault. Here sentencing practice may have to move in relatively independent grooves, with guidelines that do not add up to a comprehensive code. The axes of gravity that operate at the sentencing stage will not necessarily, or even typically, allow the gravity of each crime to be plotted relative to that of every other crime. That, in my view, is no violation of the proportionality principle, nor on the other hand an indictment of it, but rather one of its welcome implications. The idea that all crimes are covered by a single moral map has, on closer inspection, very little to recommend it.[33]

---

[31] Although, as I have assumed throughout this chapter, we all have various more limited duties of humanity towards each other. Extra-judicial punishers such as teachers and parents are covered by the State's stricter duty to the extent that they echo the State's claim to authority and its basis.

[32] In their classic article 'Gauging Criminal Harm: A Living-Standard Analysis', (1991) 11 *Oxford Journal of Legal Studies*, 1, A. von Hirsch and N. Jareborg argued that all harms with which the criminal law should be concerned are commensurable, allowing a transitive sentencing scale under the proportionality principle. I think they are wrong about the commensurability of harms, and about the commensurability of living standards on which their argument was based. But even if they are right, it is a long way from the doctrine that all harms are commensurable to the doctrine that all *wrongs* are commensurable, since a wrong is an action, and even when it is an action defined in terms of the harm done, the harm done is only one constituent of the wrong. This means that von Hirsch and Jareborg still have some way to go to show that the proportionality scale is transitive. And here I am granting the generous assumption that elements (b), (c), and (d) of the blameworthiness equation do not introduce yet further incommensurabilities. On the proliferation of incommensurability in an action-centred view of morality, see Raz, *The Morality of Freedom*, (n. 11 above) p. 321 *et seq.*

[33] See my 'On the General Part of the Criminal Law' (n. 8 above) for a much closer inspection.

5. FILLING THE DISPLACEMENT GAP

The foregoing does something to explain how the courts, as blindfolded administrators of justice, can in spite of their blindfolds systematically help to fulfil the criminal law's displacement function. Even though the justice that victims and their sympathizers want (which is primarily justice between offender and victim) is not the justice that courts are licensed and required to provide by the proportionality principle (which is primarily justice between offender and offender), the proportionality principle, correctly interpreted, nevertheless shares some of its basic moral geography with the retaliatory logic of victims and their sympathizers. For some distance, courts and retaliators travel on the same path even though the former cannot, consistent with their mission, deliberately track the latter. But as I have also attempted to show, the two paths do diverge at certain obvious points. First, as I started section 2 by explaining, to preserve the legitimacy of the criminal law's monopolization of retaliation the courts must stop short of institutionalizing the excusable but unjustifiable retaliatory excesses of victims and their sympathizers. Second, as I explained in section 3, the principle of due process means that the wrongful action at the heart of the offender's crime cannot always, in the eyes of the law, and notably for the purposes of sentencing, be the same wrongful action which inspires retaliation by or on behalf of victims. The need to restrict the trial to the substance of the charges with which it began may lead to some differences between the victim's perception and the law's rendition of what the offender has done, even when the victim is not driven to retaliatory excess. Finally, the requirement to adjust the sentence for the offender's blameworthiness may, as I just explained in section 4, drive some extra wedges between the court's sense of proportionality and the victim's retaliatory inclinations, even where those inclinations are not excessive and there are no due process impediments to their reflection in law. The court, as an agent of the State, owes a duty of humanity to all which may often exceed the duty each of us owes to other people, and which therefore requires the court to affirm each offender's moral agency and moral responsibility more conscientiously than need be the case in many of our ordinary interpersonal transactions, including transactions with those who wrong us. These three factors add up to constitute what I will call the 'displacement gap' in criminal sentencing: the gap between what retaliators want and what the courts can, in good conscience, deliver.

Traditionally, this displacement gap has been filled by the law's own wealth of symbolic significances. What was confiscated from victims and their sympathizers in point of retaliatory force has traditionally been compensated by the ritual and majesty of the law, and by the message of public vindication which this ritual and majesty served to convey. At one time it was the ritual of the punishment itself which made the greatest contribution. The pillory, the stocks, the carting, the public execution, and various other modes of punishment involving public display allowed the State to close the displacement gap by exhibiting the offender in all his shame and humiliation, in all his remorse and regret, while the proceedings remained under some measure of official control to limit retaliatory excess.[34] But of course a new penal age dawned in the nineteenth century which put the offender out of reach and out of sight in the prison, where measured punishment and control of retaliation could be more successfully combined, both with each other and with the new disciplinary ambitions of supervision and rehabilitation.[35] From then on, the burden of providing ritual and majesty to fill the displacement gap was to a large extent shifted off the shoulders of the punishment system (which was now practically invisible to the general public except in the gloomy expanse of the prison walls) and onto the shoulders of the trial system instead. The courts themselves now had to offer the would-be retaliator the kind of public vindication which would once have been provided by the act of punishment, and the ritual and majesty of the courtroom had to substitute for the ritual and majesty of the recantation at the gallows. Of course the pressure to get this substitution exactly right was eased by the fact that the prison would to some extent protect the offender against the retaliator even if the displacement gap had not been successfully filled by the court. But it was still crucial that the trial itself should offer the victim and his sympathizers some symbolic significances which would divert them from taking the matter into their own hands e.g. if the offender was acquitted, or if a custodial sentence was not used, or once the custodial sentence had expired. For this purpose the court could only rely on continuing respect, indeed deference, for its own heavily ceremonial processes and practices. If the court's processes and practices were to fall into disrepute, if they came to be seen as just distracting frippery, then the vindicatory symbolism of the trial would be lost and the displacement gap would open wide for all to see. We would then face a major legitimation crisis in the system of criminal justice.

My view is that we now face this crisis in Britain, and for the very reason I have just given. During the 1980s and 1990s the steady creep of the ideology of consumerism has led people to regard the courts, along with many other key public institutions, as mere 'service providers' to be judged by their instrumental achievements. League tables, customer charters, satisfaction surveys, outcome audits, and efficiency scrutiny became the depressing norm. Respect for valuable public institutions declined at the same time as expectations of them increased. Even among those who took themselves to be anti-individualistic, the demand that institutions should become more 'transparent' and 'accountable' came to be regarded as orthodoxy, and euphemistic talk of 'cost-effectiveness' became

---

[34] How could the death penalty ever have been consistent with limiting retaliatory excess? Surely nothing could ever have exceeded death? Wrong. That one died with one's soul cleansed by confession or recantation was one mercy. That one died after judicial proceedings in which one was able to put one's defence, and therefore treated as a responsible agent, was another. On the mistaken assumption that the widespread availability and use of the death penalty in early-modern England was a sign of sheer brutality in criminal justice policy, see J. A. Sharpe, *Judicial Punishment in England* (1990), p. 27 *et seq.*

[35] The line of thinking in this paragraph obviously owes something to M. Foucault's *Discipline and Punish: The Birth of the Prison* (1977). I hesitate to specify exactly what.

acceptable. All this was, essentially, a corruption of a sound idea, which I mentioned at the outset—the idea that modern government is the servant of its people. It was mistakenly assumed that since public bureaucracies existed to serve social functions, ultimately serving people, they ought to be judged by the purely instrumental contribution they could make to those social functions, and hence their instrumental value for people. But it was forgotten that many social functions were not purely instrumental functions, i.e. many institutions made an intrinsic or constitutive contribution to their own social functions. The mission of such institutions, to return to my earlier expression, was partly integral to their function. The National Health Service and other organs of Beveridge's welfare State are the most familiar examples in Britain; people who regard themselves as collectivists should rue the day they ever tried to defend these in purely instrumental terms, which was the day they surrendered to the creeping individualism of the consumer society. But the criminal courts exemplify the point even more perfectly. Historically they filled the displacement gap in criminal justice by their own (to the public eye) bizarre and almost incomprehensible processes, their own special black magic if you like, which lent profound symbolic importance to their work. But armed with new consumerist ideas people came to see all these processes as mere frippery. They came to ask what the courts were *achieving* by their black magic, and whether it was giving them the *product* they wanted, whether this was the *service* they were looking for, and of course those questions quickly broke the spell. The courts could no longer fill the displacement gap from their own symbolic resources, since their own symbolic resources had been confiscated by the popular expectation of raw retaliatory results.

The consequence of this rapid social change is that the displacement gap is now an open and suppurating social wound, and the threat of retaliation by or on behalf of aggrieved victims of crime looms ever larger. The courts themselves sometimes feel the pressure and feel constrained to penetrate their own veil of ignorance, abandoning their mission to do justice where, as increasingly often, it parts company with their function to displace retaliation. That seriously violates their duty as courts, which is above all the duty of justice, and which positively requires them to stay 'out of touch with public opinion' on matters of sentencing policy. Meanwhile populist politicians pander to retaliatory instincts by threatening to publish names and addresses of ex-offenders, to force ex-offenders to reveal old criminal records, even to license vigilantes in the form of private security guards—all in order 'to hand justice back to the people'. What they do not appear to appreciate is that all of this makes the justification for the criminal law less stable, not more so. For if the criminal law cannot successfully displace retaliation against wrong-doers, but instead collaborates with it, then a central pillar of its justification has collapsed.

I do not mean to suggest that the courts' recent well-documented waking-up to the existence of victims is in every way a bad thing. There has been, for as long as anyone can remember, a tendency for criminal courts, with typical bureaucratic abandon, to pretend that nobody was concerned in their processes but themselves. Victims of crime, in particular, were kept badly informed and given no quarter at all in the operation of the system. Except insofar as they were witnesses, they were expected to find out for themselves where and when the trial would take place, to queue for the public gallery, to sit with the accused in the cafeteria, etc. In their capacity as witnesses, meanwhile, no concessions were made for the special difficulty of confronting those who had wronged them. Much of this amounted to a violation of the State's duty of humanity towards the victims of crime, and to the extent that it still goes on, it still does.[36] The courts should remember that victims, as well as offenders, are thinking, feeling human beings. But this has absolutely no connection with the far more sinister contemporary campaigns to turn victims into parties to the criminal trial or administrators of criminal punishments, or in some other way to hand their grievances back to them.[37] That victims do not try, convict, sentence, or punish criminal offenders, and have no official part in the trial, conviction, sentencing, and punishment of criminal offenders, is not an accident of procedural history. It is, on the contrary, one of the main objects of the whole exercise.

[36] On which see Helen Fenwick, 'Rights of Victims in the Criminal Justice System: Rhetoric or Reality?' [1995] *Criminal Law Review* 843.

[37] A prescient manifesto for criminological consumerism was N. Christie, 'Conflicts as Property', (1977) 17 *British Journal of Criminology*, 1, which spoke of conflicts being 'stolen' by criminal law and needing to be 'returned' to the parties through procedures which were 'victim-oriented' as well as 'lay-person-oriented'.

3

Five Puzzles in von Hirsch's Theory of Punishment

ANTHONY BOTTOMS

Andrew von Hirsch's approach to sentencing theory, developed and refined in his three distinguished books *Doing Justice* (1976), *Past or Future Crimes* (1986) and *Censure and Sanctions* (1993), has been immensely influential, both in the academy and—directly or indirectly—in sentencing reforms in several legal jurisdictions. I am glad to count myself among the many who have found this body of theory both exciting and largely persuasive.[1] And yet . . . there have always seemed to me to be a number of difficulties in von Hirsch's approach to sentencing theory, and to the theory of punishment more generally: some of these difficulties are purely theoretical, while some are associated with the *application* of the theory (i.e., the important transition from theory to actual practice in the courts). The welcome opportunity to contribute to a volume of essays celebrating Andrew von Hirsch's intellectual and practical achievements has thus also become, for me, a challenge—the challenge of articulating with precision, and in the process refining, some of the intuitive reservations I have held for some time about some aspects of von Hirsch's approach. My hope is that, in writing about these reservations, I may open up some fresh lines of thought which may lead to a further strengthening and refinement of some of von Hirsch's central tenets in sentencing theory.

As the title of this chapter indicates, I shall pursue this task by considering five separate 'puzzles' in von Hirsch's theory of punishment. These 'puzzles' are not, of course, an exhaustive list of the topics in von Hirsch's work that are worthy of further debate. But they are certainly enough to be going on with—and, between them, they do, I believe, illustrate both some of the great strengths of von Hirsch's developed theory, and also some issues that perhaps require some revision or further development.

The five 'puzzles' that I have chosen are rather disparate (they range in scope, for example, from the specific nature of one particular sentence—the probation order—through to the General Justifying Aim of von Hirsch's overall theory of

---

[1] See, e.g., A. E. Bottoms, 'The concept of intermediate sanctions and its relevance for the probation service', in R. Shaw and K. Haines (eds.), *The Criminal Justice System: a Central Role for the Probation Service* (Institute of Criminology, Cambridge, 1989); A. Ashworth, A. von Hirsch, A. E. Bottoms and M. Wasik, 'Bespoke Tailoring Won't Suit Community Sentences', (1995) 145 *New L.J.* 970.

punishment). But, although disparate, the puzzles are intended to be linked. Perhaps the best way to indicate the intended linkage is to cite *verbatim* an examination question set to undergraduate law students in Cambridge in 1994:

'The idea that the punishment should fit the crime is a simple concept which appeals both to common sense and to a sense of fair play; but translating the idea into practice is not as easy as it sounds'. Discuss.

In a way, this chapter is an extended response to that examination question. The question's presuppositions, with both of which I agree, are first, that desert theory has immediate intuitive attractions, but secondly, that there are significant difficulties in translating the theory effectively into practice. In a nutshell, I shall argue that the difficulties of translation into practice have to be taken very seriously; they are, I believe, soluble, but in thinking about the solutions one is also driven to consider some modifications to the theory itself. However, I shall further argue that these suggested modifications to the theory do not weaken the power of Andrew von Hirsch's approach to sentencing theory—rather, they have the potential to strengthen it.

A Summer Holiday Incident

Before turning directly to the five selected 'puzzles', I think it is worth sharing with readers an apparently trivial incident that occurred in my presence in the summer of 1996. J. R. Lucas perceptively observes that punishment is 'a good topic to think philosophically about', since 'in attempting to clear one's mind, one is led to change it many times, as new difficulties obtrude themselves, and obstruct the latest clear and distinct ideas on the topic'.[2] The incident I shall describe is one that I have often thought about in trying to formulate the arguments of this chapter, especially those in Puzzles 3 and 4, below; and it has contributed powerfully to some of the many changes of mind on particular points that Lucas so well describes. My purpose in describing the incident at the outset of this chapter is, however, not simply autobiographical. The central point is— this was an actual incident of punishing, albeit occurring in a domestic rather than a legal setting. Undoubtedly, in penological circles, there is often a very real gap of incomprehension between, on the one hand, those concerned with abstract philosophical principles, and, on the other hand, those concerned in the courts and elsewhere with daily penal practice.[3] Inclusion of an actual incident of punishing at an early stage of the argument may therefore serve the dual purpose of first, reminding those of a theoretical bent that their theories need to be translatable to, and to make sense in, the real world; and, secondly, reminding penal practitioners that even the most trivial incidents in daily life can produce rich data for theoretical reflection upon what exactly we think we are doing when we punish someone.

---

[2] J. R. Lucas, *Responsibility* (OUP, 1993), p. 285.
[3] See R. A. Duff and David Garland (eds.), *A Reader on Punishment* (OUP, 1994), Introduction.

Here then is the 'summer holiday incident':

I was on holiday in a self-catering chalet with my wife, my daughter and her two children, then aged respectively four and two. The younger child, J, was blowing soap bubbles on the verandah of the chalet, using a small bubble-blowing kit that he had been given. The elder child, H, was in a bored mood, and started banging the door leading to the verandah. I asked her not to do this. In response, she banged the door again, and also started denigrating J, saying that the bubbles he was blowing were useless bubbles, not nearly as good as those she could blow, and so forth. H's mother intervened, firmly telling H to go and sit quietly halfway up the stairs (an understood form of punishment in their household). After a couple of minutes, H was asked by her mother to explain why she was sitting on the stairs. Her initial response ('I don't know') was rejected ('you know perfectly well'), after which she came up with the correct answers (denigration of her younger brother and door-banging). She was then reminded why these incidents had led to punishment (J was not to be denigrated just because he was younger and had fewer abilities than H; door-banging is irritating to everyone in the household). H was asked by her mother who she should say sorry to; she correctly replied 'J', and duly said sorry to him. She was then told not to behave in either of these ways again. The holiday resumed . . .

I do not intend to analyse this incident fully here (though I shall return to it from time to time in the sections that follow). At this stage, I shall simply note two important features of what transpired. The first, which is highly congruent with Andrew von Hirsch's theory of punishment (though not with that of all penal theorists), is the obvious centrality, within the incident, of an *appeal to the moral reasoning of the recipient of the punishment*. The second important feature, undoubtedly of interest to Andrew von Hirsch, but perhaps not always sufficiently stressed by him, is the rich dimension of *symbolic communication* within the incident (e.g. the reassertion of J's dignity that his mother's words and actions accomplished; and even the choice of sitting on the stairs as a kind of symbolic semi-banishment, since no one normally sits half-way up the stairs, and there is not much to do when one is there).[4] Both moral reasoning and symbolic communication will form central threads in the argument of this chapter as it develops.

Puzzle 1: A Rickety Ladder?

I turn now more directly to the five selected puzzles.

The first puzzle is derived from part of Nigel Walker's critique of von Hirsch's theory in *Why Punish?* (1991). As Walker points out, von Hirsch's sentencing theory envisages 'two ladder-like scales', each arranged in ordinal fashion, the one listing offences in order of seriousness, and the other listing penalties in order of severity. Appropriate linkages then have to be forged between the 'crime-scale'

---

[4] There is an interesting analogy here with the penalty box in the game of ice-hockey (on which see A. E. Bottoms, 'Neglected Features of Contemporary Penal Systems', in D. Garland and P. Young (eds.), *The Power to Punish* (Heinemann, 1983), pp. 176–7), though in ice-hockey no one formally engages in moral reasoning with the player punished.

and the 'penalty-scale', with one of the central requirements being that this link-age should be achieved without disturbing the ordinal order of either scale. (Or, to put it another way, the 'rungs' of the central 'ladder' that links the crime-scale to the penalty-scale must never cross.)

But according to Walker, fitting together these two scales 'is not as simple as the proportionalist makes it sound', and the net result is that the proposed over-all ladder is 'rickety'.[5] There are two central complaints. The first is that the crime-scale is usually described in terms of legal categories (murder, rape, burg-lary, etc.), yet the seriousness of a particular crime within any given legal category can vary very widely: there are, as Walker puts it, 'robberies and robberies'. Indeed there are many different kinds of robbery—ranging from, at one end of the scale, an organized and armed hold-up of a security firm's vehicle trans-porting large amounts of cash to a bank, with one of the security guards being shot and injured in the process; to, at the other end of the scale, a simple and unpremeditated push in the street, linked to the snatching of a handbag.

Walker's second complaint refers to alleged uncertainties in the penalty-scale. Here, his main argument is—following Bentham—that of individual 'sensibil-ity'. That is to say, the same 'punishment' inflicted on a group of offenders will not by any means be equivalently received by each of them; rather:

the intensity of the suffering, hardship or inconvenience which a given penalty will inflict depends on the individual offender: on sex, age, social position, and so on.[6]

In a 1993 discussion of the construction of penalty-scales, von Hirsch has responded to this criticism, indicating that he prefers a more objective 'living standard approach', as against the necessarily personal and subjective nature of 'sensibility'. This living-standard approach had previously been most fully de-veloped by von Hirsch and Jareborg[7] in relation to the topic of gauging criminal harm (one element in the construction of the 'crime-scale': see above), but von Hirsch now suggests that a similar type of analysis could also be applied in de-veloping the gradations of the penalty-scale.[8] If such an approach were adopted, he argues, this would have the advantage that the scale of severity of penalties would not be simply 'a matter of (variable) subjective unpleasantness', as a sensibility-based approach would suggest. Rather:

---

[5] N. D. Walker, *Why Punish?* (Oxford, 1991), p. 102; see also N. D. Walker, 'Legislating the Transcendental: von Hirsch's Proportionality', (1992) 51 *Camb.L.J.* 530.

[6] Walker (1991), n. 5 above, p. 99.

[7] A. von Hirsch and N. Jareborg, 'Gauging Criminal Harm: a Living Standard Analysis', (1991) 11 *Oxford J.L.S.* 1.

[8] A. von Hirsch, *Censure and Sanctions* (OUP, 1993), pp. 34–5. In very bald terms, the living-standard approach as applied to the assessment of harm in crimes with an identifiable victim requires that first, one identifies the interests transgressed by the offence (e.g. in a residential burglary, the interests of 'material amenity' and 'privacy'), and secondly, one judges the importance of these various interests by assessing their normal significance for a victim's living standard (*ibid*, p. 31). By analogy, von Hirsch (p. 34) suggests that penalties could be ranked according to the degree to which they typically affect various identified interests of the offender, for example freedom of movement, earning ability and privacy.

If the freedom of movement that incarceration interferes with is an important interest—in the sense of its importance as a standardized means to achieving a certain living-standard—then its deprivation is severe even if a particular person might have different personal sensitivities.[9]

I believe that von Hirsch has the better of this particular argument, and that we should therefore adopt the 'living standard' approach rather than the sensibility approach to the issue of the gradation of penalty-severity.[10] Yet, even if we accept this view, it is crucial to recognize that *this does not dispose of Walker's argument that measurement of the gradations of the penalty-scale can be a difficult matter, contributing to the allegedly 'rickety' nature of the eventually-constructed overall ladder.* On a living-standard analysis, the severity of sentences of imprisonment can be fairly straightforwardly measured by their length, but non-custodial penalties would have to be 'classified according to the degree to which they affect a punished actor's freedom of movement, earning capacity and so forth', an analysis that, in any full sense, has 'yet to be undertaken'.[11] Such an analysis is obviously almost certain to be rather complex, with the comparison of fines, probation, community service, and electronic tagging giving rise to a significant number of difficulties.

In short, it seems to me that significant aspects of Walker's 'rickety ladder' complaint are correct, and that the construction of neither the crime-scale nor the penalty-scale is straightforward. As regards the crime-scale, von Hirsch's[12] central proposition is that the seriousness of crimes is to be judged by the interaction of the two components of *harm* and *culpability*. But, when one thinks about the exact harm done, and the precise culpability of the actor, in any specific offence, then obviously many subtle nuances often have to be considered—and these are certainly not likely to be captured by bare legal descriptions of offences. As regards penalties, scaling the relative severity of various non-custodial penalties is clearly no easy matter.

If—as I contend—all this is true, then what are the implications for the sustainability of von Hirsch's sentencing theory? To answer this question

---

[9] Von Hirsch (1993), n. 8 above, p. 35.

[10] An example which graphically illustrates the difference between these two approaches is to be found in the eighteenth-century writings of Cesare Beccaria. In his famous treatise *On Crimes and Punishments*, Beccaria advocated that, for similar crimes, the same penalties should apply to all members of society, regardless of wealth or rank. A quarter of a century later, whilst retaining this view for major crimes, Beccaria had come round to the view that for minor crimes those of higher social rank should receive lesser punishments; for 'flogging may perhaps correct an ignorant fellow of humble condition, but it certainly would dishearten and ruin a gentleman . . . and his whole family would feel covered with the most horrible shame. Then the punishment is no longer proportionate to the crime, it is incomparably greater' (see M. Maestro, *Cesare Beccaria and the Origins of Penal Reform* (Temple UP, 1973), pp. 30, 144–5). This example is not simply of historical interest; for it is surely an inevitable consequence of the 'sensibility' approach that those of higher rank in a given society should receive lesser penalties for a given crime, precisely because giving the same penalty (e.g. three months' imprisonment) to a rich and a poor person will always be seen as hitting the former harder than the latter. A result of this kind appears, however, to be extremely difficult to defend in principled terms.

[11] Von Hirsch (1993), n. 8 above, p. 60.

[12] A. von Hirsch, *Past or Future Crimes* (Manchester UP, 1986), Ch. 6.

adequately, it is necessary, in my view, to probe more deeply into the true nature of the theory.

On the first page of his most recent book, *Censure and Sanctions*, Andrew von Hirsch suggests two main reasons for the initial intuitive attractiveness of desert theory.[13] These reasons are quite similar to, but not the same as, those suggested in the Cambridge examination question (see above): for whereas the examination question identifies 'common sense' and 'a sense of fair play' as the main sources of desert theory's initial attractiveness, for von Hirsch this attractiveness rests on the facts first, that desert theory 'provides sentencers with a degree of guidance, in a way that competing theories seldom do', and secondly, that desert theory is 'ethically plausible' to most people, since most of us consider 'that penalties should fairly reflect the degree of blameworthiness of the conduct involved'.

I shall return later to the first of these claims by von Hirsch (about 'a degree of guidance'). For the moment, let us examine a little more closely the language in which the other claim (about 'ethical plausibility') is couched:

Most of us, as part of our everyday notions of justice, think that penalties should fairly reflect the degree of blameworthiness of the conduct involved. Even children object when they notice disparities in the punishments they receive for similar acts of misbehaviour.[14]

In the second part of this quotation, Andrew von Hirsch rightly points out that even children 'object when they notice *disparities*' in punishment (emphasis added). But notice that here von Hirsch (and the children) are focusing on the *dis*parities, that is to say the perceived *in*justices or *un*fairnesses in relative punishments.[15] This is not a trivial point. Human beings have been arguing in abstract terms about 'justice' at least since the time of Socrates, and we seem no nearer to agreed solutions.[16] But in the criminal justice context, we are particularly concerned with the *application* of ideas of justice to real-life situations (which is precisely why abstract philosophies of punishment often seem meaningless to penal practitioners). And when we focus upon applications, we quickly notice—as J. R. Lucas has so insightfully pointed out[17]—that in everyday discourse justice is an *asymmetric concept*: that is to say, it is very difficult for us to specify with any precision what justice is, but it is much easier to identify *specific injustices*. And it is these specific injustices that, as von Hirsch's example reminds us, children focus upon when they denounce something done to them as 'unfair'. Indeed, the denunciation of specific alleged injustices by those disadvantaged by them (or by advocates speaking on their behalf) can often have a very real and

---

[13] Of course, von Hirsch (1993), n. 8 above, p. 2 is very well aware that the fact that desert theory has these (alleged) attractions 'does not suffice . . . to establish its merits' as a justifiable theory of punishment.

[14] Von Hirsch (1993), n. 8 above, p. 1.

[15] Here the children are focusing on disparities in sentencing *outcomes*; but very often complaints of unfairness are additionally or alternatively about allegedly unfair *procedures*: see generally T. R. Tyler, *Why People Obey the Law* (Yale UP, 1990).

[16] See, e.g., P. Pettit, *Judging Justice: an Introduction to Contemporary Political Philosophy* (Routledge, 1980).

[17] J. R. Lucas, *On Justice* (OUP, 1980), Ch. 1.

uncomfortable resonance and impact on those running the system, as the literature of (for example) the sociology of prisons sharply reminds us.[18] In short:

If I talk only about justice, I am in danger of relapsing into platitudes: *it is when I get hot
under the collar about some specific piece of unfairness, that my eloquence has an edge to
it, and I really know what is getting my goat* . . . [T]he contrast between the mild favour I
feel towards fairness and the intense fury unfairness arouses in my breast is symptomatic
of a basic asymmetry between justice and injustice which . . . is crucial to the part they play
in our conceptual structure.[19]

In modern penology, the best-known exponent of a theoretical approach
focused on *un*fairness is of course Norval Morris (though Morris is apparently
unaware of Lucas's writings on asymmetry). In Morris's theory, a consequentialist approach to punishment is taken, *except that* the punishments that one may
award are subject to 'outer desert constraints', imposed in the name of fairness or
justice. Thus, in considering a specific punishment a sentencer primarily thinks
instrumentally (of deterrence, rehabilitation, incapacitation, etc.), but what s/he
can choose to do for instrumental reasons will be to some extent constrained by
justice-based limits. Hence, for a given crime 'C1' no punishment above 'P1' may
be awarded (however instrumentally effective), since 'P1' is the upper desert constraint for crime 'C1' (that is, no offence of type 'C1' can conceivably *deserve* more
than 'P1'; it would be *unjust* to the defendant to impose such a penalty). And, similarly, for Morris, there will also be a lower desert constraint for many crimes, fixed
with an eye to fairness as viewed by the victim, and/or by society at large.

Naturally, a theory of this kind satisfies neither full-blown consequentialists
(who are unpersuaded by its introduction of some desert constraints) nor desert
theorists such as Andrew von Hirsch, who argue that Morris's 'outer desert constraints' are altogether too remote and vague to have any real practical bite.[20] In
the face of such criticisms, Morris nevertheless adheres to his theory because he is
persuaded, first, that desert or fairness considerations should play some part in a
sentencing system; yet secondly, there is usually little consensus, in any given
society, about exactly what punishment is 'deserved' for a given offence, while by
contrast there may be much greater consensus about *undeserved* punishments
(e.g. 5 years' imprisonment for a parking offence would be widely regarded as
undeserved). Hence, we find Morris offering the following Lucas-like defence of
his 'outer desert constraints' approach:

Given the reality that people's views of deserved punishment vary widely, it is unlikely
that any comprehensive system of sentencing standards will adopt a rigid scheme of
deserved punishments. Retributive considerations can, however, give guidance on *un-
deservedly* lenient or severe punishments.[21]

---

[18] See, e.g., T. Mathiesen, *The Defences of the Weak* (Tavistock, 1965), and R. Sparks, A. E. Bottoms, and W. Hay, *Prisons and the Problem of Order* (OUP, 1996).
[19] Lucas (1980), n. 17 above, p. 5 (emphasis added).
[20] See, e.g., von Hirsch (1986), n. 12 above, Ch. 4.
[21] N. Morris and M. Tonry, *Between Prison and Probation* (OUP, 1990), p. 80 (emphasis added).

As Andrew von Hirsch makes clear,[22] the most important single difference between his theory of sentencing and that of Norval Morris lies in von Hirsch's acceptance of the concept of *ordinal proportionality*. As regards actual sentences passed (the 'cardinal magnitudes' of punishment), von Hirsch and Morris are in an important respect at one, for neither defends the traditional retributivist view of *substantive commensurability* (i.e., a proposition such as 'for crime "C2", only punishment "P2" is deserved'). Hence, for both writers, desert simply imposes some limits on cardinal magnitudes.[23] However, while Morris leaves desert considerations at this point, von Hirsch insists (among other things: see, further, note 26 below) that ordinal magnitudes are also a crucial part of desert theory, in three separate respects. These are:

(i)   **Parity:** that is, 'when offenders have been convicted of crimes of similar seriousness they deserve penalties of comparable severity'.

(ii) **Rank-ordering:** that is, 'punishing crime Y more than crime X expresses more disapproval for crime Y, which is warranted only if it is more serious'.

(iii) **Spacing of penalties:** that is, if crime A is only a little more serious than crime B, but crime C is a great deal more serious than A, then the respective punishments for these crimes should reflect this difference, notwithstanding that such distinctions are 'likely to be matters of rather inexact judgement'.

Von Hirsch is surely right, as against Morris, to insist that *ordinal proportionality* (his generic term for the three matters specified above) is an important part of most people's understanding of fairness in sentencing.[24] It is certainly not at all implausible, for example, to suggest that ordinary citizens would make remarks of the following (ordinal-proportionality-based) kind:

'It's awful that A got X and B got Y when they did virtually the same thing . . .' (Informal endorsement of *parity* as part of a fair criminal justice system).

'How could they give C 5 years for breaking into that factory when D only got 3 years for that serious assault: is property worth more than human life?' (Informal endorsement of *rank-ordering* as part of a fair criminal justice system).

Yet once again, on close analysis we notice that these complaints about aspects of ordinal proportionality—complaints which have real *prima facie* bite—are couched in the form of *complaints about specific injustices* (i.e. they are about people's perceptions of *undeserved* punishments).

Reflecting upon the respective theories of Andrew von Hirsch and Norval Morris, it would seem therefore appropriate to draw two interesting conclusions.

First, a central difference between the two theorists is the inclusion or

---

[22] Von Hirsch (1986), n. 12 above, Ch. 4.

[23] Von Hirsch, like Morris, once supported both upper and lower limits of cardinal magnitude. However, while he continues to support upper constraints, he now believes, following Nils Jareborg, that 'it is preventive concerns that ultimately constrain a deflation of penalty levels, rather than considerations of cardinal desert' (von Hirsch (1993), n. 8 above, p. 38).

[24] Von Hirsch (1993), n. 8 above, p. 18. By way of example, see the following interview studies of juvenile offenders in England: A. Morris and H. Giller 'The Juvenile Court—the Client's Perspective', [1977] *Crim.LR.* 198; R. Anderson *Representation in the Juvenile Court* (Routledge, 1978), Ch. 5; H. Parker, M. Casburn, and D. Turnbull, *Receiving Juvenile Justice* (Blackwell, 1981), Ch. 6.

otherwise of ordinal proportionality. However, it seems to be extremely difficult to sustain Morris's exclusion of this concept, at any rate if one stays with the principal ground that Morris himself gives for not incorporating desert considerations (other than outer desert limits) in his theory.[25]

Secondly, however, and notwithstanding these differences between the two theorists, both appear implicitly to accept and to work with Lucas's proposition that justice is an asymmetric concept. Morris's acceptance of this proposition is obvious (see above) and requires no elaboration. Andrew von Hirsch's position is more complex, and more positive in its espousal of desert, so his relationship to Lucas's proposition is trickier to establish. However, the fact that he denies any absolute scale of commensurably deserved punishments seems ultimately crucial. For him, there is no absolute scale; but we can establish upper cardinal limits for a sentencing scale (as does Morris: and, for von Hirsch as for Morris, it would be *unfair* to offenders to transgress those limits); and we can also establish other (but only *imprecise*) principles for setting the general level of a sentencing scale.[26] We can further establish a principle that those who have committed similar offences with similar records should receive similar punishments (and it would be *unfair* to treat them otherwise); and, finally, and following on from the last point, we can establish a scale of ordinal proportionality through which those who have committed more serious crimes will receive more serious penalties than those who have committed lesser crimes (and it would be *unfair* on the latter if it were otherwise).

At this point in the argument, I think it is necessary to examine carefully one key phrase that von Hirsch uses when discussing ordinal proportionality. In his own words:

Desert should be treated as a determining principle in deciding *ordinal* magnitudes. But it becomes only a limiting principle in deciding the system's *cardinal* dimensions of severity.[27]

A difficulty with this passage, in my view, lies in the potential ambiguity of the term 'determining principle'. Read in the total context of von Hirsch's work, it seems clear that, in using this phrase, von Hirsch is doing so in a technical

---

[25] It will be recalled that this principal ground is that 'people's views of deserved punishment vary widely'. At a *substantive* level of desert, that is undoubtedly true, yet it is also true that, for example, there is very widespread agreement among citizens on the importance of the concept of parity between sentences for similar offences (a key element in ordinal proportionality): see for example the references given in n. 24 above.

[26] An often-heard criticism of desert theory has been that (as von Hirsch himself has put it), 'while it may help to order penalties relative to one another, it says little about how severe or lenient the penalty-scale as a whole should be' (von Hirsch (1993), n. 8 above, p. 4). Von Hirsch's reply to this criticism (in Ch. 5 of *Censure and Sanctions*) seems to me to be largely convincing, and I shall return to it later in this chapter. For the moment, it is sufficient to note that von Hirsch himself concedes that the principles he proposes in the chapter cited are 'not precise enough to point to a particular appropriate level of sanctions' (p. 43); further, his proposed methodology for establishing the appropriateness or otherwise of a substantive sentencing scale is the distinctly Lucasian one of 'select(ing) somewhat arbitrarily' a proposed magnitude of scale, and then assessing whether that scale fails to meet the suggested principles for setting substantive sentencing scales.

[27] Von Hirsch (1986), n. 12 above, p. 39 (emphasis in original).

philosophical sense (i.e., for him, because of the nature of desert as censure, the inclusion of ordinal proportionality is a necessary feature of a desert-based sentencing system). The difficulty, as it seems to me, is that the phrase 'determining principle' can easily be read by the unwary in a much more practical sense, as implying that it is reasonably easy to *determine*, with precision, an exact ordinal order of seriousness of all conceivable crimes. (By comparison, when considering cardinal magnitudes, much vaguer limiting principles apply.)

That von Hirsch does not intend the phrase 'determining principle' to be read in this latter (more practical) way is apparent from a reply of his to a criticism by Michael Tonry.[28] Tonry had argued that, since legal rules are capable only of a certain degree of refinement, it follows that desert theory, when applied in legal practice, must be somewhat 'aggregative' (i.e. it must in practice treat similarly some theoretically distinguishable cases). Von Hirsch's response to this criticism is robust:

A sentencing system can, to a greater or lesser extent, punish comparably blameworthy conduct similarly. No sentencing system can *completely* succeed in this respect, because of the aggregative features of sentencing rules. Nevertheless, a carefully-worked out system of standards can achieve proportionality to a reasonable degree—which is, I think, all that can sensibly be aimed at.[29]

Actually, it seems to me that von Hirsch's response here is in one respect too quick. Up to a point, what he says is clearly correct. But, on his own principles, if the aggregative tendency of a given sentencing rule is so marked that it is producing (say) a genuine lack of parity by treating dissimilar cases similarly, then clearly that result will be regarded as unfair, certainly by the offender and very probably by many others.

Yet from the previous arguments of this section it is also clear that it must be a mistake to treat the concept of 'ordinal proportionality' in too precise a fashion. That is so, first, because of the imprecisions of the calibrations of the crime-scale and the penalty-scale to which Walker drew attention. But secondly, we have seen that on close examination von Hirsch's central proportionality claims are all congruent with Lucas's emphasis on the asymmetry of justice; indeed all of von Hirsch's claims (concerning both ordinal and cardinal proportionality) are ultimately simply claims that if certain boundaries are crossed then one will find *unfairness*. These two points between them make it exceedingly unlikely that one could ever, in any practical way, produce an exact ordinal order of the seriousness of all crimes. Yet, just as importantly, they in no sense impugn von Hirsch's theoretical claims about the centrality of ordinal proportionality (properly understood) to a fair sentencing system. To reflect the propositions embodied in the two preceding sentences, I believe it would be helpful to change the language of von Hirsch's main claim about ordinal proportionality. The new formulation would avoid talk of a 'determining principle', and substitute instead a phrase such as 'ordinal fairness should be seen as a necessary feature of a desert-based sentencing system'. This would still be a robust principle, with

---

[28] Von Hirsch (1993), n. 8 above, p. 104.   [29] *Ibid* (emphasis in original).

significant practical implications (its inclusion would still, for example, sharply differentiate von Hirsch's theory from that of Norval Morris); but it would not claim any unattainable precision for ordinal proportionality.

In summary, therefore, in this section I have argued:

(1)   that some of Walker's central complaints about imprecisions in the crime-scale and the penalty-scale are correct;

(2)   that Lucas is right to see justice as an asymmetric concept;

(3)   that in this particular respect von Hirsch, like Norval Morris, is a Lucasian (notwithstanding the other differences between Morris and von Hirsch); and

(4)   that one should abandon the language of ordinal proportionality being a 'determining principle', in case anyone should infer from this that the ordinal scale of crimes is more precise than it can possibly be, if the first and third propositions above are true.

As previously indicated, it is a central aim of this chapter to maintain a continuing dialogue between penal theory and penal practice. And at this point in the argument, it is rather easy to imagine penal practitioners throwing up their hands, and saying: 'well, fine, but where does this leave the practitioner?' We have seen that von Hirsch claims there are two key features in the intuitive attractiveness of desert theory, and one of these is that desert theory 'provides sentencers with a degree of guidance, in a way that competing theories seldom do'.[30] But if the crime-scale and the penalty-scale both have imprecisions in them (as I have argued that they have), and if in any case von Hirsch's claims, on close examination, turn out to be claims about how *to avoid injustice* rather than *how to achieve exact justice* (as I have argued that they do)—if all this is true, with what real practical guidance does von Hirsch's theory supply us?

This is an important question, and one that must be squarely tackled later in this chapter. For the moment, however, I want to turn to the next two puzzles, both of which elaborate the theme, developed in the present section, that von Hirsch's proportionality theory is in fact a less precise theory than has sometimes been imagined. Puzzle 2 is about an aspect of judging the seriousness of *crimes* (the 'crime-scale'), while Puzzle 3 is about an aspect of judging the severity of *punishments* (the 'penalty-scale').

PUZZLE 2: TOTALITY AND MERCY

One of the interesting contrasts between desert theory and daily criminal justice practice is that, as Andrew Ashworth has put it, in general the writings of desert theorists 'are tied to relativities between single offences', whereas, for example, in a research study of sentencing in the English Crown Court 'some 62% of all cases involved more than one offence'.[31]

---

[30]   Von Hirsch (1993), n. 8 above, p. 1.
[31]   A. Ashworth, *Sentencing and Criminal Justice*, 2nd edn. (Butterworths, 1995), pp. 214, 207.

From a theoretical point of view, of special interest in relation to the sentencing of multiple offenders is what the English courts have called the 'totality principle' (though the approach that this principle embodies is by no means confined to England). As a leading English judge expressed the principle in 1974:[32]

When cases of multiplicity of offences come before the court, the court must not content itself by doing the arithmetic and passing the sentence which the arithmetic produces. It must look at the totality of the criminal behaviour and ask itself what is the appropriate sentence for all the offences.

As Ashworth starkly but correctly puts it, the introduction of such a principle into a legal system seems to produce 'what is in effect a discount for bulk offending'.[33] So how is such a discount to be justified?

For the consequentialist, at least in strict theory this is not too much of a problem. Since consequentialists are, by definition, interested only in the consequences, or effects, of sentences passed, theirs is a future-oriented approach. Hence, it should not matter whether a given offender is before the court for one offence, for twenty, or for two hundred; what is important is whether the sentence to be passed on this offender will have the appropriate effect of deterring him and others from future offending, reforming him, or producing appropriate incapacitation from likely future depredations.[34]

For the desert theorist, however, the 'discount for bulk offending' of the totality principle clearly presents potentially quite severe theoretical difficulties; and this is the starting point of our second puzzle. Ashworth has pointed out, following the Australian writer Marianne Wells,[35] that there are two possible

[32] D. A. Thomas, *Principles of Sentencing*, 2nd edn. (Heinemann, 1979), p. 56. See now Criminal Justice Act 1991, s. 28(2), which states that nothing in the Act shall prevent a court, 'in the case of an offender who is convicted of one or more other offences, from mitigating his sentence by applying any rule of law as to the totality of sentences'.

[33] Ashworth (1995), n. 31 above, p. 209.

[34] In consequentialist thinking, the only real relevance of a 'discount for bulk offending' would be if there were any evidence that the existence of such a discount led the offender before the court, or other potential offenders, to the view that committing multiple offences, rather than just one, was the sensible choice to make once one offence had been committed (since any additional offences would not be punished to the same extent as the first one). Precise empirical evidence on this point is lacking. However, on *a priori* reasoning, by definition only two groups of offenders would be in a position to consider such a choice. The first group would be those whose first offence was (so far) undetected, in which case committing the second offence must increase the risk of detection for *both* offences, a fact that ought in theory to offset (at least partially) any 'bulk offence sentencing discount'. The second group would be those who had been arrested for the first offence but released on bail; yet for such offenders the rule of law providing that committing a further offence while on bail aggravates the seriousness of that offence should again offset (at least partially) the 'bulk offence sentencing discount'. Of course, it does not follow from the above that offenders will actually adopt any of this reasoning. Indeed, we know from the empirical research of P. F. Cromwell *et al., Breaking and Entering: an Ethnographic Analysis of Burglary* (Sage, 1991), pp. 67–70, that, for example, solo burglars did not usually engage in multiple burglaries on the same day, yet groups of offenders could 'psych each other up', leading to burglary 'sprees' where numerous targets would be attacked on one outing. Obviously, in such an emotion-charged atmosphere, rational calculation might not count for much (and, indeed, there was a higher detection rate for burglars working in groups).

[35] Ashworth (1995), n. 31 above, pp. 214–15, following M. Wells, *Sentencing for Multiple Offences in Western Australia* (University of Western Australia Crime Research Centre, Research Report No. 6, 1992).

theoretical underpinnings to a totality principle within a framework of commensurability or proportionality. These are as follows:

(1)   first, a view that even though all the separate sentences are appropriate and proportional to the individual offences, and rightly made cumulative, *the total sentence is excessive by reference to what is the normal sentence for an obviously more serious offence committed singly*. (For example, in one English case the sentences for a multitude of (primarily) motoring offences were treated cumulatively by the court of first instance to produce a total sentence of 4 years' imprisonment, which was then reduced by the Court of Appeal on the ground that such a long sentence is normally imposed—when the offence is a single one—only for 'really serious crime'[36]).

(2)   secondly, a view that (in the same set of hypothetical circumstances), *the total sentence is excessive in relation to the total conduct involved, bearing in mind the offender's overall circumstances*.

In English law, it is the first of these two approaches that has been primarily used to justify the totality principle.[37] Where such an approach is adopted, then it clearly follows that 'no matter how many offences of a particular kind an offender is found to have committed, the sentence should remain [within] the range appropriate' for a single conviction for that type of offence.[38] As such, this approach clearly invests the 'appropriate sentencing range' for a single offence with a very considerable *symbolic importance*, within the communicative scheme that any overall sentencing system represents.[39] Yet this dimension of symbolism is not particularly prominent in Andrew von Hirsch's sentencing theory, as currently formulated. I shall return to this important theme of symbolism in the discussion of Puzzle 3.

The totality principle, or something like it, seems very deeply entrenched in practical sentencing logics, and my guess is that, if the first (symbolic) approach to the principle were not operative in England, then the courts would adopt the second approach listed above. If this conjecture is correct, then it is also necessary to examine what appear to be the strengths of the intuition that underpins the second approach. My suggestion is that only one line of reasoning about this matter carries any serious justificatory weight, and that is based on the principle of mercy.[40] That is to say, the court could take the view 'that the total sentence is

---

[36]   Ashworth (1995), n. 31 above, p. 210.

[37]   See Ashworth (1995), n. 31 above, Ch. 8, for an extended discussion. See also Nils Jareborg, 'Why Bulk Discounts in Multiple Offence Sentencing?', Ch. 5 of this book, below.

[38]   Ashworth (1995), n. 31 above, p. 214.

[39]   The concept of the 'appropriate sentencing range' for a given offence is, however, rather a vague one, and in England it has not been fully elaborated by the Court of Appeal for all types of offence. See the full discussion of sentencing ranges for different offence types in M. Wasik, *Emmins on Sentencing*, 2nd edn. (Blackstone, 1993), Ch. 12.

[40]   Another possible underpinning is akin to the principle of contributory negligence in tort law (whereby a successful plaintiff obtains less damages than he/she otherwise would have done because the plaintiff has contributed to the eventual outcome by his/her own negligence). Could one argue that the State is contributorily negligent in relation to the sentencing situation faced by the multiple offender, since the State's agents have failed to apprehend him at earlier stages in his chain of

excessive in relation to the total conduct involved' by a process of reasoning along the lines illustrated by the following case:

(1)   The defendant, D, aged 25, has committed (say) a hundred separate offences of residential burglary (sadly, this is no means an improbable scenario). Each of these burglaries, on average, might if committed as a single offence be deemed to merit (on ordinary desert-based principles of harm and culpability) a custodial sentence of (say) 6 months' duration.[41]

(2)   But 100 × 6 months = 50 years; and even if a generous early release mechanism is in operation, 50 years' nominal time is likely to mean at least 25 years real time for D. So, on standard desert-based principles, D should apparently be imprisoned for at least the next quarter-century.

(3)   But that is clearly going to deprive D, irreplaceably, of a high proportion of the prime years of his life. Despite D's multiple offending, which has caused a good deal of anger and distress to householders, it is not clear that the courts would really consider it appropriate, for such offences, to lock D up for such an extended period—in which case, the courts would show a *reluctance to exact the penalty which (on ordinary principles, treated cumulatively) is the commensurably appropriate one for D.*

(4)   Therefore, the court would exercise some mercy towards the defendant by reducing the total sentence to some degree.

Readers must judge for themselves whether I am right in regarding this process of reasoning as very likely to occur in multiple offence cases (in the postulated absence of a totality principle based on the 'symbolic' approach, as outlined above). But, having in this respect introduced the concept of mercy, it is certainly worth noting that, as Walker has very usefully pointed out, the English courts have supported, in a number of cases, a reduction in the 'just' or 'proportionate' sentence on grounds *other than* the 'standard' grounds of desert theory (i.e. harm and culpability).[42] Some such grounds seem not very defensible theoretically,[43] but others seem more ethically justifiable. Among this latter group one might perhaps include the following (in addition to the totality principle):

(i)   the offender is aged, or seriously ill;[44]

(ii)   the offender has, subsequent to the offence, shown genuine remorse for the

---

offending? The argument would appear to have plausibility only if it could be shown that the State has not even been trying to clear up earlier offences—a situation that would surely hardly ever obtain.

[41] Court of Appeal guidance (in *Mussell* (1990) 12 Cr.App.R.(S) 612) is that 'it cannot be assumed that any dwelling house burglary is an offence which automatically requires a custodial sentence. Each offence has to be judged individually'. The example given assumes that D's offences were of mixed character, but generally speaking relatively serious within the range of residential burglaries.

[42] N. D. Walker, 'The Quiddity of Mercy', (1995) 70 *Philosophy* 27.

[43] For example, what Walker (*ibid*, p. 32) nicely calls 'Christmas sentencing'; also the case of the offender who, in an incident unrelated to the offence, had recently saved a child from drowning.

[44] Walker (*ibid*, p. 33) who supports the principle of 'sensibility' (see Puzzle 1), does not include age, illness etc. as grounds for mercy; this is because sensibility requires that, as part of our standard notions of justice and proportionality, we would reduce the standard penalty where 'this would inflict more suffering on the offender in question than on most other offenders'. However, since von Hirsch rejects sensibility, for him old age and illness (unrelated to culpability) could only be taken account of through a principle of mercy.

offence (in circumstances where this could not be said to affect his culpability at the time of the offence);

(iii)   the victim has made a plea to the court to show mercy to the defendant.

In summary, therefore, my argument in relation to the second puzzle has so far
been as follows:

(1)   The totality principle presents significant theoretical difficulties for von
Hirsch's sentencing theory. The two most plausible ways of defending the
principle are, first, a 'symbolic' approach, bearing in mind the amounts of
punishment normally considered appropriate for a single more serious
offence; and secondly, a 'mercy-based' approach, arguing that a cumulative
total sentence arrived at through aggregating normal desert-based rules
would be inappropriately severe in all the circumstances. Von Hirsch's theory,
as it stands, is not particularly compatible with either of these approaches: it
is not very strong on symbolism, and neither does it incorporate any principle
of mercy (beyond the ordinary frameworks of harm and culpability).

(2)   Examination of court practice additionally shows that mercy is sometimes
extended to defendants (over and above the ordinary calculations of harm
and culpability) for reasons other than the totality principle, and that
at least some such manifestations of mercy appear ethically defensible.

This discussion therefore seems to suggest the need for, first, a more careful
look at issues of symbolism within desert theory; and secondly, a closer examination of the possible role of mercy. The first of these tasks will be pursued further
in the discussion under Puzzle 3; to the second task I now turn.

There are two possible definitions of 'mercy' that are relevant to the present
discussion, and it is important to distinguish between them. Jeffrie Murphy usefully and concisely sets out some 'fairly widely held' tenets about the concept of
mercy—including that it is an autonomous moral virtue (not reducible to any
other virtue, especially justice); that it tempers or 'seasons' justice; and that it is
not owed to the individual as a matter of right or desert.[45] The difficulty with such
an approach, if applied within a criminal justice system, is that it seems extremely
likely to lead to similar cases being treated in a dissimilar manner—since if A
receives mercy in her sentence, but identical offender B does not, then B has, by
definition, no complaint (i.e. by definition she has no rights in the matter, and so
she cannot claim that the system is acting unjustly). As Ross Harrison has fully
and persuasively demonstrated, mercy *in this sense* therefore cannot be morally
defended as a desirable feature of the acts of State authorities, since we (rightly)
expect the State to operate as a fully rational entity.[46]

But suppose we adopt a different definition of mercy? Working within a version of the retributive theory of punishment, Jean Hampton stipulates that
'mercy is the suspension or mitigation of a punishment that would otherwise be

[45]   J. G. Murphy and J. Hampton, *Forgiveness and Mercy* (Cambridge, 1988), p. 166.

[46]   R. Harrison, 'The Equality of Mercy', in H. Gross and R. Harrison (eds.), *Jurisprudence: Cambridge Essays* (Cambridge UP, 1992). Moreover, as Harrison (at p. 122) emphasizes, 'it is reason
which squeezes out mercy, not rules'.

deserved as retribution, and which is granted out of pity and compassion for the wrongdoer'.[47] Such a definition does not, in and of itself, commit us to any principle of being free to treat like cases in an unlike manner. Within such a framework, and following Lucas, the way could therefore be opened up for what might be described as *a rational exercise of mercy*. As Lucas puts it, taking as his example the remorseful offender:

A rational exercise of mercy is not unfair. If a judge passes a light sentence, on the grounds that the criminal is filled with remorse and that other potential criminals will not be the less deterred on account of his leniency, then his sentence is not unfair . . . [unless] *either the judge is failing in his duty towards society at large, or [he] is favouring with mercy one criminal, but not others similarly culpable and similarly penitent.*[48]

We saw in the discussion of Puzzle 1 that Andrew von Hirsch's central theoretical claims, closely examined, turn out to be claims about *avoiding unfairness*, including the avoidance of unfairness in relation to the key principles of ordinal proportionality (including parity). Von Hirsch must therefore reject mercy in the first of the two senses defined above ('Mercy A'), which breaches parity. However, he would seem to be in no way obliged to reject out of hand what Lucas has described as the 'rational exercise of mercy' (or 'Mercy B').[49] This seems to me to be an important conclusion in the context of the present discussion, since: first, it would make it possible for von Hirsch to defend some version of the totality principle on the grounds of mercy; and secondly, it would allow him to incorporate within his theory those other kinds of reasons (e.g. illness, subsequent genuine remorse) which the courts quite often use to mitigate sentences, but which cannot easily be included within von Hirsch's two central criteria for assessing the seriousness of crimes, namely harm and culpability.

But, at this point, we seem to return to a difficulty adumbrated at the end of the discussion of Puzzle 1. For if we complicate von Hirsch's analysis of offence seriousness by adding a principle of mercy, are we not again reducing the 'degree of guidance' that we can give to sentencers, and which is supposed to be a central merit of desert theory?

To tackle this issue, let us return to Harrison's excellent discussion of mercy. Harrison's article appears in a book of jurisprudential essays, and for a philosopher he is unusually well-informed about legal concepts and processes. He knows full well that, in practice, demands for mercy within a legal system especially arise when a given general rule seems likely to lead to an inappropriate (or unjust) result in a specific case; in other words, such demands 'are really often arguments about the need for flexibility' in the application of rules. Now flexibility is clearly very important, but, for Harrison, it is vital to distinguish:

between the mechanical operation of rules and the question of justice in the particular case. Obviously, a simple or mechanically operated rule may not take appropriate account

---

[47] Murphy and Hampton (1988), n. 45 above, p. 158.

[48] Lucas (1980), n. 17 above, p. 9 (emphasis added).

[49] Though von Hirsch would doubtless, and rightly, have some hard questions to ask about whether in any given set of circumstances the exercise of mercy really was appropriate.

of the complexity or individuality of a particular case and, if applied, justice would not be done. This is because the case is importantly different from others which are, by contrast, appropriately covered by that rule. So the rule should not be applied in this particular case. But this, it seems to me, is quite different from saying that law should be suspended, or that a mechanism is needed outside the law which can suspend it. If this is the just decision in this particular case, *then it would also be so in any exactly similar ones.*[50]

In other words (though he does not put the matter quite in this way) Harrison could defend what I have called Mercy B, but not Mercy A, as part of a criminal justice system. Yet we still seem, in practical terms, to be confronted by a very real difficulty. How can one take 'particular, possibly unique, decisions' in the special circumstances of a particular case, while at the same time remaining totally opposed to 'arbitrary decisions'?[51] And how can one, in this sort of 'flexible', individualized context, still give the sentencer some genuine guidelines?

In a nutshell, Harrison's important response to these questions is as follows:

What it requires is *the trained application of the reasons of law to individual cases . . .* If justice is to be done, the decision should be taken for reasons and be rationally defensible. *Such a rational defence will include emphasising all the special features of the particular case . . . Judgement is needed, but the best judgement is informed by, and sensitive to, reason.* The best judgement is not just about one case in isolation, but is sensitive to the possible implications of that judgement on other cases.[52]

Translating this argument specifically to the sentencing context, the consequences seem to be something like the following. Sentencing is inevitably a discretionary activity, since no set of rules or guidelines can possibly anticipate all the unique circumstances of particular cases in the future. But that does not mean that sentencers' discretion should be untrammelled. As administrative lawyers long ago realized, untrammelled discretion leads quickly to inconsistency and injustice—in short, in this context, to arbitrary sentencing. The central problem in framing just sentencing laws, therefore, is *how one provides sentencers with genuine guidelines which nevertheless are flexible enough to be adaptable to meet the special circumstances of particular cases* (bearing in mind that—see the argument above—the same approach should be adopted if another identical case with the same special circumstances were to arise). The only guidelines that seem capable of meeting this requirement are those that, in Harrison's words, require 'the trained application of reasons of law to individual cases'. Such guidelines might perhaps, by analogy from sociological writings, both draw upon and yet also develop the *deep structures* of judicial thinking about sentencing.[53]

---

[50] Harrison (1992), n. 46 above, p. 120 (emphasis added).
[51] *Ibid*, p. 121.
[52] *Ibid*, p. 122 (emphasis added).
[53] Anthony Giddens, in *The Constitution of Society* (Polity, 1984), p. 377, defines 'structures' as 'rule-resource sets, implicated in the institutional articulation of social systems'. In facing a novel (and perhaps potentially threatening) situation on a prison wing, for example, prison officers draw implicitly on their experience of similar situations in the past, plus their training, plus the formal rules and procedures of the prison system. The action that they take then itself becomes something that may be drawn on (implicitly or explicitly) in future situations. Thus, persons in particular

It is outside the scope of this essay to develop the above point in any detailed technical or practical sense. It is, however, perhaps important to offer two brief thoughts by way of elaboration—not least since a similar issue was (as we saw) also central to Puzzle 1. First, then, in the technical debate as between narrative and numerical guidelines in sentencing,[54] it seems to be the case that, given the arguments so far advanced in this chapter, narrative guidelines must have the edge. This is because we are looking for sentencers to engage in the trained application of reasons of law to individual cases, and they are more likely to be able to do this from a set of narrative guidelines than from numerical guidelines.[55] Secondly, however, it will be of central importance to ensure that these narrative guidelines are meaningful, and carry real bite—otherwise one is quickly back in the sphere of uncontrolled discretion.[56]

PUZZLE 3: THE PROBATION ORDER

The central problem to be considered in this third puzzle can be simply stated: is it possible to incorporate the probation order adequately within Andrew von Hirsch's sentencing theory? By 'the probation order' I mean, in this context, the standard probation order as it has developed in England, involving the active

occupations develop what Giddens calls a *practical consciousness* of how to 'go on' in a given situation, although they cannot articulate this kind of knowledge with any precision: these are what I here describe as the 'deep structures' of consciousness in the occupation in question. That judges develop practical consciousness of this kind is not in doubt, and indeed was implicitly indicated a decade ago by Lawton LJ as regards the 'custody threshold' in English sentencing law ('courts can recognise an elephant when they see one, but may not find it necessary to define it': *Bradbourn* (1985) 7 Cr.App.R.(S) 181); see also A. Ashworth and A. von Hirsch, 'Recognising Elephants: the problem of the custody threshold', [1997] *Crim.LR* 187). Bringing an occupation's 'practical consciousness' into the realm of formal discussion and deliberation may well be an appropriate way to begin to develop 'the trained application of reasons of law to individual cases', as Harrison puts it, precisely because the collective 'practical consciousness' often contains some extremely useful pointers to good practice. But, equally, in this process of explicit articulation of previous practice, it will very likely become apparent that appropriate good practice guidelines will need to go beyond the insights of 'practical consciousness'—which insights may at crucial points be overly vague (see Ashworth and von Hirsch (1997) above) or even, on careful reflection, actually insupportable when critically considered. Thus, the development of the kind of sentencing guidelines referred to in the main text could usefully *draw upon*, but will probably also need significantly to *develop*, the 'deep structures' of existing judicial thinking.

[54] See e.g. A. von Hirsch, 'Guidance by numbers or words: numerical versus narrative guidelines for sentencing', in M. Wasik and K. Pease (eds.), *Sentencing Reform* (Manchester UP, 1987).

[55] cf. the comments of von Hirsch (1993), n. 8 above, p. 105: 'it doubtless is a drawback of numerical sentencing guidelines such as Minnesota's that they are highly aggregative, and give so little scope within broad offence categories to differentiate on harm or culpability grounds. What that suggests is that standards should preferably be more sensitive (albeit they cannot perfectly be so) to such variations in gravity'. He adds that narrative sentencing guidelines 'permit more differentiation, as they permit development of a case-law jurisprudence that distinguishes degrees of harm or culpability within an offence category' (p. 104).

[56] See for example Ashworth and von Hirsch's (1997) (n. 53 above) discussion of the 'custody threshold' in the Criminal Justice Act 1991, s.1(2)(a). The authors argue that the Court of Appeal's interpretation of this section has been somewhat vacuous, and that it is both desirable and possible to develop firmer criteria.

supervision of an offender by a probation officer, with the threat that the probationer will be taken back to court (and possibly re-sentenced for the original offence) if he/she fails to co-operate with the supervision process, e.g. by missing appointments.[57]

Traditionally, in England, the probation order was technically speaking not a sentence, being imposed on the offender (with his/her consent) 'instead of sentencing' him/her. That earlier legal framework was radically changed by the Criminal Justice Act 1991, which provided that the probation order should be one of six 'community orders' available to the courts as sentences. Section 6(2) of the Act provides an important two-pronged test to be applied by courts when passing a sentence including one or more community orders; and this test is (in the words of the statute itself) as follows:

(a) the particular order or orders comprising or forming part of the sentence shall be such as in the opinion of the court is, or taken together are, the most suitable for the offender; and

(b) the restrictions on liberty imposed by the order or orders shall be such as in the opinion of the court are commensurate with the seriousness of the offence, or the combination of the offence and one or more offences associated with it.[58]

For present purposes, we may concentrate on part (b) of this subsection, which on the face of it appears to apply the language of desert theory to (*inter alia*) the probation order. A consideration of the background documents preceding the 1991 Act quickly confirms that this was indeed the Act's intention.[59]

Section 6(2)(b) thus apparently incorporates the view that in probation orders (as in the other 'community orders' such as the community service order (CSO))[60] there is an element of 'restriction of liberty', and it is this 'restriction' which will 'measure' the particular sentence on the desert-based 'penalty-scale' (see the discussion under Puzzle 1). So, at first sight, it looks as if there is, in England anyway, a straightforward answer to our third puzzle: that is to say, the probation order *can* be adequately understood and operationalized within the framework of

[57] The probation order may, at the court's discretion, also include additional requirements, such as a requirement of attendance at a probation centre, a requirement to participate in specified activities, etc. (for a full discussion see Wasik (1993), n. 39 above, Ch. 5). These additional requirements have become increasingly a feature of probation orders in recent years. However, most probation orders still do not include such additional requirements, and it is these orders (sometimes colloquially called 'straight probation orders' or 'standard probation orders') that are the focus of Puzzle 3.

[58] This is the text of the subsection currently in force. The original text of s. 6(2)(b) was slightly different; it was amended in 1993, but the amendment is of no consequence for the present discussion.

[59] See especially the 1990 White Paper *Crime, Justice and Protecting the Public* (HMSO, 1990), which has a much more explicitly desert-based character than the preceding Green Paper, *Punishment, Custody and the Community* (HMSO, 1988). It is of interest to the present chapter (see especially the discussion of Puzzle 5, below) that Antony Duff, in 'Alternatives to Punishment—or Alternative Punishment?' (in W. Cragg (ed.), *Retributivism and its Critics*, (Franz Steiner Verlag, 1992), p. 65) feared that the White Paper 'marks a retreat from the more appropriate ambitions which can be discerned in . . . the Green Paper'.

[60] The six community orders included within the scope of s. 6 are: the probation order, the supervision order, the CSO, the combination order, the attendance centre order, and the curfew order.

desert theory, and legislation already enshrines this. But such a conclusion would be too quick, because recent research by Susan Rex has shown that the legal framework of section 6(2)(b) does not in fact accord particularly straightforwardly with the on-the-ground reality of the probation order in practice.[61]

Some probation officers had anticipated Rex's conclusion, at least in one significant respect. Thus, in a 1993 analysis, the members of one probation service calculated that a one-year standard probation order (i.e. probation without special conditions: see note 57 above) would involve approximately 21 hours formal 'restriction on liberty' (in the form of office appointments, etc).[62] This would make such an order only about half as long as the *minimum* number of hours legally required in a CSO; yet traditionally the courts, the probation service, and the government had all equated 'standard' probation orders with short to medium-length CSOs.[63] If, therefore, one reads the phrase 'the restriction on liberty imposed by the [community] order or orders' in section 6(2)(b) as referring to *physical* restrictions on liberty, then the statutory framework seems to delegitimize the probation order as a credible sentence for any reasonably serious offence.

Susan Rex's research confirmed, but also elaborated, this picture.[64] She carried out qualitative semi-structured interviews with 60 probationers and 21 probation officers in two different probation areas after the implementation of the 1991 Act. She concluded, in a nutshell, that a mechanical analysis of 'contact hours' and the like (as in the 1993 analysis by Rhys *et al.*, and as apparently implied on a commonsense interpretation of section 6(2)(b)) was inadequate. This was because such an approach 'overlooks elements unique to probation which probationers experience as restrictive'.[65] More positively, Rex found that the probation order clearly did make 'a variety of demands' on probationers, and these demands arose centrally from 'probation officers' ability to engage probationers, [which] committed the latter to a rehabilitative task'.[66]

What kind of demands are we talking about here? To understand the nature of the demands, it is essential first to grasp that 'there was little doubt in most participants' minds' (be they probationers or probation officers) 'that the whole point of their interaction was to reduce the likelihood that probationers would offend again in the future'.[67] Hence, from the point of view of probationers, especially those who had developed a pattern of offending, clearly an element of *change of lifestyle* was being demanded. Probation officers attempted to achieve this by persuasion and influence, partly through building up a relationship of

---

[61] S. Rex, *Perceptions of Probation in a Context of 'Just Deserts'* (unpublished Ph.D. thesis, University of Cambridge, 1997).

[62] See M. Rhys, D. Godsan, and M. Wistow, *Guidance on Seriousness* (unpublished report to the Association of Chief Officers of Probation, 1993).

[63] See, e.g., Home Office, Department of Health and Welsh Office, *National Standards for the Supervision of Offenders in the Community* (Home Office, 1992), p. 27.

[64] I am extremely grateful to Susan Rex for permission to summarize some main findings from her unpublished Ph.D. thesis; and also for her more general comments on an earlier draft of this chapter.

[65] Rex (1997), n. 61 above, p. 116.   [66] *Ibid*, p. 181.   [67] *Ibid*, p. 107.

trust with probationers, and partly through developing a supervision plan focused on the specifics of the offending behaviour of the particular offender. All this was, for the most part, understood by probationers. Almost without exception probationers 'wanted to be respected' by their probation officers, and for the most part they also described 'a sense of equality' in their relationships with these officers. Nevertheless, they did not expect such relationships to be normal (reciprocal) friendships, but rather 'appreciated a certain amount of distance'.[68] This was because the relationships were seen as professional relationships focused on the rehabilitative task, and probationers:

were only really happy to share confidences with, or listen to, someone who respected them and whose professionalism they could respect.[69]

Within this kind of relationship, an element of *moral engagement* seemed often to be present. No less than half the probationers expressed feelings of personal loyalty to their supervisors, and of accountability to the supervisors for their (the probationer's) actions. Often:

probationers felt responsible for making the relationship work and beholden to a supervisor whom they saw as helping them to avoid crime (and, for some, prison). Over tasks, they felt obliged to take steps to which they had committed themselves, and to report back on these and their other activities. Probation officers seemed to underestimate the extent to which these factors impinged upon probationers.[70]

Given these various findings, Rex's central conclusion—that demands for change were being made upon probationers, and that these demands arose centrally from the rehabilitative purpose of the probation order—becomes easily intelligible. These demands for change not infrequently required considerable effort from probationers (e.g. curbing a drinking habit); and, on occasion, they could stretch into expectations of significant alterations in what would previously have been normal behaviour in spontaneously-occurring situations:

(*Probationer*): I've never walked away from a person in my life . . . [but] since I've been on [probation] I've walked away. I don't want to keep paying fines and everything. If people get my back up, I just ignore them. It's hard for me, it's really hard, but I've got to do it, that's the only way of avoiding it.

(*Interviewer*): Has anything that [your probation officer]'s said helped with that?

(*Probationer*): Oh yeah, she's come out and talked.

(*Interviewer*): How did that help?

(*Probationer*): In a lot of ways I saw from it, I could see sense at last to do it.[71]

In short, Rex's research suggests that the probation order, at least when it is working at its best, constitutes a special kind of relationship, centrally founded on the concept of rehabilitation (or behaviour change), whose impact on probationers and their lifestyle can, in practice, extend well beyond the actual hours of

---

[68] *Ibid*, p. 175.   [69] *Ibid*, p. 175.   [70] *Ibid*, p. 162.   [71] *Ibid*, p. 132 (slightly edited).

contact between probation officers and probationers—and which can even
sometimes become of deep personal significance to the probationer.[72]

Within this framework, let us take a closer look at Rex's findings about the
compulsory and formal nature of the contacts between probation officers and
probationers. Virtually all probationers did in fact regard aspects of the supervision process as physically restrictive—especially the obligation to attend
appointments at the probation office, but also other matters such as the requirement (in many cases) to receive visits from the probation officer at the probationer's home. Such obligations had to be remembered, and acted upon. Yet
many probationers did not find them particularly onerous or unpleasant, especially if they were finding the relationship with their probation officer to be beneficial, since 'the value of the experience . . . seemed to mitigate the inconvenience
of having to attend appointments'.[73] This last finding clearly takes us into the ter-
ritory of the *legitimacy* of punishments, a topic that has for far too long been
largely ignored by penal theorists and penal practitioners alike: we shall return to
this concept in discussing Puzzle 4.

Rex's research also found, however, that there were other kinds of restrictions
imposed by the probation order that were significant for probationers. Perhaps
the most important related to *privacy* and *duration*. Most probationers did in fact
disclose personal (and presumably sensitive) matters to probation officers as an
integral part of the supervisory relationship (the nature of which has been discussed above). Yet nearly half the probationers reported that either the disclosures
themselves, or prior apprehensiveness about having to make such disclosures,
caused difficulties for them (and this was especially the case for female probationers). As regards duration, about a quarter of probationers mentioned the sheer
length of the probation order as restrictive: in the case of experienced probationers, this concern 'was centred on their susceptibility to offend, while inexperienced probationers . . . were more likely to see the order as hanging over them'.[74]

As Susan Rex points out, when one takes into account all the findings of her
research, it is clear that the experience of being subject to a probation order is in
some ways radically different from being subject to a CSO. As we noted previously, the CSO almost always involves many more contact hours; but it is typically shorter in its overall duration,[75] and, in addition, 'the supervision which is the
whole point of probation is entirely different from the supervision involved in
community service, where it is the offenders' performance of a task (rather than
the offender him or herself) which is being supervised'.[76]

Hence, on the basis of Rex's research, it seems fairly clear that section 6(2)(b)
of the Criminal Justice Act 1991, with its attempt to provide a unified desert-
based 'penalty-scale' for community sentences based on 'the restrictions on liberty

---

[72] Other relationships of an intendedly therapeutic kind (e.g. with a doctor or a counsellor) of
course share many of these characteristics.

[73] Rex (1997), n. 61 above, p. 114.   [74] *Ibid*, pp. 115–16.

[75] In the CSO, the specified number of hours of unpaid work must be completed within 12 months
of the order. Probation orders are for a minimum of 6 months and a maximum of 3 years.

[76] Rex (1997), n. 61 above, p. 116.

imposed by the order or orders', makes sense only if the phrase 'restrictions on liberty' is interpreted in a very different way for different community orders.

Some might want to conclude from the findings of Rex's research that the probation order is not, in any true sense, a punishment. In an illuminating paper, written before Rex's research, Antony Duff persuasively argues against that view. Punishment, he suggests, involves 'the imposition of some kind of suffering, pain, restriction or burden',[77] and, on this test, the probation order is clearly a punishment. But that is not quite all that needs to be said:

[The] burden of being supervised is imposed on [the offender] because of the offence which he committed, and it serves those communicative and reformative aims which punishment should properly serve. For it communicates the condemnatory judgment that what he did was wrong and must not be repeated; it serves to remind him that the offence which he committed cast some doubt on his standing within the community, by undermining the mutual trust on which the community's life depends; and in doing this it aims to persuade and to help him to avoid such conduct in future. It is thus a punishment which, precisely in virtue of its punitive character as a burden which is imposed on him because he has committed an offence, aims to reinforce his understanding of the need to avoid crime in future.[78]

Three points arise from Duff's insightful analysis, as expressed in the above quotation and elsewhere in his article. First, Duff points out that philosophical discussions of criminal punishment usually focus either on the fundamental justification for punishment (why we should punish at all) or on how much we should punish (and, of course, this 'amount' problem has especially preoccupied Andrew von Hirsch). But, Duff suggests, just as important is the 'how' of punishment; that is, 'what material forms can punishment properly take?'.[79] We will return to this issue in Puzzle 5. Secondly, and notwithstanding that Duff's approach to punishment is properly described as retributive,[80] in the above quotation he emphasizes both the *communicative* and the *reformative* (forward-looking) dimensions of probation—and, as we have seen, Rex's empirical research has subsequently strongly confirmed the 'on the ground' importance of these dimensions. The relationship of the retributive and communicative/reformative dimensions of punishment is discussed in Puzzle 4. (In the meantime, it is worth noting that, at this point in the argument, the 'summer holiday incident' that I described at the beginning of this chapter begins to be highly relevant: for is it not the case that, *mutatis mutandis*, everything that Duff emphasizes in the above two points is also true for the summer holiday incident?) Thirdly, and finally, Duff argues that the immediate instinct of the desert theorist, when considering non-custodial penalties, is to look especially towards those measures that 'can be readily ranked and compared in terms of their severity'—such as the CSO and the fine.[81] But, he suggests, it is surely an important question, in the

---

[77] Duff (1992), n. 59 above, p. 43.   [78] *Ibid*, pp. 57–8.   [79] *Ibid*, p. 43.   [80] *Ibid*, p. 53.
[81] This tendency is quite marked in the important pioneering article by Wasik and von Hirsch, 'Non-Custodial Penalties and the Principles of Desert', [1988] *Crim.LR* 555, on the application of desert theory to non-custodial penalties.

overall context of a theory of punishment, 'how much weight we ought to attach to the demand for an abstract proportion between seriousness of crime and severity of punishment, as against a more richly communicative' penality?[82]

As Duff himself clearly recognizes, this last question pushes us into the realm of deep theory, and I shall postpone further discussion of it until Puzzles 4 and 5. Meanwhile, it is perhaps time to summarize the argument so far.

The discussion of Puzzle 1 suggested that, on any thorough analysis, both the crime-scale and the penalty-scale used by desert theorists contain more imprecision than such theorists sometimes concede. Puzzle 2 elaborated that criticism for the crime-scale, via an analysis of multiple offences and the totality principle, and further complicated the crime-scale by introducing what it was argued was a justifiable concept of the 'rational exercise of mercy', which can sometimes properly be exercised within a desert-based punishment system. Puzzle 3 has elaborated the criticism of Puzzle 1 as regards the penalty-scale, and has also placed in central focus the important *symbolic* and *communicative* dimension of punishment (a theme that was also apparent in some of the discussion of Puzzle 2).

But, in Puzzle 2, the elaboration of the imprecisions of the crime-scale was (at least to an extent) offset by the introduction of the concept of structured discretion, involving 'the trained application of the reasons of law to individual cases'.[83] Is there any similar device that can help us, in Puzzle 3, *both* to maintain Andrew von Hirsch's crucial emphasis upon ordinal fairness, *and* to enable us to 'measure' (for example) the comparative severity of the probation order and the CSO, while nevertheless recognizing that these two orders involve different kinds of communication with the offender, and that the demands they make upon offenders are qualitatively dissimilar? Space precludes any full treatment of this question, but briefly, I believe (with von Hirsch) that an application of a 'living standard' approach to this issue has considerable promise. We saw in relation to Puzzle 1 that, in response to Walker's 'sensibility' criticism of the penalty-scale, Andrew von Hirsch suggested (but did not elaborate) the idea of applying a 'living-standard analysis' to different punishments. Clearly, a sophisticated living-standard analysis ought to be able to cope with the problem of comparing two punishments with somewhat different operating frameworks, such as the probation order and the CSO. In such an analysis, for example, the probation order's implicit requirement of the disclosure of private information by the offender as part of the intendedly rehabilitative supervisory process (see above) would certainly count as one of the burdens (i.e. reduction of privacy) imposed on the offender by the court order, in addition to the more physical 'restrictions on liberty' upon which the 1991 Act appeared to focus.

It would obviously also be important, in such an analysis, to attempt to incorporate the symbolic dimension which is so important in punishment, as Garland

---

[82] Duff (1992), n. 59 above, p. 62. I have slightly altered the terminology at the end of this quotation to give it a wider ambit than in Duff's original.

[83] Harrison (1992), n. 46 above, p. 121.

has shown[84] (and as is confirmed by Rex's analysis of the probation order and, on a more mundane and everyday level, by the 'summer holiday incident'). The importance of the symbolic is well brought out by Anthony Giddens[85] in his sociological analysis of what he calls the 'dimensions of structure' in social life. Briefly, Giddens suggests that, in everyday life, we are surrounded by a number of social patterns (e.g. gender role expectations) that both present themselves to us as relatively 'objective' and 'external', but which yet subtly affect our own processes of thought, and our actions, in a very complex interactive process. These 'dimensions of structure' themselves consist of a complex interactive mix of dimensions of *domination* (manifesting itself in interactions of power), *signification* (manifesting itself in interactions of symbolic communication) and *legitimation* (manifesting itself in interactions of moral sanctioning). The theoretical implication of our analysis so far is, quite clearly, that desert theory needs to take *all three* of these dimensions seriously (notwithstanding that the second dimension—signification—has been inadequately considered by most desert theorists). The practical point (which is well illustrated, *inter alia*, by the 'summer holiday incident') is that all three dimensions are everywhere around us, and are to be seen manifested in action on a daily basis in (for example) the courts, prisons, probation offices, and our homes.

PUZZLE 4: WHY PUNISH AT ALL?

One of the main strengths of Andrew von Hirsch's writings on sentencing is that they constitute 'a sustained attempt to bring [a] general theory [of punishment] to bear on practical policy'.[86] Having previously considered three puzzles which were primarily concerned with various dimensions of 'practical policy', it is therefore now time to address the theoretical heart of von Hirsch's general theory of punishment, namely the arresting question 'Why Punish at All?'[87]

Interestingly, this particular aspect of von Hirsch's work on punishment has altered more than any other over the years. In his first published volume on sentencing,[88] Andrew von Hirsch endorsed the so-called 'benefits and burdens' (or 'unfair advantage') theory of retribution as a (partial) justification for the existence of punishment. Since that date, however, he has clearly distanced himself from that theory, for strong reasons that are well known and widely supported, and so need no elaboration here.[89] In *Past or Future Crimes*, a completely fresh General Justifying Aim (GJA) for the punishment system was therefore adopted.[90] In this GJA, there were two central 'grounds for punishment', namely

---

[84] D. Garland, *Punishment and Modern Society* (Oxford, 1990).

[85] Giddens (1984), n. 53 above, p. 29.

[86] Duff and Garland (1994), n. 3 above, p. 19.

[87] That question appears as the chapter-heading of Ch. 5 of von Hirsch (1986), n. 12 above.

[88] A. von Hirsch, *Doing Justice* (Hill and Wang, 1976).

[89] See Duff and Garland (1994), n. 3 above, pp. 44–5; von Hirsch (1993), n. 8 above, pp. 7–8.

[90] Von Hirsch (1986), n. 12 above, Ch. 5. The term 'General Justifying Aim' is taken from Hart's

crime prevention and reprobation (or censure). The first of these grounds was included, *inter alia*, to avoid the conclusion required by a wholly deontological rationale for punishment—such as that of Kant in his famous 'island' example[91]—namely, that 'punishment would have to be preserved even if it were found to have no preventive utility'.[92] The second ground for punishment (reprobation or censure) was, importantly, seen by von Hirsch as an *independent* element, that could not logically be 'collapsed into the preventive element'.[93]

In the same 1986 chapter, von Hirsch followed Joel Feinberg[94] in distinguishing between the twin components of 'censure' and 'hard treatment' in punishment. Perhaps not surprisingly, having adopted this terminology, the (descriptive) components of 'censure' and 'hard treatment' in punishment then became very closely aligned, in von Hirsch's argument, respectively with the 'censure' and 'crime prevention' grounds in the GJA (though these grounds are of course normative rather than descriptive). This alignment led to what von Hirsch himself subsequently described as a 'bifurcated account of punishment';[95] or, as he summarized his 1986 position in a later text:

> The penal law . . . performs two interlocking functions. By threatening unpleasant consequences [i.e., hard treatment], it seeks to discourage criminal behaviour. Through the censure expressed by such sanctions, the law registers disapprobation of the behaviour. Citizens are thus provided with moral and not just prudential reasons for desistance.[96]

But by 1993, von Hirsch had come to believe that this 'bifurcated account' was inadequate. As he put it in self-criticism, 'If the person is capable of being moved by moral appeal, why the threat? If not capable and thus in need of the threat, it appears that he is being treated like [an animal]',[97] which, it was argued, was an ontologically inappropriate way to treat a human being.[98]

famous essay, 'Prolegomenon to the principles of punishment': see H. L. A. Hart, *Punishment and Responsibility* (OUP, 1968), Ch. 1.

[91] Contained in the following well-known quotation from *The Metaphysics of Morals*: 'Even if a civil society were to dissolve itself by common agreement of all its members—as might be supposed in the case of a people inhabiting an island resolving to separate and scatter themselves throughout the whole world—the last murderer remaining in prison must first be executed, so that everyone will duly receive what his actions are worth and so that the bloodguilt thereof will not be fixed on the people because they failed to insist on carrying out the punishment'. For a fuller contextualization of this passage, in the framework of Kant's political philosophy as a whole, see H. Williams, *Kant's Political Philosophy* (Blackwell, 1983), esp. Ch. 5.

[92] Von Hirsch (1986), n. 12 above, p. 59.   [93] *Ibid*, p. 52.

[94] J. Feinberg, 'The Expressive Function of Punishment', in *Doing and Deserving: Essays in the Theory of Responsibility* (Princeton UP, 1970).

[95] Von Hirsch (1993), n. 8 above, p. 12.   [96] *Ibid*, p. 12.

[97] *Ibid*, p. 12. The original quotation reads 'like a tiger'. This refers back to a sentence on the previous page of *Censure and Sanctions*, namely: 'a neutral sanction would treat offenders or potential offenders much as tigers might be treated in a circus, as beings that have to be restrained, intimidated or conditioned into compliance because they are incapable of understanding why biting people (or other tigers) is wrong' (*ibid*, p. 11).

[98] For von Hirsch (*ibid*, p. 11) 'a condemnatory sanction treats the actor as a *person* who is capable of moral understanding . . . [This] is a matter of acknowledging his dignity as a human being' (emphasis in original). This approach is, of course, highly congruent with the Kantian demand that we should always respect other people as rational and autonomous moral agents—i.e. we should treat them as ends, never merely as means.

To overcome the perceived weaknesses of this 'bifurcated account', von Hirsch in his 1993 text *Censure and Sanctions*[99] produced what Duff and Garland have rightly described as a 'subtle reworking' of his account of the GJA.[100] In this revised account, the preventive function of the criminal sanction is seen as '*supplying a prudential reason that is tied to, and supplements, the normative reason conveyed by penal censure*'.[101] Duff and Garland have usefully summarized this revised account as follows:

Censure, which appeals to the offender as a moral agent, is the primary justifying purpose of punishment; but, recognizing that as fallible human beings we are not always sufficiently attentive to the moral appeal of the law, we also give ourselves prudential reasons for obedience. However, such prudential reasons must supplement, rather than replace, the law's moral appeal; and von Hirsch argues (1993, ch. 5) that this account of the proper purposes of punishment sets strict limits on the general severity of punishments. . . . Such a system of punishment would, he thinks, do justice to the consequentialist concern that punishment should prevent crime, whilst still respecting offenders (and potential offenders) as autonomous (but fallible) moral agents.[102]

In the same 1993 text (*Censure and Sanctions*), von Hirsch suggested, for the first time, that his views on the GJA for punishment depended upon what he described as 'a certain conception of human nature'. As he explained the matter:

Persons are assumed to be moral agents, capable of taking seriously the message conveyed through the sanction, that the conduct is reprehensible. They are fallible, nevertheless, and thus face temptation. The function of the disincentive is to provide a prudential reason for resisting the temptation. *The account would make no sense were human beings much better or worse: an angel would require no appeals to prudence, and a brute could not be appealed to through censure.*[103]

Many complex theoretical debates are potentially raised by von Hirsch's 1993 account of the GJA, and it is important to keep the present discussion within bounds. The remainder of my consideration of the fourth Puzzle will therefore first briefly consider two background theoretical issues (namely, the location of von Hirsch's account within other recent theorizing about punishment; plus some discussion of his underpinning view of human nature). Subsequently, comments will be made about the two main proffered justificatory grounds for punishment (censure and prevention), both separately and in relation to each other. Finally, I shall conclude by briefly relating the whole debate to a wider sociological dimension in punishment.

(a) Von Hirsch and recent philosophies of punishment

Theories of punishment, as everyone knows, traditionally fall into two main camps, the consequentialist and the retributive. Consequentialist theories are by

---

[99] Von Hirsch (1993), n. 8 above, Ch. 2.　　[100] Duff and Garland (1994), n. 3 above, p. 112.
[101] Von Hirsch (1993), n. 8 above, p. 13 (emphasis added).
[102] Duff and Garland (1994), n. 3 above, pp. 112–13.
[103] Von Hirsch (1993), n. 8 above, p. 13, emphasis added.

definition forward-looking. They typically 'justify punishment as a contingently efficient technique for achieving certain beneficial effects',[104] and they therefore tend to have difficulty with the apparently intrinsically backward-looking nature of punishment (exemplified in the 'summer holiday incident' in the question: 'Now, why are you sitting on the stairs?'). As J. R. Lucas has put it:

to be a punishment the [punishee's] question 'Why are you doing this to me?' *has to be met with an answer beginning 'Because you did . . .'*, where what you are accused of having done is . . . something allegedly wrong.[105]

Retributivist theories, of course, have no difficulty with backward-looking references of this kind, but such theories can all too easily appear 'to be relying on vindictive gut feelings rather than anything really rational';[106] moreover (as we have already seen), they may justify punishment even when it has no preventive utility. Both of these difficulties for retributivism arise precisely because any discussion of future consequences is laid aside in a wholly retributivist rationale.

But recent years have seen the development of 'a third kind of theory which differs from both [consequentialist and retributive] approaches, and is not merely a mixture of the two'. Theories of this third kind:

give punishment a forward-looking purpose, linking it to a goal (such as moral reform or education) which it might or might not achieve. They thus differ from purely retributivist theories, which hold that the purpose of punishment is fulfilled by the fact of punishment itself. However they also differ from consequentialist theories in that the link between punishment and its purpose is not purely contingent. Punishment, on such accounts, is an intrinsically appropriate (not merely a contingently efficacious) means of pursuing that goal.[107]

Can von Hirsch's theory properly be characterized as belonging to this third theoretical category? This seems to be a key issue in understanding his approach. On the one hand, the answer to the question appears to be clearly in the affirmative, since (as we have seen) von Hirsch's account of the GJA interlinks censuring (backward-looking) and preventive (forward-looking) justifications. On the other hand, as Duff and Garland rightly point out, theories of this third kind tend to be 'variously referred to as educative or communicative';[108] and if that is a correct description of them, then perhaps von Hirsch is not after all in this third camp, since he is clearly sceptical of, for example, theories that treat penal censure as primarily a matter of moral education,[109] and those (such as that of Duff) that regard punishment as a 'communicative attempt to bring a wrongdoer to repent her crime'.[110] Given this scepticism, perhaps von Hirsch is after all not a 'third category theorist', but belongs in the more orthodox retributive camp?

---

[104] Duff and Garland (1994), n. 3 above, p. 8.
[105] Lucas (1993), n. 2 above, p. 87 (emphasis added).   [106] *Ibid*, p. 282.
[107] Duff and Garland (1994), n. 3 above, p. 8.   [108] *Ibid*, p. 8.
[109] Von Hirsch (1993), n. 8 above, p. 11.
[110] R. A. Duff, *Trials and Punishments* (Cambridge UP, 1986); cf. the critique in von Hirsch (1993), n. 8 above, Ch. 8.

Space precludes any full discussion of the work of the 'third category theorists' here.[111] Briefly, however, my view is that von Hirsch is rightly treated as a 'third category theorist', precisely because of the interlocking of censure and prevention in his account of the GJA; moreover (and perhaps more surprisingly to some readers), I would submit that *it is correct to regard him as subscribing (inter alia) to a forward-looking communicative theory of punishment*. I shall develop these points more fully below, especially when considering the 'censure' element in von Hirsch's theory.

(b) Von Hirsch's 'conception of human nature'

Von Hirsch's 'conception of human nature', although in some respects crucial to his 1993 discussion of the GJA, is only briefly elaborated, and makes no explicit reference to the myriad theories of human nature which can be traced through 'three thousand years of . . . intellectual history, from Homer to the present day'.[112]

This chapter, equally, cannot seriously venture into this vast terrain. Nevertheless, I cannot refrain from noting the striking parallels between von Hirsch's 'conception of human nature' and that elaborated, from a Judeo-Christian perspective, by the American theologian and social critic Reinhold Niebuhr in his Gifford Lectures at Edinburgh University in 1939.[113] For the later von Hirsch as for Reinhold Niebuhr, it is humankind's 'unity of spirit and body', as Niebuhr expresses it (or the unity of the instinctual and the capacity for moral reasoning, in von Hirsch's terms) that is so important;[114] for this unity makes it impossible to consider human behaviour except as a complex interactive process involving *both* the basic instincts shared with all other animals (of greed, sexual gratification, etc.) *and*, in humankind, something more than this, including the capacity for moral reasoning. In the field of punishment, if one takes this message of the 'unity of spirit and body' really seriously, then the implication is that we can *never*, for example, consider the effect of intendedly deterrent punishments simply in instrumental terms: we must certainly consider their deterrent (instrumental) effects, but we must always do so bearing in mind that these effects will, in

---

[111] Key texts in this genre, with each author having some distinctive characteristics, include the following: Feinberg (1970), n. 94 above; Duff (1986), n. 110 above; J. Hampton, 'An Expressive Theory of Retribution', in W. Cragg (ed.), *Retributivism and its Critics* (Franz Steiner Verlag, 1992); and Lucas (1993), n. 2 above, Ch. 6.

[112] J. Passmore, *The Perfectibility of Man* (Duckworth, 1970), preface.

[113] R. Niebuhr, *The Nature and Destiny of Man*, vol. 1, 'Human Nature', (Charles Schribner, 1941).

[114] For Niebuhr, most modern secular theories of humankind are either too 'naturalistic' or reductionist (treating humans as simply a product of their biology, like other animals); or alternatively they are too 'idealistic' (in the Enlightenment sense), understanding humans too much in terms of their rational faculties only, and failing to link this 'rationality' adequately to the bodily nature of persons. 'Man's finite existence in the body . . . can be essentially affirmed, as naturalism wants to affirm it. Yet the uniqueness of man's spirit can be appreciated even more than idealism appreciates it, though always preserving a proper distinction between the human and divine. Also *the unity of spirit and body can be emphasised* in terms of its relation to a Creator . . . who created both mind and body' (Niebuhr 1941, n. 113 above, pp. 15–16, emphasis added).

real life, be inextricably intermingled with other and more normative considerations in the lives of those to whom the deterrent threat was addressed.[115]

In my view, von Hirsch's formal incorporation into his later work of this
conception of human nature, linked to his account of the GJA, is an extremely
important development in his theorization, and one that has received insufficient
attention from commentators. Perhaps its potential significance for the theory of
punishment can best be explained by an analogy. For years, sociologists have
argued about the so-called 'agency versus structure' debate: that is to say, the
extent to which human behaviour is shaped by (i) the existing (and continually
reproduced) structures of gender, class division etc. in the societies into which we
are born, as against (ii) the freely chosen actions of individuals living within those
societies. A radical contribution to this debate has been Anthony Giddens's
structuration theory, which has insisted that structures and actions are actually
indissolubly interrelated. As Giddens puts it in one key passage:

Crucial to the idea of structuration is the theorem of the duality of structure . . . The constitution of agents and structures are not two independently given sets of phenomena, a
dualism, but represent a duality. According to the notion of the duality of structure, the
structural properties of social systems are both medium and outcome of the practices they
recursively organize. Structure is not 'external' to individuals: as memory traces, and as
instantiated in social practices, it is in a certain sense more 'internal' than exterior to their
activities . . . . Structure is not to be equated with constraint but is always both con-
straining and enabling. This, of course, does not prevent the structured properties of social
systems from stretching away, in time and space, beyond the control of any individual
actors. Nor does it compromise the possibility that actors' own theories of the social
systems which they help to constitute and reconstitute in their activities may reify those
systems . . . . Even the crudest forms of reified thought, however, leave untouched the
fundamental significance of the knowledgeability of human actors.[116]

Potentially, von Hirsch's most recent theoretical account has a similar intel-
lectually revolutionary potential in the field of punishment theory. For if one
takes the argument seriously, then the integrated conception of humankind effectively rules out the 'bifurcated' view of the GJA (and of human nature) adopted in
1986 (i.e. censure = appeal to moral reasoning; crime prevention = deterrent
'hard treatment'). Instead, von Hirsch's 1993 approach seems to require a fully
interactive account of censure and prevention as the core grounds for punishment. I shall explore this interactive theme further as these two core justificatory
grounds are now more fully examined.

---

[115] Significant empirical support for this proposition is to be found in the U.S. National Institute of
Justice randomized experiments on the effectiveness of arrest in dealing with domestic violence incidents to which the police were called. A consistent pattern of results was found to support 'a hypoth-
esis that the effects of criminal punishment depend upon the suspect's "stake in conformity", or how
much he has to lose from the social consequences of arrest' (L. W. Sherman, *Policing Domestic Violence* (Free Press, 1992), p. 17); those with stronger community ties tended to be more likely to be
deterred by arrest, whereas arrest actually increased domestic violence among persons who had nothing much to lose in social terms.
[116] Giddens (1984), n. 53 above, pp. 25–6.

(c) Censure

Von Hirsch's discussion of censure is simple but compelling. Censure (or reprobation) is, he argues, following Wasserstrom and Feinberg, inherently involved in the act of punishing:

Punishing someone consists of doing something painful or unpleasant to him, because he has purportedly committed a wrong, under circumstances and in a manner that conveys disapprobation of the offender for his wrong.[117]

Yet this definitional point, von Hirsch rightly points out, does not in itself *justify* a reprobative response to the conduct in question: and, unless such a justification can be provided, punishment 'might arguably be replaced by some other [social] institution that has no blaming implications'.[118]

To provide the necessary justification, von Hirsch begins by following Strawson[119] in arguing that censure (or reprobation) is part of the process of holding people responsible, or accountable, for their wrong actions. This important point can usefully be developed using J. R. Lucas's discussion of responsibility (and bearing in mind that one can be 'responsible', in the technical sense, for praiseworthy as well as for wrong deeds):

To be responsible is to be answerable . . . or accountable. And if I am to answer, I must answer a question; the question is 'Why did you do it', and in answering that question, I give an account . . . of my action. *So the central core of the concept of responsibility is that I can be asked the question 'Why did you do it?', and be obliged to give an answer.*[120]

In the case of actions deemed by a given society to be reprehensible,[121] this process of calling someone to account therefore necessarily entails a process of censure, within the kind of moral dialogue that Lucas is describing (and which can be seen in action, for example, in the 'summer holiday incident').

But in justifying censure, von Hirsch wishes to go beyond an analysis that simply emphasizes calling the wrong-doer to account. There are, he additionally suggests, certain 'positive moral functions of blaming', of which the most important are captured in the following paragraphs (and notice again how apposite these paragraphs are to the 'summer holiday incident'):

Censure addresses the victim. He or she has not only been injured, but *wronged* through someone's culpable act. It thus would not suffice just to acknowledge that the injury has occurred or convey sympathy (as would be appropriate when someone has been hurt by a

---

[117] Von Hirsch (1986), n. 12 above, p. 35, following Feinberg (1970), n. 94 above, and R. Wasserstrom, *Philosophy and Social Issues: Five Studies* (University of Notre Dame Press, 1980).

[118] Von Hirsch (1993), n. 8 above, p. 9.

[119] P. F. Strawson, *Freedom and Resentment and other essays* (Methuen, 1974).

[120] Lucas (1993), n. 2 above, p. 5 (emphasis added).

[121] Different societies, of course, have different moral codes, and they therefore differ in what they regard as reprehensible. This social variability of moral norms is very important in some contexts, but not in the present context, since all societies will have some acts deemed worthy of censure, and that is what is crucial to the present argument.

natural catastrophe). Censure, by directing disapprobation at the person responsible, acknowledges that the victim's hurt occurred through another's fault.

Censure also addresses the act's perpetrator. He is conveyed a certain message concerning his wrongful conduct, namely that he culpably has injured someone, and is disapproved of for having done so. Some kind of moral response is expected on his part—an expression of concern, an acknowledgement of wrongdoing, or an effort at better self-restraint. A reaction of indifference would, if the censure is justified, itself be grounds for criticizing him.[122]

Very interestingly, in this passage von Hirsch adopts (but does not much elaborate) the concept of censure as involving *personal dialogues*, with a *positive moral function*, with various relevant actors ('Censure addresses the victim . . . [it] also addresses the act's perpetrator').[123] Clearly, these 'positive moral functions' in part look to the future, as well as to the past. Further, von Hirsch importantly suggests, this kind of 'communication of judgement and feeling is the essence of moral discourse among rational agents'.[124] It is for reasons such as these that von Hirsch should, I believe, properly be regarded as subscribing (in part) to a forward-looking, communicative theory of punishment (see (a) above).

The dialogue-based approach to censure is worth developing, again calling in aid the work of the Oxford moral philosopher J. R. Lucas.[125] Lucas has written separate volumes on the topics of *justice* and of *responsibility*—both of which concepts feature centrally in von Hirsch's theory of punishment, though von Hirsch does not directly refer to Lucas. In both books (as we have already seen exemplified in an earlier quotation in this subsection), Lucas advises that, in our moral analyses of these important topics, we should avoid impersonal conceptual schemes, and think actively about individualized moral dialogues with relevant actors. Take complaints of injustice, for example:

In order to justicize an action, we must either establish that any complaint of injustice is itself [factually] unjustified . . . or *adduce for deciding against a potential claimant compelling reasons of a sort whose force even he cannot evade* . . . Only then will he see that we were not acting with wanton disregard of his rights and interests, but, in spite of manifest reluctance to do him down, we still had no alternative to decide as we did. For that to be the case our reasons have to be of a special kind. They must be . . . *individualised* reasons. They must be based on facts about him, not exclusively but enough to justify, *even to him if he is reasonable*, not simply our reaching an adverse decision, but its being adverse *to him*. We have to structure the argument so that it can be seen from his point of view.[126]

If we follow this approach, then methodologically, when considering the possible existence of injustices in our sentencing system—to offenders, to victims, or

---

[122] Von Hirsch (1993), n. 8 above, p. 10 (emphasis in original).

[123] Von Hirsch adds that the criminal law (but not all forms of censure) also addresses third parties, and provides them with reasons for desistance. 'Unlike blame in everyday contexts, the criminal sanction announces in advance that specified categories of conduct are punishable' (von Hirsch 1993, n. 8 above, p. 11). This, he argues, is a normative message that is not reducible to a mere inducement to compliance.

[124] Von Hirsch (1993), n. 8 above, p. 10.   [125] Lucas (1980), n. 17 above, (1993) n. 2 above.

[126] Lucas (1980), n. 17 above, p. 45 (emphasis added).

whoever—we need to think of ourselves as having a *conversation* with those who might claim injustice, in which their point of view is fully considered, and a decision adverse to them is reached only for reasons that they ought to acknowledge as cogent[127] (though, of course, that acknowledgement might not actually be forthcoming in practice). Thus, for Lucas, though justice is unavoidably a 'cold virtue',[128] requiring, for example, judges and others who dispense it to distance themselves from prior relevant personal relationships, yet in the dispensing of justice itself, and in the identification of justice and injustice, there is necessarily a kind of *personalized methodology* at work, for 'we cannot expect [the 'done down'] to enter into our reasons if they manifest scant regard for his individuality'.[129] This emphasis on a personalized (though not *personal*) methodology, and on capturing the special features of individual cases, is of course highly congruent with the earlier conclusion of Puzzle 1 about the 'many subtle nuances' of the particular case that have to be considered when weighing the seriousness of offences; it is also congruent with the discussion of mercy in Puzzle 2.

Both of Lucas's books contain chapters on punishment, but for present purposes the chapter in the later work (on *Responsibility*) is of special interest. Here Lucas draws a distinction between two kinds of retributivism, which are described (in less than helpful language, in my view) as the 'vindictive' and the 'vindicative'. The objectives of these two varieties of retributivism are characterized as follows:

Vindictive: To pay people back for having done wrong.
Vindicative: To vindicate the law and the victim . . . [Punishment] is a disowning of responsibility for the deed. The deed was a misdeed, and society dissociates itself from it, *by deeds if necessary as well as by words*, in a way that cannot be ignored or overlooked, so that everyone shall know that the action, though an action of a member of the community, was his act alone, and not one that the community itself approves of, acquiesces in, or is in any way prepared to acknowledge as its own.[130]

In discussing 'vindicative' theories of punishment, Lucas notes the objections of consequentialists such as Walker[131] who tend to argue that theories of this kind are often disguised versions of consequentialism. Certainly, says Lucas, vindicative theory is centrally about communication, and 'communications often have consequences, and [so] give grounds for consequentialist justifications'.[132] But the real point at issue, he suggests, is whether these consequences constitute the whole rationale of vindicative punishment—and, he argues, they do not, since they cannot 'account for the individualised, backward-looking nature of the concept' of vindicative punishment.

It is fairly clear that, using Lucas's language, the 'censure' element of von Hirsch's GJA is 'vindicative' rather than 'vindictive'. Lucas's analysis of this kind of punishment does not, I believe—at least in any rigorous philosophical

---

[127] *Ibid*, pp. 67–8.   [128] *Ibid*, p. 4.   [129] *Ibid*, p. 6.
[130] Lucas (1993), n. 2 above, pp. 284, 105 (emphasis added).
[131] Walker (1991), n. 5 above, Chs. 3 and 9.   [132] Lucas (1993), n. 2 above, p. 106.

sense—require any substantial modification of von Hirsch's basic argumentation on censure. Nevertheless, I would submit that there is a real case for saying
that Lucas's insights can be used to enrich von Hirsch's discussion of censure; and
that is so, I would suggest, especially in regard to three specific issues.

First, Lucas's account probably makes it clearer than von Hirsch's that in censure-based (or vindicative) punishment one is engaged in a process of social and
symbolic communication (in von Hirsch's account, the strong emphasis on
proportionality tends sometimes to overshadow the 'symbolic communication'
element entailed in his theorization). In particular, the adoption of Lucas's
'personalized methodology' helps to breathe life into that part of von Hirsch's
justification for censure where he speaks of censure addressing the victim and the
perpetrator.

Secondly, Lucas makes the very useful point that whereas 'vindictive' (or traditional retributive) punishment leaves no room for the rational exercise of mercy,
'vindicative' punishment would, in appropriate cases, have no difficulty in
accommodating such a concept.[133] In view of the apparent importance, for desert
theory, of incorporating a principle of rational mercy (see Puzzle 2), this is a
matter of some significance.

Thirdly, it is worth drawing more explicit attention to the emphasized clause
in Lucas's previously-given quotation on vindicative punishment: namely that by
punishing, society dissociates itself from the wrongful act of the offender 'by
deeds if necessary as well as by words'. Lucas is adamant that, within his communicative, 'vindicative' theory, 'actions speak'; and, further, that this can perhaps be most clearly understood by considering how *lack of action* by the
authorities in a given situation will be understood by offenders, victims, and
others.[134] Von Hirsch has forcefully reminded us that the principle of the rank-
ordering of penalties expresses in concrete terms the comparative disapproval of
different wrongs in a given society; while the principle of the 'spacing' of penalties requires a sizeable gap between the style of expression of disapproval for a
minor infraction and a heinous crime. Given these principles, plus Lucas's very
useful reminder that 'actions speak', it is surely the case that if a censuring system
were to consist simply of a series of stronger and stronger verbal disapprovals,
this would quickly be widely construed as *societal inaction*. Hence, what Feinberg speaks of as the 'hard treatment' element of punishment seems to be intrinsically required for the 'censuring' ground of punishment, as well as for the
'preventive' ground. This is a point that von Hirsch's 1993 account does not concede,[135] but it seems to me that nothing of central importance in his overall theory
would be jeopardized by acceptance of this proposition.

In concluding this subsection on censure, I return finally to the issue of terminology. I indicated earlier that, in my view, Lucas's 'vindictive'/ 'vindicative'

---

[133] *Ibid*, pp. 107–11, 284.   [134] *Ibid*, p. 107.

[135] To be more precise, von Hirsch (1993), n. 8 above, p. 12 accepts the proposition for punishments
in non-legal contexts (e.g. for misconduct by persons in professional occupations), but he doubts
whether this kind of argument will sustain the criminal sanction.

distinction seemed rather verbally unhelpful (although I have retained it for the sake of clarity when explicitly discussing Lucas's work). I would accordingly propose that, if we follow my suggestions and (in effect) merge the central insights of von Hirsch and of Lucas on 'censure' and 'vindication', then a useful terminological adjustment would be to speak, in von Hirsch's theory, not simply of 'censure', but rather of *dialectically defensible censure*. This concept would retain the clarity of von Hirsch's emphasis on 'censure', while explicitly adding to it a reference to Lucas's personalized, dialogue-based methodology. As we shall see in a later subsection, such a term would also have the advantage of providing a helpful bridge to the related concept of *legitimacy*.

(d) Is censure primary?

An important difference between Andrew von Hirsch's accounts of the GJA in *Past or Future Crimes* (1986) and in *Censure and Sanctions* (1993) concerns the alleged primacy of censure. In his 1986 account, subsequently self-described as 'bifurcated' (see above), the twin grounds of the GJA (censure and prevention) were seen as co-equal. In *Censure and Sanctions*, however, censure is seen as primary, precisely in order to avoid the perceived difficulties of the 'bifurcated' account. The core of the argument for the primacy of censure is expressed as follows:

A condemnatory response to injurious conduct . . . can be expressed either in a purely (or primarily) symbolic mode; or else, in one in which the reprobation is expressed through the visitation of hard treatment. The criminal sanction is a response of the latter kind. It is preferred to the purely symbolic response because of its *supplementary* role as a disincentive. The preventive function thus operates only *within* a censuring framework.[136]

This line of argumentation then allows von Hirsch to suggest that, in certain social circumstances, it could be possible to abolish the institution of criminal punishment, if it were not needed for preventive purposes.[137]

I have to confess that I do not find these arguments particularly persuasive. The argument for the primacy of censure explicitly makes the assumption that there is a clear division to be drawn between 'purely (or primarily) symbolic' censure, and censure that is expressed through 'the visitation of hard treatment'; and, further, that the criminal sanction is 'a response of the latter kind'. While that is certainly true of some criminal punishments (such as imprisonment), it is much less obviously true of, for example, the probation order (see the discussion in Puzzle 3) or the conditional discharge.

Indeed, I would suggest that the whole censure/hard treatment distinction is basically unhelpful and distracting in the present context. As we have previously

---

[136] Von Hirsch (1993), n. 8 above, p. 14 (emphasis added).

[137] *Ibid*. 'The society might wish to maintain some form of official censure to convey the requisite disapproval of such acts, but with the need for prevention eliminated, there would no longer be need for so ambitious, intrusive and burdensome institution as the criminal sanction' (von Hirsch (1993), n. 8 above, p. 14).

noted, von Hirsch derives this terminology from a paper by Feinberg.[138] Consultation of the original source reveals that Feinberg introduced the distinction as part of a discussion which sought to separate 'punishments' from 'penalties'—in itself a doubtful quest, though that point need not be pursued here.[139] In the case of *punishments* (as defined by him), however, Feinberg is clear that, although the two constituent elements of censure and hard treatment 'must be carefully distinguished for purposes of analysis', nevertheless they are *'never separate in reality'*.[140] This is an important observation, to which I shall return.

In the present discussion, our main focus is upon the GJA. Von Hirsch—I believe rightly—includes both censure (or reprobation) and prevention in his GJA. But we have already argued in the preceding subsection that the (descriptive) 'hard treatment' element of punishment seems to be intrinsically required as part of the (normative) 'censuring' ground of punishment (because 'actions speak'); and it is surely also the case that the preventive ground of punishment is sometimes adequately achievable by 'censuring' or 'symbolic' responses rather than by much in the way of 'hard treatment' (see the English courts' fairly extensive use of the conditional discharge).

It follows from the above that, *in a discussion of the GJA*, we are not really obliged to concern ourselves with the censure/hard treatment distinction. *Both* 'censure' *and* 'hard treatment' may legitimately be involved in each of the two main grounds of punishment (censure and prevention). In discussing whether either 'censure' or 'prevention' is primary within the GJA, we thus do not necessarily need to become entangled in Feinberg's (descriptive) censure/hard treatment distinction.

Starting again with a clean slate, then, should either 'censure' or 'prevention' be primary within the GJA? I would argue that the answer to this question is 'no', and that the two grounds should be co-equal. One can, I think, adduce three justifications for this view—one sociological, one analytical, and one ontological.

The sociological argument picks up the previously-cited comment by Feinberg about the factual inseparability of censure and hard treatment, and applies a similar insight in a fresh context. In actual acts of punishing, is it not the case that, at least usually, censure and preventive considerations are both present, and often not at all easily separated (just as agency and structure are, in general social life, continually co-present and interactive)? In the 'summer holiday incident' for example, censure and prevention were both explicitly present in the mother's words and actions—and those words and actions were, given the nature of the

---

[138] Feinberg (1970), n. 94 above.

[139] For Feinberg (1970), n. 94 above, examples of 'penalties' (as opposed to 'punishments') are 'parking tickets, offside penalties, sackings . . . and disqualifications' (p. 96). His argument is that 'punishment' has 'a certain expressive function' (or 'symbolic significance') that is largely missing from other penalties (p. 98). Notice, therefore, that Feinberg's use of the censure/hard treatment distinction differs importantly from that of von Hirsch: for the latter, it is the 'hard treatment' element which tends above all to distinguish the criminal sanction from other sanctions (see e.g. von Hirsch (1993), n. 8 above, p. 12).

[140] Feinberg (1970), n. 94 above, p. 98.

incident, spontaneous rather than the product of deep reflection. Is not something similar true in much of our punishing? And if so, does it really make sense to speak of one or the other element as 'primary'?

This leads to the *analytic* point. We have previously suggested that von Hirsch's theory of punishment is of the sort described by Lucas as 'vindicative'; and, as Lucas has pointed out, it is actually *inherent* in the vindicative account that punishments will often be preventive. He elaborates this point as follows:

> if we generally seek to make it *ex post facto* a bad policy to have done wrong, people thinking of doing wrong will predict that it will turn out to have been a bad policy, and will therefore be deterred . . . And if punishment is a forcible reminder of society's values, the message will sometimes go home, and result in an amendment of life on the part of the wrongdoer: we often speak of teaching him a lesson, and lessons are sometimes learnt . . . Communications often have consequences.[141]

Developing the same point in another way, one could argue that the ultimate point of a *punishment system* is the prevention of undesirable behaviour, but that in any *specific instance of punishment* one initially looks back reprobatively to the act committed ('this is happening to you *because you did*' a certain deed). Analytically, then, both prevention and censure could be said in some sense to be primary: prevention as regards the institution of punishment, and censure in each specific instance of punishing. However, specific acts of punishment are always also instantiations and reproductions of the general institution of punishment.[142] Hence, prevention and censure in fact coexist and interact as justifications for punishment, and it seems to make little analytical sense to describe either as primary.

Thirdly, and finally, there is the *ontological* argument. The conception of humankind that von Hirsch briefly sketches in *Censure and Sanctions* seems to involve (see subsection (b) above) an ontological view of persons in which there is an ever-present unity of the instinctual and of the capacity for moral reasoning. Such a view of personhood would seem to be most congruent with a GJA in which censure and prevention are co-equal and interactive.

My conclusion, then, is that the case for the primacy of censure is not strong, and that von Hirsch's 1986 account of the GJA, in which censure and prevention were seen as co-equal grounds, was *in that respect* preferable to his 1993 account. Of course, as von Hirsch himself subsequently pointed out, the 1986 account was marred by the 'bifurcated' nature of the argument. Von Hirsch's solution to that problem was to avoid bifurcation by opting for the primacy of censure; however, another way of avoiding bifurcation is to retain the co-primacy of censure and prevention, *but to treat them as interactive rather than bifurcated*. That, in essence, is the case that has been argued here.

If such a view were incorporated into von Hirsch's theorization, it would of course make it clearer than ever that von Hirsch is best treated as a 'third category theorist' (see (a) above).

---

[141] Lucas (1993), n. 2 above, p. 106.   [142] See generally Giddens (1984), n. 53 above.

(e) Prevention

We turn then, finally, to the second main ground of von Hirsch's GJA, namely prevention. Essentially, only one main point remains to be made under this heading.

It is important to realize that there are different modes (or mechanisms) by which prevention can be achieved. One of these is *situational control* (or opportunity-reduction), most obviously manifested in penal systems by incapacitative imprisonment or home confinement orders, but also embracing penalties such as disqualification from driving. I have elsewhere illustrated different kinds of prevention mechanisms using the simple domestic example of a child left alone in a house with some expensive chocolates.[143] The *situational* mode of control here is of course to lock the chocolates in a cupboard and take away the key. But the parents have, at least in principle, other and more *social* modes of prevention at their disposal, of which four may be usefully distinguished:

(1) **Social Prevention Mode A: Socialization.** The child is imbued by the belief that stealing, even within the house is wrong; hence she desists from taking the chocolate, even though the cupboard door is open.

(2) **Social Prevention Mode B: Legitimation.** The child believes that her parents (whom she loves) exercise a legitimate authority over her; hence she desists from taking the chocolate because they have forbidden it, even though the cupboard door is open.

(3) **Social Prevention Mode C: Deterrence.** The child desists from taking the chocolate (the cupboard door being open again) because she fears being caught and punished, and the pain of the punishment will outweigh the pleasure of the chocolate.

(4) **Social Prevention Mode D: Reward.** The child desists from taking the chocolate from the open cupboard because, though she will not be much punished if she takes it, she has been promised a trip to EuroDisney if the chocolate remains intact until Granny's Golden Wedding—and the child dearly wants to visit EuroDisney.

Of these four, C and D can be described as *instrumental/prudential* modes of prevention (i.e. they attempt to achieve prevention by 'carrot and stick' mechanisms), whilst A and B are *normative* modes of prevention (i.e. they depend for their effectiveness on influencing the moral reasoning of the persons to whom they are addressed).

In the context of a sentencing system, D is not very relevant. But A and C are familiar enough to sentencers (the probation order, for example, can be regarded as an attempt at resocialization through a court order, while the fine is intendedly deterrent in impact). Much less often discussed, however, is B—i.e. legitimation as a mechanism of prevention.

---

[143] See Sparks, Bottoms, and Hay (1996), n. 18 above, Ch. 9, and A. Liebling, G. Muir, G. Rose, and A. E. Bottoms, *An Evaluation of Incentives and Earned Privileges: Final Report to the Prison Service* (unpublished research report by the Institute of Criminology, University of Cambridge), Ch. 5.

Empirical evidence has recently been accumulating, especially in the field of police studies, to suggest that the ways in which persons in contact with the legal system are treated by representatives of the system can powerfully affect their perception of the legitimacy of State institutions (for example, persons treated with respect and with fair procedures when stopped by the police are more likely to regard the police force as legitimate than those given more brusque treatment). Additionally—and of special importance for present purposes—there is growing evidence that people who regard the police as having acted fairly, and as having shown respect to them as citizens, are more likely subsequently to obey the law.[144]

Thus, one way of helping to achieve prevention seems to be for legal authorities (in the case of sentencing, the court and its ancillary officers) to act fairly and to treat defendants with respect. Hence, and contrary to von Hirsch's 1986 'bifurcation' assumptions, there is empirical evidence that prevention can embrace a normative as well as an instrumental ('hard treatment') dimension; and this normative dimension can involve legitimation as well as rehabilitation.

(f) Legitimacy and the wider social context

But the potential significance of legitimation for a sentencing system is not confined to its contribution to prevention.

Consider, for example, the following well-known set of facts. In September 1944, the Nazi occupying forces in Denmark arrested the entire Copenhagen police force, and from then until the liberation all policing was carried out by an improvised (and ineffective) watch corps. Andenaes takes up the story:

> The number of cases of robbery increased generally in Copenhagen during the war, rising from ten per year in 1939 to ten per month in 1943. But after the Germans arrested the police in 1944, the figure rose to over a hundred per month and continued to rise. Larcenies reported to the insurance companies quickly increased tenfold and more. The fact that penalties were greatly increased for criminals who were caught and brought before the courts did not offset the fact that most crimes were going undetected.[145]

Now suppose that D committed a robbery (on a Danish civilian) after the Nazi action, was caught, and was sentenced to the new, higher penalty for that crime. Suppose too that D was aware of the Nazi proclamation about higher sentences for robbery when he committed the offence.

Would this be a justified sentence, in moral terms? The following points could be adduced in support of that view:

(i)   D has committed a wrongful act, and deserves censure for it;

(ii) punishing D will probably contribute to crime prevention, especially in the absence of a regular police force (in which circumstances, the role of sentencing in overall crime prevention is enhanced);

---

[144] See especially Tyler (1990), n. 15 above, and R. Paternoster, R. Brame, R. Bachman, and L. W. Sherman, 'Do fair procedures matter? The effect of procedural justice on spouse assault' (1997) 31 *Law and Society Review* 163.

[145] J. Andenaes, *Punishment and Deterrence* (Michigan UP, 1974), p. 51.

(iii) given (i) and (ii), the two grounds suggested by von Hirsch as the GJA of a punishment system (censure and prevention) are both present;

(iv) the defendant was aware that in committing this act he risked the higher penalty, so he cannot claim arbitrary imposition of penalties;

(v) the higher penalty was prescribed by those in power in Denmark at that time.

Intuitively, however, we may feel that, despite all the above points, there remains a serious doubt about the moral justifiability of the enhanced sentence. Arguments in support of that view would be:

(a) the higher penalty levels were prescribed by the Nazi authorities solely as a consequence of their own imprisonment of the entire Copenhagen police force, an action of extremely doubtful morality;

(b) the Nazis, although in unquestioned power in Denmark, had achieved that power solely through an armed invasion which had been (and still was) strongly opposed and resented by the great majority of the Danish people. Moreover, this lack of overall political legitimacy had led directly to the Nazis' action against the Copenhagen police (who, basically, the occupying power did not trust)—and hence, had led also to the enhanced sentence levels;

(c) given (a) and (b) above, the higher penalty levels prescribed—and now imposed upon D—cannot reasonably be considered to have been prescribed within a legitimate criminal justice system.

However one might finally assess this particular example, the example does, I believe, fairly conclusively indicate that one cannot wholly justify punishment, in any given social situation, simply by reference to the two grounds of 'censure' and 'crime prevention'. Rather—and as I have previously suggested in a semi-popular essay[146]—it would appear that, in sentencing as elsewhere in criminal justice studies, there is a need to pay explicit attention to the issue of the legitimation of authority.[147] More specifically, I would suggest that there is a clear case for incorporating an additional element into the GJA, namely: 'To operate as part of a legitimate and legitimated system of authority'. But, if so, what exactly is legitimacy? Space forbids any full treatment of this question here, but the following brief account, following the work of David Beetham, might be helpful.[148]

Beetham contends that, although the particular content of legitimating beliefs and principles has been extremely historically and culturally variable, nevertheless we can identify a common underlying structure of legitimacy which is very general.[149] On Beetham's account, that underlying structure has three dimensions or criteria, in terms of which the legitimacy of any actually existing distribution

---

[146] A. E. Bottoms, 'Avoiding Injustice, Promoting Legitimacy and Relationships' in J. Burnside and N. Baker (eds.), *Relational Justice* (Waterside Press, 1994), p. 61.

[147] See, e.g., R. Sparks and A. E. Bottoms, 'Legitimacy and Order in Prisons', (1995) 46 *British Journal of Sociology* 45.

[148] The following paragraphs are adapted from Sparks *et al.* (1996), n. 18 above, pp. 85–7, which in turn draws on the more extended discussion in Sparks and Bottoms (1995), n. 147 above.

[149] D. Beetham, *The Legitimation of Power* (Macmillan, 1991), p. 22.

of power and resources can be expressed and evaluated. Such criteria are almost never perfectly fulfilled, and each dimension of legit-imacy therefore has a corresponding form of non-legitimate power (see Figure 1).

Figure 1: Beetham's Dimensions of Legitimacy[150]

Criteria of legitimacy	Corresponding form of non-legitimate power
1. Conformity to rules (legal validity)	Illegitimacy (breach of rules)
2. Justifiability of rules in terms of shared beliefs	Legitimacy deficit (discrepancy between rules and supporting shared beliefs, absence of shared beliefs)
3. Legitimation through expressed consent	Delegitimation (withdrawal of consent)

The three dimensions shown in Figure 1 roughly correspond to the traditional preoccupations of three different academic specialisms which have considered issues of legitimacy: first, lawyers (has power been legally acquired, and it is being exercised within the law?); next, political philosophers (are the power relations at issue morally justifiable?); and finally, social scientists (what are the actual beliefs of subjects about issues of legitimacy in that particular society?).[151] However, a central plank of Beetham's argument is that social scientists have been wrong to follow Max Weber[152] in defining legitimacy as simply 'belief in legitimacy on the part of the relevant social agents'.[153] To promote this view, Beetham argues, is to leave social science with no adequate means of explaining why subjects may acknowledge the legitimacy of the powerful in one social context, but not in another. Beetham accordingly argues for an alternative formulation of the social-scientific view of legitimacy—'a given power relationship is not legitimate because people believe in its legitimacy, but because it can be *justified in terms of their beliefs*'.[154] This may seem to introduce a rather fine distinction, but the alternative formulation is seen as fundamental, because it injects a crucial element of moral judgement into the social-scientific definition.[155]

Beetham argues against some currently influential views of power (especially those flowing from 'rational choice' models) which tend to ignore the fact that systems of social power inherently generate normative as well as prudential or self-interested elements.[156] It follows that, in his view, social situations in which legitimacy is *not at all* necessary to the powerful will be very rare. Ironically,

---

[150] Source: Beetham (1991), n. 149 above, p. 20.   [151] Beetham (1991), n. 149 above, p. 4 *et seq.*

[152] M. Weber, *Economy and Society* (California UP, 1968).

[153] Beetham (1991), n. 149 above, p. 6.   [154] *Ibid*, p. 11.

[155] Additionally to this point, Beetham also suggests that the simple 'belief in legitimacy' view takes no account of those aspects of legitimacy that have little to do with beliefs at all, such as conformity to legal rules.

[156] Beetham (1991), n. 149 above, p. 27; and cf. (e) above.

of course, the modality of power that stands most in need of legitimation is not democratic discussion, which claims to be inherently self-legitimating, but force. For 'the form of power which is distinctive to [the political domain]—organized physical coercion—is one that both supremely stands in need of legitimation, yet is also uniquely able to breach all legitimacy. The legitimation of the State's power is thus both specially urgent and fateful in its consequences'.[157]

Legitimacy and power are, on this view, actually two faces of the same problem, and this point is certainly relevant to any State sentencing system, which on occasions is very obviously involved in the practice of 'organized physical coercion'. Hence, in a criminal justice system (and any other system of power relations), the content and strength of legitimating beliefs can radically affect all parties (especially as only legitimate social arrangements generate normative commitments towards compliance). Indeed, the need for legitimation not infrequently constrains the actions of the powerful since, as Giddens puts it, 'to speak of legitimacy in the usual sense implies the existence of standards external to he [sic] who claims it'.[158]

More could, of course, be said about legitimacy, but the preceding brief argument is perhaps sufficient to make at least an outline case for incorporating legitimation as an important dimension, additional to censure and prevention, into any adequate account of the GJA in a punishment system.

We may finally note that, if such a step is taken, then there are two interesting consequences. First, the issue of legitimacy will also interact with (though it will not be reducible to) the concept of 'dialectically defensible censure'(see (c) above). And secondly, the debate—ultimately crucial to desert theory—about whether it is possible to offer 'just deserts in an unjust society'[159] will have to be radically reconceptualized if one adds to the GJA the requirement for the criminal justice system 'to operate as part of a legitimate and legitimated system of authority'. Personally, I would regard such a reconceptualization as both constructive and exciting; but to pursue this point in any detail would require another chapter.

(g) *Conclusion*

In conclusion, then, in this lengthy discussion of Puzzle 4, I have argued that the GJA of a punishment system should be formulated as containing three elements. A formal statement of these elements might take something like the following form:

A punishment system, and any specific instance of punishment, is justified where:

(1)   the person punished deserves censure, and the fact and the extent of that censure can be dialectically defended in rational discussions with relevant persons (the offender, the victim, third parties, etc.); *and*

---

[157] Beetham (1991), p. 40.
[158] A. Giddens, *Studies in Social and Political Theory* (Hutchinson, 1977), p. 92.
[159] See von Hirsch (1993), n. 8 above, pp. 106–8.

(2) the punishment system contributes to the prevention of wrongful acts; *and*

(3) the punishment, and the punishment system, operates as part of a legitimate and legitimated system of authority.

PUZZLE 5: FROM THEORY TO PRACTICE

In this final puzzle, we move away from high theory back to the world of penal practice, focusing specifically on the implications of the GJA discussion in Puzzle 4 for the sentencing system.

In early drafts of this chapter, Puzzle 5 had a rather narrow focus. In both *Past or Future Crimes* and *Censure and Sanctions*, Andrew von Hirsch defended a conception of the GJA that embraced (albeit in different ways) both censure and prevention; yet, in both books, when discussing *the actual distribution of the amount of punishment by the courts in daily practice*, the proposed dominance of the principle of proportionality meant that prevention was squeezed into a rather minor role. An important issue for von Hirsch's theory is, therefore, whether the apparent disparity between the role of prevention in the GJA, and its smaller role in fixing the amount of punishment, can be adequately defended.

That remains a key question, but I would now prefer to set it within a somewhat wider context—namely, the general implications for sentencing practice of the proposed revised account of the GJA that I have offered in Puzzle 4. That wider context requires one to consider not only the *amount* of punishment awarded; but also the issues of the *types* of punishment that are appropriate (given the conclusions re the GJA), and the *extent of the choice* of punishments that should be available to the courts.

Let us begin with the amount issue. Von Hirsch is himself well aware of the core problem here, and indeed he describes it as a potential 'Trojan Horse' for his overall account of the sentencing system. As he puts the matter:

If punishment's existence is justified even in part on preventive grounds, might prevention be involved in deciding comparative severities of punishment? Were that permissible, proportionality would be undermined.[160]

Essentially, von Hirsch's response to this difficulty is to say that, since the amount of punishment is inextricably linked to the extent of the censure, proportionality must be preserved in a sentencing system. He adds that 'making prevention part of the justification for punishment's existence, in the manner that I have, does not permit it to operate independently as a basis for deciding comparative punishments'.[161]

This response, I believe, is broadly appropriate, yet it does not go quite far enough. The key word is 'independently'. Von Hirsch rightly suggests that a preventive purpose can be regarded as immanent (my word, not his) in a sentencing system whose 'amount' principles are based solely on proportionality. Allowing

---

[160] *Ibid*, p. 16.   [161] *Ibid*, p. 17.

prevention to operate *independently* in fixing amounts of punishment would destroy proportionality—but of course that does not deny the fact that, in a real sense, prevention underpins the whole sentencing system.

But given all this, logic surely requires us to take one further step. If prevention is really to be considered as having a justified place in the GJA, then it should follow that *it must be able to influence the punishment where this does not interfere with the principle of proportionality*. This point is likely to be most relevant, in practice, in the sphere of non-custodial penalties. If D is convicted for an offence which does not (on proportionalist grounds) require a prison sentence, then there might still be a choice of different non-custodial penalties (e.g. probation, short CSO, fine) which could be regarded as of equivalent penal severity.[162] In such a situation, it might be the case that, for that particular offender with his/her special characteristics, there are no strong indications which penalty would—in crime preventive terms—be the more successful. But, as knowledge of effective interventions improves,[163] there will certainly be occasions when one of the penalties with equivalent penal severity seems likely to be the most (crime-preventively) successful. The logic of the joint censure/prevention GJA then seems to require that the potentially most successful penalty (at the appropriate point on the penal severity scale) should normally be the court's choice.

There is one other important general issue as regards the amount of punishment. In Chapter 5 of *Censure and Sanctions*, von Hirsch argues robustly against critics who had suggested that desert theory has little to say about the overall severity of sentencing scales; and, as we have seen, he then puts the case for low punishment levels (albeit ones that are not precisely specified: see note 26 above). A number of persuasive arguments are put forward for this conclusion, including the view that (based on living-standard analysis) 'punished persons' vital interests are being trivialised when . . . drastic deprivations are used to convey merely a mild degree of censure'.[164] It is not necessary to discuss all these arguments here. However, in view of the discussion of Puzzle 4 above, we must note that one of von Hirsch's central arguments in his Chapter 5 relies heavily on the alleged primacy of censure over prevention:

Crucial to such a conception of prevention is that it be implemented through a modest range of sanctions. Such sanctions would provide a supplementary prudential incentive for compliance, which may help offset the temptation to offend. But since the threat levels are not so devastating, the moral reasons expressed through the sanction's censuring features still count. The actor would not suffer irretrievable damage to his life prospects were he to ignore the threat and suffer the penalty. In such a situation, the actor's response to the normative message of the sanction still has some practical relevance to his decision. The supplementary prudential disincentive is just that, supplementary: it does not loom so large as to co-opt or displace the normative message.[165]

---

[162] See further Bottoms (1989), n. 1 above, and von Hirsch (1993), n. 8 above, Ch. 7.

[163] J. McGuire and P. Priestley, 'Reviewing "What Works": past, present and future', in J. McGuire (ed.), *What Works: Reducing Reoffending* (Wiley, 1995).

[164] Von Hirsch (1993), n. 8 above, p. 37.   [165] *Ibid*, pp. 42–3.

My own conclusion, of course, is that the case for the primacy of censure in the GJA has not been substantiated (see Puzzle 4). Does that then destroy the above argument for reasonably modest penalty scales? In a nutshell, I believe that the answer to this question is 'no'. The nub of von Hirsch's argument, in the above-cited paragraph, is that the normative (moral reasoning) dimension of punishment must not be so overwhelmed by harsh, allegedly preventive, punishments that, from the point of view of the punished person, no credible moral reasoning dimension remains. Such an argument appears to be just as valid where censure and prevention are seen as truly co-equal and interactive partners in the GJA as it is when censure is seen as primary. The need for 'dialectically defensible censure' remains (see Puzzle 4), and those dialogues will provide an important check on the overall severity levels of punishment, linked also to the issue of legitimacy.

We turn now from the *amount* of punishment to its *type*; and this is perhaps the point at which von Hirsch's own account of sentencing theory, and my own revisionist interpretation of his approach, diverge the most sharply.

Von Hirsch's principal discussion of types of punishment is to be found in a chapter (joint-authored with Uma Narayan) on 'Degradingness and Intrusiveness'.[166] Degrading punishments are rejected for the Kantian-style reason that 'they fail to treat the offender with the dignity due to a human being', so that they interfere 'with any legitimate moral response the censured person may make'.[167] Thus, it is argued, censure treats the offender as a person, and as a moral agent; degradation does not.

So far, so straightforward; but some of the suggested applications of this principle are more debateable. So, for example, von Hirsch and Narayan develop the concept of 'acceptable penal content', which is the idea that a punishment 'can be administered in a manner that is *clearly* consistent with the offender's dignity'.[168] They then go on to suggest that home visits, as part of a non-custodial sentence, are:

not part of acceptable penal content: it is not plausible to assert that the penalty for a given type of offence should be that agents of the State periodically snoop into the offender's home.[169]

This seems a rather strong statement, and its message is not by any means fully supported by Rex's subsequent research. While in Rex's study (and in other recent research studies on probation in England) probationer-probation officer contacts primarily took the form of office interviews, nevertheless nearly two-thirds of the probationers in Rex's sample had received home visits. While few showed active enthusiasm for such visits, there was 'little preference for office- or home-based contact', though this was at least partly accounted for by the fact that many probationers 'seemed to accept it as an inevitable part of being supervised that their officer would come to their home'.[170] This resigned acceptance of

---

[166] *Ibid*, Ch. 9.   [167] *Ibid*, p. 82.   [168] *Ibid*, p. 84 (emphasis in original).

[169] *Ibid*, p. 85. Von Hirsch does, however, allow that home visits could be justifiable as (but only as) a mechanism to assist the enforcement of another sanction that is of 'acceptable penal content'.

[170] Rex (1997), n. 61 above, p. 117.

the inevitable, however, was clearly not felt to be over-intrusive by most probationers,[171] given the overall framework of the (often positively-viewed) probationer-probation officer relationship (see the discussion in Puzzle 3).

I have dealt with the home visits issue in some detail principally because it seems to me to be a practical illustration of a more general tendency in Andrew von Hirsch's writings to emphasize that the sentencing system should deal with offenders '*externally*', rather than attempting 'to elicit certain *internal* states'.[172] And I doubt that this emphasis is completely justifiable, on any full elaboration of the justifications for desert-based punishment, as extensively discussed in Puzzle 4.

One way of summarizing some of the discussion in Puzzle 4 would be to say, with Antony Duff, that:

On this view punishment is therefore retributive, in that it aims to impose on the offender the suffering (the pain of condemnation [etc.] . . .) which she deserves for her crime. But precisely in virtue of its character as an appropriate retribution for a past offence, punishment also looks to the future.[173]

This is clearly not the place for any full discussion of the intriguing debate on punishment between Duff and von Hirsch.[174] But those knowledgeable about that debate will realize that the position outlined in this chapter draws on both writers, yet without fully agreeing with either. On the one hand, 'dialectically defensible censure' is still *censure*, and hence is not, in terms, a direct attempt to induce penitence/repentance (cf. Duff). On the other hand, I have argued that a full development of von Hirsch's censure-based approach nevertheless perhaps requires a more future-oriented and more individualized (and so *less external*) view of the offender than von Hirsch sometimes concedes (and in this respect, my position is closer to that of Duff).

Indeed, an exclusive emphasis on the external has its own severe dangers, as is graphically evident from the following (intendedly neutral) description of desert theory in a very recent pamphlet issued by a reputable British organization:

The just deserts approach . . . focuses on the offence rather than the circumstances of the offender who, it is assumed, has the capacity to redeem himself (or more rarely herself) and to lead a law-abiding life.[175]

A desert theory founded upon a GJA combining dialectically-defensible censure, prevention, and legitimacy (see Puzzle 4) is of course in no way committed to

---

[171] Though there was one clear exception: 'I think they just come to your home to be nosey, that's what I think. You've got to watch them, they ain't daft, you see, they don't tell you what they write down about you' (Rex (1997), n. 61 above, p. 129).

[172] Von Hirsch (1993), n. 8 above, p. 72.

[173] Duff (1992), n. 59 above, pp. 53–4.

[174] See more generally Duff (1992), n. 59 above, and von Hirsch (1993), n. 8 above, Ch. 8.

[175] Centre for Explorations in Social Consciousness, *The Regeneration of Criminal Justice* (The Grubb Institute, 1997). The Centre for Explorations in Social Consciousness is a unit of the respected Grubb Institute. The report cited was produced after discussions with a 'Criminal Justice Concern Team' which included a Circuit Judge, a Chief Constable, a Chief Probation Officer, a member of the Prisons Board, and a well-known criminologist.

such a proposition. Yet it is not impossible to see how even fairly well-informed observers of the penal scene could reach a conclusion of the above kind, given desert theory's traditional (and, up to a point, certainly justifiable) emphasis on proportionality, and hence initially on the offence rather than the offender.[176]

The difference of interpretation and emphasis between a more 'external' or a more 'internal' censure-based theory can have very significant practical consequences as regards the question of types of punishment. This is, essentially, the important conclusion reached by Antony Duff in the question previously noted (see Puzzle 3 above), namely, the issue of:

How much weight we might attach to the demand for an abstract proportion between seriousness of crime and severity of punishment, as against the demand for a more richly communicative [penality]? [177]

As Duff himself explicitly avers,[178] proportionality is a very important principle; yet his conclusion—which I share—is that it cannot be allowed to become over-dominant in a sentencing system, bearing in mind the overall point and purpose of punishment (see Puzzle 4). For Duff, the overall point and purpose of punishment is somewhat different from that sketched in the discussion of Puzzle 4, and this would lead to some difference between Duff and myself on the issue of types of punishment.[179] But we are both quite clearly 'third category theorists' of punishment (see Puzzle 4, (a) above), and, for both of us, that entails that punishment includes (but is not limited to) forward-looking goals such as prevention which the particular punishment 'might or might not achieve'. This would differentiate us both, as regards the range of punishments in a sentencing system, from those desert theorists who would wish to allocate a very predominant role to proportionality. For such theorists, as Duff has noted,[180] 'the penalties available to the courts must be such that they can be *readily* ranked and compared in terms of their severity' (emphasis added). For Duff and myself, a principle of this kind would be too restrictive; it would lead to too narrow a range of types of available penalties, bearing in mind the overall goals of the punishment system. For example, such a principle would probably involve, *inter alia*, abolishing, or relegating to a very minor role, the traditional probation order; but, as the discussion of Puzzle 3 has hopefully shown, that would lead to an overall impoverishment of the sentencing system.

[176] For a brief indication of the historical reasons for desert theory's emphasis on the offence rather than the offender, see for example Bottoms (1994), n. 146 above.

[177] Duff (1992), n. 59 above, p. 62.

[178] *Ibid*, pp. 61–2.

[179] For example, Duff's theoretical approach, in which analogies with penance play a significant role, tends to produce demands for a 'communicative and concrete fit between the nature of the [specific] crime and the character of the punishment imposed for it'; and also a 'more participatory penal process which gives a more active role to the offender and to the victim' (Duff (1992), n. 59 above, p. 62). The first of these suggestions is not particularly congruent with the account of the GJA that I have sketched in Puzzle 4. The second suggestion is more congruent with my approach, yet there is no requirement (from the theory sketched in Puzzle 4) to go all the way towards 'victim-oriented' or 'restorative' justice.

[180] Duff (1992), n. 59 above, p. 46 (emphasis added).

But this leads me, finally, to consider the *extent of the choice* of punishments (especially, of course, non-custodial punishments) that should be available to sentencers. As Andrew von Hirsch has been at pains to point out, if this choice becomes too wide, then it becomes in effect impossible to sustain any realistic scale of ordinal proportionality for non-custodial sentences.[181] Since ordinal proportionality is a key dimension of the censuring element of punishment, that is a danger that must be avoided. Thus, as so often in establishing sentencing systems, we have a balance to strike: on the one hand, the range of non-custodial sentences available must not be so great that it will, in practice, swamp the principle of proportionality; on the other hand (see earlier discussion) the principle of proportionality must not be allowed to become so dominant that it will (in effect) swamp other justifiable grounds of punishment by insisting that the criminal justice system includes only penalties that can be 'readily ranked and compared in terms of their severity'.[182]

CONCLUSION

Through an analysis of five specific 'puzzles', this chapter has attempted to offer both a defence and some reconceptualization of von Hirsch's theory of punishment. This has involved, *inter alia*, some emphasis on the difficulties of producing appropriate ordinal scales for both crimes and punishments; it has also involved a suggested reformulation of von Hirsch's overall justification for punishment ('the GJA'). If my arguments have merit, then in order to apply this approach to a sentencing system, further hard work would be needed—for example, in urgently developing 'living standards' analyses of non-custodial penalties, embracing their subtler as well as their more obvious demands (see Puzzle 3); and in developing sentencing guidelines that would enable judges to develop confidently (and not vacuously) what Ross Harrison calls 'the trained application of the reasons of law to individual cases' (see Puzzle 2).

As a final word, it seems worth emphasizing that, despite the suggested modifications to von Hirsch's theory that this chapter contains, I see the overall thrust of my analysis emphatically as a defence of von Hirsch's general approach to punishment. I suspect that, in the long run, von Hirsch's principal contributions to punishment theory will be seen to have been, first, his strong emphasis on ordinal proportionality, and secondly, his defence of a GJA that embraces both censure and prevention (linked, more recently, to a particular theory of humankind). These are both extremely important points, as regards each of which (in my judgement) von Hirsch's basic argumentation is both convincing and highly original. The more critical comments of the present chapter are thus offered only within that framework of core agreement and admiration.[183]

[181] See, e.g., von Hirsch (1993), n. 8 above, Chs. 7 and 8; Ashworth *et al.* (1995), n. 1 above.
[182] Duff (1992), n. 59 above, p. 46.
[182] I am grateful to Antony Duff and to Michael Tonry for valuable comments on a late draft of this chapter: these comments enabled we to make important minor amendments at proof stage. I regret that, when writing this chapter in 1997, I was unaware of Duff's important 1996 article (R. A. Duff, 'Penal Communications' (1996) 20 *Crime and Justice* 1).

Part II

Troublesome Issues in Sentencing Theory

Aggr.
or
Mitigating
Factors.

4

Crime Seriousness and the Offender-Victim Relationship in Sentencing

MARTIN WASIK

1. INTRODUCTION

The questions 'why punish?' and 'how much?' are located within political and social theories for which the relationship between the State and the criminal offender is the defining concern.[1] We ask in what circumstances the imposition of punishment on the offender by the State can be justified at all and, where it can, what limitations should be placed upon the form and duration of that punishment. Here the focus is upon what may be termed the 'State-offender axis'. In contrast, the relationship between the offender and the victim, what might be called the 'offender-victim axis', has been taken to be only marginally relevant to these debates.[2] Thus, in a leading modern collection of essays on sentencing theory,[3] victims of crime are mentioned in only one small section of the text, and the topic is presented there so as to suggest that the relevance of the victim lies 'beyond the sentence' in the spheres of prosecutorial discretion, compensatory arrangements, and in the rather marginal 'alternative' schemes of criminal justice, based upon reparation and mediation.[4]

A degree of mis-match between theory and practice is, however, clearly evident in this area. In everyday sentencing practice the offender-victim axis is assumed to be closely connected with the assessment of both harm and culpability. Empirical studies of sentencing practice support this view.[5] In

---

[1] See Andrew von Hirsch, 'Proportionality in the Philosophy of Punishment: From "Why Punish?" to "How Much?" ' (1990) 1 *Criminal Law Forum* 259.

[2] Valuable discussions may be found in A. Ashworth, 'Punishment and Compensation: Victims, Offenders and the State' (1986) 6 *Oxford Journal of Legal Studies* 86; P. Duff, 'The "Victim Movement" and Legal Reform' in M. Maguire and J. Pointing (eds.), *Victims of Crime: A New Deal?* (1988), at p. 147; and J. Dignan and M. Cavadino, 'Towards a Framework for Conceptualising and Evaluating Models of Criminal Justice from a Victim's Perspective' (1996) 4 *International Review of Victimology* 153.

[3] A. von Hirsch and A. Ashworth, *Principled Sentencing* (1992).   [4] *Ibid*, pp. 399–403.

[5] See, for example, E. Green, 'Sentencing Practices' in N. Johnston, L. Savitz, and M. E. Wolfgang, *The Sociology of Punishment and Correction* (1962), p. 69, at p. 70: 'an analysis of the data on

Nunn,[6] the Court of Appeal observed that it was 'an elementary principle that the damaging and distressing effects of a crime on the victim represent an important factor in the sentencing decision', and recently revised sentencing guidelines for magistrates' courts now require sentencers in every case to weigh the 'impact on the victim' when assessing offence seriousness.[7] As part of the recognition of 'rights' of victims within the criminal justice system, pre-sentence reports should contain information about the effect which the offence has had on the individual victim.[8] Other jurisdictions have gone further in this direction, by allowing the routine presentation of a 'victim impact statement' for the sentencer's consideration, or by allowing the victim to address the court on the question of sentence.[9] Also, following concern expressed by the Royal Commission on Criminal Justice[10] over the extent to which some offenders, at the sentencing stage, try to shift much of the blame for the offence on to the victim, the Criminal Procedure and Investigations Act 1996 now permits the judge to order that there should be no press reporting of such comments.[11] To what extent can these various developments be squared with traditional sanctioning theory on the (ir)relevance of the victim?

Utilitarian theories of punishment place reliance upon the requirement of general social protection, but they rarely address the situation of individual victims. This is understandable. Although utilitarian goals have their ultimate force in their claim to achieve net community benefit through punishment, their immediate purpose is either to motivate a change in the offender's[12] behaviour (through individual deterrence, or rehabilitation) or to restrain the offender from committing further crime (through incapacitation). In each of these strategies, circumstances of past offences are much less important than assessment of the offender's propensity to offend in the future. Such assessment is based on the weighing of precipitating factors: the offender's psychological profile, his social circumstances, and his (lack of) response to previous sentences. For incapacitation, the issue is the risk posed by the offender to the general public, rather than the harm done to any particular victim in the past.[13] In rehabilitation, the emphasis is on the offender's social circumstances, his character, and his willingness to change

the distribution of sentences for the various types of crimes indicate that they consist of three variables, each an aspect of the offender-victim relationship'. Green found these variables to be (i) 'the specificity of the victim' (by which he meant whether the victim was 'the public' generally, or an individual), (ii) the degree of personal contact between the offender and the victim occasioned by the offence, and (iii) the degree of 'bodily harm' resulting from the offence.

[6] [1996] 2 Cr.App.R. (S) 136, at 140.

[7] Magistrates' Association, *Sentencing Guidelines* (1997).

[8] Home Office, *National Standards for Pre-Sentence Reports* (1995). See further David Thomas, 'Viewpoint' (1994) 4 *Sentencing News*, 12.

[9] For a collection of relevant materials see Martin Wasik (ed.), *The Sentencing Process* (1997).

[10] *Report* (Cm 2263, 1993), Ch. 8, para. 47.

[11] See also the Criminal Justice and Public Order Act 1994, s. 31, which places the defendant's shield in jeopardy if, during the trial, he casts an imputation upon the character of the deceased victim.

[12] Or, in the case of general deterrence, would-be offenders.

[13] An exception arises in the case where the offender always offends against the same victim. In *Nicholas* (1994) 15 Cr.App.R. (S) 381 it was held that a preventive sentence could be imposed on grounds of public protection where there was a serious ongoing risk to the offender's wife, but not to anyone else.

his behaviour. It is true that some rehabilitative techniques require the offender to confront the suffering incurred by the victim of the offence,[14] and may involve mediation with the victim. Even so, rehabilitation is mainly concerned with re-adjusting the offender's attitudes to the requirements of the community generally, rather than to the particular victim.

Turning now to desert theory, it is clear that most forms of retributivism have taken victims into account indirectly, and only to a limited extent[15]. Modern desert theory, of course, stresses the importance of proportionality between the seriousness of the offence and the severity of the punishment. Andrew von Hirsch has maintained that offence seriousness comprises two elements: the magnitude of the harm caused (or risked) by the offender *and* the offender's culpability with respect to that harm.[16] The harm incurred by the victim is certainly one factor to be taken into account when gauging the seriousness of an offence,[17] but that injury always has to be related to the culpability of the offender. The proportionalities which are central to desert theory are those which obtain between the offender and the offence, and hence between one offender and another, but *not* between the offender and the victim. So, it follows that little attempt has been made within desert theory to analyse the circumstances of victimization generally, still less to assess the aetiology of individual cases.

Desert theory, unlike utilitarian theories, claims to offer a fair degree of practical guidance in the implementation of theory into everyday sentencing practice.[18] The reality of sentencing in court stands at several steps removed from the promulgation of general theory, but it is with the relevance and application of desert theory to practice that the present chapter is concerned. The present author shares many of the concerns which have been expressed by other writers about victims becoming more intimately involved in the sentencing process.[19] The comments of the Court of Appeal in *Nunn*, to the effect that the victim's view as to the appropriate level of punishment for the offender cannot provide a sound basis for sentencing, are surely to be welcomed.[20] Otherwise, cases with identical features

---

[14] R. Prentky, 'A Rationale for the Treatment of Sex Offenders' in J. McGuire (ed.), *What Works: Reducing Reoffending* (1995), p. 155.

[15] There are exceptions. One version of retributive theory holds that the general justification for punishment lies in the satisfaction of the grievance desires of victims. See T. Honderich, *Punishment: The Supposed Justifications* (1971), p. 29: 'The relationship may be described as holding between the grievance caused to the victims of the offence and others, on the one hand, and, on the other hand, the satisfactions given them by the offender's penalty'.

[16] Andrew von Hirsch, *Past or Future Crimes* (1986), p. 64 *et seq.*

[17] Contrast the '*Lex Talionis*', where an exact equivalence between the punishment and victim's injury is sought.

[18] Andrew von Hirsch, *Censure and Sanctions* (1993), p. 1 states that the idea of desert 'provides sentencers with a degree of guidance [while] competing utilitarian theories seldom appear capable of providing much guidance at all'.

[19] Donald J. Hall, 'Victims' Voices in Criminal Courts: the Need for Restraint' (1991) 28 *American Journal of Criminal Law* 233; Andrew Ashworth, 'Victim Impact Statements and Sentencing' [1993] *Criminal Law Review* 498 and also his *Sentencing and Criminal Justice*, 2nd edn. (1995), p. 309. See further J. Gardner in Ch. 2 of this book, above.

[20] See also the Scottish case of *H.M. Advocate* v. *McKenzie* 1990 SLT 28, where it was said to be invidious for a sentencer to seek the views of the victim as to the proper sentence, since that would

nd to be dealt with in widely differing ways, depending substantially upon
rce of the victim's advocacy. These issues are not pursued further here. The
ma... aim of this chapter is to demonstrate a number of important ways in which
the offender-victim axis *does* impinge upon harm and culpability issues in sentencing. In these situations, and to that extent, it is argued that desert theory must
give more attention to the offender-victim axis than it has done in the past.

2. Victims and Offence Definitions

The desert model of sentencing requires us to rank offences in terms of their relative seriousness. Paul Robinson has argued that in drafting a rational sentencing
system which takes account of principles of proportionality it will be necessary
for broad offence classifications to be broken down into a number of distinct sub-
categories.[21] What should limit the number of sub-divisions, according to Robinson, is the requirement that such categories should remain reasonably
distinguishable from each other, and should continue to reflect 'meaningful differences' in offence seriousness. There are a number of ways in which offences
might be sub-divided to reflect such differences. For example, in American sentencing guideline systems theft offences are commonly divided into three, four or
more sub-categories on the basis of the value of property taken. Or the offence of
robbery might be sub-divided according to whether the offender carried a
weapon, or not. A frequently-used criterion for sub-division of offences, however, is victim-based. Some State systems, for example, double the mandatory
minimum sentence for drug dealing offences where the drugs were supplied to a
minor, to a pregnant woman, or in the vicinity of a school.[22]

In England, nineteenth century legislation, such as the Offences Against the
Person Act 1861 and the (now repealed) Malicious Damage Act of the same year,
made many victim-based sub-divisions of offences. Under the former Act, for
example, separate and distinct offences of assault are committed depending upon
whether the victim is a clergyman officiating at a place of divine worship, or a
magistrate authorized to preserve a vessel in distress.[23] Although at the time when
these provisions were drafted, the distinctions drawn must have seemed important enough, they would clearly not now reflect, to use Robinson's term, 'meaningful differences' in offence seriousness.[24] Modern law reform bodies in England

---

'expose the complainer to a risk of public pressure by passing any comment on matters that lie outside her experience'.

[21] Paul Robinson, 'A Sentencing System for the 21st Century?' (1987) 66 *Texas Law Review* 1, at
17–20.

[22] See further D. Husak in Ch. 8 of this book, above.

[23] Offences Against the Person Act 1861, ss. 36 and 37.

[24] The 1861 Act also marks out different offences by reference to the *means* by which injury is
caused: choking, suffocating, poisoning, starving, exposing to the elements, etc. See further John
Gardner, 'Rationality and the Rule of Law in Offences Against the Person' (1994) 53 *Cambridge Law
Journal* 502.

have advocated the sweeping away of these distinctions, arguing that 'the special relationship [between offender and victim] and the circumstances are generally relevant to sentencing and not to the definition of the substantive offence'.[25] The examples given above still represent the law, but a radical overhaul of the Act is pending.

The introduction of more broadly drafted legislation of the kind advocated, such as was achieved in the Theft Act 1968 and the Criminal Damage Act 1971, means that the nature of the offender-victim relationship is no longer apparent on the face of the offences themselves. Where relevant to the appropriate punishment, matters relevant to the relationship then fall to be identified and taken into account by the sentencer.[26] The crime of incest, for example, is a broad single offence defined by reference to a range of prohibited familial sexual relationships.[27] The maximum penalty is 7 years' imprisonment, except where a man commits incest with a girl aged under 13, where the maximum is life. For sentencing purposes, it has proved necessary for the Court of Appeal to develop subdivisions within the 7-year offence, by specifying different sentencing brackets for offenders within different categories and victims falling within different age-groups. The relevant sentencing guideline judgment of the Court of Appeal distinguishes, in some detail, between cases where the female victim was aged under 13, was aged between 13 and 16, or was aged over 16.[28] Other sentencing cases delineate the principles applicable where other familial relationships are involved, such as brother and sister,[29] or mother and son.[30] It is a matter for debate whether it is better in legislative terms to adopt a scheme of narrow offences or to go for a single broad offence with a high maximum penalty. What is clear, however, is that if the latter approach is adopted, the relevant distinctions in offender-victim relationships still have to be made by the sentencer.

It is not difficult to find examples in English law where the status of the victim qualifies the case for inclusion within one category of offence rather than another. A good example is burglary. Although the Theft Act 1968 adopted the approach of placing all forms of burglary within a single offence, this position was reversed in 1991, so that there are now two distinct offences, one involving invasion of a person's home and one covering burglary of non-domestic premises, such as shops, offices, and schools.[31] Although the criminal conduct required of the offender in the two offences is identical, different maximum sentences are involved,[32] different mode of trial provisions apply, and different

[25] Criminal Law Revision Committee, 14th Report, *Offences Against the Person* (1980), para. 3.

[26] See, further, D. A. Thomas, 'Form and Function in Criminal Law' in P. R. Glazebrook (ed.), *Reshaping the Criminal Law* (1978), p. 21 and Michael Tonry, 'Criminal Law: The Missing Element in Sentencing Reform' (1982) 35 *Vanderbilt Law Review* 607.

[27] Sexual Offences Act 1956, s. 10(1): 'It is an offence for a man to have sexual intercourse with a woman whom he knows to be his grand-daughter, daughter, sister or mother'.

[28] *Attorney-General's Reference (No. 1 of 1989)* (1989) 11 Cr.App.R. (S) 409.

[29] Examples are *Harding* (1989) 11 Cr.App.R. (S) 190 and *P* (1993) 15 Cr.App.R. (S) 116.

[30] For example, *F* (1991) 13 Cr.App.R. (S) 358.

[31] Theft Act 1968, s. 9, as amended by Criminal Justice Act 1991, s. 26.

[32] Thus establishing that they are distinct offences: see *Courtie* [1984] 1 AC 463.

sentencing guidelines operate. Another example is the Sexual Offences Act 1956, which separates the offence of unlawful sexual intercourse with a girl aged under 13 from the offence of unlawful sexual intercourse with a girl aged under 16. There are also the offences of assaulting a police officer in the execution of his duty and assaulting a person with intent to resist lawful arrest, which mark out such victims from all other victims of assault.[33] These examples relate to the status and characteristics of the victim of the offence. The prior relationship between the offender and the victim can also be a defining feature of offences. The clearest example is where the deceased victim is shown to have provoked the offender to kill, such that the crime is reduced from murder to voluntary manslaughter. The issue of provocation is considered further, below. There are other examples. A number of European countries have separate offences of unlawful sexual intercourse where the victim was a person under the care or control of the offender. There is no such general offence in England, but a distinct offence of unlawful sexual intercourse is committed where the victim is a mentally impaired woman,[34] and the offence is different again where the victim was mentally impaired and the offender was a person employed to take care of her.[35]

Reference may also be made to recent changes in England in respect of the offence of rape. Until the landmark decision of the House of Lords in *R*,[36] non-consensual sexual intercourse committed by a man upon a woman amounted to rape, *except* where the man and the woman were married to each other. The marital status of the victim, in this situation, meant that the unwanted sexual intercourse fell outside the offence of rape and constituted a lesser crime or, depending on the circumstances, no offence at all. Statutory revision to the offence of rape in 1994 confirmed the effect of *R*, and further extended the scope of the offence so as to include males within the range of applicable victims.[37] These very significant shifts in the definition of the offence of rape are closely correlated with the range of victims thought to fall appropriately within or beyond the scope of that particular offence. The offence of rape is thereby broadened by the legislature but, when sentencing for rape of a wife, courts may still have regard to the relationship which existed between the parties before the commission of the offence.[38]

This range of examples shows that there is often a need to mark out 'meaningful differences' between and within offences in accordance with the offender-victim axis. To the extent that the legislative trend is to favour broader offences and to eschew detailed sub-divisions, perceived differences in harm and culpability on the offender-victim axis still need to be addressed and taken into account by the sentencer. Apart from these questions relating to the structure of

---

[33] Police Act 1996, s. 89; Offences Against the Person Act 1861, s. 38. Oddly, for more serious assaults such as assault occasioning actual bodily harm, attracting a maximum sentence of 5 years on indictment, no such distinctions are drawn, and it is left to the sentencer to take into account that the victim was a police officer or was a person effecting a citizen's arrest.

[34] Sexual Offences Act 1956, s. 7(1).

[35] Mental Health Act 1959, s. 128; *Goodwin* (1995) 16 Cr.App.R. (S) 144.

[36] [1992] 1 AC 599.   [37] Criminal Justice and Public Order Act 1994, s. 142.

[38] See, for example, *Stephen W* (1993) 14 Cr.App.R. (S) 256.

criminal offences, there are other ways in which issues of harm and culpability emerge from the offender-victim relationship. The next three sections of this chapter examine, in turn, three of the most important ways in which these have been recognized by sentencers—cases involving gratuitous harm to the victim, cases where the victim is regarded as especially vulnerable, and cases where the victim may be seen as having contributed to the offence.

3. INFLICTION OF GRATUITOUS HARM

There is a broad and generally applicable aggravating factor, recognized in many sentencing schemes, where the offender has occasioned to the victim a degree of harm which is gratuitous, in the sense of being over and above the harm implicit in the nature of the offence itself.[39] Clear examples are cases where additional force is used upon a victim who has already submitted to the offender's demands, such as where handcuffed robbery victims are sprayed with mace,[40] or where the offender subjects the victim of a violent or sexual offence to additional gross insult or offence.[41] The function of the aggravating factor here is to indicate that the sentencing bracket should normally be significantly above that which is appropriate for a case where that factor is absent. It is important to note that additional severity in sentence can only be justified in such circumstances where the aggravating factor is either admitted by the offender or is proved against him to the requisite standard.

An enhancement of sentence here is clearly appropriate on desert grounds, since the harm occasioned to the victim is significantly greater in these circumstances, and so is the culpability of the offender. The notion of 'gratuitous' harm implies that such additional harm was indeed intended, or at least knowingly risked, by the offender. This is the kind of enhancement of seriousness which might in principle be marked by the charging of one or more additional counts against the offender, although in practice this is often not done. Thus, the circumstances of a rape are aggravated by the fact that the offender abducted the victim, or threatened to use, or did use, a weapon, and the sentence for the rape can be enhanced by these aggravating factors without the need to charge separate counts of kidnapping or assault.[42] The circumstances of a domestic burglary are aggravated by ransacking and damage in the house, and the sentence for the burglary can be enhanced by this aggravating factor without the need to charge a separate count of criminal damage.[43] But if these aggravating factors are not admitted by the defendant, nor proved against him to the requisite standard, then they cannot form part of the factual basis for the sentence.

[39] See, for example, *Minnesota Sentencing Guidelines*, II.D.103, (b)(2): 'The victim was treated with particular cruelty for which the individual offender should be held responsible'.

[40] *State* v. *Schantzen*, 308 N.W.2d 484 (Minn. 1981).

[41] See, for example, the guidelines on rape in *Billam* [1986] 1 WLR 349. The infliction of gratuitous violence and injury in assault was at its worst in *Legge* (1988) 10 Cr.App.R. (S) 208.

[42] *Billam*, n. 41 above.　　　[43] *Brewster* [1998] 1 Cr.App.R. (S) 181.

Enhancement of seriousness for gratuitous harm is typically to be found in racially motivated offending, which is an aggravating factor relevant across a range of different offences. The racial element here constitutes an extra dimension of harm, since it amounts to an additional attack upon the victim's legal rights,[44] and offender culpability is high because the victim has been singled out for the purpose of the attack. The Court of Appeal has said that considerable weight should be given to this aggravating factor.[45] It is the kind of victim-related consideration which could in principle justify the creation of a separate 'aggravated' form of the offence,[46] or a distinct sub-category of the offence. The creation of a separate offence of racially motivated violence was urged by the Commission for Racial Equality and others during the passage of the Criminal Justice and Public Order Bill in 1994, but was opposed by the Government on the basis that to define an offence in terms of racial motivation would create an extra hurdle of proof which it would be difficult for the prosecution to overcome.[47] This may well be true but, as we have seen, whether racial motivation is treated as a defining element of the offence, or as an aggravating factor in sentencing, it still requires proof to the requisite standard.

4. VULNERABLE VICTIMS

A second group of victims is commonly identified for distinct treatment in sentencing schemes. These are the so-called 'vulnerable victims'. Commission of a given offence against a vulnerable victim is taken to aggravate that offence significantly. Victims who invariably seem to fall within this class are children and the elderly. The group sometimes also includes people who have a physical or mental disability and some other categories may qualify. In the USA, sentencing guideline schemes identify victim vulnerability as a general aggravating feature in the setting of sentencing levels.[48] The American Federal Sentencing Guidelines, for example, provide in section 3A1.1 for an *automatic* two-level increase in sentencing severity, in respect of *any* offence, if:

the defendant knew or should have known that a victim of the offense was unusually vulnerable due to age, physical or mental condition, or that a victim was otherwise particularly susceptible to the criminal conduct.

---

[44] Ashworth (1995), n. 19 above, p. 130.

[45] See, for example, *A.G.'s References Nos 29, 30 and 31 of 1994* (1994) 16 Cr.App.R. (S) 698 and *Craney* [1996] 2 Cr.App.R. (S) 336.

[46] The Crime and Disorder Bill 1997 makes provision for aggravated versions of assault, harassment and public order offences and, when sentencing for other offences, requires the court to treat racial motivation as an aggravating factor.

[47] See further Martin Wasik and Richard Taylor, *Blackstone's Guide to the Criminal Justice and Public Order Act 1994* (1995), pp. 98–100, and Editorial, 'Hate Crimes' [1994] *Criminal Law Review* 313.

[48] See, for example, Minnesota Sentencing Guidelines, II.D.103, (b)(1): 'The victim was particularly vulnerable due to age, infirmity, or reduced physical or mental capacity, which was known or should have been known to the offender'.

In England, the Magistrates' Association's Sentencing Guidelines refer to 'vulnerable victim' as an aggravating consideration in a large number of the offence guidelines.[49] Vulnerable victims are also referred to in guideline judgments of the Court of Appeal on particular offences. In *Billam*,[50] the guideline judgment on rape, for example, commission of the offence on a victim who is either very old or very young is specified as a serious aggravating factor.

Another group of vulnerable victims accorded special status in some sentencing schemes is those involved in law enforcement in the broadest sense, including police officers, emergency service crew, and traffic wardens. Associated with this group are ordinary citizens injured while trying to uphold the law, such as by intervening to protect another person, or by trying to prevent a crime. Members of these groups do not have the physical or mental frailty of children, the elderly, or the disabled, so a different account for their special status must be provided. Again, this has often been found within deterrence. The argument is that such people, for the community's benefit, place themselves at greater risk of becoming victims of crime, and so whenever they are victimized a more severe sentence is appropriate.[51] A desert-based argument can also be made out. As Ashworth puts it, a person who knowingly attacks a public official such as a police officer chooses to strike against a fundamental institution, as well as assaulting the individual concerned,[52] and indeed it is recognized in the cases that sentence should not be enhanced if the defendant was genuinely *unaware* that the victim was a police officer.[53] Often included together with the last group, but in principle distinct from them, are cases involving victims who do not represent the State, but who simply have jobs in areas which incur a greater than average risk of being victimized. Included within this group would be private security officers, bus drivers, taxi drivers,[54] sub-postmasters, and licensees.

The sentencing category of 'vulnerable victim' is, on reflection, a puzzling one. One meaning of 'vulnerable' is 'at risk', but it is clear that this special status has very little to do with the likelihood of a particular person actually becoming the victim of crime. We can see from victim surveys, such as the British Crime Survey, that the 'vulnerable victim' for sentencing purposes bears no relationship to the social, economic, and demographic characteristics of the victim population. We know that a person's lifestyle makes a significant difference to the relative likelihood of their falling victim to crime,[55] 'lifestyle' being construed broadly here so

---

[49] Magistrates' Association, *Sentencing Guidelines* (1997) (see the relevant guidelines for assault, indecent assault, wounding offences, affray, theft, obtaining by deception, making off without payment, and taking vehicle without consent). While most of these categories are readily understandable, in what circumstances will a victim be 'vulnerable' in respect of either of the last two offences?

[50] [1986] 1 W L R 349.

[51] The Criminal Law Revision Committee (1980) at para. 162, considered whether there should be 'special offences of assault' to reflect the prevalence of assaults on public officials, but decided against so recommending. See the text at n. 33 above.

[52] Ashworth (1995), n. 19 above, pp. 131–2.   [53] *Stosiek* (1982) 4 Cr.App.R. (S) 205.

[54] An example is *Johnson* [1998] 1 Cr.App.R. (S) 126.

[55] See John H. Laub, 'Patterns of Criminal Victimization in the United States' in R. C. Davis,

as to include a person's domestic relationships.[56] We know that young, fit, and socially active people are most at risk of violent crime. Children, the elderly, and the handicapped, are more likely to be victimized at home than elsewhere. These groups are not specially at risk from crime, although the elderly do suffer disproportionately from fear of crime.[57] 'Vulnerability', in the sense of 'at risk', also suggests relative ease of access to the victim by the offender. Offenders generally live in the same areas as their victims, and not infrequently occupy the same house. People who live in high crime areas with low socio-economic status, high population density, low standard housing, and reliance upon welfare benefits, are the most 'vulnerable' to property crime.[58] We are also now increasingly aware of the highly skewed nature of victimization—that for most citizens victimization is a quite rare event, whilst some 'repeat' victims are affected by crime routinely, perhaps almost continuously.[59] Yet victims most at risk in these important senses are not generally regarded as 'vulnerable victims' in law.

A second, overlapping, meaning of 'vulnerability' is to do with the relative ease with which the person may be victimized. Some victims may be seen as easy targets, likely to offer little resistance, and may be targeted for that reason.[60] On grounds of deterrence, at least, sentences may be more severe where 'vulnerable victims' are involved, to provide a disincentive from singling them out. Judges sometimes express themselves in that way when passing sentence on an offender who has committed an offence against an elderly victim, or a child. We can set the deterrence claim on one side here, since we are concerned in this chapter to ask whether it is appropriate to recognize 'vulnerable victims' as a separate category in desert terms. According to the general theory there are two aspects to consider—harm and culpability. Unlike cases of gratuitous harm, considered above, the category of vulnerable victim does not necessarily entail additional harm or additional culpability. Both these elements, and the relationship between them, must be considered here.

To what extent is *harm* increased when crime is committed against a vulnerable victim? We might start by observing that, as a matter of principle, sentencers should avoid drawing distinctions of this kind amongst victims. An offence committed against one adult victim is the same harm as a similar offence committed against a different adult victim. Some empirical evidence suggests that sentencing levels may vary in accordance with the social status or moral standing of the

A. R. Lurigio, and W. G. Skogan, *Victims of Crime*, 2nd edn. (1997), p. 9; Antonia Cretney and Gwynn Davis, *Punishing Violence* (1995), Ch. 2.

[56] See S. Walklate, *Victimology* (1989), pp. 6–13.

[57] R. Mawby, 'Age, Vulnerability and the Impact of Crime' in M. Maguire and R. Pointing (eds.), *Victims of Crime: A New Deal?* (1988). M. Hough, Home Office Research Study No 147 (1996).

[58] See Lucia Zedner, 'Victims' in M. Maguire, R. Morgan, and R. Reiner (eds.), *The Oxford Handbook of Criminology*, 2nd edn. (1997), Ch. 18.

[59] See G. Farrell and K. Pease, *Once Bitten, Twice Bitten: Repeat Victimization and its Implications for Crime Prevention*, Home Office Police Research Group CPU Paper 46 (1993); H. Genn, 'Multiple Victimisation' in Maguire and Pointing (1988), n. 57 above, p. 90.

[60] See Schafer's category of 'weak' victims, below.

victim,[61] or with their ethnic origin.[62] If this suggests that injury to one adult victim is 'worth' more in terms of punishment than the same injury to a different adult victim, it is surely indefensible.[63] A more promising tack, however, is to say that a given offence, such as an assault, perpetrated upon an elderly person or a child, will *necessarily* cause greater harm to them than it would to a non-vulnerable victim. Vulnerable victims are, *ipso facto*, less well able to defend themselves through one or another form of physical or psychological limitation, so that the impact of the assault upon them is bound to have a deeper and more prolonged effect than it would on a non-vulnerable victim. The difficulty here is that this is an empirical claim which will often, but not always, be true. Not *all* older people are frail; many are resilient. The impact of crime on a child can sometimes be devastating and may have long-term deleterious effects, but some children seem to recover rapidly from trauma, perhaps more rapidly than an adult might from the same offence.[64] If it *is* the additional harm which makes the difference when sentencing in cases of vulnerable victims, that additional harm surely requires to be proved, rather than simply presumed. As with the case of gratuitous harm, discussed earlier, especially harmful consequences of the offence should not be taken to aggravate the offence unless admitted by the offender or proved to the requisite standard. Yet the American Sentencing Guidelines have an *automatic* enhancement of sentence severity of two levels whenever a victim falls within the requisite category. The Magistrates' Association's guidelines can also be seen as defective in this respect, since they simply refer to 'vulnerable victim' as an aggravating feature in sentencing, without requiring proof of any greater than average loss in the particular case.

So, it seems, the 'vulnerable victim' category is a *status* which has been accorded to certain types of victim, such status not being dependent on proof that the victim actually *did* suffer additional harm from the offence. A degree of moral accounting seems to be taking place here, with the respective merits of the victim and the offender being compared and contrasted. There is a close link between the 'vulnerable victim' and the 'ideal victim', identified in criminological literature. The ideal victim is upright, innocent, passive, and morally uncompromised, displaying 'contrasting characteristics to those of the offender'.[65] This is most obviously the case where offences are committed against the elderly, or against children. There is also an element of moral accounting where offending is against the police, since a lawbreaker stands in the sharpest contrast to an officer of the law, or to a person

---

[61] An example is rape of a prostitute. See *Kennan* [1996] 1 Cr.App.R. (S) 1 and *AG's Reference (No 28 of 1996)* [1997] 2 Cr.App.R. (S) 206.

[62] See further B. Hudson in Ch. 9 of this book, below.

[63] A more plausible claim for distinguishing among victims, perhaps, is that the killing or injuring of a child is a greater harm *per se* than the killing or injuring of an adult. Should a child's life, being so unfulfilled, be valued more highly than that of an adult's?

[64] See Jane Morgan and Lucia Zedner, *Child Victims* (1992), Ch. 3.

[65] See J. Shapland, J. Willmore, and P. Duff, *Victims in the Criminal Justice System* (1985), at pp. 188–9. The American 'ideal victim' is said to be 'a clean cut, polite war veteran with a Purple Heart for losing an arm while saving a buddy': William F. McDonald, 'Introduction' to McDonald (ed.), *Criminal Justice and the Victim* (1976), p. 17, at p. 42.

who is injured in the course of upholding the law. Also, though less clearly perhaps, where the victim is a citizen who, through his or her work, finds themselves in the 'front line' against lawbreaking, such as the sub-postmaster, the bus driver or the bank teller. The American case of *U.S.* v. *Jones*[66] provides a useful illustration. In that case the issue was whether a bank teller was a vulnerable victim within the meaning of section 3A1.1. The defendant had entered a bank with a jacket covering one hand and had presented a note to the teller demanding money. It was argued on appeal that the sentence should not have been increased under the vulnerable victim provision, since the teller had been surrounded by a protective screen, cameras, alarms, and trained security personnel, and because she herself had been trained in how to react in a threatening situation. The Appeals Court held, however, that an enhanced sentence was correct, since what mattered was not the *actual* vulnerability of the victim on the facts nor whether they had in fact sustained any injury but, rather, the general status of bank tellers as vulnerable victims. The Court held that they were vulnerable victims *per se*, and so the degree of protection and training accorded to the particular bank teller, or the extent of any injury actually suffered by them were not, in principle, relevant.

Apart from harm, then, the other element in crime seriousness is offender *culpability*. Crimes which involve the *targeting* of victims are viewed as particularly serious. As the U.S. Court of Appeals commented in one case, it is the selection of the vulnerable victim by the offender which 'show[s] the extra measure of criminal depravity which s.3A1.1 intends to more severely punish'.[67] Culpability is at its highest where the offender has deliberately targeted the victim, such as in the case of an assault on a child, a frail or disabled person,[68] or a theft, deception, or robbery practised on an elderly victim.[69] Frequently the targeting of a vulnerable victim will be associated with the further aggravating factor of breach of trust, such as where a child or elderly person has been abused by a carer.[70] Where culpability is so high, it may well not be necessary to demonstrate much if any additional harm to justify sentence enhancement. In the English case of *Lewis*,[71] residential burglaries committed against recently bereaved householders were treated as being more serious than an 'ordinary' house burglary and, indeed, the 'recently bereaved' might qualify as a further category of vulnerable victim. One can see that the effect of a burglary on the victim in such circumstances would be more than usually upsetting. There was also, however, clear evidence of targeting in *Lewis*. The offender, when arrested, was found to be in possession of a cutting from the 'deaths' column of a newspaper. The culpability of the offender in selecting such victims, rather than the degree of the harm itself, was probably the main reason for enhanced seriousness of the offence in this case.

---

[66] 899 F. 2d 1097 (11th Cir., April 30, 1990).

[67] *U.S.* v. *Moree* 1990 U.S. App. LEXIS 4588 (5th Cir. March 29, 1990).

[68] An example is *Bayfield* [1996] 1 Cr.App.R. (S) 441.

[69] Recent examples are *Tucker* [1997] 1 Cr.App.R. (S) 337 and *Eastap* [1997] 2 Cr.App.R. (S) 55.

[70] Examples are *Mason* (1995) 16 Cr.App.R. (S) 860 and *Taylor* [1997] 1 Cr.App.R. (S) 36. See the text to n. 34 above.

[71] (1993) 14 Cr.App.R. (S) 744.

It should be noted, however, that the relevant provision of the Federal Sentencing Guidelines, cited above, is not confined to cases of targeting. Indeed, it is much more liberally drafted, so as to include cases where the defendant 'knew or should have known' that the victim was vulnerable. So, aside from cases where a burglar has specifically targeted the homes of elderly people, to what extent should he be held responsible for the additional degree of shock, distress, and injury which is occasioned to a particular householder on a particular occasion? Should punishment be enhanced only where the burglar can be shown knowingly to have run the risk that the house was occupied by an elderly person, or does the burglar simply take the victim as he turns out to be? Many house burglars can be said to run the risk that the victim of their offence may, in a particular case, suffer far more than might have been expected. If that risk materializes, should the burglar suffer additional punishment in consequence? In recent sentencing guidelines issued by the Court of Appeal for the offence of house burglary in *Brewster*[72] the Lord Chief Justice drew no distinction between more than usually harmful consequences which are foreseen by the offender and those which are not. Domestic burglaries were, he said, more serious if 'they are targeted at the elderly, the disabled and the sick' or 'if they are shown to have a seriously traumatic effect on the victim'. The Magistrates' Association's guidelines are also defective here, referring simply to 'vulnerable victim', without specifying *any* degree of awareness of that fact on the part of the offender. The respective elements of harm and culpability, and the importance of each in relation to the other, need to be separated out here. Some sentencing differential is surely appropriate to reflect significant additional harm to the victim, and a further differential is appropriate where that additional harm was intended or foreseen by the offender.

It would probably be widely agreed that an offence targeted at an elderly, or very young, person is especially culpable and should attract additional punishment even where no greater than average harm is incurred. If so, the real gravamen in 'vulnerable victim' cases is the culpability of the offender, rather than the harm occasioned to the victim. To place the focus primarily on culpability in vulnerable victim cases renders the status and characteristics of the selected victim of less importance than it currently is. It could be argued that in *any* case where a victim has been targeted by the offender a significant enhancement of sentence should result. Take the example of a woman who has been physically abused by her partner. If violence recurs, should the abused woman not be regarded as a vulnerable victim? Such victims offer an easy and familiar target for the abusing partner, and are thus likely to be subjected to renewed assault. Repetition of attack against the same victim is especially harmful, since a further assault will tend to rekindle the fear which was associated with the earlier assault.[73] In cases where the assaults continue despite court warnings there is also a high degree of

---

[72] [1998] 1 Cr.App.R. (S) 181.

[73] Repetition of offending against the same victim was recognized as an aggravating factor in *Brewster*.

culpability. Until recently, at least, a domestic assault was commonly viewed as less serious than an identical assault committed by a stranger outside the home. The Court of Appeal has indicated that an assault committed in a domestic setting should be sentenced on the same basis as any other assault (i.e. rather than more leniently),[74] but this does not go far enough. Are not abused women almost archetypal 'vulnerable victims', so that attacks upon them should justify enhanced rather than reduced sentencing levels? This seems not to have been advanced as an argument in the sentencing context. The reason is probably the persistence of the view that some degree of fault attaches to the battered spouse, by reason of the prior relationship between the parties, and because of the victim's failure to leave the aggressor after earlier attacks. The battered spouse thereby lacks the moral standing of the 'ideal' vulnerable victim. The issue of contributing victims is considered further below.

Before concluding the dicussion on vulnerable victims, it is appropriate to ask whether there are any categories of victim where crime may properly be regarded as being *less* than normally serious for sentencing purposes? There is one such example. In general, crimes committed against corporate or commercial victims are seen as somewhat less serious than the equivalent crime committed against an individual. This is often sustainable on the harm dimension of desert theory. The commercial victim is generally better able to bear the loss, since the loss is (usually) not suffered by a single individual and is more likely to be insured. Apart from that, we have already noted the differential sentencing tariffs for burglary committed on commercial premises and burglary committed in a person's home, the latter involving such an invasion of private space that it is appropriately seen as a quasi-personal injury crime. Victims of burglary in the home will be more deeply and personally affected, while corporate victims will generally find it easier to pay for repairs and to recover from the offence. The commercial/domestic distinction should not, however, be pushed too far. The distinction becomes blurred in the context of small family businesses. In a number of decisions the Court of Appeal has held[75] that robberies or attempted robberies from small shops and off-licences *are* to be regarded as serious crimes, since these businesses (in contrast with banks and building society branches), are unlikely to be able to pay for expensive security, carry a fair amount of cash, and are often open for long hours. The Court observed that these factors rendered such premises 'especially vulnerable' to attack.

5. Contributing Victims

One of the most pressing claims made by pioneers in the field of victimology was that crime should be understood in the context of any pre-existing relationship

---

[74] See, for example, *Nicholas* (1994) 15 Cr.App.R. (S) 381.
[75] See *AG's Reference (No 9 of 1990)* (1990) 12 Cr.App.R. (S) 7, followed in several subsequent cases including *Attorney General's Reference (Nos 23 & 24 of 1996)* [1997] 1 Cr.App.R. (S) 174.

between the victim and the offender.[76] In a leading text, Stephen Schafer observed that[77] 'the fact that the victim may play the role of the major contributor to a crime has been known to the courts all over the world for a long time. The offender is usually sentenced accordingly'.[78] Since that comment was written, the 'victim movement' has distanced itself from the kind of (admittedly crude) offender-victim typologies which were generated by Schafer and his colleagues. Attention has since moved to a different agenda—that of caring for the needs, and improving the rights, of victims of crime. This change of focus has meant that the occasional suggestion that victims might bear some responsibility for crimes committed against them, or that citizens might be required by law to take better care of themselves or their property, has been greeted with scepticism.[79] It does seem, however, that so-called 'victim precipitation' can raise issues of harm and culpability (as well as a fair amount of confusion), and that desert theory should have something to say about it.

Schafer suggested that there were the following classes of victims:[80]

(i)   victims having no prior relationship with the offender;

(ii) provocative victims, who rouse or incite the offender and where, Schafer suggested, offender culpability is lessened and responsibility should be 'heavily shared';

(iii) precipitative victims, whose 'thoughtless behaviour instigates, tempts or allures the offender to commit a crime', such victims 'bearing some responsibility' for the offence; and

(iv) weak victims, who provide easy prey for the offender but who clearly bear no responsibility for the offence.

One criticism which has been made of such typologies is that they are simplistic, and detract from the valuable detailed studies of offender-victim interaction which have been carried out. The typology creates a drift to a generalized stance of 'victim blaming', where victims come to be seen as largely responsible for their own plight. Such a response is often encountered in relation to victims of violent and sexual offences, but is also encountered elsewhere, such as in white-collar crime.[81] At its worst, victim precipitation arguments seem to lead to the conclusion that victims of crime have no one except themselves to blame, so it is hardly surprising that they have 'attracted only criticism'.[82] Indeed, Schafer seems to assume that if the parties were known to each other before the offence, responsibility *must* be 'shared', at least to some extent: his typology does not even allow

---

[76] The work of H. von Hentig and B. Mendelsohn, conveniently summarized by S. Schafer, 'The Beginnings of Victimology' in B. Galaway and J. Hudson (eds.), *Perspectives on Crime Victims* (1981), p. 15.

[77] S. Schafer, *Victimology: The Victim and His Criminal* (1977).   [78] At p. 70.

[79] See David Miers, 'The Responsibilities and the Rights of Victims of Crime' (1992) 55 *Modern Law Review* 482.

[80] Schafer (1977), n. 77 above, at p. 45. Other proposed categories, of 'self-victimizing victims' and 'political victims', are left out of account here.

[81] M. E. Walsh and D. D. Schram, 'The Victim of White Collar Crime: Accuser or Accused?' in G. Geis and E. Stotland (eds.), *White Collar Crime* (1980).

[82] Zedner (1997), n. 58 above, p. 579.

for a case where offender and victim knew each other and where no fault attaches to that victim for a subsequent crime.

The aspect of Schafer's approach which we need to consider further in this chapter is his claim that there is a certain total amount of 'responsibility' to be allocated for each crime, and that such responsibility may be placed wholly upon the offender, or distributed in varying proportions between the offender and the victim. My contention is that this view is mistaken, and that this mistake has taken the issue of victim precipitation down the wrong track. To begin with, it cannot be doubted that there *are* many cases falling within Schafer's group (ii), in which the ultimate victim of an offence (particularly a violent offence) has, earlier in the exchange which culminated in the crime, conducted himself or herself in a manner which is causally crucial to its commission. The victim may have initiated the confrontation, by waylaying, assaulting, or taunting the offender. In these circumstances the roles of offender and victim can run very close together. Both are substantially at fault in their behaviour and, at the end of the exchange between them it is largely a matter of chance which of the participants turns out to be the victim, and which the offender.[83] Or, if not actually initiating the exchange, the victim may have been perfectly willing to trade insults with the offender, and may have chosen to stand their ground, and meet force with force, rather than taking the chance to flee or retreat. Or the victim may have disengaged initially, perhaps even left the scene, but then returned to pursue the matter. Reported sentencing cases are full of such examples.[84]

The classic example is that of provocation. The paradigm case of provocation in murder[85] involves a degree of fault on the victim's part, such as where the victim assaults, torments, or goads the offender and thereby precipitates their killing. Thus Andrew von Hirsch and Nils Jareborg explain the rationale of provocation in terms of the principle of 'resentment'—the offender has acted in anger at the victim, and has good reason for being angry, by virtue of some wrong or impropriety suffered at the victim's hands.[86] Moving from the standard case is appropriate in provocation cases not because the harm occasioned to the victim is less than it would have been without the provocation (clearly it is not), but because the culpability of the offender is thereby (somewhat) reduced. Legal writers differ over whether this reduction in culpability is best explained in terms of partial excuse, partial justification, or some mixture of the two.[87] The partial excuse approach focuses on the offender's loss of self-control, while the partial justification view invites comparison between what the victim did to the offender and what the offender did to the victim, suggesting that, to some extent, the victim 'asked for it'.

---

[83] Numerous examples can be found in Cretney and Davis (1995), pp. 34–8. See also *Grainger* [1997] 1 Cr.App.R. (S) 369.

[84] See, for example, *Rowbotham* [1997] 1 Cr.App.R. (S) 187.

[85] Homicide Act 1957, s. 3.

[86] Andrew von Hirsch and Nils Jareborg, 'Provocation and Culpability' in F. Schoeman (ed.), *Responsibility, Character and the Emotions* (1987), p. 241 at p. 248.

[87] J. Dressler, 'Provocation: Partial Justification or Partial Excuse?' (1988) 51 *Modern Law Review* 467; Andrew Ashworth, *Principles of Criminal Law*, 2nd edn. (1995), pp. 225–9.

Nobody argues that a crime committed under provocation is fully justified, but could it be partially justified? One problem with this approach is that, to the extent that the victim's behaviour was sufficiently culpable itself to deserve punishment, such as where the victim assaulted the offender first, the defendant lacks the appropriate authority to carry out that punishment.[88] A second point is that, as English law now stands, provocation does not require that the victim has been at fault. The issue of provocation in murder may be left to the jury even where the offender has reacted violently in the face of the victim's perfectly lawful behaviour, such as the persistent crying of the offender's young child in *Doughty*[89] or, in *Dryden*,[90] a planning officer's efforts to enforce the law by demolishing buildings on the offender's land. There will, however, be few murder cases in which a jury would accept the second element of the defence—that a reasonable person (endowed with the 'relevant characteristics' of the accused) would have killed in response to inoffensive conduct.

The victim's conduct before the offence, whether itself culpable or not, which precipitated the offender's violent reaction, can properly reduce (sometimes marginally, sometimes greatly) the offender's culpability for the offence. While there is a strong expectation that citizens normally should be able to retain self-control in the face of provocation, in the face of some kinds of behaviour the defendant's loss of self-control is, to a greater or lesser extent, understandable.[91] Whether one stresses the element of partial excuse or the element of partial justification, the doctrine of provocation really has nothing to do with the respective allocation of fault between two parties (as Schafer's typology suggests). It is concerned with the degree of culpability of the offender alone. To the extent that the victim *is* at fault, their fault is separate from (and additional to) the offender's fault. The victim's conduct prior to the offence is relevant to the offender's liability insofar as it provides an evidential basis to account for the offender's reaction to it.[92]

Apart from homicide cases, provocation by the victim has long been accepted as reducing the seriousness of crimes, and this is clearly recognized by the Magistrates' Association in its sentencing guidelines on assault and public order offences triable summarily.[93] The definition of provocation in section 3 of the Homicide Act 1957 has no direct application to non-murder cases, and provocation tends to become a much looser concept when weighed as a mitigating factor,

---

[88] See von Hirsch and Jareborg (1987), n. 86 above, at p. 242: 'Penalizing malefactors is not a legitimate role for an individual; it is a state function, to be undertaken with appropriate due process safeguards'.

[89] *Doughty* (1986) 83 Cr.App.R. 319. See further Jeremy Horder, 'The Problem of Provocative Children' [1987] *Criminal Law Review* 655.

[90] [1995] 4 All ER 987.

[91] I take this to include cases of 'cumulative provocation', as well as cases of immediate reaction to overwhelming provocation.

[92] It was held in *Acott* [1997] 2 Cr.App.R. 94 that before the issue of provocation can be left to the jury there must be some specific evidence of what had been done or said by the victim to provoke the loss of self-control.

[93] Magistrates' Association (1997), guidelines on affray, assault occasioning actual bodily harm, common assault, violent disorder, and unlawful wounding.

rather than an issue on which direction must be given to a jury.[94] In mitigation, circumstances of provocation tend to shade into other states of mind such as extreme annoyance, frustration, and ill-temperedness. Sometimes it makes little sense to refer to 'provocation' as a separate issue on sentence, rather than to see it as part and parcel of relevant mitigation.[95] There are, for example, numerous sentencing cases involving similar factual situations to that of *Doughty*, referred to above. When sentencing for non-fatal assaults on young children, the courts have drawn a distinction between cases of 'deliberate wickedness' and cases occurring in circumstances of severe personal stress where the parent has been unable to cope with caring for a young child.[96] Provocation, loosely interpreted, figures to some extent in such cases. It is also encountered in many instances of street assault and public disorder, where it may be complicated by the offender's (often drunken) (mis)interpretation of the victim's conduct. The Magistrates' Association's guidelines also admit of the possibility of provocation reducing offence seriousness in cases of criminal damage,[97] which might perhaps apply where one person reacts to another's behaviour by smashing up the latter's belongings. Smith and Hogan assert that 'mere circumstances, however provocative, do not constitute a defence to murder'[98] but there is clearly more flexibility in mitigation for other crimes. However, in assault cases, just as in murder cases, provocation has little to do with the allocation of fault between two parties—the degree of culpability of the offender alone is at issue. In an assault case, where the victim assaulted the offender first, the victim may be subject to legal sanction for their own conduct. Again, the victim's conduct prior to the offence is relevant insofar as it provides an evidential basis to account for what the offender did.

It has been argued that taking account of provocation in sentencing is appropriate not because the harm occasioned to the victim is less than it would have been without the provocation, but because the culpability of the offender may be (somewhat) reduced. In what circumstances might a victim's 'thoughtless behaviour'[99] before the offence, their imprudence or gullibility, be relevant to the offender's culpability? One way of putting the claim here is to say that the careless victim has contributed to the crime through their own 'contributory negligence'. Contributory negligence is a tortious doctrine which (typically) operates in a situation where both defendant and plaintiff have been negligent, such as where the defendant driver has not been keeping a proper look out and the plaintiff pedestrian has stepped into the road without taking care. Its operation requires that compensation paid by the defendant to the plaintiff be reduced by an amount commensurate with the plaintiff's own fault. The contributory negligence analogy is, however, profoundly unhelpful in the sentencing context. In

---

[94] See generally Martin Wasik, 'Excuses at the Sentencing Stage' [1983] *Criminal Law Review* 450.

[95] On 'provocation' and 'irritating conduct' see *Attorney General's Reference (No 45 of 1996)* [1997] 1 Cr.App.R. (S) 429 at 432.

[96] See, for example, *Smith* (1984) 6 Cr.App.R. (S) 174.

[97] Magistrates' Association (1997), n. 93 above, p. 12.

[98] J. C. Smith and B. Hogan, *Criminal Law*, 8th edn. (1996), p. 363.

[99] To use Schafer's phrase: see his category (iii) above.

most crime situations the offender has acted with *mens rea* while the victim, at most, has been negligent, so that the victim's 'contribution' is causally eclipsed by the defendant's wrongful act. This argument, however, may not be enough standing alone. There is authority that contributory negligence can operate to reduce compensation in cases of intentional torts, such as battery.[100] A similar claim might plausibly be made in a criminal case—that the victim's negligence is relevant even where the defendant acted with intent. But there is a stronger reason for rejecting a role for 'contributory negligence' in crime. This is that civil litigation is designed to restore the balance between plaintiff and defendant and is purely a dispute between the parties. Sentencing for a criminal offence, at least on the desert view, is fundamentally different. Here, as we have seen, the role of the victim is relevant only where it affects the harm occasioned to the victim, or is relevant to the offender's culpability. In the great majority of cases the victim's imprudence or gullibility is irrelevant to these concerns.[101]

At one time it was suggested that a rape victim's imprudence in accepting a lift from a stranger, or in wearing revealing clothes which had the effect of tempting the offender, represented a degree of fault on the victim's part which thereby reduced the seriousness of the offence.[102] The offence was seen as being partly the victim's own fault. The courts have now recognized, in the sentencing guideline case of *Billam*,[103] that even where the victim has been naive, unwise, or imprudent in their behaviour, this cannot in itself affect the seriousness of the rape. This is surely correct, since the earlier view confused two distinct meanings of 'responsibility'. The victim's conduct in such cases is clearly causally relevant to the commission of the offence, and so the victim is partly 'responsible' for subsequent events in that sense. But causality should be distinguished from blame. It is wrong to ascribe to the victim blame for the rape, since the victim had no culpability with respect to that outcome—the victim did not want to be raped nor, presumably, did she knowingly run the risk that she would be.[104] The *Billam* guidelines try to forge a distinction between cases where the victim has simply been imprudent and cases where 'the victim has behaved in a manner which was calculated to lead the defendant to believe that she would consent to sexual intercourse'.[105] Depending upon the precise facts, a case of the latter type may reduce the offender's culpability for rape, to some extent. Here the defendant can make the plausible claim that, in the light of the victim's conduct, he believed that she would consent. What matters for liability for rape is, of course, the defendant's belief about consent at the time of the act itself, but a realistic belief held by the

---

[100] See *Murphy* v. *Culhane* [1977] QB 96 and A. H. Hudson, 'Contributory Negligence as a Defence to Battery' (1984) 4 *Legal Studies* 332.

[101] A case involving a highly gullible victim is *Mundle* [1997] 2 Cr.App.R. (S) 160.

[102] See S. Jeffreys and L. Radford, 'Contributory Negligence or Being a Woman? The Car Rapist Case' in P. Scraton and P. Gordon (eds.), *Causes for Concern* (1984), p. 154.

[103] [1986] 1 WLR 349.

[104] See 'Blaming the Victim' in Julie A. Allison and Lawrence S. Wrightsman, *Rape: The Misunderstood Crime* (1993), pp. 103–14.

[105] At p. 351.

defendant during the time leading up to the act, that she would consent, makes the rape somewhat less culpable than if there had never been such a belief. Again, the issue in rape has nothing to do with allocating a total amount of responsibility between offender and victim; the proper question is whether the victim's conduct prior to the offence impinges upon the offender's culpability.

A further controversial area is that of sexual offences committed against children. Judges sometimes draw distinctions in the sentencing of sex offences against children by noting that in some cases the child involved was already sexually experienced, or was a willing participant in the offence or, indeed, encouraged or instigated the commission of the offence.[106] The contrast with our earlier discussion is striking here since, as we have seen, children are generally regarded as vulnerable victims. If a child appears to encourage sexual familiarity in what circumstances, if at all, can this make the offence less serious? Mitra[107] suggests that to take account of the child's instigation is to place part of the blame for the offence on the child. But this is to make the same mistake as Schafer, to assume that there is a certain amount of blame for a crime which has to be allocated. The appropriate question to ask is whether the child's role in the offence affects the seriousness of the offence, and so a proper assessment of harm and culpability has to be made. This is not straightforward. The first issue is to identify the harm committed, which is sexual familiarity with a minor. The minor cannot in law consent to sexual familiarity, so consent is not relevant to liability. What is its relevance for sentencing purposes? For adult victims, there is a considerable difference in harm and in culpability between non-consensual sexual familiarity and consensual but illegal sexual familiarity.[108] But for child victims, the distinction is of much less importance. As far as culpability is concerned, there are some distinctions to be drawn between offenders, but the great majority of cases are aggravated *either* by the fact that the offender has deliberately sought out and violated the child *or* the fact that the offender has abused a position of trust. As we have seen, targeting of vulnerable victims is an important aggravating factor, and the duty on the offender to resist temptation is very strong, or absolute, where he is in a position of trust in relation to the victim. A small minority of cases will fit neither of these categories, such as where the child truly instigates the offence. Especially where associated with other well-known mitigating factors, such as the closeness of the victim's age to the age of consent, the relative youth of the offender, and other factors, the culpability of the offender is thereby somewhat reduced.[109] But a somewhat lower sentence in such a case is explicable in terms of the absence of key aggravating factors and/or the presence of mitigating factors. It does *not* involve an part-apportionment of guilt upon the victim. This last small group of cases apart, the conclusion must be that in cases of child abuse

---

[106] See the current sentencing guidelines for incest, n. 28 above.

[107] Charlotte L. Mitra, 'Judicial Discourse in Father-Daughter Incest Appeal Cases' (1987) 15 *International Journal of the Sociology of Law* 121.

[108] See *Newton* (1982) 4 Cr.App.R. (S) 388.

[109] Examples are *Oakley* (1990) 12 Cr.App.R. (S) 215 and *Polley* [1997] 1 Cr.App.R. (S) 144.

the conduct of the child rarely has relevance to sentence at all, since it will not impinge significantly either upon the degree of harm occasioned to the victim, or upon the culpability of the offender.

Comparable issues arise in relation to property offences.[110] Take the case of a motorist who carelessly leaves his car unlocked when parked on the street. The car door is opened by a thief and property is taken. Until recently, the Magistrates' Association's sentencing guidelines on theft indicated that 'car unlocked' was a factor which made theft from a car less serious, and should thereby reduce the offender's sentence.[111] At first sight this is misleading, to the extent that it perpetuates the view that fault on the part of the victim reduces the offender's fault accordingly. On the analysis given in this chapter, 'car unlocked' should be irrelevant to the seriousness of the theft, since it seems to affect neither the extent of the harm, nor the culpability of the offender. On further reflection, however, there is a way in which the victim's leaving the car unlocked might be regarded as relevant. The question is whether the standard case of 'theft from a vehicle' assumes that the car was locked, so that the offender must have damaged the car to effect entry, such as by smashing a window. If so, 'car unlocked' *is* a matter affecting seriousness, since it is a significant deviation from the standard case of theft from a vehicle. The element of criminal damage which is normally factored in to the standard case is missing here, and so the offence is, relatively, less serious than the norm. The matter is dealt with differently in the 1997 edition of the guidelines, with 'related damage' being listed as an aggravating factor for theft.[112] The 'standard case' of theft from a vehicle thus becomes theft without damage.

6. Individual Victim Susceptibility

How should the sentencer deal with cases where the offender has occasioned much more, or much less, harm to the victim than was foreseen or was foreseeable? In an article which develops principles by which the relative seriousness of different crimes may be assessed, Andrew von Hirsch and Nils Jareborg[113] have focused on this 'harm' dimension of seriousness. The authors posit a 'standard case' of a given species of crime, where the harm is incurred by a victim 'who is neither especially vulnerable nor resilient'.[114] They note, however, that 'how hurtful a given intrusion is depends on the situation of the victim, and the

---

[110] See John Baldwin, 'The Role of the Victim in Certain Property Offences' [1974] *Criminal Law Review* 353.

[111] Magistrates' Association (1993), p. 39.

[112] Magistrates' Association (1997), n. 93 above, p. 28.

[113] Andrew von Hirsch and Nils Jareborg, 'Gauging Criminal Harm: A Living-Standard Analaysis' (1991) 11 *Oxford Journal of Legal Studies* 1.

[114] *Ibid*, p. 4. von Hirsch and Jareborg refer to '*the* standard case of an offence'. This suggests, on the face of it, that there is only *one* standard case victim to be identified *per* offence, but illustrations given later in the article, show that there might be more—perhaps two, three, or four standard cases *per* offence.

particular victim's situation varies greatly',[115] arguing that such variations should be taken into account in mitigation or aggravation of sentence. Despite a dearth of authority in the past, in a number of recent decisions the Court of Appeal has declared it to be an 'elementary principle of sentencing'[116] that the especially damaging and distressing effects of a crime upon the victim,[117] or upon the close surviving family of a deceased victim,[118] should be made known to, and taken into account by, the sentencer.

Since harm is one of the two defining elements of crime seriousness, it seems obvious that information about the harm occasioned to the victim should be before the sentencing judge. It was said in *Hobstaff*[119] that it must be clearly established that this additional harm has actually been caused, and that the information should be couched in proper evidential form. Where this leads to a sharp division between prosecution and defence views of the facts of the offence, a *Newton*[120] hearing is the appropriate forum in which to resolve the difference, with the prosecution being required to establish the existence of any additional harm beyond reasonable doubt. It is clear in principle that the offender should not be sentenced for a crime in respect of which he has not been convicted nor pleaded guilty.[121] There are, however, often complexities in practice, since the prosecution is not bound to charge the most serious offence which could conceivably be made out on the facts. In the majority of cases the harm occasioned to the victim will fall somewhere within a range of broadly what might have been expected, in which case it can safely be left to the judge to take the expected degree of harm into account. This is what is described by von Hirsch and Jareborg as the 'standard case'. It seems right in principle, and sensible in practice, for the sentencer to be able to assume that a case falls within the 'standard case' range without specifically hearing evidence on the matter, although there is some doubt whether this represents the current law.[122]

Suppose, however, harm has been occasioned to the victim which is of a kind normally to be anticipated for that offence, but where much more harm of that kind is occasioned than was foreseeable—the so-called 'thin skull' case. Should the offender simply take his victim as he finds him, should sentence be limited strictly in accordance with the offender's own culpability, or should some middle course be steered, with sentence being enhanced to a certain extent, but not to the same degree that would have been appropriate had the offender intended the full consequences? Although desert theory tells us that harm and culpability are the twin dimensions of seriousness, the theory offers no clear answer to such cases. Andrew Ashworth, for one, has argued consistently that culpability should be the prime determinant of sentence, so that 'sentence should be governed not by the

---

[115] *Ibid*, p. 4.   [116] *Nunn* [1996] 2 Cr.App.R. (S) 126.
[117] See *Doe* (1995) 16 Cr.App.R. (S) 718. The point is also referred to in the rape guidelines in *Billam* [1986] 1 WLR 349.
[118] See *Nunn*, n. 116 above.   [119] (1993) 14 Cr.App.R. (S) 605.
[120] (1982) 4 Cr.App.R. (S) 388.   [121] See cases listed in *Current Sentencing Practice*, L2.
[122] See *O'S* (1993) 14 Cr.App.R. (S) 632.

vagaries of chance but by what the offender believed he was doing or risking'.[123] Andrew von Hirsch has observed that:[124]

Culpability, in turn, affects the assessment of harm. The consequences that should be considered in gauging the harmfulness of an act should be those that can fairly be attributed to the actor's choice. This militates, for example, against including in harm the unforeseeable consequences of the act.

This approach *may* be slightly less subjective than Ashworth's, suggesting that the prime determinant of seriousness ought to be the harm occasioned to the victim, although viewed through the prism of culpability. If this is a correct interpretation of von Hirsch's view, it would involve the offender being held responsible for some results of his offending to which the full subjective requirements of criminal liability would not extend. Other versions of desert theory might, of course, place far more emphasis upon the nature and extent of the harm occasioned and less upon the offender's culpability.[125] Historically, versions of constructive liability have held the offender responsible for a range of unforeseen further harm, consequential only upon proof of an initial offence committed with subjective fault.

Consider again the example of a professional house burglar who, although not targeting the elderly, has on the present occasion burgled the house of an elderly occupant living alone. Property of great sentimental value to the victim, well in excess of its market worth, is taken. The invasion has a serious emotional effect. The victim requires medical treatment for anxiety and, because he or she no longer feels secure in their home, sells up and moves into sheltered accommodation. Now, property loss and distress to the victim are foreseeable, indeed standard, consequences of house burglary, but the impact of the property damage to the particular victim, and the extent of his or her emotional distress, is not foreseen by the offender. Should this additional degree of harm be left out of account in sentencing, or can it 'fairly be attributed to the actor's choice', as von Hirsch puts it? In the view of the present author the harms listed here *can* fairly be attributed to the offender. This is because the harms which were occasioned were harms of a type which were certainly to be expected and lay within a foreseeable range of suffering. It seems that a certain degree of moral toughness is appropriate here, and it ought not to lie in the mouth of the offender to argue that he did not realize that the house might be occupied by an elderly person, or that he did not realize that the victim might be particularly badly affected by the burglary. The offender *should* be held responsible for these extra degrees of harm. Apart from the attribution of such harm to the offender being morally appropriate, there is also the issue of practicality to be borne in mind—it is not possible at the

---

[123] Ashworth *Sentencing and Criminal Justice*, 2nd edn. (1995), p. 108; see also A. Ashworth, 'Taking the Consequences' in S. Shute, J. Gardner, and J. Horder, *Action and Value in the Criminal Law* (1994).

[124] Andrew von Hirsch, *Past or Future Crimes* (1986), pp. 64–5.

[125] See, for example, John Gardner, 'Rationality and the Rule of Law in Offences Against the Person' (1994) 53 *Cambridge Law Journal* 502.

sentencing stage to investigate in minute detail whether each and every aspect of the harm which was occasioned to the particular victim was foreseeable. Again, this is why sentencers should start from the assumption that the harm falls within the normal range, with argument on the matter being heard by the sentencer only where the additional evidence, if accepted, would make a marked difference to the sentence to be imposed. At what point should the offender's responsibility for consequential harm come to an end? Where should the line be drawn? It seems wrong to hold the offender responsible for harm of a kind, or of an extent, which is itself an extraordinary outcome of the crime committed, and which was an outcome well outside the offender's contemplation at the time when he committed it.

The converse situation is a case where the victim has suffered less harm from the offender than might reasonably have been expected. On a view such as Ashworth's, which emphasizes culpability in sentencing, this fortunate outcome for the victim should make little or no difference to the sentence, but on a view which stresses harm it should affect the outcome to an extent. If it turns out that the burglary victim was fully insured, that the stolen items were readily replaced, and that the victim was able to deal with the offence stoically, these factors indicate a sentence somewhat nearer to the lower end of the normal range. No greater reduction is appropriate, however, since the lesser degree of seriousness is not related to the offender's culpability, and hence does not redound to his credit. A comparable issue has arisen in the context of rape, where sentences have been reduced in cases where the victim has been less seriously affected by the offence than might have been expected. One example is the 'Ealing vicarage rape case', where the sentencing judge noted that 'the trauma suffered by the victim [was] not so great'.[126] In a group of recent cases, of which *Hind*[127] is an example, the Court of Appeal has reduced sentence where the rape victim has apparently forgiven the offender. It was said in *Hind* that although forgiveness by the victim is not sufficient reason in itself for reducing an otherwise proper sentence, forgiveness might indicate to the sentencer that the suffering of the victim was less severe than would normally result from such a crime, and a reduction could properly be made. Great care needs to be taken here, since efforts made by the victim after the offence to 'put her life together and minimise the trauma'[128] need not entail that the impact of the offence was any the less for her.[129] However, in principle, if there has been significantly less harm from the offence than might have been expected, that does impinge on one of the dimensions of crime seriousness, and indicates a sentence somewhat nearer to the lower end of the normal range for the offence. No greater reduction in sentence than this is appropriate, however, since the

---

[126] See *The Times*, 2 February 1987. The comment, and the manner of expressing it, caused considerable outrage at the time.

[127] (1993) 15 Cr.App.R. (S) 114. See also *Hutchinson* (1993) 15 Cr.App.R. (S) 124.

[128] Susan Edwards, *Sex and Gender in the Legal Process* (1996), p. 360.

[129] Forgiveness by a child victim of sexual offences was held not to be relevant to sentence in: *Attorney-General's Reference (No 75 of 1995)* [1997] 1 Cr.App.R. (S) 198.

lesser degree of seriousness is not related to the offender's culpability and hence does not redound to his credit.

7. CONCLUSION

The purpose of this article has been to argue that the relevance of the relationship which existed between the offender and the victim at the time of the offence should be given closer attention in sentencing theory and, in particular, by desert theorists. The offender-victim axis continues to be of considerable importance in the way in which offences are defined, structured, and sub-divided. The centrality of the offender-victim relationship is also demonstrated in practice by the existence of recurrent general features of sentencing schemes, such as the 'vulnerable victim' and 'contributing victim' categories. It has been argued in this chapter that both of these categories are flawed as they are currently worked out in practice, and an attempt has been made to apply the harm and culpability components of crime seriousness more rigorously in their analysis. It has been argued that it is not a function of the sentencing courts to draw moral comparisons between the lifestyles of offenders and victims, nor is it their function to apportion blame between offenders and victims.[130] It has been suggested, however, that the offender-victim axis provides a number of challenges for desert theory, and requires its further development and refinement. It is not enough simply to state that the constituent elements of crime seriousness are harm and culpability. It is necessary to go further, to analyse the respective importance of these two elements across a range of sentencing situations. There is still plenty of work to be done in this area, but one of the great strengths of desert theory is that it offers a framework within which such concerns may be refined and addressed.

---

[130] Recognized by the Court of Appeal in *Bacon* [1997] 1 Cr.App.R. (S) 335.

5

Why Bulk Discounts in Multiple Offence Sentencing?

NILS JAREBORG

1. Introduction

The law of most countries provides for mitigation for first offenders, with the result that a repeat offender receives a more severe sentence. The law of most countries also provides for a discount where an offender has committed more than one crime and the court sentences him on one occasion for these. (I will use the term 'bulk discount' for such discounts.) For the recidivist, the second crime costs more than the first one. For the multiple offender, the second crime costs less than the first one.

A rational explanation for this difference could possibly be found in a special-prevention sentencing rationale. If the punishment is to be determined with a view to prevent the individual offender from re-offending, his response to previous punishment is normally relevant for what is 'needed' as punishment. But that is not the case with multiple offending, since there is no apparent connection between the offender's personality and the number of offences charged. It is also possible that the difference could be explained from a general-prevention point of view if it stresses that crime is an expression of disobedience or rebellion. The disregard of the (additional) warning inherent in the previous sentence would then be seen as a particularly important ground for treating recidivists (as a category) differently. But many general-prevention theorists would probably argue that bulk discounts weaken the deterrent force of the law, and consequently that they should not be allowed. I believe that the empirical claim has no foundation, but the matter is complicated and my concern here is quite different: could the difference be explained from the point of view of desert theory?

I will leave recidivists aside, and only speak about multiple offenders in the sense indicated. Desert theorists disagree to some extent on the moral nature of recidivism, and therefore also on the just deserts of recidivists. But the question has at least been extensively discussed. The just deserts of multiple offenders has hardly been discussed at all. One reason for this could be a fear that focusing on proportionality in this context may lead to severer sentences.

The main purpose of this chapter is to examine whether a discount theory can be rationally defended from a proportionalist perspective, i.e., a sentencing perspective that makes the severity of the sentence primarily dependent on the harmfulness of the crime and the culpability of the offender. This area should not, however, be entered without a comment on the shakiness of the distinction between single and multiple criminality.

2. MULTIPLE CRIMINALITY

Concurrence of crimes is arguably the most complicated topic in criminal law—in those countries that care about it at all. Whether the topic is important depends on a number of things. As already indicated, it is more important if sentencing is based on a proportionalist rationale, and less important if it is based on a preventative rationale. It is very important, if the prosecutor has a duty to prosecute all detected, provable criminality, and of little importance, if the prosecutor is allowed to charge specimen crimes. It is much more important in a country that does not know of plea bargaining or guilty pleas than in a country that bases its criminal processes on these two institutions. It is more important in a country where the prosecutor binds the court by providing an account of the defendant's behaviour than where the prosecutor binds the court by charging the defendant with a particular crime. For example, it is much more important in Sweden than in a common law country.

Irrespective of whether they are regarded as important or not, in any modern legal system the following main points should be addressed in a concurrence doctrine.[1]

(a) Rule concurrence

A first question of concurrence concerns concurrence on an abstract level, concurrence between the area of application of different provisions. This is a conceptual concurrence, and the only one that can in practice be solved by legislative means, namely by using so-called subsidiarity clauses.

If the area of application of one provision lies completely within the area of application of another provision (subordination) this is normally intended. It is, for example, obvious that a conviction of petty theft is meant to exclude conviction of (ordinary) theft, and that conviction of aggravated theft or burglary is meant to exclude conviction of (ordinary) theft. If the areas of application overlap (interference) it might be much more difficult to tell whether both provisions or only one provision should be applied. Sometimes it is also difficult to tell whether the areas do overlap. Theft by consuming food in a shop is also causing damage to another's property.

---

[1] In a particular legal system, the number of basic distinctions could be greater. I have dealt with Swedish law in *Straffrättens gärningslära* (Stockholm: Fritzes förlag, 1995), pp. 158–239.

(b) Deed unit

On the level of concurrence between concrete deeds (acts or omissions) one unavoidable question is what criteria to use in deciding what constitutes one deed under a particular provision. In theory, a great number of crimes could be attributed to the offender where we find it 'natural' to say that only one crime has been committed. But acts have no natural boundaries, and, for example, in a series of blows and kicks a provision on assault could be applied several times. Counting crimes always implies normative decisions. The criteria normally used have to do with the number of victims or persons otherwise affected, the unity of the incident in time and space as regards e.g. place, activity, or caused states or processes, or the number of distinct crime objects, including criminal products. The choice of relevant criteria is, of course, mainly guided by pragmatic reasons and tradition, and cannot be expected to be the same in different countries. In addition, the law is largely unknown by those who count crimes, and the police may use criteria that are quite different from those used by the courts. Any statistics on reported crime should be regarded with the utmost suspicion, and comparisons should be recognized as meaningless. A striking example from Swedish law is that the number of instances of the offence of insulting conduct is determined by the number of people that are reached by the insult. So an utterance of a few seconds addressed to millions of TV-viewers will result in millions of crimes.

(c) Co-punished deeds

Even if it is quite clear that the offender has committed more than one crime it may also be quite clear that he is not to be convicted of more than one crime. In German literature, this phenomenon is known under the designation '*mitbe-strafte Vor-, Neben- und Nachhandlungen*', i.e. preceding, concomitant, and subsequent deeds that are co-punished with the most important crime committed.[2] A simple example is that someone who has committed theft should not also be convicted of receiving stolen goods even if his handling of the goods fulfils the prerequisites of the latter crime.

Is it really necessary to make the implied distinction between a 'suppressed' deed[3] being classified as a non-crime (as when one provision is regarded as taking precedence over another) and as a co-punished crime? It is necessary to the extent that the operation of provisions concerning responsibility for complicity, confiscation and similar measures, absence of prescription, and special rules on prosecution could be blocked unless the normally suppressed deed constitutes a crime.

---

[2] See, e.g., Hans-Heinrich Jescheck and Thomas Weigend, *Lehrbuch des Strafrechts: Allgemeines Teil*, 5th edn. (Berlin: Duncker & Humblot, 1996) pp. 735–7.

[3] The term normally used outside common law countries is that a deed is 'consumed' by another deed. This means that the presence of another act or omission makes the deed irrelevant for purposes of conviction and sentencing.

One purpose of this simple overview has been to throw doubt upon unreflected conclusions to the effect that multiple criminality is as such a factor that speaks for a severer sentence. Desert theory must look behind the legal classifications. A moral judgment of the offender's proved criminal conduct may have nothing to do with the number of crimes that he is deemed to have committed, or the number of charges that the prosecutor has found convenient to include in the indictment.[4]

Another purpose has been to give some background to the use of a distinction between different sorts of concurrence of crime where the decisive question is whether the crimes were committed by the 'same' act or belong to a 'single' incident or transaction. I will return to this question in the next section.

3. Principles and Models

The legislative models used in regulating the sentencing of multiple offenders are reflections of three principles: the principles of *cumulation, absorption*, and *asperation*. The words 'cumulation' and 'absorption' need no explanation, but 'asperation' may not even exist as an English word. It is the internationally used term for 'docked' cumulation, i.e. a combination of limited cumulation and limited absorption.

The principles can be made operative on two levels. First, they can concern the *penalty scales*. Cumulation would then mean that the available maximum is the sum of the applicable maxima of all crimes committed. Absorption would mean that the available maximum is identical with the highest individual maximum applicable among the crimes committed. And asperation would mean something in between. Swedish law provides an example. According to the Criminal Code, chapter 26, section 2:

A sentence of imprisonment may be imposed for several offences collectively if such sentence may be imposed for any one of the offences committed.

A sentence of imprisonment may be imposed for a fixed term longer than the severest of the penalties imposable for the offences but shall not exceed the sum total of the maximum terms imposable for the individual offences. And it shall not exceed the severest penalty imposable by more than

1. one year if the severest penalty is shorter than imprisonment for less than four years,
2. two years if the severest penalty imposable is imprisonment for four years or more but less than imprisonment for eight years,
3. four years if the severest penalty imposable is imprisonment for eight years or more.

In sentences imposed by virtue of the second paragraph, a fine shall be considered as corresponding to imprisonment for fourteen days.

A sentence of imprisonment for a term shorter than the longest of the minimum terms may not be imposed.

---

[4] The same conclusion is reached by Andrew Ashworth, *Sentencing and Criminal Justice*, 2nd edn. (London: Butterworths, 1995) p. 204.

Secondly, the principles can concern the *actual sentences* for the crimes committed. Cumulation would then mean what in common law countries are known as consecutive sentences, and absorption would mean what are there known as concurrent sentences. Again, asperation would mean something in between, let us call such sentences 'total sentences' (the German term is '*Gesamtstrafe*').[5]

In all three cases, the sentence is aggregate, i.e. the court has first to determine the sentence for each proved crime. As can be learnt from the first paragraph of the cited section, Swedish law is different. Like Austrian law,[6] for example, it uses the method of 'collective sentences' (the German term is '*Einheitsstrafe*'). The court does not first determine a sentence for each crime but proceeds directly to determining a sentence for the totality of crimes. The principle of asperation is not explicitly recognized as operative on this level; the message is implicit in the prescribed construction of the penalty scales. There is, of course, no guidance given to the courts.

As I mentioned above, in many countries a distinction is made between two types of concurrence. If the crimes are judged to be committed by the same act or omission (in German '*Idealkonkurrenz*') or held to constitute a single incident or transaction, there is a tendency to shape the law according to the principle of absorption, at least on the level of the penalty scales. For other cases (in German '*Realkonkurrenz*') the other two principles dominate, although sometimes a third category, 'continuous criminality' (in German '*fortgesetze Tat*'), is recognized and normally treated according to the principle of absorption.

An example is found in German law. According to the Penal Code, section 52, only one penalty is imposed where the offender has infringed several penal provisions or the same penal provision several times in a single transaction. The penalty scale is constituted by the highest maximum and the highest minimum involved. In other cases, a total sentence has to be imposed (section 53). Section 54 concerns the construction of the total sentence:

(1) Where one of the individual sentences is imprisonment for life, the total sentence is imprisonment for life. In all other cases, the total sentence is constructed by enhancing the severest punishment, and if different types of punishment are involved by enhancing the severest type of punishment. The construction is based on a comprehensive judgment of the offender's person and the individual offences.

(2) The total sentence must be lower than the sum of the individual sentences. Where imprisonment for a fixed term is imposed, it must not be higher than fifteen years. Where fines are imposed, it must not be higher than seven hundred and twenty day-fines.

(3) Where the total sentence is constructed from both imprisonment and fines, one day-fine shall correspond to one day of imprisonment.

---

[5] The term 'total sentence' is used by The Canadian Sentencing Commission in *Sentencing Reform: A Canadian Approach* (Ottawa: Canadian Government Publishing Centre, 1987). See pp. 217–27, where the Commission recommends that the use of consecutive and concurrent sentences for multiple offence sentencing be replaced by the use of the total sentence.

[6] The Austrian Penal Code, s. 33. Multiple criminality is regarded as a special aggravating factor.

A reason for making the distinction between one and more than one transaction is that (as the previous section demonstrates) it is largely a matter of chance, tradition, or ignorance whether some conduct is judged to constitute one crime or more than one crime, and that this is the case primarily where there is some connection (time, place, planning, etc.) between the acts. A reason against making the distinction is that it is in practice very difficult to handle concepts like 'same act', 'continuous criminality', and 'single transaction'. To use them is an invitation to endless argument, and the response from the courts may well be a formalism that draws attention away from the real issues. Such experiences made Sweden abandon the distinction almost 60 years ago, and Finland has recently done the same.

For the rest of this chapter I will simply disregard the existence of cases of *Idealkonkurrenz*. They constitute a special form of discount for bulk offending for which I have little sympathy.[7] My main concern is to examine whether bulk discounts can be rationally defended in a proportionalist context, and for the sake of clarity the discussion will proceed on the basis of obvious cases of *Realkonkurrenz*, such as ten burglaries committed on the 10th of ten different months in ten different cities.

I will also disregard solutions based on the principle of cumulation. They have been a speciality of American jurisdictions, and sometimes astonished newspaper readers in other countries when offenders have been sentenced to hundreds of years of imprisonment to be served consecutively.

Present-day English law and also the law of other common law jurisdictions seem, however, to be guided by the principle of asperation in that the so-called *totality principle* requires a court to 'look at the totality of the criminal behaviour and ask itself what is the appropriate sentence for all the offences'; 'the court must not content itself by doing the arithmetic and passing the sentence which the arithmetic produces' (Lawton LJ).[8] There is also some evidence that judges sometimes initially use the model of a collective sentence, not the model of a total sentence, i.e. they start with the totality principle and the individual sentences are determined afterwards to complete the picture.[9] Disregarding national differences among common law jurisdictions, in general one could say, in Austin Lovegrove's words, that the 'effect of the totality principle is that the effective sentence imposed for a case is normally less, sometimes very much less, than the sum of the sentences appropriate to the individual comprising counts. In this sense the totality principle is properly regarded as limiting, but it is also

---

[7] Ashworth comments ((1995) n. 4 above, p. 205): 'It is very difficult to construct a workable definition of a "single transaction", especially since it seems to be little more than a pragmatic device for limiting overall sentences than a reflection of a sharp category distinction. Indeed, the Court of Appeal has taken advantage of this fuzziness to extend the principle considerably beyond what might be expected.'

[8] In *Barton* (unreported, 1972), cited by D. A. Thomas, *Principles of Sentencing: The Sentencing Policy of the Court of Appeal Criminal Division*, 2nd edn. (London: Heinemann, 1979) pp. 56–7.

[9] The totality principle is discussed by Ashworth (1995), n. 4 above, pp. 209–14. It was originally analysed by Thomas (1979), n. 8 above, pp. 54–9.

determining, since it enjoins the sentencer to impose, within some ill-defined limit, an effective sentence in accordance with overall seriousness'.[10]

4. THE GERMAN SENTENCING PATTERN

As stated above, German law prescribes bulk discounts but gives no genuine guidance to the courts. Thanks to a remarkable sentencing study by Hans-Jörg Albrecht[11] we have, however, some knowledge of how the courts use the law.

Albrecht's empirical research as regards bulk discounts concerns cases of repeated burglaries, rapes, and robberies. The discounts were hardly noticeable where the sum of the punishments was imprisonment for less than one year: the average total punishment was 78 per cent of the sum of the individual punishments. For almost each additional one-year interval the percentages fell: (2) 73 per cent, (3) 69 per cent, (4) 58 per cent, (5) 56 per cent, (6) 47 per cent, (7) 38 per cent, (8) 45 per cent, (9) 31 per cent. Above a sum of 9 years the percentage was oscillating between 30 and 20. The average 'cost' for one burglary was 7.9 months, for three burglaries 15.6 months (97 per cent added for two more crimes), for five burglaries 22.9 months (47 per cent), for seven burglaries 24.6 months (7 per cent) and for nine burglaries 26 months (6 per cent added for two more crimes). A rough norm resulting from the data indicates that the total sentence is found halfway between the punishment for the most serious crime and the sum of the punishments for all crimes. It was also apparent that the upper limit of the scale of penalties used in practice (not the statutory maximum) had a steering effect. This is strikingly similar to English Court of Appeal practice.

The most interesting discovery was that the severity of the separate punishments and the amount of discount were explained by the same factors. Paradoxically, these factors were the harmfulness of the crime and culpability of the offender. Desert theory dominates sentencing when the punishment is determined for a separate crime. When the total sentence is determined, desert theory seems to be turned upside down: the more serious the aggregate criminality is (the more harm and culpability there is), the greater is the bulk discount.

Can this reality, which I believe is the reality also of other countries, be integrated into a proportionality scheme?

German criminal law theory knows of five different (attempted) explanations of the phenomenon of bulk discounts. One is that the total sentence in fact is a collective sentence, and that the individual sentences are added as window-dressing. Another is that the individual sentences and the total sentence are based on

---

[10] I have profited from an unpublished article by Austin Lovegrove, 'Towards Consistency of Approach in Sentencing the Multiple Offender'.

[11] Hans-Jörg Albrecht, *Strafzumessung bei schwerer Kriminalität: Eine vergleichende theoretische und empirische Studie zur Herstellung und Darstellung des Strafmasses* (Berlin: Duncker & Humblot, 1994). For the research concerning multiple offenders, see pp. 387–98.

different relevant factors. Both explanations have been proved empirically false by Albrecht's research, and they have also been heavily criticized from a theoretical point of view.[12] A third explanation is that repeated offending lessens the amount of culpability: since the offender gets used to offending, it is easier for him to commit new crimes. Joachim Bohnert dismisses this explanation, arguing that it would make the law inconsistent and that it would create insoluble procedural difficulties.[13] In any case, it seems to depend on the curious idea that an offender has a certain amount of culpability at his disposal and that culpability can be consumed.

The official German explanation is that *the intensity of punishment increases with increased length of incarceration*. This is the explanation advanced in the *travaux préparatoires*, repeatedly invoked by the Supreme Court, and normally propounded in textbooks and handbooks. Fairness accordingly dictates that in prison the clock should go faster when the second sentence is served, still faster when the third sentence is served, and so on.

A first objection to this rationale of increased intensity is, of course, that it is empirically unsound. It is not a fact that in general a number of punishments are experienced as more severe when they are served immediately after each other than when they are served with a period spent outside prison in between. Different people react differently, and the phenomenon of prison acclimatization is well known. A second objection is that an offender's exceptional sensitivity is an ordinary ground for sentence mitigation, so discounts that can be rationally defended have already been made. Bohnert also points to other inconsistencies with the surrounding law, and he concludes, in my view correctly, that the official explanation is just a sham.[14]

A further objection is that it is a mystery why the increased intensity should be felt only when the first individual punishment has been served. If there is any truth in the theory, the increased intensity will start to be felt also by a single offender, and at the end of a sentence for a single offence the prison clock should go considerably faster than in the beginning. This would make current sentencing to imprisonment utterly enigmatic. The correct procedure would be to proclaim punishment in punishment units that would then be translated into time to be spent in prison after consulting a handbook that states the values that follow from the standard increased-intensity curve.

According to Bohnert, bulk discounts have nothing to do with harm or culpability, or anything else concerning the offence or the offender. They have nothing to do with substantive criminal law. Total sentences are in fact meant to be unproportional. They cannot be normatively explained but they are still humanly 'correct'. Bulk discounts are the natural results of *the inclination of human beings to view things perspectively*. The formal elements of a perspective are of four kinds: spatial, temporal, quantitative, or qualitative. Our reaction to

---

[12] See Joachim Bohnert, 'Warum Gesamtstrafenbildung?', *Zeitschrift für die gesamte Strafrechtswissenschaft* 105 (1993), pp. 846–70, at pp. 853–8. Bohnert's article contains complete references to the German literature.

[13] Bohnert (1993), n. 12 above, pp. 851–3.   [14] Bohnert (1993), n. 12 above, pp. 847–51.

a crime committed in another part of the world or long ago is weaker than our reaction to a crime committed in our neighbourhood or recently. Bohnert thinks that such factors should affect the sentence for each individual offence, so the bulk discounts depend only on the two other elements. If someone steals a hundred times, the quantity does not mean anything to the victims, for them all offences retain their full disvalue, but the judge loses interest after considering some instances: at some point quantity breeds the quality of indifference. Similarly, a great difference in offence seriousness makes the less serious offence 'shrink' in the eyes of the judge. An elephant is visible and a mouse is visible but if they are placed beside each other the mouse is almost invisible.[15]

Bohnert thinks that the best way to proceed is to make the operation of the indicated human inclinations more foreseeable by introducing a few simple formulae. I will not go into details, but only give a few examples of their effects. If five offences are each worth one year of imprisonment (a sum of 5 years) then the total sentence will be 3.64 years. If five offences are worth 1, 2, 3, 4, and 5 years respectively (a sum of 15 years) then the total sentence will be 9.85 years. If five offences are worth 1, 5, 5, 5, and 10 years respectively (a sum of 26 years) then the total sentence will be 16.6 years.[16]

Bohnert's theory may fit the facts of German sentencing practice at least in general outline (although some of the resulting sentences are too severe) but that does not mean that it is of any help. A theory that is avowedly non-normative is useless when we want to explain why there should be bulk discounts. And it implies that total sentences are explicitly unproportional—a conclusion that desert theory cannot accept.

5. Bulk Discounts and Proportionality

Empirically, we meet the same general sentencing pattern in, e.g., Germany and Sweden as in England and other common law jurisdictions. Each added offence contributes less and less to the aggregate or total or collective sentence. At some point the curve flattens out so that an additional offence makes no difference at all. Normally, this occurs well below the maximum provided for the most serious of the offences. Thomas says that Court of Appeal practice reveals that 'the aggregate sentence should not be longer than the upper limit of the normal bracket of sentences for the category of cases in which the most serious offence committed by the offender would be placed'.[17] This may be a formula that cannot be used in all cases, but it indicates what sort of reality we have to explain.

Thomas's explanation is essentially a reference to the sentencing rationale of rehabilitation: the aggregate sentence should not be 'crushing', given the offender's prospects for reform. This is of no interest for our purposes.

---

[15] Bohnert (1993), n. 12 above, pp. 859–66.   [16] Bohnert (1993), n. 12 above, pp. 867–70.
[17] Thomas (1979), n. 8 above, p. 59.

Ashworth states 'that overall proportionality should be preserved. This means that, no matter how many offences of a particular kind an offender is found to have committed, the sentence should remain in the range appropriate to that type of offence'.[18] He explains that this involves a choice between two possible applications of the proportionality doctrine. Strict proportionality resulting in cumulative sentences is one thing, and overall proportionality is another thing. 'Since there are arguments on either side, it is fitting that the principle of restraint in the use of custody should decide between them.'[19] On the whole, I think Ashworth is right. The remainder of the article is little more than an attempt to strengthen his position.

No one has done more than Andrew von Hirsch to demonstrate that it is essential for desert theory to distinguish between ordinal and cardinal proportionality.[20] Ordinal proportionality concerns relative seriousness of crimes among themselves. Cardinal proportionality has to do with relating the ordinal ranking of crimes to a scale of punishments; it requires that the punishment should not be out of proportion to the seriousness of the crime involved. We have to begin with some questions of cardinal proportionality.

I think that anyone legislating on multiple sentencing must proceed from two premises. Somewhat flippantly I will refer to them as the *'life is short argument'* and the *'wet noodle punishment argument'*, the latter phrase being inspired by oral presentations by Andrew von Hirsch. The wet noodle punishment argument is that it is in practice impossible to punish, e.g., a committed rape with beating the offender with a wet noodle. In theory, crime could be met by censure in a ritual form, but in real life some hard treatment is necessary, and this treatment must be such that it convincingly reflects the seriousness of the crime. Different jurisdictions rely on different levels of repression, but even the least repressive ones provide for fairly severe sentences for very serious crimes. A criminal code that punishes armed robbery and aggravated rape with a fine would hardly gain any respect in contemporary societies.

The implication of the life is short argument is that the law must prescribe an absolute punishment maximum. Many jurisdictions do have an absolute punishment maximum as regards imprisonment for a fixed time, and I think that a minimum of moral decency requires that a ceiling is created for State intervention in human lives. Although the principle of parsimony[21] is of relevance for all levels of punishment, it is of special importance in this connection.

Some may think that the very worst criminals deserve incarceration for the rest of their lives, but I fail to see that this changes the principle. The ceiling is

---

[18] Ashworth (1995), n. 4 above, p. 214.   [19] *Ibid*, p. 215.

[20] Andrew von Hirsch, *Past or Future Crimes: Deservedness and Dangerousness in the Sentencing of Criminals* (Manchester: Manchester UP, 1986), Chs. 4–7; Andrew von Hirsch, *Censure and Sanctions* (Oxford: OUP, 1993), pp. 17–19, 36–8.

[21] See von Hirsch (1993), n. 20 above, Ch. 5, and Ashworth (1995), n. 4 above, pp. 80–1. Ashworth treats the principle of restraint in the use of custody as a separate principle (pp. 77–8), but it could also be regarded as a sub-principle of the principle of parsimony.

certainly raised, but life is still short. In any case, I do not believe that the public would accept such a raised ceiling for other than very serious criminality, so I choose to disregard this possibility.

I conclude that the legislator has to move within a range of punishments, that the punishment for a single serious offence must be substantial, and that the available range is unable cumulatively to accomodate more than a limited number of additional counts of similar seriousness. If an offender has committed ten rapes, each of them worth 5 years' imprisonment, and the absolute maximum is 15 years, the offender 'hits the ceiling' after the third rape, if a principle of strict proportionality is applied.[22]

Given this, a legislator has two options. One could use strict proportionality for multiple offences with the result that it would be easy to reach the ceiling, or one could, so to say, let the presence of the ceiling be felt immediately after the first (most serious) offence. The second option—bulk discounts—should be preferred for two reasons. One is that it better satisfies the principle of parsimony. The other is that it better satisfies requirements of ordinal proportionality. In the circumstances, it gives more scope for ordinal ranking of combinations of offences.

The existence of bulk discounts entails an increasing 'stiffness' of the penalty scale for multiple offences. It gets harder and harder to reach the next level. And by the way, what is the next level? I think it is a common experience that the longer sentences of imprisonment are, the larger are the steps used by the court. In Sweden, for example, at the lower end the courts use weeks as imprisonment units, but from 8 years they rarely use smaller steps than one year.[23] This implies a sort of 'quantum theory' for sentencing: it is increasingly harder to reach the next level in use. And for multiple sentencing it implies that additional criminality of minor or even intermediate seriousness becomes increasingly irrelevant for the effective sentence.

The conclusion is, I think, that bulk discounts are unproblematic from the point of view of cardinal proportionality. So, if there are any problems they have to do with ordinal proportionality.

First of all, it must be remembered that ordinal proportionality is primarily a rank ordering; it is not necessary to express it in any sort of units or punishment values. Secondly, even if ordinal proportionality is expressed in quantitative terms, the possibilities for making rational use of such models are quite limited. Assessing the seriousness of crime is like assessing art or wine in that beyond a certain point there are no common criteria available for an evaluation. It may be possible to find common criteria for all victimizing crime,[24] but hardly for all

---

[22] For example, in Swedish law the penalty scale for aggravated rape or aggravated robbery is 4–10 years, whereas the penalty scale for multiple offences is 4–14 years.

[23] For a discussion of English sentencing practice, see Ashworth (1995), n. 4 above, pp. 98–100.

[24] A first attempt is made in Andrew von Hirsch and Nils Jareborg, 'Gauging Criminal Harm: A Living-Standard Analysis', (1991) 11 *Oxford Journal of Legal Studies* 1–38. See also von Hirsch (1993), n. 20 above, pp. 29–33 and Ashworth (1995), n. 4 above, pp. 93–8.

types of crime.[25] Assessing seriousness of crime is, of course, much facilitated by the underlying value structure of the criminal law system. This system contains a number of fixed points. But the rationality exhibited is to some extent purely pragmatic: for example, the worst of one sort (murder) is ranked together with the worst of a totally different sort (high treason).

If ordinal proportionality is regarded as merely rank ordering, bulk discounts as such are not problematic. The difficulty is to explain why the curve flattens out well below the available maximum, why additional crime does not make a difference above a certain level. I do not think there is a good explanation from the point of view of ordinal proportionality. I fail to see that the assertion that the sentence should remain in the range appropriate to the actual type of offence is a proportionality argument[26] unless we (against better knowledge) introduce a proportionality principle regarding not the offence, but the offender. Surely, ordinal proportionality requires *some* increase for each additional offence.[27] It should, however, be remembered that the principle of proportionality is but a principle, and I do think that at this stage it is properly overridden by the principle of parsimony (even if 'the moral message' of the criminal law is some-what blurred).

Not all will be satisfied with this explanation. Admittedly, a bulk discount will in many cases depend less on principles of proportionality and deserved blame than on the principle of parsimony and purely pragmatic considerations. Some will maybe say: 'What sort of proportionality is this? It is utterly unfair that one person should pay much less for a certain crime than someone else just because he has committed other crimes'. Criminal law is guided by several principles of equality but I do not think there should be a principle of equality of such a narrow scope as this objection presupposes. There is no market for crime, crime is not a commodity that can be bought with punishment. Punishment is in some respects comparable to a currency but it is not at the disposal of the offender.[28] What an offence is 'worth', what is a proportionate response to a committed crime, depends on the design of the criminal law system and this is more complex than most people tend to think. There are always a number of circumstances that can make a difference.

---

[25] I do think that it is possible to develop rational general criteria for grading crime seriousness. But with the expression 'common criteria' I refer to criteria developed out of a particular value or interest perspective to form a yardstick for grading crime seriousness. The impossibility of develop-ing such criteria depends on the impossibility of reducing individual interests, group interests, collec-tive interests, and State interests into one interest category (except in a totalitarian State).

[26] An exception would be where a (long) series of minor offences are compared with serious offences.

[27] See the discussion by Paul H. Robinson, 'A Sentencing System for the 21st Century' (1987) 66 *Texas Law Review* 1–61, at pp. 45–7.

[28] It is, of course, true that some minor offences, e.g. road traffic offences, are treated as if they car-ried price tags. But in some countries they are not regarded as criminal offences at all, but as adminis-trative offences, and how they are handled should for all that not be imitated in the sentencing of more serious criminality.

6

Dangerousness and Citizenship

R. A. DUFF*

1. INTRODUCTION

My focus in this chapter is on *persistent*, *serious*, *violent* offenders, who are fully responsible for their crimes (I assume, but will not argue now, that this class is not empty). 'Persistent' offenders are not merely repeat offenders who break the law more than once (or who repeat the same kind of offence): they are those whose repeated crimes cannot, given the character and contexts of their commission, be seen merely as a succession of discrete aberrations in otherwise law-abiding lives; they rather display a *pattern* of offending, which persists despite regular convictions and punishments. 'Serious', 'violent' offenders are those who commit crimes of serious violence against the person: most obviously murder and other life-threatening attacks, rape, and other serious sexual assaults. At least some such offenders are, we think, wholly responsible for their crimes: we are not tempted to see them as the victims of pathological impulses, or of unfortunate circumstances, which drive them to crime.

Such offenders are likely to be called 'dangerous'. The 'danger' which they pose consists not just in the fact that they persistently cause, or risk causing, serious (physical) harm to others: that much is also true, for instance, of persistently reckless or drunken drivers or of firms which persistently operate unsafe procedures. Those who standardly figure in public debate as 'dangerous' offenders are, rather, those who persistently *attack* others.[1]

The danger posed by such offenders, the failure of normal penal measures to dissuade or reform them, has led some to suggest that we should try to incapacitate them from continuing their violent criminal careers: more precisely, that they should be subject to extended terms of imprisonment, to incapacitate them from committing further crimes against anyone other than fellow prisoners or prison officers—since no other incapacitative measures, which were not intolerably cruel, would be effective. Imprisonment can, of course, generally be seen either as serving a partly incapacitative purpose, or as having welcome incapacitative side-effects: but the suggestion which interests me here is that persistent,

* Grateful thanks are due to colleagues at Stirling, and especially to Sandra Marshall, for helpful comments and criticisms.
[1] See my *Criminal Attempts* (1996), pp. 363–6.

serious, violent offenders should be subject to what I will call 'special selective detention' (SSD). SSD is 'special' in that it involves longer periods of imprisonment than those to which the offenders would normally be liable for their most recent offences; it is 'selective' in that it is focused selectively on offenders, or groups of offenders, who are thought to be particularly likely to commit further serious crimes if released at the end of a normal prison term.

The reasons for focusing on persistent offenders, rather than on those who have committed just one (or no) serious crime will become clear later. The reason for focusing on serious, violent offenders, rather than on other kinds of persistent offender, is that the arguments for SSD seem strongest in this context. Other, minor offenders might often have been captured by provisions for extended preventive sentences;[2] others, especially persistently drunken drivers or firms who operate unsafe procedures, might cause more consequential, physical harm than offenders typically classified as 'dangerous'.[3] There is, however, more room to argue that other kinds of measure might be more effective in dealing with these kinds of offender; or that—in the case of relatively minor offenders—their crimes are a price we should be willing to pay to maintain a moderately just and minimally humane penal system. Furthermore, if the case for SSD cannot be made out for persistent serious offenders it certainly cannot be made out for other offenders; while if it can be made out for such offenders, we can ask how far (if at all) beyond that category it could extend.

The apparent urgency of the question of whether SSD can be justified, and of demands for such provisions, will depend upon (amongst other factors) the prevailing frequency and length of normal prison sentences. The question will seem more urgent, those demands will be louder, when penal policy moves towards making less use of imprisonment: towards non-custodial sentences for more offenders and shorter prison terms for most of those who are imprisoned.[4] The issue would become yet more urgent if von Hirsch's 'decremental strategy' was to be seriously followed: if imprisonment was reserved for serious violent offences, and serious white-collar offences; and if the longest normally available prison sentence became 3 years, or 5 years for homicide.[5] There are ample reasons (of justice, efficiency, and humanity) to urge such radical reduction in our use of imprisonment. But any serious movement in this direction would predictably provoke greater concerns about persistent, dangerous offenders, more of whom

---

[2] See A. J. Ashworth, *Sentencing and Criminal Justice* (1992), pp. 141–2; D. Katkin, 'Habitual Offender Laws: A Reconsideration' (1971) 21 *Buffalo LR* 99, 106.

[3] See A. E. Bottoms, 'Reflections on the Renaissance of Dangerousness' (1977) 16 *Howard Journal* 70; J. E. Floud and W. Young, *Dangerousness and Criminal Justice* (1981), pp. 6–7, 10–15.

[4] Hence the policy of 'bifurcation' (see Bottoms (1977), n. 3 above; M. Cavadino and J. Dignan, *The Penal System* (1997), pp. 23, 26): punishments are reduced for 'ordinary' offenders, but made harsher, on partially incapacitative grounds, for 'dangerous' offenders. See also the special provisions for violent and sexual offenders in the Criminal Justice Act 1991, s. 2(2)(b): on which see A. von Hirsch and A. J. Ashworth, 'Protective Sentencing under Section 2(2)b' [1996] *Criminal LR* 175; and N. Padfield, 'Bailing and Sentencing the Dangerous', in N. Walker (ed.), *Dangerous People* (1996), p. 70.

[5] A. von Hirsch, *Censure and Sanctions* (1993), p. 43; *Doing Justice: The Choice of Punishments* (1976), Ch. 16.

would be more quickly released; and louder demands for some species of SSD to deal with such offenders. Could such demands be justified?

2. SELECTIVE INCAPACITATION: FOR AND AGAINST

There are familiar arguments for and against SSD which need only be briefly rehearsed here. In their purest forms, they seem irreconcilably opposed: one set of arguments sees no objection of principle to SSD; the other portrays SSD as in principle wholly unjustifiable, because inconsistent with the basic principles of punishment.

The most familiar argument for SSD comes from what can be called an aggregative consequentialist perspective: consequentialist, since it justifies SSD in terms of its benefits as a cost-effective method of reducing crime; aggregative, because its focus is not on individual offenders, but on groups of offenders, and on the overall number of offences we can hope to prevent by subjecting suitably identified groups to SSD. Such proponents of SSD hope to find suitable sets of 'indicators', which would identify categories of high-rate offenders: by subjecting offenders falling within those categories to SSD (and reducing the levels of punishment for other offenders) we could prevent a much greater number of crimes, more cost-effectively, than do our present sentencing practices.[6]

There are of course plenty of practical difficulties in actually constructing a system of SSD—including the problem of defining the kinds of offender who could usefully be subjected to such a measure, and of finding indicators which will identify such offenders without intolerably inefficient inaccuracy. Such problems might (at present, or for the foreseeable future) be insoluble: perhaps we cannot hope, given present predictive techniques, to construct any cost-effective system of SSD. On this view, however, there is no objection of basic principle to a system of SSD: it would be justifiable if it could be expected to be a cost-effective way of reducing crime.

To call those who favour SSD on such grounds 'consequentialists' is not to imply that they must be *pure* consequentialists, who think that *only* the consequences matter; we will see that they may accept side-constraints of justice on our pursuit of the consequentialist aim of preventing crime, such as the constraint that only convicted offenders should be liable to SSD. Nor is to imply that they must be *utilitarian* consequentialists, who measure the benefits and costs of actions in terms of one final good (such as happiness), defined in non-moral terms: a consequentialist can recognize justice, rights, or autonomy as intrinsic moral values. On a non-consequentialist reading, those values forbid or require certain actions, regardless of further consequences: we must not act unjustly, or

[6] See P. Greenwood and A. Abrahamse, *Selective Incapacitation* (1982); J. Q. Wilson, *Thinking about Crime* (1983), Ch. VIII; M. H. Moore, S. Estrich, D. McGillis, W. Spelman, *Dangerous Offenders: The Elusive Target of Justice* (1984); also M. M. Feeley and J. Simon, 'The New Penology' (1992) 30 *Criminology* 449.

violate rights. By contrast, on a consequentialist reading such values are goods to be maximized: we should act in ways which will in the long run maximize the extent to which justice is done and injustices avoided, or rights respected or autonomy preserved.[7] Such consequentialists could accept that SSD does serious injustice to some of those subjected to it, or violates their rights, or infringes their autonomy. But, they can argue, crime does serious injustice to its victims, violates rights, and infringes autonomy. A system of SSD which cost-effectively reduced crime would prevent more injustice, rights-violations, and autonomy-infringements than it caused: it would thus be justified as serving the values of justice, rights, and autonomy. One question will be whether we should interpret such values in this consequentialist way.

Another question, however, concerns the relation between such an aggregative consequentialist justification of SSD and the demand for something like SSD which ordinary citizens may make. That demand is typically provoked by a particular case. A serious offender who has been released from prison commits another similar violent crime; or he is simply released: people might protest that he should have been kept in prison for much longer, or even for life, to protect others from him. Such protests may be ill-informed. But even theorists who reject aggregative consequentialism might have sympathy for the concerns which motivate them: for the feelings of those victimized, or directly affected, by the released offender's new serious crime; for the anxieties of those who fear for their own, or their loved ones', safety. Such sympathy is not merely of the kind that we feel for any crime victim or for anyone who is (reasonably) fearful of being victimized. It is for the protest that the criminal justice system has, by releasing this offender, exposed others to the serious danger (or the actual harm) of being victimized by him.

Aggregative consequentialists might claim to be offering a rational foundation for such protests. I will argue, however, that they can be better understood as expressing a different moral perspective—one which focuses not on aggregated categories of offender, but on individual offenders and their actual or potential victims; on what we owe them as individual citizens. I will also argue that this perspective can generate a distinctive rationale for a limited practice of SSD: a rationale which lays upon those who oppose any practice of SSD the onus of explaining to citizens who are victimized, or endangered, why they should accept that serious harm or risk.

The familiar consequentialist argument in favour of SSD meets an equally familiar retributivist response: that there are basic objections of principle to such a practice. Such a response may come from pure retributivists who see retribution as the *aim* of punishment; or from impure retributivists, who accept that punishment must be justified in crucial part by its consequential benefits, but hold that it must also be justified as being deserved for a past offence.[8]

---

[7] See e.g. J. Braithwaite and P. Pettit, *Not Just Deserts* (1990).

[8] See e.g. von Hirsch (1993), n. 5 above, pp. 12–14; on the distinction between the two forms of retributivism see D. Dolinko, 'Some Thoughts about Retributivism' (1991) 101 *Ethics* 537, 539–43.

One common objection is that, given the imprecision of our existing or plausibly achievable predictive techniques, any practice of SSD would inevitably detain an intolerably high proportion of 'false positives': people judged to be 'dangerous' who would not have committed more crimes of the relevant kind had they not been subject to SSD.[9] Retributivists who seek to justify any human system of punishment must of course accept that any such system will sometimes in fact mistakenly convict and punish an innocent person: but this does not commit them to accepting, as analogously justified, the rate of 'false positives' which SSD would involve. The proportion of 'false positives' would be much larger than the proportion of mistaken convictions: the most that seems currently achievable is a rate of two false positives for every true positive (two people wrongly identified as 'dangerous' for every one who is accurately identified); and even optimistic advocates of SSD do not aspire to a 'false positive' rate much lower than 50 per cent.[10] The fact that those subjected to SSD are anyway guilty of serious offences might justify tolerating a higher rate of errors than we accept for mistaken convictions: but, critics argue, we cannot justify a system as grossly inaccurate as this.

However, just as the stronger arguments against consequentialist theories of punishment focus on their treatment of the guilty rather than of the innocent, the stronger argument against consequentialist justifications of SSD focuses on their treatment not of false positives, but of true positives, who would indeed commit further serious crimes if released. The former arguments are stronger because effective even against a side-constrained consequentialism which forbids the deliberate punishment of an innocent; and the latter is stronger because it would show that even a more accurate system of SSD would be in principle unacceptable.

The argument flows from a retributivist conception of punishment as deserved for past crimes: but different versions of retributivism offer different accounts of why, and how, crime deserves or requires punishment. I will focus on the version that von Hirsch and I partly share, which justifies punishment as the communication of deserved censure for past wrongdoing.[11]

If punishment is to communicate the censure an offender deserves for his past crime; and given that the seriousness of the censure is communicated by the severity of the punishment: the level of punishment must be proportionate to the seriousness of his crime. The idea of *cardinal* proportionality, of punishments that are absolutely (not just relatively) appropriate to particular offences, might not

---

[9] See e.g. A. von Hirsch, *Past or Future Crimes* (1986), Ch. IX; M. Tonry, 'Selective Incapacitation: The Debate over its Ethics', in von Hirsch and A. J. Ashworth (eds.), *Principled Sentencing* (1992), p. 165, at pp. 171–4; N. Lacey, 'Dangerousness and Criminal Justice' (1983) 36 *Current Legal Problems*, 31, 38–42.

[10] See N. Walker, 'Unscientific, Unwise, Unprofitable, or Unjust' (1982) 22 *British Journal of Criminology* 276. For the argument that this is inevitable if we are trying to predict the commission of serious and thus relatively infrequent crimes, see Bottoms (1977), n. 3 above, p. 80; von Hirsch (1986), n. 9 above, p. 113.

[11] See von Hirsch (1993), n. 5 above, Ch. 2; and my 'Penal Communications' (1996) 20 *Crime and Justice* 1, 41–57.

have a clear sense or application. But punishments must at least be *ordinally* proportionate: any difference in the severity of the sentences received by two offenders must be justified by, as proportionate to, a difference in their criminal culpability. Disproportionately severe punishments are unjust, and so unjustified: for they communicate harsher censure than is justified.[12]

If SSD is to be reserved for persistent serious offenders, those subject to it will admittedly be already liable to relatively severe punishments for their current offence; and on von Hirsch's view, they could not expect the kind of reduction in the otherwise deserved punishment which a first-time or non-persistent offender could properly receive. But a record of persistent previous crime could not, for von Hirsch, normally justify any *increase* in the sentence beyond what is deserved for the latest offence: proportionality should be preserved between the seriousness of that offence and the severity of the punishment. The offender's prior record could only (and very occasionally) justify an increase in sentence if some aspect of it revealed an aggravating factor in the *current* offence which was not otherwise apparent—for instance a pattern of racial motivation.[13] But, first, proponents of SSD do not favour basing the predictions of future crimes, on which the imposition of SSD is to depend, purely on prior record:[14] of two offenders guilty of similar crimes, with similar records, one might be eligible for SSD, because judged 'dangerous', whilst the other is not. Secondly, for von Hirsch no feature of the offender's past criminal record, however serious, could justify a large enough increase in present punishment to meet the demands of effective incapacitation. Thus a practicable system of SSD would involve imposing radically disproportionate, and therefore unjust, sentences.

Furthermore, since SSD is imposed for the sake of future, crime-preventive benefits, it treats the offender merely (insofar as it is disproportionately harsh) as a means to others' good. His additional term of imprisonment cannot be justified (as it must be justified if he is to be respected as an autonomous agent) as an appropriate response to what he has done; it is (inappropriately) justified in terms of the benefits it will bring to others.

It is true that if SSD would efficiently reduce crime, a refusal to impose SSD sentences is also a refusal to do what would prevent a number of crimes, which inflict serious injustices on their victims. But even if a consequentialist calculus of justice would show that a system of SSD could on balance prevent more injustice than it caused (although it is not clear how such a calculus could be carried out), that would not justify such a system, since we should not understand the values of justice, rights, or autonomy in purely consequentialist terms.[15] What they demand is not (merely) that we should aim to *maximize* the extent to which they

---

[12] See von Hirsch 'Selective Incapacitation: Some Doubts' in von Hirsch and Ashworth (1992), n. 9 above, p. 158. On ordinal and cardinal proportionality see von Hirsch (1993), n. 5 above, pp. 18–19, Ch. 5.

[13] See von Hirsch (1986), n. 9 above, Ch. 7; M. Wasik and von Hirsch, 'Previous Convictions in Sentencing' [1994] *Criminal LR* 409.

[14] See e.g. Greenwood and Abrahamse (1982), n. 6 above.   [15] See at n. 7 above.

are (consequentially) actualized, but that we respect the *constraints* they set on our treatment of others: we must not commit injustice against others, or violate their rights or their autonomy, even if by doing so we would prevent greater future injustices, rights-violations, or autonomy-infringements. It is, thus, misleading to talk of the need to 'balance' offenders' rights not to be subjected to SSD, against potential victims' rights not to be victimized.[16] Such 'balancing' might be necessary, in a situation in which any available course of action would directly violate someone's rights. But, although SSD would directly violate the rights of those detained, a refusal to introduce SSD does not directly violate the rights of future victims—their rights are directly violated by their attackers; and respect for rights as non-consequentialist constraints requires us to refrain from rights-violations, even if this would be an effective way of preventing rights-violations by others.

We thus seem to face a familiar, but stark, conflict between the consequentialist demand for efficient crime-prevention, and the retributivist demand that punishment should be imposed *for*, and should therefore be determined in its severity by, the offence of which the offender has been convicted. Is this conflict irresoluble; or can we somehow reconcile SSD with the demands of retributive justice?

3. CRIMINAL AND CIVIL PREVENTION

SSD, as I have defined it, would consist in special incapacitative sentences, imposed on convicted offenders. There are, of course, other kinds of preventive detention which might be imposed on people who have not been convicted of any offence; and the actual length of time convicted and sentenced offenders spend in prison can depend on predictive judgements about their 'dangerousness', without any formal system of SSD.

First, there are non-criminal procedures by which those who have not been charged with an offence can be detained for harm-preventive reasons: the seriously mentally disordered can be detained in psychiatric institutions; carriers of dangerous diseases can be subjected to compulsory quarantine. Such detention is justified as being necessary to prevent the serious harms which those detained might cause to others if left free;[17] their release depends upon being judged to be no longer 'dangerous' in the relevant way. Decisions made within the criminal process can also depend on whether someone is judged to be dangerous: police or prosecutorial decisions about whether, or on what charge, to prosecute; and most notably judicial decisions about whether to grant bail.[18] Bail can be refused if there is substantial reason to believe that this defendant will fail to appear for

---

[16] See e.g. A. E. Bottoms and R. Brownsword, 'Dangerousness and Rights' in J. Hinton (ed.), *Dangerousness: Problems of Assessment and Prediction* (1983), p. 9.

[17] Or, in the case of the seriously mentally disordered, to prevent the harm they would otherwise do to themselves.

[18] N. Morris and M. Miller, 'Predictions of Dangerousness' (1985) 6 *Crime and Justice* 1, 2–4.

trial, or will commit offences whilst on bail, or interfere with the course of just-ice.[19] Admittedly, detention on remand should be much shorter than the terms of SSD would be: but people who have been convicted of no offence are still detained in order to prevent harms or wrongs which it is thought they might otherwise do.

Secondly, systems that allow for early release on parole typically make such release dependent on a judgment about whether the offender is 'dangerous': i.e. how likely he is to reoffend if released.[20] The actual length of time a prisoner serves, and so the actual severity of his punishment, thus depends on such predict-ive judgments; of two offenders who committed similar offences with similar prior records, one might be released on parole, whilst the other is refused parole and thus serves what might be a much longer sentence.

Such provisions pose a question to consequentialist advocates of SSD; and a challenge to those who oppose SSD on grounds of justice.

Consequentialists will regard such provisions as justifiable, in principle, if they can be expected to produce a net balance of good. The question they face is: why should SSD be reserved for *offenders*; why not advocate a broader system of pre-ventive detention for *anyone* reliably judged to be 'dangerous', whether they have been convicted of a crime or not?[21] One consequentialist answer might be that past criminal conduct is the only reliable predictive indicator of future crim-inal conduct.[22] Another answer might be that our pursuit of the consequentialist goal of preventing harm must be constrained by demands of justice: for instance, the demand that responsible citizens should (normally) be subjected to State coercion only when they have voluntarily broken the law.[23]

The challenge to a non-consequentialist opponent of SSD comes in two stages. In the first stage the objections to SSD are interpreted as objections to it as a *puni-tive* measure: it is unjustified because it is unjust as punishment. But the critic can-not now, it is argued, object to a system of *civil* preventive detention quite distinct from punishment;[24] and she should also argue for the abolition of parole.

I cannot discuss parole here, save to suggest that a parole system does not indeed differ significantly from a system of SSD in its substantive moral charac-ter (it selectively subjects those judged to be likely to reoffend to longer periods of imprisonment, on preventive grounds); and that retributivist critics of SSD

[19] Bail Act 1976, s. 4(1), Sch. 1, Part I, para. 2. See A. J. Ashworth, *The Criminal Process* (1994), Ch. 7; Padfield (1996), n. 4 above.

[20] See Cavadino and Dignan (1997), n. 4 above, pp. 181–97; R. Hood and S. Shute, 'Parole Cri-teria, Parole Decisions and the Prison Population' [1996] *Criminal LR* 77. For the last Government's proposals to abolish parole, see Home Office, *Protecting the Public* (1996), para. 9; Hood and Shute, 'Protecting the Public: Automatic Life Sentences, Parole, and High Risk Offenders' [1996] *Criminal LR* 788.

[21] See F. D. Schoeman, 'On Incapacitating the Dangerous' (1979) 16 *American PQ* 27; D. Wood, 'Dangerous Offenders and the Morality of Protective Sentencing' [1988] *Criminal LR* 424.

[22] See N. Walker, 'Protecting People', in Hinton (1983), n. 16 above, p. 30; and Morris and Miller (1985), n. 18 above, pp. 14–15.

[23] See famously H. L. A. Hart, *Punishment and Responsibility* (1968). 'Normally' marks the need to explain how compulsory quarantine could then be justified.

[24] See Wood (1988), n. 21 above.

should therefore also object to parole as being inconsistent with the requirements of proportionality (for of two offenders whose criminal culpability is the same one might serve a significantly longer prison term than the other, for preventive reasons).

Retributivists can, however, reject a system of civil preventive detention, by making explicit the moral foundations of the retributivist demand that punishment must be *for* a past crime: that the fact and severity of punishment must be determined by the offender's past offence. For if we ask why we should maintain a system of *punishment* as thus defined, rather than a more cost-effective, consequentialist system of crime prevention, the answer is that this is needed if the state is to respect its citizens' autonomy as responsible agents who are rationally capable of determining, and who ought therefore to be left free to determine, their own actions. Such respect is consistent with a system of law which claims to impose obligations on citizens, so long as the law is justified *to* those it claims to obligate;[25] it is consistent with a system of punishment, if punishment functions as an appropriate response to a past crime. But it is inconsistent with a system of purely preventive detention which detains those deemed to be dangerous: for such a system does not leave citizens free to decide for themselves whether to obey the law.

This response, however, opens the way to the second stage of the challenge to those who oppose SSD on grounds of justice. If a proper respect for autonomy precludes SSD, it must also forbid the kinds of non-punitive detention and restriction noted above: pre-trial detention when bail is refused; quarantine for the carrier of a dangerous disease; and preventive detention for the mentally disordered.

I cannot deal with the issue of pre-trial detention now, save to note that it presents a genuine problem for anyone, retributivist or not, who takes seriously the non-consequentialist demands of justice and respect for autonomy, since it involves detaining those who have not been convicted of any offence on the basis of a prediction about what they might do if left free.[26]

By contrast, the preventive detention of the mentally disordered can be consistent with the demands of justice and autonomy—given a suitably restrictive definition of the kinds of disorder which could justify it. We can define mental disorder as a condition involving a serious impairment of the agent's capacities for rational thought or action, and thus of their capacity for rational self-determination. The mentally disordered are less than normally autonomous; in severe cases, they are not autonomous agents at all. The requirement that a state respect its citizens' autonomy, whilst it requires respect for such autonomy as disordered agents do retain, and efforts to restore them to full autonomy, does not preclude their detention, to prevent serious harms which they would otherwise be likely to cause (because of their disorder) to themselves or others.[27]

---

[25] See my *Trials and Punishments* (1986), Ch. 3.

[26] See my (1986), n. 25 above, pp. 139–40; Ashworth (1994), n. 19 above, Ch. 7; Cavadino and Dignan (1997), n. 4 above, pp. 77–84.

[27] See my (1986), n. 25 above, pp. 174–5. Contrast Bottoms and Brownsword (1983), n. 16 above, p. 17, arguing that such detention (justifiably) infringes their rights.

What then of quarantine?[28] Consider first the less dramatic case of one who is likely to harm others, by infecting them, only if she engages in a particular activity, such as working with food. She may be forbidden to engage in that activity, just as an epileptic can be forbidden to drive. Such prohibitions admittedly constrain those who are subject to them. But, first, they can be seen as applications of the general moral demand that we should not knowingly subject others to unreasonable risks of harm: a requirement which admittedly, given their unfortunate condition, bears more hardly on these people. Secondly, such prohibitions address those subject to them as responsible agents who must decide for themselves whether to obey them. So while such prohibitions do aim to constrain freedom of action (to persuade those affected to constrain their own actions), they do not infringe autonomy.

We can understand the more dramatic example of quarantine in the same way. Quarantine is appropriate for someone who would, given the seriously contagious or infectious nature of the disease he carries, seriously endanger others not just by engaging in particular activities, but by going out into the world at all. If the danger to which he would expose others is serious enough, he may be prohibited from going out in the world, be required to stay in a designated place of quarantine, for as long as he would thus endanger others. Again, one can see this as a particularized (and, unluckily for him, more onerous) application of a general moral requirement not to expose others to unreasonable risks of serious harm. This requirement respects his autonomy, as does any justified legal requirement. If he attempts to breach it, by refusing to go to or by trying to leave the designated place, it may be legitimate to keep him there by force—just as one can legitimately use force to prevent someone from carrying out the criminal action on which she has embarked.

Floud and Young are thus on the right track, when they distinguish detention which protects others against wilful harm, from detention which protects them against unintentional harm.[29] Someone who knows that she carries a seriously infectious disease does endanger others wilfully if she nevertheless goes out into the world, since whether she endangers others depends on her own choice to go into the world. But if she goes out in the world, she cannot then help but endanger others; the danger she then causes will not be under her control. By contrast, the 'dangerous' offender who might be subject to SSD would not inevitably—*whatever* further choices he makes—endanger others merely by going into the world; whether he harms, or endangers, them will depend on his further choices—on whether or not he chooses to commit further crimes. In forbidding the dangerously infected person to go into the world, or preventing her from doing so, we forbid her to engage or prevent her from engaging in an intrinsically dangerous activity; and

[28] See Schoeman (1979), n. 21 above: Floud and Young (1981), n. 3 above, pp. 40–5; Walker (1983), n. 22 above, pp. 26–7; Wood (1988), n. 21 above, pp. 429–31; A. E. Bottoms and R. Brownsword, 'The Dangerousness Debate after the Floud Report' (1982) 22 *British Journal of Criminology* 229, 235–9; von Hirsch (1986), n. 9 above, pp. 55, 60; and my (1986), n. 25 above, pp. 175–6.

[29] Floud and Young (1981), n. 3 above, pp. 40–5; see Wood (1988), n. 21 above, pp. 429–31; Schoeman (1979), n. 21 above, pp. 33–4.

her choice to go out into the world would be a choice to endanger others. In detaining a 'dangerous' offender, however, we prevent him from engaging in an activity which is not *intrinsically* dangerous, because of further choices we predict he will make. That is why SSD infringes autonomy, whilst quarantine need not.

Someone who opposes SSD as being unjust, and inconsistent with a proper respect for autonomy, can thus deal with at least most of the other kinds of case in which people might be detained on the grounds that they are 'dangerous' to others. In particular, she can reject a general practice of civil detention for the 'dangerous'; and she can distinguish, as being consistent with a proper respect for autonomy, quarantine and the protective detention of the mentally disordered.

But can we really be satisfied with this principled rejection of SSD? More precisely, even if it provides an adequate response to the aggregative consequentialist justification of SSD, by showing how it fails to respect the moral status of individual citizens, including serious offenders, is it an adequate response to the more particular concerns for individual victims, or potential victims, which I noted above?[30] Can we honestly say to the victim of a persistent, serious offender who was released after a normal prison term, that while her victimization is indeed a terrible wrong, which demands our sympathy and indignation, it is the price that we (and particularly and sadly she) must pay for a criminal justice system which respects the moral standing of every citizen? If we feel uneasy, as I do, about saying this, we may wonder whether some type of SSD could not be reconciled with the demands of justice.

4. CRIMINAL DANGEROUSNESS

I want to discuss two connected arguments which aim to show that a (strictly limited) system of SSD need do no injustice to those who are detained. Basic to both arguments is an account of what makes a person criminally dangerous, i.e. dangerous in a way that could justify SSD. That is the topic of this section; and in section 5 I will offer a rationale for subjecting those thus identified as criminally dangerous to SSD.[31]

The first argument is a version of one of Floud and Young's central arguments for SSD.[32] Any liberal society which takes seriously the values of autonomy and freedom must tolerate a significant level of crime—whose costs will be most directly borne by its victims. It will forswear certain methods of efficient crime prevention, such as the preventive detention of those who have not yet committed a crime, because they would infringe the autonomy of those subject to them.

---

[30] See p. 144 above.

[31] By 'criminally dangerous', I mean 'dangerous because likely culpably to commit serious crimes', as distinct from other species of dangerousness, including that of infectious disease-carriers, and of those whose severe mental disorder might lead them to commit (but not culpably) serious crimes.

[32] See Floud and Young (1981), n. 3 above, especially Ch. 4; also Morris and Miller (1985), n. 18 above, pp. 21–4.

Rather than imposing on non-criminal citizens the costs of effective crime prevention, we expect all citizens to bear the costs (in increased crime) of a less effective but autonomy-respecting penal system. We can thus talk of a 'right to be presumed harmless'—'to be presumed free of harmful intentions'.[33] Even if we are confident that a citizen will form and try to actualize a serious criminal intention, respect for his autonomy forbids us to coerce him to prevent him carrying that intention out, unless and until he begins to put it into action.

However, the right to be presumed harmless is not unconditional; the presumption of harmlessness is not irrebuttable. If someone persists in committing serious crimes, the presumption can be rebutted: not merely because we now have empirically sound evidence that he is not 'harmless' (that he might well commit further such crimes); but because he has, by his own criminal conduct, undermined his right to that presumption. Given a suitably reliable prediction that he would probably commit further such crimes, if released after a normal term of imprisonment, we can therefore justifiably redistribute the costs of crime, or its prevention, onto him: we can impose on him the cost of being detained beyond the term of imprisonment he would otherwise serve for his current offence, rather than leaving other citizens to bear the costs of his probable future crimes.

This first argument can be buttressed by another, which seeks to show that the difference between 'true' and 'false' positives is not as important as critics of SSD have thought; and that someone who is appropriately judged to be 'dangerous' is not detained *purely* on the basis of a possibly mistaken *prediction* of what he might do.

If we take the judgement that a person is 'dangerous' to consist, essentially, in the prediction that he will commit serious crimes if released, the problem of 'false positives' seems to be serious: even if our predictions could achieve 50 per cent accuracy, we would detain many who were not actually dangerous (of whom that prediction was false). However, that is not how we should understand dangerousness. A judgement of 'dangerousness' 'is a statement of a present condition, not the prediction of a particular result'.[34] An unexploded bomb is dangerous even if it does not explode; to call it dangerous is not just to offer the possibly mistaken prediction that it will explode.[35] So too, a person could be in the relevant sense 'dangerous', even if he will not actually commit a serious crime in the future. Thus, first, 'false positives' can still be dangerous, though they would not actually have committed further offences. Secondly, to detain a dangerous offender is not merely to detain him because of what he might do; it is to detain because of his *present* condition.

Now Morris misrepresents his bomb analogy, by talking as if what might make the prediction that this bomb will explode false, without undermining the

   [33] Floud and Young (1981), n. 3 above, p. 44.

   [34] N. Morris, 'Incapacitation within Limits', in von Hirsch and Ashworth (1992), n. 9 above, p. 139; see Morris and Miller (1985), n. 18 above, pp. 18–20; Floud and Young (1981), n. 3 above, pp. 47–9, 55–8.

   [35] Morris (1992), n. 34 above, pp. 139–40; see von Hirsch (1986), n. 9 above, pp. 175–6.

judgement that it is dangerous, is just the fact that it is defused, or otherwise rendered safe. That mode of prediction-falsification does not indeed undermine a judgement of dangerousness. Similarly, if what falsifies the prediction that this offender will reoffend is the fact that he is detained, that would not falsify the judgement that he is dangerous. But this is irrelevant: a 'false positive' is someone who would not have reoffended even had he not been detained. To show, by analogy with unexploded bombs, that the 'false positive' could still be dangerous, Morris needs to show that we can count as dangerous a bomb which would not have exploded, even had it not been defused.

But he can of course do this: for to say that an unexploded bomb is dangerous is not to say that it will inevitably explode unless it is defused. Dangerousness is a dispositional property which involves being in some present condition, or having existing characteristics, which *would* produce the relevant effect *if* certain (roughly) specifiable circumstances obtained. To say that a bomb is dangerous is to say that it would explode if certain circumstances (which are likely to obtain) came to obtain: for example, if it was exposed to certain weather conditions, or was kicked or dropped. Such circumstances, of course, might never obtain (might not have obtained had the bomb not been defused). So it could be true that this bomb never explodes, or would never have exploded even if it had not been defused, but still also true that it is dangerous.

Analogously, to say that a person is criminally dangerous is to say that he has characteristics which are such that he *would* commit serious crimes *if* certain (quite likely) circumstances, having to do primarily with the situations he is likely to find himself in if not detained, obtained. So someone could be criminally dangerous even if (though he is not subjected to SSD) he never in fact commits serious crimes—if the reason why he does not do so is that the appropriate circumstances never in fact come to obtain.[36]

We must, however, distinguish two kinds of judgement of 'danger': the judgement that 'A is dangerous, because likely to do X', from the judgement that 'there is a danger that A will do X'. Suppose we find what looks like an unexploded bomb. We can reasonably say that there is a danger that it will explode: given what we now know about this object, and about the dispositional properties of objects resembling it in the respects we can identify, there is a high probability that it will explode in certain likely circumstances. Suppose now that an expert finds that it is not a bomb, but a clever fake; or that it is a bomb, but is in such a condition that it could not explode. We can still say that *there was a danger* that it would explode—because it could well have been an explodable bomb. Our judgement that there was a danger was not just reasonable, given the limitations on our knowledge, but true: for 'there is a danger . . .' is true, roughly, if a person

[36] See Floud and Young (1981), n. 3 above, pp. 24–5. How likely must it be that those circumstances will obtain? That depends on how serious the crime would be if they obtained: but they must be circumstances which frequently obtain in ordinary life; their ordinary frequency must be such that it would be a matter of luck if they never obtained (for to say that A is 'dangerous' is to say in part that it will be lucky if he does not cause harm).

applying normal powers of reasoning to such facts as would be recognized by normal people would make such a judgement. But we cannot now say that the object is, or was, *dangerous*: for we have found that it was not in a condition, it did not have any properties, such that it 'would have exploded if . . .'.

This distinction between two kinds of judgements of danger has an important bearing on the issue of what kinds of fact can justify the judgement that a person is criminally dangerous, and in particular on the issue of how far 'actuarial' predictions can be appropriate.[37] A prediction is actuarial if it is based on the person's membership of a group identified by a set of characteristics which are contingently correlated with the relevant outcome. Thus the fact that a person is male, young, unemployed, not in a stable domestic relationship, and a user of illegal drugs, justifies an actuarial prediction that he will commit crimes of a certain kind if there is a high empirical correlation between membership of the group identified by those characteristics and the commission of such crimes. We can then say that *there is a danger* that this person will commit such crimes, and also quantify that danger: if N per cent of that group commit such crimes, there is a N per cent risk that this person will. His membership of the group is indeed not merely evidence from which we can infer that judgement of danger: it *entails* that judgement. However, this is not to say that this person is *dangerous*; only that there is a danger that he is dangerous.

Why is this? The answer is partly conceptual: that dangerousness requires a closer connection between those characteristics in virtue of which a person counts as 'dangerous', and the commission of those crimes which actualize that danger, than obtains between the characteristics which define this group and the commission of such crimes. The latter connection is *indirect*. Being young, male, unemployed, and a drug-user does not lead *directly* to the commission of such crimes. Rather, those characteristics are contingently connected to dispositions or attitudes that typically lead those who have them to commit such crimes in the kinds of circumstance in which they are likely to find themselves; it is those dispositions and attitudes, not merely membership of a group most of whose members have such dispositions, that make a person criminally dangerous. However, the answer is also partly moral: if we are to identify someone as criminally dangerous, as grounds for subjecting him to incapacitative detention, we *ought* not to define his dangerousness merely in terms of his membership of an actuarially identified group. To justify this claim, I should first indicate how criminal dangerousness ought to be defined.

Criminal dangerousness is constituted by the possession of character traits (dispositions, attitudes, patterns of motivation) which will manifest themselves in serious criminal conduct in the kinds of situation in which their possessor is likely to find himself. Thus a man is criminally dangerous as a potential rapist[38] if he has sexual desires which could (only) be fulfilled by forcing sexual intercourse

---

[37] See Morris (1992), n. 34 above, pp. 140–1.

[38] Of women; see the Criminal Justice and Public Order Act 1994, s. 141 for the extension of the English law of rape to include rape of males.

on women without their consent, and has attitudes towards women which would encourage, or not inhibit, seeking to fulfil such desires. On this account, the connection between the character traits which make a person criminally dangerous, and the criminal conduct which would manifest those character traits, is logical, not contingent. To have those character traits *is* to be disposed to behave in those criminal ways in situations of the appropriate kind; to say that the criminal conduct manifests those character traits is to say that that conduct constitutes the public actualization of those traits.

Indeed, we should go further, to hold that someone is criminally dangerous only if he *has* displayed those character traits, in criminal conduct of the appropriate kind. If he has not done so, because he has not yet found himself in a situation in which those character traits would be manifested in action, we might be sure that he *would* do so if such a situation arose. However, what we are now sure of is not that he *has* a definitively criminal character trait, which will be manifested in the appropriate situation, but that he *will develop* such a character trait in the appropriate situation.[39]

To say that someone is in this sense criminally dangerous is not to say that he will certainly commit further serious crimes, if not prevented by incapacitative measures. For, first, he might (luckily) never again find himself in a situation in which his character trait will be actualized in criminal conduct; and secondly, it is conceivable that he will undergo some reformative change of heart before he again finds himself in such a situation. It is rather to say that he will commit such crimes, *if* he finds himself in the relevant kind of situation (as is likely) *unless* he undergoes such a change of heart.

We can now see the moral ground for defining criminal dangerousness in this way, rather than actuarially. Respect for autonomy, and the 'presumption of harmlessness' which follows from it,[40] forbid us to ascribe criminal dangerousness to anyone, unless and until by his own criminal conduct he constitutes himself as having such a character. Until then, even if we have good empirical grounds for predicting that he will come to manifest such a criminal character, we owe it to him to presume that he will not: to presume that he will, when it comes to the point, refrain from crime even if tempted to commit it.

Two preliminary conclusions follow from this argument. First, a criminal record involving persistent commission of serious crimes of the relevant type is the only possible legitimate ground for a judgment of 'criminal dangerousness' that could justify SSD. For only if SSD is justified by the offender's dangerousness as thus defined can we hope to meet the objection that SSD coerces a person not for what he has done, but for what he will or might do—by arguing that the offender is subject to SSD because of what he has made himself.

Secondly, Morris is wrong to rely on actuarial predictions, as the basis for judgments of dangerousness.[41] Actuarial judgments might be predictively more

[39] See my (1996), n. 1 above, pp. 183–90.   [40] See at n. 33 above.
[41] See Morris (1992), n. 34 above, p. 141; Morris and Miller (1985), n. 18 above, pp. 12–18, 33–4.

accurate, as judgments that *there is a danger* that this person will commit serious crimes: but they cannot justify the judgment that he is *dangerous*, or the ascription of a 'present condition' of dangerousness.

Morris might reply that, whilst the offender's criminal record is an essential basis for a judgement of dangerousness, for the sake of accuracy it must be supported by actuarial evidence; and though such evidence does not make it true that the offender is dangerous (his membership of the relevant group does not *constitute* dangerousness) it is good evidence of dangerousness. But we must ask whether such actuarial evidence should be relevant at all to judgements of criminal dangerousness which are to justify SSD; and a comparison of such judgements with ordinary legal verdicts of guilt or innocence suggests that it should not be.

Suppose that a defendant belongs to an actuarially defined group whose members are very much more likely than others to commit crimes of the kind of which he is accused. Of course, even if the probability that members of this group would commit such crimes was greater than 50 per cent, this would not even make it more likely than not that *this* member committed *this* crime. But should such evidence be relevant in his trial, as adding *some* weight to whatever other evidence there is of his guilt? The answer must surely be 'No'. The fact that a defendant is a young, male, unemployed drug user might justify an actuarial prediction that he will commit a violent crime, but it should not be allowed to add *any* probative weight to the charge that he committed this particular violent crime: not because it would add *insufficient* weight, but because it is the wrong *kind* of evidence. To respect the defendant as a responsible citizen, we must treat and judge him as an autonomous agent, who determines his own actions in the light of his own values or commitments. His membership of this actuarial group is part of the context of that self-determination; and as observers, we might think it very likely that he will have determined himself as a criminal. As judges of his guilt, however, we must rely only on evidence related to him as an individual agent, not on evidence related to him only as a member of an actuarial group.

The same should be true if the issue is not whether he committed a particular crime, but whether he has, by his own criminal conduct, defined himself as criminally dangerous. For the question is what he has made of himself; and it must be answered by attending to what he has done, not to his membership of an actuarially defined group.

The question now is: if we define criminal dangerousness in this way, and insist that it be proved solely by reference to this defendant's current offence and prior criminal record, could a system of SSD be consistent with justice and respect for autonomy?

5. A JUSTIFICATION OF SELECTIVE INCAPACITATION?

A defendant is convicted for an offence of serious personal violence. His prior record reveals, not just three or four crimes of the same kind (crimes which, at least if separated by long intervals, and committed under different and unusual circumstances, might be seen as discrete aberrations that he himself genuinely disowns): but a pattern of such crimes, with which he has persisted despite the punishments he received for his earlier crimes. Could it be consistent with the demands of justice, and a due respect for the offender as a responsible agent, to impose on him an incapacitative sentence far longer than would otherwise be justified by his current crime—and far longer than retributivist critics of SSD would allow in the light of his prior record?[42]

It will be useful to compare SSD with various kinds of (quasi-)punitive disqualification,[43] and various kinds of exclusionary punishment, which people might suffer, within and outwith the criminal justice system.

There is a range of activities which citizens can legally engage in only if they obtain a licence, or which they can be forbidden to engage in, or be disqualified from engaging in. Disqualification can be permanent or temporary; and if temporary, restoral of the licence might require a test. These activities include ordinary activities, like driving or keeping a pet; and more specialized activities, like doctoring, lawyering, or running a company: such activities typically involve particular risks to others' safety or interests greater than those normally involved in activities which are not subject to such provisions. People can be disqualified, or excluded, from such activities if they are judged incompetent and thus likely to conduct themselves in ways that would (unreasonably) endanger others; or if they have a condition, such as an illness, such that they would endanger others.

Whilst such disqualifications can be onerous (for example, for a driver who loses her licence; or for a doctor forbidden to practice on medical grounds), they need reflect no culpability in the person disqualified. We can see them either (in the case of ordinary activities) as applications of the general requirement that we should not expose others to unreasonable risks;[44] or (in the case of more specialized activities) as reflecting the view that a citizen's right to engage in such specialized and risky activities is conditional upon her ability to engage in them safely. Quarantine is an extreme form of temporary disqualification: a dangerously infectious person is temporarily disqualified from engaging in ordinary life at all.

However, such disqualifications can also result from reckless or wilful malpractice, when they take on a partly punitive character. A reckless or drunken driver may be disqualified; a malpractising doctor may be struck off. They are forbidden to engage in that activity in which they engaged improperly; and those prohibitions can be seen both as punishments which they deserve for their malpractice, and as measures which protect others (at least for a time) from them. Their disqualification or exclusion may be temporary: but in cases of serious and persistent malpractice, it could be permanent.

---

[42] See at n. 13 above.

[43] On which see especially A. von Hirsch and M. Wasik, 'Civil Disqualifications Attending Conviction' (1997) 56 *Cambridge LJ* 599.

[44] See p. 150 above.

Consider too how a university might deal with members—staff or students—who flout its rules, particularly rules which express the ends and values that define a university as an academic institution. Single serious breaches of those rules may be penalized by temporary suspension or exclusion: but persistent serious breaches may be penalized by permanent exclusion—dismissal or expulsion.

Such disqualifications and expulsions (whether temporary or permanent) can be understood and justified in punitive terms; and while they can be seen as serving a protective purpose (to protect others, or an institution or practice, from harms or wrongs that this person might do), their justification need not depend on a morally dubious prediction. If they are punishments, they must of course be proportionate to the character and seriousness of this person's wrong-doing: but we could justify even permanent exclusions (I will use this term to cover both disqualifications and expulsions) in these terms.

A temporary exclusion communicates an appropriate message to the wrong-doer: that in her wilful misconduct she flouted those values on which the activity she was engaged in depends—for its existence or for its safe practice. She has put in question her 'fitness' to participate in the activity: a 'fitness' that involves not just certain skills or competences, but certain attitudes or commitments. She has undermined the mutual trust on which the activity depends: the trust that patients must be able to have in their doctors, that road users must be able to have in other drivers or that academics must be able to have in each other. Her exclusion aims to bring home to her these implications of her misconduct, but it also offers her a prospect of readmission. It is temporary because she is, we think, owed another chance: a chance to recognize the error of her previous conduct, and to so reform her future conduct that she can once again participate in the activity.

One question is whether there are any single wrong-doings in such activities as these which are so serious that permanent exclusion is justified or even required. But the relevant question now is whether a persistent pattern of serious malpractice could justify permanent exclusion. It surely could. An academic who persistently plagiarizes others' work; a doctor who persistently betrays his patients' trust; or a driver who persists in drunken or reckless driving: such people show themselves to be, have constituted themselves as, unfit to take part in the practice; they may, and should, be permanently excluded. They *may* be permanently excluded (this would not be unjust), because they have in effect excluded themselves by such persistently serious refusals to respect those values on which the practice depends. They *should* be permanently excluded because their continued participation would endanger others, or the practice itself. That judgement of danger is of course predictive: it depends on the likely character and effects of their future conduct. But that 'future conduct' will consist in the continuation of that pattern of conduct which they have already displayed, of the dispositions it manifests. We might owe it to them to respond to them in the light of the standing possibility (which partly defines them as autonomous agents) that they could yet reform themselves. But that can be true only up to a certain point, after which we cannot be expected to give them yet another chance.

This is not to say that such exclusions must be *irreversible*. To say that they should be permanent is to say that they should be *presumptively* permanent: but it might in some contexts be possible, and morally appropriate, to leave open the possibility for the wrong-doer to regain admission by offering convincing evidence of her reform.

By comparing these partial kinds of exclusion with a practice of SSD, we can both outline an argument in favour of SSD that reflects, not the crime preventive aims of an aggregative consequentialism, but a more particular concern for actual and potential victims;[45] and see what kind of moral principle we must be able to accept if we are to reject such a system.

We can see normal sentences of imprisonment as analogous to temporary exclusions from activities or institutions. The message which imprisonment aims to communicate to the offender is that his offence flouted a value (expressed in the law that he broke) of vital importance to the community. By flouting such a value he denied the bonds of community (the normative bonds which are essential to the community), and thus cast his own membership of that community into doubt. Imprisonment, as exclusion from the normal community, gives concrete form to that implication of his crime: it marks a recognition (which we hope he will come to share) that his crime made it impossible for us to continue to live with him as fellow-members of a community. In most cases that exclusion is not and should not be permanent: we owe it to the criminal, as one who is still a fellow-citizen and to whom civic respect and concern are still owed, to allow him back into community after a fixed term of imprisonment. The question is, however, whether such readmission is *always* owed.

One question is whether there are any single crimes which are so serious, so destructive of community, that there might or should be no way back: that a, if not the only, morally legitimate response is *permanent* exclusion, by imprisonment which is really for life (if we rule out capital punishment). But that is not our present question—although it raises similar issues about what we owe to a wrong-doer, and whether it could ever be morally permissible, or inevitable, to see him as having put himself beyond the possibility of restoration to normal community.

The more relevant question is whether we can ever properly judge that a criminal has so persistently, inexcusably flouted significant social values that we can or should exclude him from full community: not just for whatever limited term can be justified in the usual way as an appropriate punishment for his present crime, but permanently.

The moral grounds for such exclusion can be spelled out in a way analogous to the grounds for exclusion from an activity or an institution. The offender's persistent pattern of serious (and previously punished) criminality can only be interpreted as manifesting a continuing attitude of utter contempt for, and rejection of, the values which are essential to our community. He has thus, by his own

---

[45] See p. 144 above.

wrongful actions, rendered himself unfit for continued community; he has
destroyed the claims he had to the restoration of community; and we can (and
perhaps for the sake of others should) exclude him from it. We do owe it to any
citizen to give them another chance even if they have done a serious wrong: to
restore them to normal community, even if we think it probable that they will do
serious wrongs again. But there comes a point when they lose such a claim: having persistently spurned community with us by their crimes, they can no longer
claim (and we no longer owe) the restoration of community.

In response to this, it might be said that we can never properly treat anyone as
being beyond redemption: however serious and persistent his crimes, we should
still treat him as someone who could come to repent those crimes and reform
himself.[46] But just what does this require of us? It requires us not simply to destroy
him, physically or psychologically; we must offer him the chance to redeem himself, through a repentant moral understanding of his past crimes; we must offer
him the chance of being restored to community by demonstrating such a genuinely redemptive repentance (thus his detention should be presumptively, not
irreversibly, permanent). With most criminals, a due respect for them, as
autonomous fellow-citizens who could repent their wrongs and reform themselves, requires us to subject them only to limited, and we hope restorative, punishments, despite the danger that they will reoffend. Other citizens must, as
potential victims, accept that risk: they should trust the now punished offender
(or at least behave as if they trusted him) as they should trust any other citizen.
Hence the 'presumption of harmlessness',[47] which could also be expressed as a
presumption of trustworthiness. But that presumption, the argument claims,
should not be irrebuttable: we should not require our fellow citizens to continue
accepting that risk, to continue showing that trust, come what may. There can
come a time when, by his persistent criminal conduct, the offender replaces that
presumption by its opposite: by a presumption of harmfulness.

That new presumption has, of course, a predictive dimension: the prediction
that this person will probably reoffend as he has persistently offended until now.
But that prediction is based on (and only on) the dispositions manifest in his persistently criminal conduct—it is one which he has invited, or forced on us, by his
own conduct. It is a prediction that he will continue to behave as he has persistently behaved so far; and whilst it might be false (since, were he not detained, he
might have found no further criminal opportunities, or might have reformed
himself), he cannot expect us to rely on its possible falsity.

Could such presumptively permanent detention be proportionate to the seriousness of the persistent offender's wrong-doing? It is categorially more severe
than the normal sentence which could be imposed for his current offence (even if
that sentence could be increased in the light of his prior record). But the argument
is that there could come a time when persistently serious criminality can make
just such a categorial difference to our response to a wrong-doer. We no longer

---

[46] See my (1986), n. 25 above, pp. 265–6.
[47] See n. 33 above.

see his crimes as lying on a continuum of seriousness with those of other, ordinary offenders; that categorial shift in the character of his offending is what makes it appropriate to subject him to a categorially different kind of punishment. SSD can thus in principle be justified for a serious, persistent offender as an appropriate, deserved response: not to his most recent crime (that would not be SSD) but to his persistent and serious criminality; if restricted in the way suggested here, it can be consistent with the demands of retributive justice and proportionality.

So am I offering a justification for the kinds of 'Three strikes and you're out' provisions which have gained popularity with British and American governments?[48] The argument I have offered does provide a principled foundation for measures of this kind: but *not* a justification for those particular measures. In particular, those measures are very much broader than could be justified by this argument, capturing offenders of whom we certainly could not (or should not if we are to display any real regard for them as fellow-citizens) say that they have so persistently and seriously flouted the most basic, central values of our community that they have excluded themselves from normal community. Those measures are, furthermore, focused on *repeat* offenders, making the mere fact of repetition a sufficient condition for extended detention, whereas the argument I have offered requires *persistent* offending: what must be shown is that the pattern of this person's past and current offending is such that we can interpret it only as displaying his utter and continuing disregard for the values on which our community depends.

Any attempt to give a practicable institutional form to a system of SSD of the kind that the argument given here could justify would, of course, face severe difficulties: difficulties both of definition (just how should we define the kinds of crime and criminal for which such detention should be a possibility?) and of institutional structure (what should the conditions of detention be; what should be the provisions for review or release?). I will not discuss most of those difficulties here. For my concern is with the basic issue of principle (of whether any kind of SSD could in principle be consistent with the demands of penal justice), rather than with the question of how or whether we could in practice give morally acceptable institutional form to such a system; and I want to go on to ask whether we could have any principled grounds for resisting the argument I have offered in favour of a very limited kind of SSD—as distinct from grounds which appeal to the difficulties involved in giving practicable form to such a system. However, I should say a little more about the distinction which I have emphasized, between 'repeat' and 'persistent' offenders: for unless I can show that this is a genuine distinction, my argument that SSD could be justified only for persistent, and not for merely repeat, serious offenders will lack substance.

What could justify SSD, I have suggested, is not merely the fact of repeated offending, but that the pattern of this person's past and current offending is such that we can interpret it only as displaying his utter and continuing disregard for

---

[48] See the Crime (Sentences) Act 1997.

the values on which our community depends, and which the law aims to protect. Now especially in the case of serious offences, which I have suggested should be a necessary condition of SSD, the very fact of repeated offending might well create a presumption that these offences manifest such a disregard: for that might well be the natural and obvious way to interpret them. Such a presumption should, however, certainly not be irrebuttable, since any of the following factors could provide grounds for rejecting it: that the offences were widely separated in time (and not just because the opportunities or temptations to commit them were thus separated); that the offender did display, and does now display, a genuine recognition of the wrongfulness of his conduct, and a serious concern to reform himself; that the offences, though all falling within the same legal category, differed from each other in their particular characters and circumstances, so that we could interpret them as discrete aberrations rather than as parts of the same pattern. It might not often be plausible, in the case of an offender who has now been convicted of his fourth or fifth similar offence of serious personal violence, to suppose that that natural presumption might be rebutted; and obvious and serious procedural problems will arise when we ask how the distinction between 'repeat' and 'persistent' offending is to be established in court: but all I aim to have done here is to show that more than the mere fact of repeat offending is required, to ground the in-principle justification of SSD which I have sketched.

I want to finish, however, by asking what principled grounds we could have for resisting this argument and its conclusion.

The analogy I have drawn between presumptively permanent exclusion from particular activities and presumptively permanent exclusion from normal community might seem at best misleading. The former kind of exclusion might have serious implications for those excluded, but leaves them free to lead a life in the wider community; whereas detention under a system of SSD cuts the offender off altogether from the community, and from any kind of normal life within it. Can we be justified in doing this to a person, whatever he has done?

It is possible to answer 'No' to this last question: but only if we can honestly accept a stringent, absolutist view of the character of citizenship. Membership of those kinds of institution from which, as I noted above, wrong-doers may be permanently excluded, is conditional rather than unconditional: conditional, if not on positive good conduct, at least on refraining from the kind of persistent wrongful conduct which denies those values essential to the institution. What must now be claimed is that membership of political community is not thus conditional: the right to participate in the normal life of the community is absolute (subject only to limited terms of imprisonment for crimes committed); it cannot be lost, however serious the wrongs that the person commits. But can we really hold to such a view?

It is certainly not a view which typically informs our more personal relationships. Consider friendship, for example, as a model to which communitarian theorists might plausibly appeal.[49] Now there is a sense in which true friendship is 'unconditional': my love for my friend is not contingent on the benefit I gain from her; its content is not conditional ('I love her so long as . . .'), but unconditional ('I love her'). Nonetheless, friendships can be destroyed by persistent betrayal; a time can come when I can no longer regard or treat the other person as my friend. Love between parents and children can have a more radically unconditional character; so also, perhaps, can the mutual love and concern that defines a marriage.[50] But should we (can we) model our concerns for our fellow-citizens on such intimate relationships as these? Or if we prefer more liberal foundations for our political theory, can we honestly insist that the rights of citizenship are unconditional and inalienable? Certainly those who talk in roughly contractualist terms cannot readily take such a view: for contracts must of their nature involve some mutual reciprocity, some mutual consideration; we cannot say that a social contract is unconditionally binding even with those who refuse to recognize it, or to pay any serious attention to its most basic terms.

I must end, therefore, on a note of uneasy uncertainty. There is an argument (distinct from that based on an aggregative consequentialism) in favour of a limited system of SSD. A clear recognition of just what SSD does to those who are subject to it (what it does both materially, as a detention that might be for life, and symbolically, as excluding them completely from normal community) should certainly disturb us. But we can reject any such practice in principle only if we can hold that the basic rights or status of citizenship are truly unconditional; and I am not sure whether we can believe that.

[49] See S. E. Marshall, 'The Community of Friends' in E. Christodoulidis (ed.), *Communitarianism and Citizenship* (Ashgate, forthcoming).

[50] A good example, which also brings out the radical and demanding character of such unconditional concern, is Stephen Blackpool in Charles Dickens' *Hard Times*.

7

Sentencing Young Offenders

1. INTRODUCTION

Desert theory has conferred significant benefits upon young offenders sentenced by the criminal courts. It has introduced a host of due process rights into the sentencing process, curtailed the range of factors considered in deciding the sentence, and placed strict limits upon the length and nature of the sentence imposed. In so doing it has reasserted the rights of young people to enjoy levels of certainty, consistency, and parsimony in sentencing which were often denied them in the past. These achievements rely upon the reorientation of sentencing under desert theory toward the seriousness of the offence and the priority given to proportionality of punishment.[1] In pursuit of these goals, desert theory draws attention away from the offender, his or her background, problems and needs, indeed all those individual characteristics which were the target of welfare-orientated strategies.[2] Instead the offender is constructed as an anonymous actor whose individual characteristics, qualities, and failings are beyond the legitimate purview of the sentencer. For young offenders long habituated to being treated for the failings of their character or home life rather than punished for the specific offence of which they stand convicted, the achievements of desert theory are highly valuable. This said, the ascendancy of just deserts is not unproblematic in its application to young people. Focus on the gravity of the offence might seem to suggest that there is little justification for differentiating between adult and juvenile offenders.[3] And yet, the sentencing of juvenile offenders has powerfully resisted being subsumed into the general body of sentencing theory for adults.

Late adolescence is the peak age of offending, and youth crime dominates the news media,[4] prompting administrators to introduce an ever-changing array of

* I am most grateful to Professor Roger Hood, All Souls College, Oxford, for comments and criticisms.

[1] As Hudson has observed, 'contemporary penal policy is concerned with crimes, not criminals': B. Hudson, *Penal Policy and Social Justice* (London: Macmillan, 1993), p. 57.

[2] The importance of these characteristics, together with their concomitant problems and needs, is not denied but it is argued that they should be dealt with outside the criminal justice process, by family, schools, or welfare services.

[3] S. Asquith 'Justice, Retribution and Children' in A. Morris and H. Giller (eds.), *Providing Criminal Justice for Children*, (London: Edward Arnold, 1983) p. 13.

[4] See generally, G. Pearson, 'Youth, Crime, and Society', in M. Maguire, R. Morgan, and

policies, and politicians to exercise their legislative imaginations with an intensity not inspired by any other section of the offending population.[5] As a result, the sentencing of young offenders continues to enjoy (or perhaps better, to endure) a rapidity of change and innovation not found in the rest of the system. It is as if the sentencing of young offenders represents an experimental laboratory where new ideas (to say nothing of ministerial whims) flourish with little regard to research findings, still less to any theoretical or conceptual framework.[6] In this respect the sentencing of young offenders continues to stand apart from and often, as it turns out, ahead of mainstream sentencing.[7]

This chapter explores why it is that young offenders are subject to continuing differentiation and assesses whether this continues to be tenable. Examining the applicability of desert theory to the sentencing of young offenders, the chapter explores its appeal and the difficulties raised by its application to the young. In particular, it will question the reliance of desert theory upon a presumption of responsibility in respect of those young offenders who lack sufficient autonomy or maturity to be held fully accountable. Given the complexities entailed in the current solution of reascribing responsibility to parents, the chapter concludes by suggesting some alternative approaches.

2. SHOULD YOUNG OFFENDERS BE DIFFERENTIATED?: THE PROBLEM OF WELFARISM

The category of young offender is generally accepted as self-evident. Yet it might well be asked why young offenders should enjoy distinct fora (in the form of juvenile or youth courts), specially adapted penalties, and, most importantly for our purposes, their own body of sentencing theory, when other groups of offenders might make equally persuasive claims for differentiation. Despite extensive empirical research and theoretical debate, other categories such as race, class, and gender have not generated their own bodies of sentencing theory. One possible explanation for the successful differentiation of juvenile justice from other potential categories lies in the emergence of welfarism and the predominance of the rehabilitative model during much of the nineteenth and twentieth centuries. It was welfarism which helped develop and sustain the category of the juvenile offender, by recognizing the particular needs created by the relative immaturity, social inadequacy, and structural disadvantages suffered by many young people

---

R. Reiner (eds.), *The Oxford Handbook of Criminology* (Oxford: Clarendon Press, 1994), pp. 1161–206.

[5] Witness the string of pronouncements and proposals by both Conservative and Labour Governments in the 1990s regarding the sentencing and punishment of young offenders.

[6] See R. Harris, 'Towards Just Welfare'(1985) 25 *British Journal of Criminology* 43.

[7] In England, the welfare model was applied first and most vigorously to juveniles. Likewise, the justice model was applied first to juveniles under the Criminal Justice Act 1982 and only extended to the sentencing of adults nearly a decade later under the Criminal Justice Act 1991.

coming before the courts.[8] The question remains how far the very categorization of young offenders as meriting or requiring distinct treatment relies upon the continued acceptance of welfarist ideology.

Put simply, welfarism recognizes that failures of psychological or physiological development and social factors such as poverty, dysfunctional family background, poor schooling, or unemployment profoundly limit young people's capacity for moral development and their exercise of free choice.[9] Avowedly paternalistic in its approach, welfarism claimed for the State the conventional parental role of disciplining youngsters in such a way as to persuade or coerce them to internalize society's moral standards.[10] It sought to raise the age of criminal responsibility and to abolish judicial proceedings for young offenders in favour of welfare-orientated tribunals.[11] It promoted a sentencing structure predicated upon responding to the young offender's needs through individualized and indeterminate treatment programmes.[12] In its heyday, welfarism characterized young offenders as neglected children who, if provided with appropriate countervailing influences upon their development, were potentially reformable. The demise of faith in the rehabilitative ideal has, however, undermined this presumption of reformability and tended instead to pathologize young offenders. Where young offenders were once presented as the appropriate subjects of welfare, they are now demonized as standing outside decent society, a threat to the well-being of ordinary citizens. As Duff suggests, we would do better to ask 'how we as fallible moral beings should encourage *ourselves* to obey the law. We should, that is, still treat those who might commit or be tempted to commit even serious crimes as fellow members of the moral community'.[13]

Nowhere is this tendency to distance and disassociate more pronounced than in regard to offenders who do not resemble those who have the power to punish. The more dissimilar their characteristics, the more powerful is the distancing act. Women, members of racial minorities, and young offenders in particular are more readily characterized as 'other' than adult, white, middle class, male offenders. The present tendency to demonize young offenders is possible precisely because they are so far removed from those who stand in judgement upon them. Their

---

[8] In the 1850s the reformer Mary Carpenter had already established the principle that juveniles should be treated differently in the interests of their particular welfare needs. In England, the Children Act 1908 first established the juvenile court with specific instructions that it should take account of the child's welfare in any disposition it made. In so doing, Garland argues the Act 'did endorse the conception of the child or juvenile as a special category': D. Garland, *Punishment and Welfare* (Aldershot, Gower: 1985), p. 222, see also pp. 22–3.

[9] B. Hudson, *Understanding Justice* (Buckingham: Open University Press, 1996), p. 28.

[10] N. Lacey, *State Punishment* (London: Routledge, 1988), p. 31.

[11] See discussion in A. Morris and H. Giller, *Understanding Juvenile Justice* (Beckenham: Croom Helm, 1987), p. 77 *et seq*.

[12] Albeit ones characterized by informalism and executive decision-making. See L. Gelsthorpe and A. Morris, 'Juvenile Justice 1945–1992' in M. Maguire, R. Morgan, and R. Reiner (eds.), *The Oxford Handbook of Criminology* (Oxford: Clarendon Press, 1994), p. 973.

[13] R. A. Duff, 'Penal Communications: Recent Work in the Philosophy of Punishment', (1996) 20 *Crime and Justice* 16. See also A. von Hirsch, *Censure and Sanctions* (Oxford: OUP, 1993), p. 5.

status as 'rational moral agents',[14] against which standard offenders are judged, is cast into doubt and their rights are likely to be ignored as a consequence.[15] The difficulty, of course, is that many young offenders do lack mature powers of reasoning and are not yet capable of acting as full moral agents. Where this is so, it can hardly be a sign of disrespect to treat them as less than capable. Indeed, and this is central to my argument, one might contest that to recognize their relative lack of capacity is not merely honest but more likely to promote justice than pursuing the fiction that they are rational moral agents when they are not.[16]

The danger is that, to the degree that young people are considered incapable of fulfilling the responsibilities of citizenship, they are liable to be subject to intrusive reformative, curative, or treatment programmes. In theory, though more rarely in practice, a single infraction of the law renders offenders subject to highly intrusive responses by the State. Consequentialist theories, like welfarism, provide few safeguards against extensive intervention, much of which is rationalized as being in the offender's 'best interests'. Most worrying of all is the fact that incarceration has been justified on the grounds that, separated from their habitual 'contaminating' milieu, offenders will be more receptive to the curative impact of treatment and reform programmes. Belated recognition that custodial institutions are themselves fertile sources of contamination which expose offenders to the adverse moral influence and expertise of the criminal community has done much to undermine these claims. Growing concerns about the corrupting or demoralizing effects of institutional life on young offenders, the younger and less experienced of whom are liable to find themselves exposed to offenders older, more recalcitrant, and refractory than themselves, have challenged the welfarist orthodoxy that such institutions are places of safety in an otherwise corrupting world.[17]

It is, however, a matter of continuing live debate whether the abandonment of the welfarist dream necessarily entails subjecting young offenders to adult models of justice. Even if principles of legalism, due process, and proportionality are accepted, it may be that there are some sections of the population whose interests are best safeguarded by more intrusive measures. The mentally disordered are an obvious category, but children too are not well placed to know their own best interests. It is generally accepted that children should be compulsorily subject to full-time schooling and, in some jurisdictions, to health and immunization programmes also. These are administered in the child's interest, irrespective of whether they would wish it for themselves, and do not provoke moral outcry for the very reason that children are recognized as lacking the capacity to determine their own best interests. According to the same logic, can therapy or treatment legitimately be imposed upon young offenders? So long as these penal interven-

---

[14] Duff (1996), n. 13 above, p. 10.   [15] Hudson (1996), n. 9 above, p. 42.

[16] This point will be pursued in greater depth below in relation to the attribution of responsibility under the justice model.

[17] The designation of prisons as 'schools of crime' nicely captures this capacity of custodial institutions to have precisely the counter effect to that intended.

tions can be shown to be in the offender's interests and are not used only as the means to some wider social good, the primary objection to welfarism evaporates.[18]

We have shown that the differential treatment of young offenders and the promotion of welfarism are intimately linked. Many of the objections mounted against welfarism do not apply with the same force to young offenders as they do to adults. It is also questionable whether such objections as do apply are inherent and inescapable characteristics of consequentialist approaches or whether they arise only from abuses in their practical application. Of welfarism, Harris claims that 'it is not necessarily incompatible with consistent sentencing so long as certain procedures are invoked to restrict its scope and monitor its progress'.[19] He goes on to propose a restraining mechanism whose operation might parallel the role of proportionality in desert theory. The principle of 'limiting welfare', which he promotes, recognizes that 'an offender's welfare can be met negatively (by doing as little as possible) as well as positively (by doing as much as possible)'.[20] In this manner welfarism might be brought closer to the justice lobby's demand that State intervention be limited by the requirements of consistency with the responsibility of the offender and the seriousness of the offence.

Without such constraints welfarism is undoubtedly open to abuse and, it may be argued, it is most prone to abuse when applied to those vulnerable members of the population least able to resist its intrusive momentum. Only through the imposition of strict limits upon the exercise of judicial discretion, and the introduction of clearly stipulated criteria for the use of custody, can the untrammelled discretion characteristic of welfarism be constrained and the intrusive powers of the State be limited. The principal appeal of desert theory is that it promotes uniformity in sentencing and places limits upon punishment in such a way as to minimize discretionary and potentially discriminatory decision-making. And yet desert theory is not without its own conceptual and practical difficulties, some of which are generic, and some which apply with particular force to young offenders. In the following section we will explore the fundamental premises of desert theory and consider their specific application to young offenders. We will show that there is often a lack of fit between the model, which takes as its object the free-willed adult,[21] and its application to those who fall short of autonomous agency.[22]

3. Are Young Offenders Responsible?

The criminal law excludes from liability those who are clearly deficient in powers of reasoning, for example those whom it classifies as insane and those so

---

[18] Lacey (1988), n. 10 above, p. 31.   [19] Harris (1985), n. 6 above, p. 36.

[20] Harris (1985), n. 6 above, p. 38.

[21] A model which is itself problematic in that it assumes a uniform level of intellectual ability, rational facility, and freedom to act which belies the realities of many adult lives.

[22] A problem recognized by most advocates of desert theory. See, for example, A. Ashworth, *Principles of Criminal Law* (Oxford: OUP, 1995), pp. 245–6.

situated as to be unable to exercise their will.[23] In respect of young offenders the position is more complicated. The younger the offender, the more obviously immature they are, the less plausible is the ascription of responsibility to them.[24] Psychological studies of childhood provide ample evidence that child development to full adult powers of reasoning is a progressive and variable process.[25] Age categories marking the progression from childhood to full adult responsibility recognize this fact, though, as Harding and Koffman acknowledge: 'such categories are necessarily arbitrary and are vulnerable to changing moral and social conceptions'.[26] All jurisdictions declare very young children to be below the age of criminal responsibility in recognition that they have neither the experience nor reasoning powers to understand what it is to do wrong. The importance of setting an age below which young offenders are not held liable is stressed in international law: the Commentary to the Beijing Rules insists that if the age set is too low or is non-existent the concept of responsibility becomes meaningless.[27] And yet, the age at which criminal responsibility is set varies strikingly, from 7 years in Ireland to 15 in Sweden. Given that it is unlikely that children mature at such widely differing rates in near neighbouring countries, these differences would seem to confirm that the age of criminal responsibility is a social construct determined more by differences in legal, social, and political culture, by differential attitudes to juvenile delinquency, and the use of criminal sanctions, than differential rates of juvenile development.[28]

During early adolescence the device of a rebuttable presumption against liability used to protect most children from prosecution, allowing the law to punish only those who could be shown to understand that what they did was seriously wrong.[29] The doctrine of '*doli incapax*' applied to children between the ages of 10 and 14 and recognized that responsibility grows only with maturity and that children mature at different rates.[30] Accordingly, children of this age were not automatically considered fully criminally responsible and were prosecuted only if it could be shown that they knew that what they did was 'seriously wrong'.[31] The doctrine of *doli incapax* was first seriously challenged by the case of *C* v. *DPP*, in which Laws J sought to abolish the presumption of incapacity, arguing that 'the conditions under which this presumption was developed in the earlier law now have no

---

[23] A. Ashworth, *ibid*.   [24] A point recognized in the Labour Party policy document *Tackling Youth Crime* (London: Labour Party, 1996), p. 9.

[25] M. Rutter and D. Smith, *Psychosocial disorders in young people: time trends and their causes* (London: John Wiley, 1995).

[26] C. Harding and L. Koffman, *Sentencing and the Penal System* (London: Sweet & Maxwell, 1995), p. 350.

[27] G. van Bueren, 'Child-Oriented Justice: An International Challenge for Europe' (1992) 6 *International Journal of Law and the Family* 387.

[28] M. King, 'Comparing Legal Cultures in the Quest for Law's Identity', in D. Nelken (ed.), *Comparing Legal Cultures* (Aldershot: Dartmouth, 1997), p. 128 *et seq*.

[29] C. Ball, K. McCormac, and N. Stone, *Young Offenders: Law, Policy and Practice* (London: Sweet & Maxwell, 1995), pp. 79–82.

[30] Penal Affairs Consortium, *The Doctrine of 'Doli Incapax'* (London: PAC, 1995), p. 5.

[31] T. G. Moore 'In defence of Doli Incapax', *Justice of the Peace*, 27 May 1995, p. 347.

application'.[32] This decision was subsequently overruled by the House of Lords who argued that the doctrine of *doli incapax* was still necessary to protect children from the full force of the criminal law. Legal debates ranged over the changing levels of maturity of children; over the possible injustice of ascribing a more developed moral appreciation of wrong-doing to children from 'good homes' and thus penalizing them unjustly; and over whether and by what means children should be held less accountable than adults.[33] The Lords' judgment emphasized that studies of child development and learning confirm that children mature at different rates over differing time-spans and that the law should, therefore, take into account differing levels of maturity. Given this judicial acceptance of differential maturation within the doctrine of *doli incapax*, the Government's decision to abolish the presumption in the Crime and Disorder Bill 1998 can hardly be welcomed.

The imposition of uniform ages at which all young people acquire full criminal liability seems arbitrary and potentially unjust. Although it may be practical to set a standard age at which liability arises, to do so conspicuously ignores continuing differences in levels of experience, understanding, and maturity. One course of action is to vary the degree of responsibility ascribed on a case by case basis, according to the relative maturity of the particular individual.[34] Another, more practicable solution might be to take up Ball's suggestion that we should, as a matter of principle, make lesser demands of youth on the grounds that their culpability is reduced.[35] Either approach would help to resolve unfairness caused by the present fiction that children move abruptly into adulthood on a pre-specified, universal date.

The fact that the criminal law holds young people liable for their actions does not provide a complete answer to the question of their responsibility in respect of sentencing. In the literature on desert theory the offender's responsibility is rarely subject to enquiry but, rather, is simply assumed. Whereas the difficulties of determining the level of harm caused or relating the severity of the punishment to the gravity of the offence are much discussed,[36] the means by which one might establish whether an offender is fully responsible is rarely debated.[37] And there is relatively little discussion of how one might measure possible variations in the degree of responsibility ascribable to any given offender. This is a curious

---

[32] *C (a minor)* v. *Director of Public Prosecutions* [1994] 3 WLR 888 and [1995] 2 WLR 383.

[33] Penal Affairs Consortium (1995), n. 30 above, pp. 4–5. See also the subsequent cases of *T* v. *DPP*, *L* v. *DPP*, *H and others* v. *DPP*, [1997] *Criminal Law Review* 127–9.

[34] This was a course recommended by the 1990 Government White Paper which recognized that teenagers 'are at an intermediate stage between childhood and adulthood' and that 'there should be some flexibility in the sentencing arrangement for this age group'. Home Office, *Crime, Justice and Protecting the Public* (London: HMSO, 1990) p. 43. See also N. Stone 'Sentencing the Near Adult', 158 *Justice of the Peace* (1994) 580, 595.

[35] Ball, McCormac, and Stone (1995), n. 29 above, p. 116.

[36] See, for example, A. von Hirsch and N. Jareborg 'Gauging Criminal Harm: A Living-Standard Analysis', (1991) 11 *Oxford Journal of Legal Studies* 1–38.

[37] The Labour Government's announcement that it 'is determined to reinforce the responsibility of young offenders' simply sidesteps the issue: Home Office, *No More Excuses—a New Approach to Tackling Youth Crime in England and Wales* (London: HMSO, 1997), p. 12.

oversight given that the complexities of gauging and assigning responsibility are considerable. Responsibility goes beyond mere capacity (intellectual or physical) to embrace issues of status and situation and it should be recognized that children neither enjoy nor can be offered the immediate prospect of enjoying full citizenship rights. To the extent that young offenders enjoy less than equal status and less than a full share of rights, it is questionable whether they should be held strictly to account for their actions. As Ball *et al* argue, 'young people tend to have less stake in society with reduced benefits and recognition and thus their communal liabilities and sense of responsibility or obligation should be correspondingly lower'.[38] Many of those coming before the courts are the products of impoverished, disadvantaged upbringing or from families disrupted by separation, divorce, or illness. Many have had a disrupted educational career whether as a result of poor educational performance, truancy, or school exclusion, and many have problems with alcohol or drug abuse.[39] The presumption under desert theory that offenders are autonomous actors thus disregards the fact that many young offenders operate within a very constrained realm of choices, that their prospects are limited, and that external pressures on them, be it from peers, parents, or others, severely limits their scope for free choice. Hudson argues that 'Legal reasoning seems unable to appreciate that the existential view of the world as an arena for acting out free choices is a perspective of the privileged'.[40] She might have added that it is the perspective of the privileged *adult* which legal reasoning adopts, a perspective far removed from that of most young offenders. Even the most deprived and disadvantaged of adults are unlikely to experience the constraints on free will suffered by their juvenile counterparts.

For desert theory to accommodate emphasis on larger social or structural considerations within its primary emphasis on individual responsibility would involve significant reorientation. Norrie, for example, argues that 'we hold the individual responsible for what he has done to society, when in reality, his crime is the product of what society has done to him'.[41] Whether desert could embrace such a massive extension of its parameters without losing its trademark reliance upon the ascription of responsibility is open to doubt. Ashworth has grappled with the problem of how far desert theory can take account of the offender's social situation in mitigation.[42] He asks: 'should it be relevant to sentencing that the offender suffered abuse as a child, had an alcoholic father, lost his mother at an early age, or otherwise had a deprived childhood?'[43] He concludes that there is

---

[38] Ball, McCormac, and Stone (1995), n. 29 above, pp. 115–16.

[39] A. Hagell and T. Newburn, *Persistent Young Offenders* (London: Policy Studies Institute, 1994), Ch. 7.

[40] Hudson, 'Punishing the Poor: A Critique of the Dominance of Legal Reasoning in Penal Policy and Practice' in R. A. Duff *et al* (eds.), *Penal Theory and Practice*, (Manchester: Manchester University Press, 1994), p. 292; see also Chapter 9 below.

[41] A. Norrie, *Crime, Reason and History* (London: Weidenfeld and Nicolson, 1993), p. 208.

[42] Though see A. Ashworth 'Desert, Determinism and Deprivation', *Criminal Justice Ethics* (Winter/Spring 1994), pp. 8–10.

[43] A. Ashworth (1994), n. 42 above, p. 8.

scope even within desert theory for mitigation 'based upon significant social disadvantage and deprived upbringing'. If the argument in favour of mitigation can be made in respect of adults, who may have had subsequent opportunities to overcome their early disadvantage, how much stronger it is in respect of young offenders, who are so much more proximate to these mitigating factors.

4. IS PUNISHING THE YOUNG JUST?

A central tenet of desert theory is that offenders be punished equally. It is a tenet which relies upon the assumption that all offenders are rational autonomous agents, equal before the law.[44] Equality before the law appears to demand that young offenders, to the extent that they can be held responsible, be punished the same as adult offenders. Yet the principle of equality of impact imposes the competing demand that sentencing 'should strive to avoid grossly unequal impacts on offenders with differing resources and sensitivities, because that would be unjust'.[45] It is readily recognized that financial penalties must be adjusted to take account of young offenders' limited financial resources.[46] Less readily recognized is the fact that other penalties may bear differently upon the young and be more burdensome upon them than on adults. Sentencing to custody, for example, raises the question of whether a month or year in prison is not more onerous for a young person than the same period experienced by an adult. Do we, as Duff argues, need to recognize that 'a sentence of one year's imprisonment will bear more harshly on some than others, depending both on the age and character of the offender'.[47] In respect of longer sentences in particular, the impact of incarceration on a teenager in this formative period of development may be more profound, and more devastating, than a similar sentence suffered by someone 10 years older. The deprivations of incarceration—limited spatial mobility, curtailed life experiences, restricted opportunities—together with the stigma suffered on release are arguably both more painful and more damaging to the young than their elder counterparts. Whilst creating differential financial penalties is relatively straightforward, graduating custodial penalties so as to ensure equality of impact on young offenders is far more problematic. It calls for reference to factors beyond strict proportionality to the gravity of the offence.[48] Accordingly, Duff suggests that we should distinguish between formal proportionality and the 'substantive appositeness of "match" or "fit" between the particular substantive

---

[44] Asquith (1983), n. 3 above, p. 10.

[45] A. Ashworth, *Sentencing and Criminal Justice* (London: Butterworths, 1995), p. 80.

[46] Unless the parents are to be held liable for their payment, in which case it is the parents' disposable income which is at issue.

[47] Duff (1996), n. 13 above, p. 59.

[48] It is worth noting that one of the principles laid down in international law is that penalties should be proportionate not only to the offence but to the circumstances of the child. See van Bueren (1992), n. 27 above, p. 385.

punishment and this particular crime and this particular criminal'.[49] Inevitably, sensitivity to the appositeness of the penalty to the particular offender tends to promote more individualized sentencing than a strict adherence to proportionality would allow. The tension between pursuing consistency in sentencing and creating punishments which 'fit' the particular offender highlights the conflict between formal justice and a more flexible conception of justice which does not presume uniformity among offenders and is prepared to vary sentences to ensure equality of impact.

A second assumption of the justice model is that the offender is a rational actor who enjoys full citizenship and can justly be held responsible for his or her wrong-doing. Rejecting the claim that social disadvantage excuses wrong-doing, von Hirsch poses the question: 'that culpability is reduced is at least arguable . . . But is culpability actually *eliminated*?'[50] Curiously, the potential injustice of holding to account those whose capacity is in question is deemed less objectionable than risking the potential consequences of acknowledging that some may lack responsibility. Von Hirsch warns that 'Persons deemed incapable of responsibility for their actions tend to be seen as less than fully adult, and can become the target of proactive forms of state intervention that may be still more intrusive than the criminal law'.[51] It is questionable, however, whether these objections apply with the same force where offenders are in fact 'less than fully adult' and where non-criminal interventions may, as a consequence, be perfectly appropriate.[52]

Critics have been quick to point out that not all offenders are endowed with equal powers of reasoning and that not all are situated so as to be able to exercise their will freely.[53] As Asquith observes, to presuppose the offender's rationality 'poses particular problems for any social institution dealing with those whose status as morally autonomous agents needs careful consideration'.[54] The obvious difficulty is that the assumed figure of the offender as rational actor accords more closely with the mature powers of adult decision-making than it does with the limited capacities of many young offenders.[55] This lack of fit is not plausibly overcome by promoting a mythical reconstruction of young offenders as rational calculating actors freely exercising their will to choose wrong-doing. Ascribing rationality in this way relies upon a collective denial of any indications that the offender is immature or highly impressionable which call into question their capacity for autonomous agency. Reconstructed as deliberate wrong-doers with

---

[49] Duff (1996), n. 13 above, p. 62.

[50] A. von Hirsch, 'The politics of "just deserts" ', (1990) 32 *Canadian Journal of Criminology* 409 (reworked as Ch. 9 of his *Censure and Sanctions* (1993). A less absolutist approach might be to ask 'is culpability reduced?'

[51] Von Hirsch (1990), n. 50 above, p. 409 (and von Hirsch (1993) Ch. 9).

[52] Though, as we have already argued, to condone welfarist intervention is not to condone limitless intervention.

[53] Hudson (1993), n. 1 above, Ch. 2.; A. Norrie, 'The Limits of Justice: Finding Fault in the Criminal Law', (1996) 59 *Modern Law Review* 540–2.

[54] Asquith (1983), n. 3 above, pp. 10–11.   [55] Ashworth (1995), n. 45 above, p. 245.

all the powers of mature reasoning, young offenders are ascribed a degree of responsibility sufficient to justify punishing them. The result, as Giller has observed, is that the young offender is no longer treated as a child in trouble[56] but is caricatured as a 'predatory actor who acts with callous calculation with the intention of achieving maximum gain for himself while demonstrating a reckless indifference to others'.[57] It is, of course, open to question whether this reconstruction of the young offender is a necessary by-product of developments in sentencing theory or whether it is rather that changing attitudes towards youth have promoted a particularly punitive variant of the justice model over welfarism.[58] As von Hirsch's own writings make clear, desert theory is primarily intended as decrementalist strategy for limiting punishment not, as it is often misrepresented, for increasing its bite.[59]

Recognizing the stark variations in autonomy enjoyed by offenders according to age, race, gender, and class demands a much more sensitive appreciation of the impact of the offender's structural situation on the exercise of free will than desert theorists have been prepared to countenance.[60] Their claim that to admit indicia of social disadvantage into the sentencing equation is likely to produce greater injustice presumes the lack of constraints tolerated by most consequentialist theories.[61] Yet such injustice is likely only if factors such as poverty, unemployment, or broken homes are introduced in ways which are prejudicial to the offender. It would obviously be prejudicial, for example, to use the poverty of the young offender's home life as grounds for protective incarceration. But it would be equally prejudicial to deny the impact of that home life on their capacity to choose. A possible solution would be to develop a model of sentencing which admitted social factors deemed relevant to the responsibility of the offender in order to determine what precise level of responsibility pertains. Admitting social factors to determine responsibility alone, within the strict constraints of desert theory, need not create the dangers commonly associated with utilitarian approaches. And it would have the considerable advantage of recognizing that offenders do not operate in a sterile vacuum, untouched by the material conditions of their surroundings. It may be that von Hirsch is right to argue that criminal justice cannot be made an instrument of social justice, but neither should it be made an instrument of injustice.

---

[56] Note the change in labels used in government policy documents. The title of the White Paper preceding the Children Act 1969 spoke of 'children in trouble', that preceding the Criminal Justice Act 1982 referred more starkly to 'young offenders': Home Office, *Children in Trouble* (London: HMSO, 1968); Home Office, *Young Offenders* (London: HMSO, 1980).

[57] H. Giller, 'Is there a Role for the Juvenile Court?' (1986) 25 *Howard Journal of Criminal Justice* 161–71 at 165. For more general discussion of the construction of youth crime, see J. Muncie, G. Coventry, and R. Walters, 'The politics of youth crime prevention: developments in Australia and England and Wales' in L. Noaks *et al* (eds.), *Contemporary Issues in Criminology* (Cardiff: University of Wales Press, 1995), pp. 339–43.

[58] Pearson (1994), n. 4 above, p. 1192 *et seq.*

[59] A. von Hirsch, *Censure and Sanctions* (Oxford: OUP, 1993), Ch. 5.

[60] This is not, of course, to claim that young offenders lack free will, but rather to argue that its exercise is very often curtailed to a degree not shared by most adults.

[61] Von Hirsch (1993), n. 59 above, Ch. 9.

5. SHOULD PARENTS BE HELD RESPONSIBLE?

Recognition that children's responsibility grows only as they mature and that it may be substantially vitiated by social deprivation has caused sentencing theorists to look around for a proxime to supply that portion which is as yet 'missing'. A ready solution has been to ascribe graduated responsibility to parents (or guardians) according to the age, maturity, and experience of the child.[62] In this way it is always possible to locate a responsible party upon whom punishment may justly be visited or from whom fines or compensation payments may be extracted.[63] Ascribing responsibility to the parents of delinquent youth may be a convenient solution but its logical foundations, ideological framework, and practical application demand careful scrutiny.

Responsibility is ascribed to parents of young offenders on several grounds. Unhappily, these are not wholly consistent with one another.[64] Perhaps the most obvious ground is that, as we have noted, very young children bear no legal responsibility for their actions. Accordingly, any wrong-doing on their part is held to be the responsibility of the parents.[65] As children mature they are deemed to assume ever greater individual responsibility for their actions and the parents' level of responsibility correspondingly declines.[66] This 'traditional' ground for ascribing responsibility rests upon an idealized vision that parents should exercise effective authority over the activities of their offspring.[67] It is a vision which accords ill with the lives of many young people in conflict with the law. A newer 'realist' account recognizes instead that many parents fail to exercise due authority and, further, that their own lifestyles may be such as to inhibit their children's acquisition of the responsibilities of full citizenship. Those who abuse alcohol or drugs, whose relationships break down, and who otherwise fail either to offer a 'good example' or to exercise proper control, are ascribed a negative form of responsibility for creating the conditions in which their children's anti-social

---

[62] 'Case law has determined that parental responsibility itself diminishes as the child acquires sufficient understanding to make his or her own decisions': The Labour Party, *Parenting: A discussion paper* (London: Labour Party, 1996), p. 8. See also Home Office, *No More Excuses—a New Approach to Tackling Youth Crime in England and Wales* (London: HMSO, 1997), Ch. 4.

[63] The Crime and Disorder Bill 1998 introduces parental responsibility in clauses 8 and 9: these give the courts the power to impose 'parenting orders' and, in certain cases, require them to do so. This tactic is hardly new. In 1847 a Select Committee of the House of Lords recommended that, wherever possible, part of the cost of convicting and punishing young offenders should be charged to the parents. L. Radzinowicz and R. Hood, *The Emergence of Penal Policy in Victorian and Edwardian England* (Oxford: Clarendon Press, 1990), p. 656.

[64] As the Labour Party in discussion of parental responsibility acknowledges: 'the very breadth of the term produces its own problems in defining what is expected of parents': Labour Party (1996), n. 62 above, p. 8.

[65] See Home Office, *Preventing Children Reoffending* (London: HMSO, 1997), p. 8.

[66] Home Office (1990), n. 56 above, pp. 40–4.

[67] The Conservative Government's view was as follows: 'From their children's earliest years parents can, and should, help them develop as responsible, law-abiding citizens. They should ensure that their children are aware of the existence of rules and laws and the need for them; and that they respect other people and their property. Most parents try to carry out these duties conscientiously': Home Office (1990), n. 56 above, p. 40.

behaviour flourishes. The former Conservative Government adopted this vision wholesale:

The single most important influence on a child's development is that of the family. Those children who show signs of criminal behaviour at an early age are those who are most likely to end up as serious or persistent offenders. Such children often come from communities and families which are unstable, chaotic and suffer from a number of problems. Their parents are likely to have a criminal record, to neglect their children, or to exercise low levels of supervision and harsh and erratic discipline, and themselves to come from similar families.[68]

According to this second account, parental responsibility rests precisely in their failure to act as responsible parents. Caught between the twin prongs of this attack, parents cannot easily escape responsibility: either they are 'good' disciplinary parents who must be held to account for the failure of that discipline or they are 'bad' reckless parents whose lack of authority and poor example is the cause of their offspring's misdeeds.[69]

The ideological bases of parental responsibility are also confused. On the one hand, holding parents responsible fitted comfortably within the Conservative ideology of a minimal State and the maximization of individual and family autonomy.[70] In pursuit of these goals, State withdrawal is said to allow for the flourishing of parental responsibility. An alternative, more sceptical reading is that the imposition of greater responsibility upon parents 'is being used as a mechanism to legitimate the withdrawal of the State'.[71] This withdrawal can be read in a number of ways: as a tacit acknowledgement that the State has failed to control juvenile crime, as a reaction against the unfettered intrusion of the 'nanny State' into the lives of young people, promoted under welfarism, or as a simple cost-cutting measure. Even the Labour Party has acknowledged this third ground, arguing: 'turning the tide of delinquency and crime means looking at the early years of people's lives, their upbringing and the way parental responsibilities are discharged. If we are not prepared to do this then we are doomed to spend more on police, security, insurance, courts and prisons'.[72]

Withdrawal is also commonly justified on the grounds that State interference usurps the parental role and tends to induce dependency and a progressive abandonment by parents of the exercise of their duties. By restricting the disciplinary activities of criminal justice agents, it is hoped that parents may be induced to reassert control. This notion of dependency culture rests upon the highly questionable assumption that it is interference by State agencies which inhibits parents' willingness to act responsibly. It ignores the many possible extraneous

---

[68] Home Office (1997), n. 65 above, p. 11.

[69] The Conservative Government made just such a distinction in its own policy documents. See Home Office (1997), n. 65 above, p. 23.

[70] M. Drakeford, 'Parents of Young People in Trouble', (1996) 35 *Howard Journal of Criminal Justice* 242–55.

[71] S. Edwards and A. Halpern, 'Parental Responsibility as an instrument of social policy', (1992) 22 *Family Law* 113.

[72] The Labour Party (1996), n. 62 above, p. 7.

reasons for their failure, upon which State withdrawal will have little effect, and it overlooks the fact that some individuals and some families are simply not able to flourish without support. As the State withdraws, the inability of such families to prosper becomes all too apparent. As Stenson and Factor observe: 'the effort to reduce dependency on state provision starkly spotlights those who are seen as unwilling or incapable of acquiring the requisite capacities for (legally acceptable) survival in the market place'.[73] The hope that the policing and disciplinary duties previously borne by the State may be shouldered by families and communities reveals itself as naively optimistic.

A second, contrary reading is that the promotion of parental responsibility extends, rather than limits, State control.[74] As Edwards and Halpern have argued: 'the psychological device of parental responsibility is used . . . as a mechanism which allows the state to exercise greater control over the individual than before by more determinedly enforcing that responsibility'.[75] On this reading, the assignment of responsibility represents not the granting of a freedom but the imposition of a duty which, if not satisfactorily fulfilled, renders the parents directly answerable to the court.[76] The child's delinquency serves as a justificatory device to embrace the parents within the disciplinary gaze of the court.[77] Extension of responsibility expands the ambit of sentencing, beyond desert theory's focus upon the offence, to reimport distinctly welfarist concerns about family background. It is as if the child's crime is deemed proof enough of parental delinquency rendering them liable to be found guilty of a failure of control, publicly censured for their inadequacies, and sanctioned.[78]

This highly interventionist State response to criminal behaviour stands in striking contrast to the commonly propagated view that the more autonomy parents are given the more likely they are to act responsibly toward their child.[79] As Eekelaar observes, 'where activity threatens the general public, government policy has been ready to intervene by extending the scope, or the penalties, of the criminal law. Nothing less, it is claimed, will establish "responsible behaviour" '.[80]

---

[73] K. Stenson and F. Factor, 'Governing youth: new directions for the youth service', in J. Baddock and M. May (eds.), *Social Policy Review* 7 (Canterbury: Social Policy Association, 1996), p. 180.

[74] For a historical account of these trends, see J. Donzelot, *The Policing of Families* (London: Hutchinson, 1979).

[75] Edwards and Halpern (1992), n. 71 above, p. 118.

[76] The Labour Party asserts 'there is a growing consensus that enforcement of parental authority is needed if problems of youth disorder and crime are to be tackled': The Labour Party (1996), n. 62 above, p. 18.

[77] The Conservative Government alluded to this disciplinary quality thus: 'attendance at court is a powerful reminder to the parents of their duty both to their children and to the wider community': Home Office (1990), n. 56 above, p. 41.

[78] In England and Wales, under the Criminal Justice Act 1991, the court can require the parents or guardians to attend court with their offspring (s. 56), make the parents responsible for the payment of any fines on compensation orders (s. 57), and be bound over to take proper care and exercise proper control over the child (s. 58(2)(a)). If they refuse unreasonably they can be liable for a fine of up to £1,000.

[79] This philosophy clearly underlies the Children Act 1989.

[80] J. Eekelaar 'Parental responsibility: state of nature or nature of state?', (1991) 37 *Journal of Social Welfare and Family Law* 46.

On this reading, then, parents are not being involved as the informal police of their own families, but rather are held to account by the State.[81] Policing is as much of, as by, the parents. And the State, whilst appearing to withdraw, simultaneously extends its ambit of control. Parents now made responsible for the payment of their offspring's fines or compensation orders or bound over to ensure their good behaviour are necessarily subject to greater, not lesser, controls. And to the extent that they fail to exercise the controls required of them, parents are liable to find themselves subject to further judicial controls and penalties (see the Crime and Disorder Bill 1998, clauses 8 and 9). The irony is that these controls are imposed with few of the legal safeguards or due process rights theoretically associated with the justice model. Parents facing penalties for offences committed by their children are unlikely to be eligible for State-aided legal representation and although they may seek advice from their offspring's lawyer, it is doubtful whether this is a sufficient or appropriate source of legal representation. As one commentator has pointed out, if the child's defence advocate acts also for the parents 'there is a conflict of interest between the child and his parents, since any mitigation which suggests the defendant is other than utterly beyond control or redemption is quite deliberately an argument in favour of an order against the hapless parents'.[82] This potential conflict of interests is objectionable not only on legal grounds but also in its likely effects on family life.

The confused and conflicting ideological grounds upon which parental responsibility is located raise several problems for sentencing practice. First, the identification of parents as responsible agents obdurately ignores the fact that very many parents of young offenders are quite incapable of exercising authority over them.[83] Parents whose own lives are chaotic or out of control, single mothers intimidated by strapping teenage sons, or those struggling with multiple problems of poverty, ill-health, or poor housing are unlikely to be well placed to perform the role of responsible parents. In so far as the imposition of responsibility signals notice of parental failure, it is naive to expect the mere impact of court censure to prompt immediate exercise of responsibilities hitherto neglected.[84] As Drakeford has observed, its message is 'a variation of the Langian double-bind; be competent you incompetent parent'.[85] It is all too likely that these 'incompetent' parents are just those who will agree to be bound over to

---

[81] On the fining of parents, the Conservative Government freely admitted its motives: 'the imposition on the parents of a formal requirement to pay has an important effect. It brings home to them the reality of the consequences of their children's behaviour and the implications for their own actions': Home Office (1990), n. 56 above, p. 41.

[82] R. W. Noon, 'Binding over parents under Section 58 Criminal Justice Act 1991—some practical problems', (1992) *Justice of the Peace* 803.

[83] A fact recognized more readily by the courts than by sentencing theorists. For example, in England and Wales in 1993 in only 6% of cases of young offenders sentenced for indictable offences were parents or guardians required to pay fines on their behalf and in only 14% of these cases were they ordered to pay compensation. Source: Penal Affairs Consortium, *Parental Responsibility, Youth Crime and the Criminal Law* (London: Penal Affairs Consortium, 1995), p. 2.

[84] Edwards & Halpern (1992), n. 71 above, p. 118.

[85] Drakeford (1996), n. 70 above, p. 253.

control their offspring and to accept conditions they cannot possibly fulfil. The seeds of failure are planted in the very conception of this approach.

A second problem is that publicly censuring parents sends out a message to young offenders that, to the extent that their parents are held responsible, their own culpability is proportionately reduced. Any attempt to impress upon young offenders that they are in any way responsible for their actions will tend to be undermined by the countervailing message that their parents are at fault. As the Penal Affairs Consortium has observed: 'penalising parents rather than children does not help to reinforce the vital need for young offenders to face up to their responsibility for their own actions: if anything it sends out the contrary unhelpful message that young people can slough off responsibility on to their parents'.[86] The power of sentencing as a device of censure, impressing upon young offenders that they have done wrong and will be held to account, is simultaneously dissipated by the message that it is their parents and not they who, ultimately, will be held to account.

A third and wholly counterproductive effect of threatening the parents with sanctions, should they fail to prevent future misdeeds, is to shift the power balance between parent and child. The threat of sanctions arms manipulative children, encouraging them to threaten to engage in the very delinquent conduct which will require their parents' return to court. Parents eager to avoid such an eventuality may be driven to demand that their offspring leave home in order to bring an end to their own continuing responsibility.[87] The attribution of parental responsibility is thus liable either to infantilize young offenders by confirming their dependency status or, worse still, to furnish them with the means of manipulating parents faced with the threat of further court sanctions. Far from achieving its stated aim of bolstering families as agents of social discipline, the State is liable to succeed only in contributing to their dissolution.[88]

In the light of these numerous difficulties, it is instructive to examine concrete proposals for the imposition of parental responsibility made by the leading political parties. The former Conservative Government proposed to introduce a 'Parental Control Order' as a means of sanctioning those parents who failed both to control their children and to respond to help offered.[89] It proposed that the order should be available both in place of a parental bind-over where the child had been convicted of an offence and, more controversially, 'in its own right where no offence had yet been committed'. To propose to sanction parents pre-emptively when their child had not yet been found guilty of any offence suggests a striking disregard for justice and a disturbing readiness to expand the ambit of punishment. The Conservative Government sought to evade this charge by

---

[86] Penal Affairs Consortium (1995), n. 83 above, p. 3.

[87] A practising solicitor poses the risk thus 'Is it totally unrealistic to suggest that such desperate remedies may recommend themselves to a significant number of hard-pressed parents?': Noon (1992), n. 82 above, p. 804.

[88] Penal Affairs Consortium (1995), n. 83 above, p. 2.

[89] Home Office (1997), n. 65 above, p. 23 *et seq.*

arguing that 'in deciding whether to impose the Order, the court would not be convicting the parents or the child of an offence, but considering whether the parents had exercised proper care and control'.[90] And yet the penal nature of the order together with the proposal that failure to consent to or comply with its conditions be a criminal offence for which recalcitrant parents be subject to further penalty would clearly extend the ambit of punishment. Nor has the Labour Government been immune to the appeal of parental responsibility. Their proposals to use local by-laws to enforce child protection curfews to keep young children off the streets and to introduce 'Parenting Orders' at first appear reminiscent of Conservative Government policy.[91] In practice, however, the Parenting Order would not be available prior to offending behaviour and renounces disciplinary sanctions in favour of requirements that parents attend counselling and guidance sessions (see the Crime and Disorder Bill 1998, clause 8). These more constructive proposals explicitly recognize that 'simply requiring parents to exert more control over their children by itself is unlikely to produce results, since problems within the family often run far deeper than this'.[92] Here, at least, appears some glimmer of recognition that disciplining parents is not merely a convenient proxy for punishing their delinquent offspring and that responding to young offenders invites a more constructive response than punishment alone.[93] Disquiet at the futility of a strictly penal approach to crime may be what is driving this new focus on social policies for promoting parenting skills.[94] It remains open to question, however, whether this disquiet is sufficient to displace punishment altogether as the dominant paradigm in responding to young offending.

6. Is Punishment of the Young Necessary?

The justice model requires that the legal system acknowledge and respond to violations of the criminal law. There is, it is said, 'an intuitive connection between desert and punishment'.[95] Punishment is justified as necessary to the satisfaction of public feelings of vengeance, to respecting the moral agency of individuals, and to the safeguarding of individual rights.[96] Of the latter, Asquith observes:

---

[90] Home Office (1997), n. 65 above, p. 24.

[91] These were first announced in the Labour Party's discussion paper *Parenting* (London: Labour Party, 1996), p. 19 and introduced in the Crime and Disorder Bill 1997–98, clauses 8 and 9.

[92] Labour Party (1996), n. 62 above, p. 19.

[93] 'Parents of young offenders may not directly be to blame for the crimes of their children, but parents have to be responsible for providing their children with proper care and control. The courts need powers to help, and support parents more effectively to keep their children out of trouble: Home Office (1997), n. 62 above, p. 12.

[94] As one academic suggests: G. Slapper 'Stepping behind the family—1', (1997) *New Law Journal* (10 January) p. 11.

[95] Ashworth (1995), n. 45 above, p. 69.

[96] U. Narayan, 'Adequate Responses and Preventative Benefits: Justifying Hard Treatment in Legal Punishment', (1993) 13 *Oxford Journal of Legal Studies* 166–82.

'Advocacy of children's rights and of punishing is, within the terms of a justice approach, conceptually linked: only in a system in which children are punished for what they have done can their rights best be protected'.[97] International law takes a different view: the commentary to the Beijing Rules suggests that in many cases concerning juveniles non-intervention would be the best response.[98] Even where punishment is demanded, the Rules suggest that deprivation of liberty, if used at all, should be 'used only as a measure of last resort and for the shortest appropriate period of time'.[99] Restraint from punishing young offenders can be justified on several grounds. Not only can they not be expected to reason with the full capacity of adulthood, they lack experience to appreciate fully the consequences of their actions. The damage, harm, pain, or distress to others which a sentient adult might be expected to recognize as likely consequences of their actions, may not be apparent to the young offender. Indeed it is arguable that it is only through experimentation during adolescence that youngsters can, by trial and error, appreciate the consequences of their actions. Far from rushing to punish young offenders for their errors, Ball *et al* argue, 'they should be given more scope to learn from their mistakes without undue penalisation or stigma'.[100]

A further argument is that 'delinquent behaviour of some kind among young people, if not universal, is at least far too widespread to be regarded as abnormal'.[101] Official criminal statistics appear to show that whilst offending peaks markedly in the late teens, it falls away rapidly thereafter.[102] A significant proportion of the crime for which young people are prosecuted and punished falls into the category of 'status offences', that is acts which would not attract the attention of the law if perpetrated by adults.[103] Committed by young people, these status offences are read as indicia of more generalized delinquency and responded to with a gravity which they do not merit. If some degree of delinquency is a normal facet of adolescent exploration, a necessary part of growing up, then the grounds for penal intervention are open to question.[104]

Several strategies suggest themselves as apposite ways of limiting the potentially damaging impact of punishing young offenders. First, re-examining the scope of the criminal law to identify those offences which discriminate against the common activities of young offenders and to excise those whose potential to

---

[97] Asquith (1983), n. 3 above, p. 8.   [98] van Bueren (1992), n. 27 above, p. 388.

[99] Art. 37(b) of the 'Beijing Rules'.

[100] Ball, McCormac, and Stone (1995), n. 29 above, p. 115.

[101] N. Morris and G. Hawkins, *The Honest Politician's Guide to Crime Control* (Chicago: University of Chicago Press, 1970), p. 45.

[102] Home Office, *Digest of Information on the Criminal Justice System 3* (London: HMSO, 1995), p. 22; D. Farrington, 'Age and Crime', in M. Tonry and N. Morris (eds.), *Crime and Justice* vol. 7 (Chicago: Chicago University Press, 1986).

[103] Pearson gives the examples of riding a motorbike, purchasing cigarettes or alcohol, or engaging in sexual activity under age. All of these derive their criminality from the young offender's very status as a youth: Pearson (1994), n. 4 above, p. 1187.

[104] The commonly vaunted counter argument, that without the formal protections of criminal proceedings the offender's due process rights are liable to be overridden, presumes some form of State intervention. If there is no intervention at all, the concomitant need for legal protection vanishes.

cause harm to others is minimal.[105] Secondly, recognizing the triviality of much delinquent behaviour and refraining from punishing that which would not attract punishment if committed by an adult. Thirdly, placing a brake upon the automatic move from establishing capacity to attributing blame; recognizing that structural factors may limit blame even where a young person is technically responsible. And finally, pausing to question whether no response is likely to be productive of more good than any response, penal or otherwise. Encouraging strategies of non-intervention through cautioning, diversion, and 'no action' in these ways would absolve those at the sentencing stage from inflicting damaging sentences upon those who, arguably, should not be before them in the first place.[106]

Ironically, despite the commitment of successive governments to be 'tough on crime' and the vigorous promotion of a rhetoric of punitiveness in respect of young offenders, the reality of criminal justice practice is that the use of diversionary strategies has increased steadily. Cautioning of young offenders remains at very high levels and, despite attempts to limit the use of repeat cautions, is by far the most common response to offending by those under the age of 18.[107] Whether this dichotomy between the rhetoric of punitiveness and the more humane diversionary practices of the police reflects conflicts in policy, simple confusion, an attempt by politicians to mask the realities of criminal justice practice, or by practitioners to mitigate the demands of punitivism remains open to question.

7. Some Alternative Strategies

Presuming, for the moment that, *pace* the demands of the abolitionists, some young offenders will continue to be brought before the courts for sentence, what suggestions can we make to ensure that sentencing practice is appropriate to their age? We might start by questioning whether a communicative theory of sentencing, in which the declaration of the punishment is intended to convey social condemnation, is appropriate for young offenders. An account of sentencing as a means of censure assumes offenders to be rational 'moral agents capable of understanding others' assessment of their conduct'.[108] This assumption is open to considerable doubt in the case of the young and inexperienced. Since communicative accounts of sentencing presume that those subject to sentence are not merely passive recipients but active participants in their punishment, the capacity of young

---

[105] A reversal of the direction taken by the Criminal Justice and Public Order Act 1994, many of whose provisions criminalize the social and political activities of the young.

[106] See Jung's advocacy of 'strategies of no action', H. Jung, 'Structural Problems of Juvenile Justice Systems', (1982) 27 *The Journal of the Law Society of Scotland* 327.

[107] In 1994, 70% of known offenders under 18 were cautioned for indictable offences: source G. Barclay (ed.), *Information on the Criminal Justice System Digest 3* (London: HMSO, 1995), p. 27. However, the Crime and Disorder Bill 1998 is set to introduce a more formalized system of reprimands and warnings, which might affect the diversion rate for young offenders.

[108] Von Hirsch (1993), n. 59 above, p. 10. See also A. von Hirsch 'Proportionality in the Philosophy of Punishment: From "Why Punish?" to "How Much?" ', (1990) 1 *Criminal Law Forum* 273.

offenders to understand is important.[109] Those who are very young, immature, of limited intelligence or learning may not have the cognitive skills necessary to reflect upon and absorb the condemnation made of them or their peers. If they are incapable of reflecting upon their actions in such a way as to appreciate their wrongfulness, then the efficacy of the act of censure is severely diminished.[110]

The assumption that the most effective means of communicating censure to adults will be equally appropriate for young offenders is clearly open to challenge. Whereas adult offenders may be more readily, though perhaps not universally, impressed by the majesty of the law, the drama of the court, and the solemnity of the judgment, young offenders are liable to be left merely intimidated and confused.[111] The strictures of legalism demand that young offenders enjoy the same procedural safeguards at sentence as adults and have done much to ensure that the procedural injustices associated with rehabilitation are avoided. Yet it is arguable that a more educational approach might be more appropriate and effective in expressing censure in ways which the young offender is capable of understanding. Far from taking such a form as to bypass the offender's status as a moral agent altogether,[112] such punishment would address the young offender directly and in language more apposite than any formal judicial pronouncement. This model of punishment as a form of 'moral education' has been criticized when applied to adults on the grounds that 'we can "educate" someone only if there is something she does not yet know or understand, which we aim to teach her ... we must surely see that many criminals know full well that they are doing wrong'.[113] It is far less likely to be objectionable in the case of young offenders who may well not appreciate that what they are doing is morally wrong nor why.

Censure assumes that we share moral standards by which to judge the wrongness of conduct and the actor's fault.[114] This aspect of censure too rests upon certain questionable assumptions. It presumes a uniformity of moral standards[115] where a plurality exists, and universal adherence to those moral standards enshrined in criminal law where adherence is variable or non-existent. Whilst young offenders may be brought through censure to understand and appreciate the moral standards embodied in the criminal law, they may not regard these standards as ones to which they would willingly subscribe. Either we concede that whilst some moral standards are shared, others are imposed, or we set about

---

[109] Duff (1996), n. 13 above, p. 47.

[110] Even if one denies the importance of the offender's receptivity to censure as von Hirsch does in respect of shame, repentance etc., the capacity to understand surely remains a basic requirement: von Hirsch (1993), n. 59 above, p. 73.

[111] Certainly research on child victims in the same age group reveals high levels of confusion and anxiety about the various actors and activities of the trial process: J. Morgan and L. Zedner, *Child Victims* (Oxford: OUP, 1992) p. 142.

[112] A fear raised by von Hirsch in respect of 'neutral' non-condemnatory sanctions: von Hirsch (1990), n. 108 above, p. 273.

[113] Duff (1996), n. 13 above, p. 47.   [114] Von Hirsch (1993), n. 59 above.

[115] Von Hirsch claims 'It is because we share certain moral standards that a response is required that recognizes both the conduct's wrongfulness and the actor's fault': von Hirsch (1990), n. 108 above, p. 272.

finding ways of persuading young offenders to enter into a moral community they have yet to join. Here we can find guidance in the model of sentencing for young offenders promulgated by international law under the broad heading of 'reintegration'.[116] This approach neither assumes full responsibility on the part of young offenders nor presupposes that they inhabit the same moral world as rational, responsible adults. Rather, the goal of reintegrative punishment is that 'children should be assisted within the community to develop a sense of responsibility which can only be accomplished if the child begins to develop a sense of belonging'.[117] This approach reacts against the tendency of welfare-orientated approaches to focus upon the individual failings of the child in isolation from their wider social environment. Rather, the goal of restoring young offenders to full membership of their community explicitly recognizes the importance of that community to young people's well-being. Forms of penalty which might damage their prospects of successful reintegration or even increase the likelihood of their alienation are to be avoided.[118] And stigmatizing or exclusionary penalties such as incarceration are resisted in favour of those which allow youngsters to maintain normal relations with their family, school, and community. Experiments in New Zealand and Australia with reintegrative shaming techniques such as family group conferences have received strong interest amongst British criminal justice professionals impressed by the powerful psychological impact that confronting young offenders with their victims may have.[119] Originating in Maori dispute resolution, family group conferences bring together the young offender, their family, the victim, and anyone else with a legitimate interest, in the presence of a youth justice co-ordinator who acts as mediator. The primary aim is to get young offenders to take responsibility for what they have done, to recognize the harmful effects of their actions upon the victim and, not least, to create the possibility of reintegrating them into society.

It is questionable whether the labelling of this approach as *re*integration accurately describes the process at hand. If young offenders have never enjoyed the benefits of full citizenship, it is unclear how these can be restored to them. A more honest descriptive tag would recognize that this process is simply 'integrative',

---

[116] Under art. 14(4) of the International Covenant on Civil and Political Rights reintegration has replaced the concept of rehabilitation as the concept upon which juvenile justice should be based. This Covenant, together with the United Nations Standard Minimum Rules for the Administration of Juvenile Justice (the Beijing Rules) (1985); the United Nations Guidelines for the Prevention of Juvenile Delinquency (the Riyadh Rules); and the United Nations Rules for the Protection of Juveniles Deprived of their Liberty, form a corpus of international law laying down principles upon which the sentencing and punishment of young offenders should be based. See van Bueren (1992), n. 27 above, pp. 381–99.

[117] van Bueren (1992), n. 27 above, pp. 381–2; J. Braithwaite, *Crime, Shame and Reintegration* (Cambridge: Cambridge UP, 1990), p. 134.

[118] For a fuller account of the potential of penalties to reintegrate see Braithwaite (1990), n. 117 above.

[119] J. Braithwaite, 'What is to be done about criminal justice?' (unpublished paper); A. Morris, G. Maxwell, and J. Robertson, 'Giving Victims a Voice: A New Zealand Experiment', (1993) 32 *Howard Journal of Criminal Justice* 304–21; NACRO, *A new three Rs for young offenders: responsibility, restoration and reintegration* (London: NACRO, 1997), p. 25.

that is it enables young offenders to acquire both the rights and reciprocal responsibilities of full adult membership of the community. This approach is unashamedly consequentialist in that it seeks to ensure that young offenders develop into full and responsible members of the moral community. Its forward-looking orientation is emphasized in the United Nations Convention on the Rights of the Child (1989) which requires that young offenders be treated in a manner consistent with their age and 'the desirability of promoting the child's reintegration and the child's assuming a constructive role in society'.[120] Unlike rehabilitation, which all too often works *on* the offender through reformative or curative programmes, (re)integration purports to work *with* the offender so that they become the agent of their own reform. This approach has several advantages: it reduces the likelihood that young offenders will be subject to other people's conception of their own good, it deflates the objection that they are made the means to other goals, and it is said to increase the likelihood that the intervention will be effective. Obvious objections, made in respect of all such mediatory techniques, are that they are potentially unfair, entail disproportionate intervention, and foster inconsistency of outcome among like offenders.[121] The question remains whether these potential disadvantages are irresolvable or, indeed, whether they outweigh the potential advantages claimed by the reintegrative approach.

8. Conclusion

Desert theory is predicated upon the justice of punishing responsible actors. Where the actor is less than fully responsible, justice would seem to demand that they receive lesser punishment. To punish third parties in their place simply side-steps the issue of responsibility and, where parents are incapable of exercising effective control, may simply be futile. Nor is the reconstruction of young offenders as calculating rational actors universally plausible. This development is an understandable reaction to the overly determinist accounts prevalent under welfarism, but to the extent that it relies upon a fictional attribution of responsibility where little or none pertains, its legitimacy must be open to doubt. Just as children were found to be suffering multiple deprivation, lacking in experience, learning, and judgement in the 1960s, so today children are not free autonomous, rational actors. At each historical moment the young offender is in part a construct of the sentencer's vivid imagination. The further this construct stands from the realities of children's lives, the less likely it is to form the basis of a just or effective system. Only when sentencing theorists pause to recognize that young offenders pose particular problems for the underlying premises of their theories, can the creation of a thoroughly differentiated, apposite model begin.

---

[120] Art. 40 of the United Nations Convention on the Rights of the Child.
[121] L. Zedner 'Reparation and Retribution: Are they Reconcilable?', (1994) *Modern Law Review* 244–7.

8

Desert, Proportionality, and the Seriousness of Drug Offences

DOUGLAS N. HUSAK

Andrew von Hirsch's central contribution to legal philosophy has been his sustained defence of a desert model of punishment and sentencing. In this chapter I endeavour to apply desert theory and the principle of proportionality to assess the seriousness of drug offences. In section 1, I briefly place the issue of the seriousness of drug offences in the larger context of the ongoing debate about drug policy. In section 2, I raise questions that must be answered before desert theory and the principle of proportionality can be applied to gauge the seriousness of a given offence. In section 3, I describe specific drug offences—and their relative seriousness under current law. In section 4, I explain my reasons for focusing largely on the simple offence of drug possession. Sections 5 and 6 are the heart of this chapter. In these sections, I attempt to apply the theory sketched in section 2 to assess the seriousness of the offences described in section 3—especially to the offence of drug possession. I discuss the harmfulness of drug offences in section 5, and the culpability of drug offenders in section 6. My efforts to apply desert theory to drug offences will prove unsuccessful, perhaps to the point of complete failure. In section 7, I draw some tentative conclusions from my inability to provide a helpful measure of the seriousness of drug offences.

1. THE DRUG POLICY DEBATE AND THE HARM-REDUCTION COMPROMISE

Contemporary debate about the 'drug problem' tends to be polarized by two extreme positions. Prohibitionists usually concede that current policies have achieved only modest success, but promise that tougher laws, stricter enforcement, and longer sentences will eventually lead to victory in the 'war on drugs'. On the other hand, a small but growing number of academics and politicians have come to believe that the use of some or all illicit substances should not be criminalized at all. They typically argue that drug prohibitions are ineffective and counterproductive,[1] and confidently predict that many social and economic benefits would follow if the use and possession of some or all drugs were decriminalized. Moderate alternatives are easily neglected when the debate is focused on extremes.

Suppose, however, that a case can be made in favour of what I will call the **harm-reduction compromise**. According to this intermediate position, drug offences should be regarded as less serious, even though most or all drug users should continue to be punished. Many of the evils caused by the severity of drug prohibitions—congested courts and overcrowded prisons, for example—would be reduced if drug offences were punished less harshly. This alternative would also satisfy some of the concerns of drug prohibitionists. Commentators who defend the status quo are worried that decriminalization would 'send the wrong message' to prospective users who should be instructed in no uncertain terms that society regards drug use as wrongful. Retaining criminal sanctions but reducing the sentences of drug offenders would not be interpreted as a wholesale surrender in the war on drugs.

Implementation of the harm-reduction compromise would be responsive to many of the criticisms of present policy made by concerned citizens and legal officials. Groups such as Families Against Mandatory Minimums—FAMM—were created to urge Congress to repeal the mandatory minimum sentences of drug offenders, not to repeal drug offences altogether. Although only a handful of judges have publicly defended decriminalization,[2] many have expressed outrage about the severity of the punishments they are obligated to impose.[3] Like all compromises, of course, the proposal to lessen the seriousness of drug offences will not satisfy extremists. Ultimately, it will not satisfy me. Nonetheless, the harm-reduction compromise offers obvious benefits as a matter of social policy.

The practical advantages of the harm-reduction compromise are easily demonstrated. But why restrict the focus of debate to drug *policy*? The case in favour of reducing the punishment of drug offenders must not depend solely on political expediency. Persons should be treated as they deserve, and not used merely as a means to serve the State's utilitarian ends. What *do* drug offenders deserve? Attempts to answer this question require a willingness to engage in deep and original thought about the moral principles that underlie a desert theory of punishment. Desert theory consists of deontological principles, rejecting the consequentialist framework so pervasive throughout the history of criminal law and sentencing policy. Much of the foundation for thinking about principles of desert

---

[1] The best summary of this position is presented by Ethan Nadelmann: 'Drug Prohibition in the United States: Costs, Consequences, and Alternatives', (1989) 245 *Science* 939.

[2] One such judge is Robert Sweet. See 'A Federal Judge Enlists', in Arnold Trebach and Kevin Zeese (eds.) *Drug Prohibition and the Conscience of Nations* (Washington: Drug Policy Foundation, 1990), p. 205.

[3] One federal judge wondered whether in coming years he and his fellow jurists would have to assert the Nuremberg Defence—'I was only following orders'—to justify the number of people sentenced to prison for decades. See Jim Newton, 'Judge Denounces Mandatory Sentencing Law Courts; Jurist Gives First-Time Drug Offender a 10-Year Term But Calls System That Imposes the Federal Guidelines "Barbaric" ', *Los Angeles Times*, 19 December 1992, p. B1. See also n. 118 below.

has been built by von Hirsch. Unfortunately, much less scholarly effort has addressed matters of principle in the context of drug offences. Almost all of the participants in the contemporary debate have endeavoured to identify the ideal drug policy—that optimizes the ratio of costs and benefits.[4] But why suppose that whatever approach is ultimately defensible on cost/benefit grounds will succeed in treating persons as they deserve?[5] Principled thought about drug offenders must break new ground.

2. DESERT THEORY AND THE PRINCIPLE OF PROPORTIONALITY

Desert theory, as explicated by von Hirsch, addresses both the question of *why* punishment is justified, as well as the question of *how much* punishment is justified. According to von Hirsch, these two questions are intimately related because penal sanctions convey blame. Punishment both conveys (as a matter of fact) and ought to convey (as a normative matter) censure and disapprobation. If punishment expresses blame, the quantum of punishment should bear a reasonable relation to the blameworthiness of the crime.[6]

The cornerstone of desert theory is the **principle of proportionality**: the severity of punishment should be a function of the seriousness of the offence. Although von Hirsch allows that consequentialist considerations may be incorporated into the overall structure of a desert theory of punishment, he is unwilling to allow these objectives to compromise the principle of proportionality.[7] In part, this position stems from his scepticism that sentencing policy is an effective tool for reducing crime.[8] More importantly, however, this unwillingness derives from his commitment to understand sentencing as an integral part of a theory of justice. The principle of proportionality is an almost inviolable requirement of justice that should not be overridden at the uncertain prospect of utilitarian gains.

The severity of the punishment can be made proportionate to the seriousness of the crime only if degrees of seriousness can be distinguished. However, the judgement that one crime is more or less serious than a very different crime seems much like dealing with apples and oranges. Applications of desert theory and the principle of proportionality to any given offence thus require a solution to what

---

[4] I do not mean to suggest that all proponents of harm-reduction favour the compromise I have described. Many different proposals, including decriminalization, have been defended in the name of harm-reduction. Recent books on harm-reduction policy include Nick Heather, Alax Wodak, Ethan Nadelmann, and Pat O'Hare (eds.), *Psychoactive Drugs & Harm Reduction: From Faith to Science* (London: Whurr Publishers, 1993); and P. O'Hare, R. Newcombe, A. Matthews, E. C. Buning, and E. Drucker (eds.), *The Reduction of Drug-Related Harm* (New York: Routledge, 1992).

[5] See Douglas Husak, 'Two Rationales for Drug Policy: How They Shape the Content of Reform', in Jefferson Fish (ed.), *How to Legalize Drugs* (New York: Jason Aronson, forthcoming, 1997).

[6] Andrew von Hirsch, *Censure and Sanctions* (Oxford: Clarendon Press, 1993), p. 9.

[7] According to von Hirsch, upward departures from proportionality are questionable even to prevent 'an intolerable level of crime': *ibid*, p. 48.

[8] *Ibid*, p. 97.

might be called the **problem of incommensurables**. The difficulty posed by this problem has led many legal philosophers to despair about the prospects of applying desert theory to the real world. It is easy to sympathize with the vague and general proposition that the severity of the punishment must be a function of the seriousness of the crime. It is far more difficult, of course, to apply this abstract claim to particular cases. In order to solve the problem of incommensurables, a common currency is needed to express varying degrees of seriousness.

The problem of incommensurables is compounded because the seriousness of crime is a function of *two* variables. According to von Hirsch, 'the gravity of a crime depends on the degree of harmfulness of the conduct, and the extent of the actor's culpability'.[9] Applications of the principle of proportionality to concrete cases thus require *two* scales: the first to measure the relative harmfulness of offences, the second to gauge the relative culpability of offenders.[10]

Begin with the former variable—harm. The first step in applying the principle of proportionality to a particular case is to identify the harm sought to be prevented by the offence. Usually, this determination requires no ingenuity. To be sure, the exact nature of the interests violated by a few crimes remains controversial. Typically, however, the far more difficult issue is not to identify which harm an offence is designed to prevent, but to assess whether one such harm is greater or lesser than another. In order to rank-order the harms caused by different kinds of offences, some criterion is needed to decide whether violations of our interest in economic security, for example, are more or less harmful than violations of our interest in liberty. The problem of incommensurables is most formidable at this stage of the inquiry.

The search for a common denominator in which to express various kinds of harms has consumed much of von Hirsch's scholarly attention.[11] In collaboration with Nils Jareborg, he came to settle on what they describe as a **living-standard** analysis to gauge the relative harmfulness of various crimes.[12] Von Hirsch writes: 'Victimizing harms are to be ranked in gravity according to how much they typically would reduce a person's standard of living'.[13] The importance of the various interests violated by different crimes is placed on a common scale by assessing their normal significance for a person's living standard. Mayhem is

---

[9] Ibid, p. 29.

[10] Of course, a third scale is needed as well—to assess the *severity* of punishments. Modes of punishment other than imprisonment introduce a new layer of complexity into the analysis. Von Hirsch has attempted to gauge the severity of some of these different modes of punishment. See Andrew von Hirsch, Martin Wasik, and Judith Greene, 'Punishments in the Community and the Principles of Desert', (1989) 20 *Rutgers Law Journal* 595.

[11] At one time, von Hirsch favoured using the concept of *choice* as the common denominator to measure the relative seriousness of different kinds of harms. A violation of our interest in economic security, for example, is more grave than a violation of our interest in physical well-being if and to the extent that the former more greatly curtails the options available to the persons who suffer these harms. See Andrew von Hirsch, *Past Or Future Crimes* (New Brunswick: Rutgers University Press, 1985), pp. 65–71.

[12] Andrew von Hirsch and Nils Jareborg, 'Gauging Criminal Harm: A Living-Standard Analysis', (1991) 11 *Oxford Journal of Legal Studies* 1.

[13] Von Hirsch (1993), n. 6 above, p. 30.

more harmful than burglary, for example, because the overall quality of the maimed person's life is more adversely affected.[14]

A few aspects of this analysis will prove especially important for my purposes. Particular crimes are **act-tokens** rather than **act-types**. The harm caused by different tokens of the same type can vary enormously. Sam's act-token of theft might cause almost no harm—his victim is relieved to be rid of the defective automobile that is stolen—while Dave's act-token of theft might cause enormous hardship. Yet judgements about the seriousness of crime are about act-types rather than act-tokens. Von Hirsch bridges the gap from tokens to types by using what he calls a 'standard case'. Recall that harms are ranked in gravity according to how they *typically* reduce a person's standard of living.[15] If Sam's token of theft is unlike to a typical case, principles of aggravation or mitigation can be applied to increase or decrease the severity of his punishment. Von Hirsch has not commented in detail about how standard cases are to be constructed. In what follows, I will assume that standard cases are constructed statistically;[16] the harmfulness of a typical case of theft, for example, depends on empirical data about the extent of economic loss (and other possible kinds of losses) caused by the statistically average theft. Since standard cases are derived statistically, theorists should be prepared to revise their presuppositions about the harmfulness of a given type of offence in the light of new empirical data. As von Hirsch and Jareborg insist, 'judgments of blameworthiness of conduct (including those of harm) reflect how much the offender and his conduct **ought** to be blamed, not just how reprehensible this or that decision-maker or constituency happens to think the conduct is'.[17]

Notice that this approach is viable only if legislators have done an adequate job in creating and defining offences. The use of statistical averages to identify the harmfulness of an act-type is meaningful only if that type is defined with the appropriate degree of breadth. Suppose that legislators have done their job poorly, and enacted only one crime—'the infliction of bodily injury'—to protect our interest in physical well-being. In this imaginary jurisdiction, defendants who kill would commit the same crime as defendants who merely scratch their victims. Attempts to identify the quantum of harm caused by the statistically average instance of 'infliction of bodily injury' would not be very informative about particular cases. The amount of harm caused by tokens of this crime would vary so widely that nearly every case would qualify for mitigation or aggravation.

Von Hirsch has said relatively little about culpability—the second variable used to measure the seriousness of crime. He has focused less attention on this variable because he is generally satisfied with its treatment in positive law.[18] Von Hirsch largely concurs with the culpability structure of the Model Penal Code, which assigns greater blame to persons who commit a given criminal act

---

[14] *Ibid*, p. 31.   [15] *Ibid*, p. 30 (emphasis added).
[16] Other alternatives may be available. Perhaps there exist a number of standard cases within a given offence, each representing different types of that offence.
[17] Von Hirsch and Jareborg (1991), n. 12 above, p. 6.
[18] See von Hirsch (1993), n. 6 above, pp. 29–30.

negligently, recklessly, knowingly, or purposely.[19] He is prepared to tinker with this structure, but any refinements he might propose would be unimportant for the purpose at hand.

However these two variables are combined into a coherent solution to the problem of incommensurables, the most serious crimes will cause a major harm performed with a high degree of culpability, and the least serious crimes will cause a minor harm performed with a low degree of culpability. These generalizations should prove helpful in assessing the seriousness of drug offences. If drug offences should be regarded as serious, they must involve both a great deal of culpability and a large quantum of harm.

3. The Seriousness of Drug Offences Under Current Law

Theorists who are convinced that drug offenders are punished too severely usually present their case through aggregate statistics. Despite their familiarity, these figures still retain their capacity to shock. I will only summarize some of the more extraordinary data.

The USA now incarcerates more persons than any country.[20] By the end of 1995, more than 1.58 million inmates were in Federal and state prisons and local jails.[21] This tremendous rate of incarceration is due largely to increased penalties for drug offenders. The more than $68 billion invested in domestic and foreign drug enforcement by the Federal Government since 1981 has radically altered the profile of the prison population.[22] The number of drug offenders convicted in federal courts has more than tripled in the past decade, and drug offenders now occupy 61 per cent of the beds in federal prisons.[23] 21.5 per cent of all federal inmates are low-level drug offenders with no record of violence and no involvement in sophisticated criminal activity.[24] 42.3 per cent of these offenders were couriers or persons who played peripheral roles in drug trafficking schemes.[25] The average sentence for all drug offenders is 86 months, which requires them to serve an average of 72 months.[26] More than $20,000 a year is needed to house a federal inmate, so the total cost to taxpayers is over $115,000 per prisoner for the duration of his sentence.[27] Despite these remarkable rates of incarceration, about

[19] See Model Penal Code, 2.02.
[20] See Margaret Spencer, 'Sentencing Drug Offenders: The Incarceration Addiction', (1995) 40 *Villanova Law Review* 335, 338.
[21] U.S. Department of Justice, Bureau of Justice Statistics, *Prison and Jail Inmates, 1995* (Bulletin, August, 1996).
[22] See Eva Bertram, Morris Blachman, Kenneth Sharpe, and Peter Andreas, *Drug War Politics* (Berkeley: University of California Press, 1996), p. 10.
[23] Spencer (1995), n. 20 above, p. 365.
[24] U.S. Department of Justice, 'An Analysis of Non-Violent Drug Offenders with Minimal Criminal Histories', (1994) 54 *Criminal Law Reporter* 2101, 2108–9.
[25] *Ibid.*
[26] U.S. Department of Justice, Bureau of Justice Statistics, *Drugs and Crime Facts* (1994), p. 18.
[27] See 'Low Level Drug Offenders Fill One-Fifth of Prison Space', *Washington Post*, 5 February 1994, p. A4.

23 million Americans continue to use illegal drugs each year, and half do so at least once a month.[28] The vast majority of drug offenders evade detection and prosecution. About seven-eighths of the persistent cocaine and heroin users, for example, are unpunished.[29]

But these aggregate statistics, however appalling, are not especially helpful in attempts to assess the seriousness of drug offences. These figures may be more meaningful to taxpayers who hope to save money than to citizens who aspire to a just system of sentencing. Are the punishments imposed on drug offenders deserved and consistent with the principle of proportionality? An attempt to address this question must begin by examining specific drug offences and the sentences imposed on particular persons who violate them. Thus I begin with a brief look at drug statutes.

Most commentaries on drug offences focus on federal law. This emphasis is misplaced. By any measure, states are far more active in enforcing drug prohibitions than the Federal Government, as almost 1.5 million persons were arrested for drug offences by state and local police in 1995.[30] In what follows, I will use the drug laws of New Jersey as illustrative of state law, while examining federal drug law in somewhat less detail. With the Comprehensive Drug Reform Act of 1987, New Jersey has recently overhauled its drug offences, giving the statutory scheme a degree of coherence sometimes lacked in other states—or under federal law.[31]

The most basic drug offence in the New Jersey hierarchy of drug crimes prohibits the actual or constructive possession of any substance on the state's schedule of 'controlled dangerous substances'.[32] The degree of the crime depends on the identity of the substance and the quantity possessed. Mere possession of most controlled substances subjects defendants to a term of imprisonment between 3 and 5 years and a fine of as much as $25,000. Possession of more than 50 grams of marijuana calls for a sentence of up to 18 months in prison and a fine of the same amount. Possession of less than 50 grams of marijuana is punished by a term of imprisonment not to exceed 90 days and a $1,000 fine.

A more serious offence applies to persons who manufacture, distribute, or dispense controlled substances, or who possess with intent to distribute or dispense such substances.[33] This statute is generally used when the quantity of the controlled substance is greater than that governed by the simple possession statute. Possession of more than 5 ounces of heroin or cocaine (or possession of more than 100 milligrams of LSD) results in a term of imprisonment between 10 and 20 years and a fine of up to $300,000. Defendants must serve between one-third and

---

[28] *National Household Survey on Drug Abuse, Population Estimates 1995* (Washington D.C.: U.S. Government Printing Offices, 1996).

[29] Elliot Currie, *Reckoning: Drugs, the Cities, and the American Future* (New York: Hill and Wang, 1993), p. 151.

[30] U.S. Department of Justice, Federal Bureau of Investigation, *Crime in the United States, 1995, Uniform Crime Reports* (1995), p. 208.

[31] Federal drug law contains a bewildering patchwork of offences scattered in various places. A nice summary can be found in Theodore Valliant, *Prohibition's Second Failure* (Westport, Conn.: Prager, 1993), Appendix A.

[32] New Jersey Criminal Code, 2C:35–10.   [33] *Ibid*, 2C:35–5.

one-half of this sentence, during which time they are ineligible for parole. Possession of between half an ounce and 5 ounces of heroin or cocaine subjects offenders to a term of imprisonment between 5 and 10 years and a fine of $100,000. Possession of less than one-half ounce of heroin or cocaine carries a term of imprisonment between 3 and 5 years and fines as high as $50,000. Again, marijuana is governed by separate provisions.

These two basic offences in New Jersey are supplemented by a number of additional statutes that apply in circumstances in which defendants are believed to be especially culpable or drug use is regarded as excessively dangerous. Repeat offenders are subjected to extended terms of imprisonment.[34] Most important are those several provisions that increase the seriousness of drug offences that involve minors. Fines and terms of imprisonment are doubled if a defendant distributes a controlled substance to a person 17 years of age or younger.[35] Persons who distribute or possess with intent to distribute a controlled substance within 1,000 feet of school property must be sentenced to imprisonment of at least one year in the case of marijuana, or at least 3 years in the case of other controlled substances.[36] An adult who directs or employs a person 17 years or younger in a drug distribution scheme is sentenced to a mandatory term of imprisonment of at least 5 years with no prospect of parole.[37] In view of recent increases in teenage marijuana use, politicians have denounced these punishments as inadequate to deter minors. New Jersey Governor Christine Whitman has recently promised to propose legislation to 'increase penalties for drug pushers'.[38]

The most serious drug offence in New Jersey imposes 'strict liability for drug-induced deaths'.[39] Any person who manufactures or distributes most of the well-known controlled substances such as heroin, cocaine, or marijuana to someone who dies as a result of using that substance is criminally liable for the death. The provisions governing the causal relationship between conduct and result that pertain to other homicide offences do not apply when a defendant is charged with this strict-liability crime.

New Jersey has created a somewhat novel way to deal with situations in which laboratory tests reveal that the substance possessed or distributed by the defendant was not in fact a controlled substance. Some defendants are aware that their substance is uncontrolled, and seek to cheat their customers; others have been cheated themselves, and are surprised to learn that their substance is uncontrolled. Since a defendant cannot be guilty of possessing or distributing a controlled substance if the substance he actually possesses or distributes is uncontrolled, these situations are typically treated as ordinary attempts. New Jersey, however, has created a separate crime for persons who represent that a substance is controlled, or who create circumstances that would lead a reasonable person to believe that a substance is controlled.[40] This statute applies even when the recipient is aware that

---

[34] New Jersey Criminal Code, 2C:43–6(f).   [35] *Ibid*, 2C:35–8.   [36] *Ibid*, 2C:35–7.
[37] *Ibid*, 2C:35–6.
[38] See 'Drug Use Is Up in High Schools', *New York Times*, 9 October 1996, p. B1.
[39] New Jersey Criminal Code, 2C:35–9.   [40] *Ibid*, 2C:35–11.

the substance is not in fact controlled, but is told that it has the appearance of a controlled substance so that he will be able to distribute it as such.

In addition to the foregoing penalties, persons found guilty of a drug offence in New Jersey are subject to a number of additional sanctions beyond fine or imprisonment.[41] For example, some persons convicted of mere possession of small amounts near a school zone are required to perform at least 100 hours of community service.[42] Perhaps the most important of these sanctions requires all drug offenders to forfeit their driver's licences for at least 6 months but not more than 2 years.[43] Although many legal philosophers have neglected these sorts of additional sanctions, von Hirsch recognizes that those that are clearly punitive—such as the above—are subject to the limitations of proportionality and desert that apply to more conventional modes of punishment.[44] In what follows, I will not even mention what is perhaps the most punitive of the civil sanctions used against drug offenders—the forfeiture of assets such as homes and cars that are alleged to be used in the commission of a drug offence.[45]

Several states differ from New Jersey in one important respect. Although every state treats the possession of marijuana as an offence, several states impose only a fine on persons convicted of possessing small amounts.[46] Arizona, as a result of a recent voter referendum, prohibits a jail sentence for first-time possessors of any illegal drug.[47] Alaska actually affords constitutional protection to the use of marijuana in the home.[48]

Federal drug offences are similar to those in New Jersey. Sentencing, however, is altogether different. Under federal law, punishments are derived from the interaction of mandatory minimum statutes with the sentencing guidelines.[49] The Anti-Drug Abuse Act of 1986 eliminated the flexibility of federal judges to tailor sentences to the circumstances of particular cases by including a number of mandatory minimum sentences for drug offences. The 1988 Amendments to the

---

[41] Federal law also provides for a number of additional sanctions for drug offenders. For example, residents of public housing are evicted if any member of the household or guest is involved in certain drug offences. Moreover, new welfare legislation imposes a lifetime ban on cash assistance and food stamps for persons convicted of a drug felony. President Clinton has recently proposed that persons be required to pass a drug test as a condition for receiving a driver's licence.

[42] New Jersey Criminal Code, 2C:35–10(4).

[43] *Ibid*, 2C:35–16.

[44] See Andrew von Hirsch and Martin Wasik, 'Civil Disqualifications Attending Conviction' (1997) 56 *Cambridge LJ* 599.

[45] See Henry Hyde, *Forfeiting Our Property Rights* (Washington: Cato Institute, 1995). See also Leonard Levy, *License to Steal* (Chapel Hill: University of North Carolina Press, 1996).

[46] This approach is sometimes misleadingly described as 'decriminalization'. For a non-technical summary of state law, see Richard Boire, *Marijuana Law* (Berkeley: Ronin Pub. Co., 1993), p. 21.

[47] 'Votes on Marijuana Are Stirring Debate', *New York Times*, 17 November 1996, p. A16.

[48] See *Ravin* v. *State*, 537 P.2d 494 (Alaska 1975).

[49] The sentencing guidelines create a table of 43 levels. These base levels are adjusted by the defendant's prior record, his acceptance of responsibility for his criminal conduct, and the extent of his particular role in the offence. Unless the court concludes that a departure is justified, the sentencing table determines the appropriate sentencing range. For a clear summary, see William Wilkins, Phyllis Newton, and John Steer, 'Competing Sentencing Policies in a "War on Drugs" Era', (1993) 28 *Wake Forest Law Review* 305.

Anti-Drug Abuse Act imposed mandatory minimums for simple possessory offences, and the Violent Crime Control and Law Enforcement Act of 1994 significantly increased these mandatory minimums.[50] For example, 2 years' imprisonment and/or a fine of $1,000 is imposed for simple possession of a controlled substance. The average sentence actually imposed for mere possession under federal law is 22 months.[51] Simple possession of more than 5 grams of cocaine results in a minimum sentence of 5 years and a maximum of 20 years. The punishments imposed for possession of crack are especially harsh. The maximum term of imprisonment for possession of up to 5 grams of crack is one year, but a first offender convicted of simple possession of more than five grams receives a mandatory minimum of 5 years. 500 grams of cocaine are needed before defendants receive a 5 year mandatory minimum, thus creating the notorious 100–1 sentencing disparity that has given rise to outraged commentary.[52] In 1995, the Sentencing Commission recommended that Congress re-evaluate the disparity in punishment between cocaine and crack. Both Houses of Congress rejected the Commission's recommendation.

Federal punishments for manufacture or distribution are severe. Persons convicted of possession with intent to distribute at least 100 grams of heroin, 500 grams of cocaine, 5 grams of crack, or 100 kilograms of marijuana receive a 5 to 40 year sentence, without probation or parole. Defendants who intend to distribute larger amounts—one kilogram of heroin, 5 kilograms of cocaine, 50 grams of crack, 10 grams of LSD, or 1,000 kilograms of marijuana—receive a sentence of 10 years to life, again without probation or parole. These mandatory minimums are doubled for defendants with a prior conviction for a drug felony, and are increased still further if drugs are distributed to a person under 21, to a pregnant woman, or near a school.

Under federal law, a defendant may evade the mandatory minimum sentence in only one way. Upon a motion by the prosecution—which remains within his discretion—the sentence can be reduced for 'substantial assistance' in the investigation or prosecution of other drug offenders. This exception, of course, is far more likely to be available to persons who play central roles in drug distribution schemes. Far more prevalent are sentence enhancement provisions. Offenders with a prior criminal history, or who use a gun, or who create a substantial risk of bodily harm to others, or who victimize someone especially vulnerable, are all subject to increased sentences.

[50] Mandatory minimums are extraordinarily unpopular with judges and commentators. For one recent discussion, see Karen Lutjen, 'Culpability and Sentencing Under Mandatory Minimums and the Federal Sentencing Guidelines: The Punishment No Longer Fits the Criminal', (1996) 10 *Notre Dame Journal of Law, Ethics & Public Policy* 389. Among other difficulties, the 'cliff' established by these guidelines has been subjected to frequent criticism. See Stephen Schulhofer, 'Rethinking Mandatory Minimums', (1993) 28 *Wake Forest Law Review* 199.

[51] U.S. Department of Justice, Bureau of Justice Statistics, *Drugs and Crime Facts* (1994), p. 18. In state courts, the average prison sentence for persons convicted of drug possession is 4 years and one month, of which the estimated time to be served is 13 months. *Ibid*, p. 20.

[52] See Gerald Heaney, 'The Reality of Guideline Sentencing: No End to Disparity', (1991) 28 *American Criminal Law Review* 161.

Are these sentences disproportionate to the offences for which they are imposed? No assistance in answering this question is likely to be offered by courts. For all practical purposes, the Supreme Court has held that the 'cruel and unusual punishment' clause of the Eighth Amendment does not contain a requirement of proportionality.[53] Not surprisingly, this holding was reached in the context of a drug offence, where differences of opinion about the seriousness of the crime are likely to be especially great.[54] A first-time offender convicted of simple possession of 672 grams of cocaine had been sentenced to life imprisonment without parole—the most severe punishment allowed in his state. Since the Court was largely unwilling to apply the principle of proportionality, it evaded the difficult issue of identifying the degree to which drug possession is a serious offence. An answer to this question must come from legal philosophers rather than from the judiciary.

4. The Focus on the Offence of Simple Drug Possession

With the foregoing statutory provisions in mind, the groundwork has almost been prepared for an examination of the seriousness of drug offences. In what follows, I will focus largely (but not exclusively) on the seriousness of the simple offence of drug possession. Contrary to what many persons tend to assume, drug possession is typically a single offence—that is, all persons who illegally possess a controlled substance commit the very same crime, regardless of *what* drug they possess.[55]

I focus on the offence of simple possession for theoretical as well as for practical reasons. Conceptually, this offence is the most basic in the hierarchy of drug crimes. I see no prospects for assessing the seriousness of other drug offences without a prior understanding of the seriousness of possession. If drugs were not possessed (and ultimately used), it is hard to see why anyone would be worried about them.[56] All of the evils of drugs, real or imaginary, stem from their use.[57]

---

[53] See *Harmelin* v. *Michigan*, 501 U.S. 957 (1990). In light of the complexity and sheer number of the separate opinions written in this case, any conclusion about the status of proportionality review is necessarily tentative.

[54] In dissent, Justice White wrote that 'the "absolute magnitude" of petitioner's crime is not exceptionally serious': *ibid*, 1024. 'Mere possession of drugs—even in such a large quantity—is not so serious an offence that it will always warrant, let alone mandate, life imprisonment without possibility of parole': *ibid*, 1022. But in a separate concurrence, Justice Kennedy alleged that the defendant's 'suggestion that his crime was nonviolent and victimless, echoed by the dissent, is false to the point of absurdity': *ibid*, 1002.

[55] I describe the implications of treating drug possession as a single offence in Part 6 below.

[56] Most jurisdictions fail to punish drug use *per se*. I do not attach any deep significance to this failure. An offence of possession is far easier to enforce and to prove than an offence of use. I regard the offence of drug possession as a surrogate for an offence of drug use.

[57] On the other hand, most (but not all) jurisdictions allow a person to be convicted for simple drug possession even though the quantity or quality of the drug possessed could *not* be used. A seed of marijuana vacuumed from the carpet of a car, or a residue of heroin scraped from a spoon cannot be used to obtain a drug 'high'—but are usually sufficient to allow a conviction.

The more serious offence of distribution seems designed to prevent the more widespread use of drugs.[58] If the seriousness of the offence of drug possession can be identified, the principle of proportionality might be easier to apply to more serious drug offences. Or so I will assume.

From a practical point of view, simple possession is the most frequently enforced crime in the arsenal of drug offences. In the last decade, between 70 and 75 per cent of all drug arrests have been for simple possession.[59] Many of these arrests involve marijuana; approximately 350,000 persons are arrested for marijuana possession every year,[60] and over two-thirds of all persons sentenced for simple drug possession in federal courts possessed marijuana.[61] Insofar as any trend in law enforcement can be detected, there is little reason to believe that substantial efforts are underway to shift resources toward the arrest and prosection of higher-level drug offenders. In an era of 'zero tolerance', possession is still 'the stuff of criminal justice work'.[62]

A critical appraisal of the desert of persons convicted of simple drug possession is urgently needed. It is noteworthy that the quantum of punishment for drug offences generally, and for possession in particular, has steadily increased.[63] For the most part, this trend has not been supported by new empirical findings that illicit drugs are more dangerous than previously believed. Instead, the rationale for more punitive measures is that deterrence is perceived as inadequate. Although the number of drug offenders has decreased from its modern peak around 1979,[64] the level is still regarded as unacceptably high. This rationale for severe punishments, of course, is at odds with desert theory.

In short, the offence of simple possession is both theoretically and practically challenging for a desert theory of punishment and sentencing. It is theoretically challenging because it raises many conceptual difficulties in understanding and applying desert theory. Admittedly, other existing offences—such as blackmail—raise vexing conceptual problems as well.[65] But a theory can survive intact as long as difficulties in application are relatively infrequent and unimportant. The conceptual problems that arise in applying desert theory to drug possession, however, pose a unique practical challenge. This offence is enforced with such frequency that the problems in applying desert theory cannot be dismissed as insignificant anomalies. If these problems turn out to be substantial,

---

[58] For an argument (which the author ultimately rejects) that construes the harm of drug distribution as analogous to exploitation and blackmail, see Peter Alldridge, 'Dealing with Drug Dealing', in A. P. Simester and A. T. H. Smith (eds.), *Harm and Culpability* (Oxford: Clarendon-Press, 1996), p. 239.

[59] Office of National Drug Control Policy, *National Drug Control Strategy* (Washington, D.C.: U.S. Government Printing Office, 1992), p. 99.

[60] Mark Kleiman, *Against Excess* (New York: Basic Books, 1992), p. 267.

[61] United States Sentencing Commission, *Cocaine and Federal Sentencing Policy* (1995), p. 155.

[62] See Mike Collison, 'Drug Crime, Drug Problems and Criminal Justice: Sentencing Trends and Enforcement Targets', (1994) 33 *Howard Journal of Criminal Justice* 25, 37.

[63] See Spencer (1995), n. 20 above.

[64] See Bertram *et al* (1996), n. 22 above, p. 269.

[65] See the Symposium in (1993) 141 *University of Pennsylvania Law Review* 1565–989.

commentators may be forced to rethink the justifiability of the offence of drug possession—or the viability of desert theory itself.

I finally turn to a discussion of these problems.

5. The Seriousness of Drug Offences: Harm

Two separate inquiries are needed to apply the principle of proportionality to assess the seriousness of drug offences. Since the seriousness of crime is a function of harm and culpability, each of these two dimensions of drug offences must be examined. In this section, I investigate the harmfulness of drug offences; I turn to a consideration of culpability in section 6.

Applications of the principle of proportionality require, first, that the harm of a given offence be identified. Usually, this determination is straightforward. In the vast majority of cases, the interests violated by particular offences are readily described. Thus, von Hirsch expends more effort attempting to express these various interests in the common currency of his living-standard analysis than to provide detailed instructions about how to identify the nature of the harm in the first place.

In the present context, however, the task of identifying the harm sought to be prevented is more problematic. There simply is no consensus about the nature of the harm that the offence of drug possession is designed to curb.[66] Nor is there an authoritative source in which the 'official' rationale for drug prohibitions can be found. I see little alternative but to rely on the writings of commentators who have argued in favour of the justifiability of drug offences. Even this device will prove far from definitive, as commentators provide very different answers to the question of what harm the offence of drug possession seeks to prevent. In order to avoid begging questions, I will refer to the harm(s) that the offence of drug possession is designed to prevent as harm X.[67] In what follows, I cannot discuss each and every opinion that anyone has ever advanced about the nature of harm X. One commentator or another has purported to link drugs to every imaginable

---

[66] Perhaps the offence of drug possession is not designed to prevent a harm at all. Drug possession might be proscribed simply because it is regarded as immoral. Legal moralists contend that the immorality of conduct, apart from any harm it might cause, provides sufficient reason to proscribe it. Legal moralism has played a prominent role in the thought of commentators who have endeavoured to support the seriousness of drug offences. Yet the legal moralist defence of drug prohibitions as serious offences encounters three difficulties, each of which I believe to be insuperable. First, legal moralism itself has been widely discredited. Secondly, no good reason has been given to believe that drug use is immoral, apart from the harm it might cause. Thirdly, no one has a clue about how to apply the principle of proportionality to assess the seriousness of immorality apart from its harmfulness. If immorality were sufficient for criminality, one would expect that the seriousness of crime would be proportionate to the extent of its wrongfulness. But *harmless* immoralities, if they exist at all and are justifiably subjected to criminal punishment, can hardly be among the most wrongful acts that a moral theory would recognize. The best discussion is found in Joel Feinberg, *Harmless Wrongdoing* (New York: Oxford University Press, 1989).

[67] Although I will refer to the harm of drug possession as singular rather than plural, I do not suppose that there must be just *one* state of affairs this offence is designed to prevent.

social evil. All I can hope to accomplish is to briefly survey some of the more plausible candidates. I will proceed by sorting these candidates into two general kinds: paternalistic and non-paternalistic rationales for drug prohibitions.

Unfortunately, the ensuing analysis will be complicated by at least three factors. First, notice that von Hirsch and Jareborg acknowledge that 'there is no unitary account that can explain the harm dimension in all kinds of crimes'.[68] They invoke their living-standard analysis only to assess the harmfulness of what they call *victimizing* offences—characterized as criminal conduct 'which injures or threatens *identifiable victims*'.[69] For other categories of crimes—they cite the example of cruelty to animals—'something other than a living-standard analysis would be needed'.[70] Is drug possession a victimizing offence? If not, it may be inappropriate to assess its seriousness by a living-standard analysis, and my whole inquiry becomes misplaced.

It is hard to be certain. The concept of a 'victimizing offence'—a crime that injures or threatens 'identifiable victims'—is not altogether precise. First, consider the requirement that the crime must create a victim. Unless conduct causes a bad state of affairs, it is hard to see why anyone would want to proscribe it. And it is equally hard to see how conduct *could* cause a bad state of affairs unless it were detrimental to some person who thereby is *victimized*.[71] Next, consider the requirement that the victim must be identifiable. A psychopath who kills by randomly firing his gun into a crowd surely creates *victims*—but are they *identifiable*? Victims can be identified *ex post*, after the carnage is complete; is there any good reason to demand that they must have been identifiable *ex ante*, prior to the criminal conduct? I hope to avoid (at least temporarily) some of the difficulties that arise in confining the scope of the inquiry to victimizing offences. Fortunately (for my project), few of those commentators who argue that drug offences are relatively serious would be willing to concede that these crimes lack identifiable victims. They prominently display the faces of all-too identifiable victims on televisions every day. Before abandoning my project, a good-faith effort is needed to try to understand drug possession as a victimizing offence. If this inquiry stalls, the classification of drug possession as an offence that creates identifiable victims can be reconsidered.[72]

A second complication emerges from the need to measure the harm of a given offence by reference to a standard case. Generalizations about the harm caused by drug possession should not be derived from unusual scenarios involving pilots, brain surgeons, pregnant women, or the like. The criminal law might enact (and, for the most part has enacted) specific statutes to proscribe the harms caused by drug use in these atypical situations. The need to construct a standard case, however, jeopardizes my proposal to rely on the opinions of commentators

---

[68] Von Hirsch and Jareborg (1991), n. 12 above, p. 34.   [69] *Ibid*, p. 3.   [70] *Ibid*, p. 34.
[71] In other words, drug use is unlikely to be categorized as what Feinberg describes as a 'free-floating evil'—that 'are not the ground of plausible grievances' and 'have no adverse effects on anyone's well-being'. See Feinberg (1989), n. 66 above, p. 20.
[72] See below.

to identify the nature of the harm X sought to be prevented by possessory offences. Much of what these commentators have said about the evils of drugs is based on worst-case scenarios. The identifiable victims displayed on television screens may not have been created by standard cases of drug use at all. Empirical data, not anecdotal evidence, are required to construct a standard case. But the use of empirical data to construct a standard case is further complicated by the fact that drug possession is a single offence, regardless of the kind of drug possessed. A single offence to proscribe the possession of each and every controlled substance is extraordinarily broad. It is hard enough to be confident about the nature of the harm X to be prevented by a standard case of the possession of a given drug such as marijuana. But if the class of proscribed activities is enlarged to include the possession of all illicit substances, the use of a statistical average to identify a standard case is even less meaningful. The harm to be prevented by the possession of an inexpensive and non-addictive substance such as LSD may be quite unlike the harm to be prevented by the possession of a costly and addictive substance such as heroin.

A third preliminary complication is as follows. In identifying the harm X to be prevented by a standard case of drug possession, it is surely inappropriate to include the harms that would not have been caused were possession of that drug not illegal. Theorists who favour a fundamental change in drug policy never tire of pointing out that many of the harms typically attributed to drugs are more plausibly attributed to drug prohibitions.[73] The harms caused by drugs themselves, however, are difficult to disentangle from the harms caused by drug laws. Consider, for example, the high incidence of economic crime associated with drugs—in particular, the thefts committed by addicts to gain money to buy drugs. Is this harm caused by drugs, or by drug prohibitions? To answer this question, one would have to contrast the rate of economic crime in otherwise identical worlds that have and lack drug prohibitions. Needless to say, no such controlled experiment could be conducted. The plausibility of the claim that economic crime would be drastically reduced if drugs were not proscribed depends in large part on how the number of users and the price of drugs would be affected by the repeal of drug prohibitions—and any such estimates are highly speculative. Still, no can deny that *some* of the harms associated with drugs—perhaps a great many—are properly attributed to drug prohibitions, and thus have no place in an assessment of the seriousness of drug possession.

Despite these three complications, I finally turn to the central issue: What *is* the harm X to be prevented by the offence of drug possession? Competing kinds of answers to this question can be contrasted by reference to the different persons alleged to be victimized by drug possession. Perhaps the person most likely to be victimized is the defendant himself. Much (and probably most) of the hardship caused by drug use is suffered by the drug user. According to this school of thought, the offence of drug possession is an instance of criminal *paternalism*,

---

[73] See Nadelmann (1989), n. 1 above.

designed to prevent the various injuries[74] that users inflict on themselves. If construed as an instance of paternalism, an assessment of the harmfulness of the offence of drug possession depends largely on the degree to which a standard case is injurious to the user. A lifetime of empirical research would be required to settle this matter. I will restrict myself to five brief observations about paternalistic rationales for drug prohibitions.[75]

First, drug use does not appear to be especially dangerous to standard persons. The majority of drug users are under the age of 25, after which time most 'mature out' of drug use.[76] As a class, there is little reason to conclude that these persons are less physically healthy than abstainers of comparable age. Of course, the health hazards of different drugs must be distinguished. Not surprisingly, the most popular drugs are the least unhealthy. Despite years of federal funding, there is no reliable evidence of any substantial adverse effects on the health of regular smokers of marijuana.[77] But what of psychological effects? If drugs were very detrimental to psychological well-being, one would expect that differences between the mental health of users and non-users would be detected by longitudinal studies of these two classes of persons. The most extensive such study concludes that adults who used moderate amounts of drugs as adolescents (and who outnumbered either heavy drug users or total abstainers) are 'the psychologically healthiest subjects, healthier than either abstainers or frequent users'.[78]

Secondly, any data about the severity of the injuries suffered by drug users must be placed in context by comparing the dangers of drugs with the dangers of various other activities. After all, judgements about the seriousness of crime are essentially comparative. Data about licit substances such as tobacco—which kills far more people than all illicit substances combined—are relevant here. But the severity of injuries suffered by persons who engage in activities that do not involve the use of substances—such as mountain climbing and boxing—are equally relevant. These risky activities are not (and presumably ought not to be) crimes at all. Illicit drug use is not prominent among the vast array of activities that are injurious to persons.

[74] I describe the states of affairs to be prevented by paternalistic legislation as *injuries* rather than as *harms* because I understand a harm to be a violation of a right. Unless persons can have rights against themselves, those who break paternalistic laws do not violate rights. Although it is doubtful that persons *can* harm themselves, I assume that persons *are* able to *injure* themselves—notwithstanding the maxim '*volenti non fit injuria*' (what is done to a man with his voluntary consent cannot be injury).

[75] For further discussion, see Douglas Husak 'Recreational Drugs and Paternalism', (1989) 8 *Law and Philosophy*, p. 353.

[76] Although more than 16% of persons aged 18 to 25 reported recent use of an illegal drug in 1988, about half this many persons (8.3%) continued to report recent illegal drug use when they reached the ages of 26 to 34. Only 2.8% of persons 35 or over reported recent drug use in 1995. Thus, most persons who use illegal drugs quit. See each annual *National Household Survey on Drug Abuse, Population Estimates* (Washington D.C.: U.S. Government Printing Office).

[77] See the discussion and references in Lynn Zimmer and John Morgan, *Exposing Marijuana Myths: A Review of the Scientific Evidence* (New York: Open Society Institute, Lindesmith Center, 1996).

[78] See Jonathan Shedler and Jack Block, 'Adolescent Drug Use and Psychological Health', (1990) 45 *American Psychologist* 612, 625.

Thirdly, no data about *aggregate* injuries seem especially meaningful here. A defendant becomes liable by a single act of possession; he need not have engaged in persistent drug use to be eligible for punishment. Thus the relevant statistic would identify the extent of physical or psychological injury to users *per* offence. But even if accurate data about the aggregate health hazards caused by drugs could be obtained, any attempt to divide this total by the number of offences—to identify the quantum of injury per offence—would be problematic. No theoretical problem arises in counting the number of burglaries, for example, and dividing this figure into the total economic loss caused by all burglaries to identify the harm of a statistically average case of burglary. But no clear method is available for identifying a *unit* of a possessory offence, or for *individuating* the number of possessory offences. How can one decide *how many* possessory offences are committed over a given period of time? Unlike burglary or most other crimes, possession does not seem to be an act; it is a *continuous* offence. To be sure, one can estimate how many *persons* commit possessory offences over a given period of time. But that figure would be no more helpful for the purpose at hand than is the number of burglars rather than the number of burglaries. In all likelihood, the relevant unit of offence is the number of instances of illegal drug *use*.[79] Although I have seen no respectable estimate of this number, approximately 23 million drug users surely commit well over a billion illegal acts of drug use every year. When the aggregate injuries to all drug users is divided by this massive number, one must conclude that the injury caused by a standard drug possessory offence is not very great.[80] Although the total injury caused by millions of drug users committing billions of acts of drug use may be substantial, the quantum of injury per offence probably qualifies as trivial. The injury caused by particular acts of drug use is perhaps so minuscule that one wonders why it does not fall under the legal principle of *de minimis*.[81]

Fourthly, no reasonable calculation of the harmfulness of a given activity should treat injuries caused to others on a par with injuries caused to oneself.[82] Surely the fact that an injury is self-inflicted should receive *some* weight on the scales of harmfulness. Autonomous choice must become relevant at some stage

---

[79] This (otherwise reasonable) suggestion is problematic insofar as persons can be convicted of possession even when the drugs they possess *cannot* be used—because they are too small in quantity for the body to detect them. See n. 57 above.

[80] One commentator has endeavoured to calculate the amount of public harm caused per average dose of drug consumed. His estimates are presented as part of his case that tort liability for users of various kinds of drugs would be ineffective because 'the ordinary user of alcohol, tobacco, heroin or cocaine is not worth suing': Chester Mitchell, *The Drug Solution* (Ottawa: Carleton University Press, 1990), p. 203.

[81] See Model Penal Code, 2.12(2). This provision requires that a prosecution be dismissed when the defendant's conduct causes the harm or evil sought to be prevented by the offence 'to an extent too trivial to warrant the condemnation of conviction'. This provision is almost never invoked in drug offences.

[82] One defender of a harm-reduction approach to drug policy writes that 'drug use is evaluated in terms of harm to others, and, to some extent, harm suffered by users. The latter is regrettable, but acceptable if it arises from informed choice': Stephen Mugford, 'Harm Reduction: Does It Lead where Its Proponents Imagine?' in Heather *et al* (1993), n. 4 above, p. 21.

of the analysis. If the criminal law generally regarded autonomous choice as unimportant, there would be no reason to regard consent as a defence to the vast majority of offences.[83] Of course, reasonable minds will disagree about how *much* significance should attach to the fact that injury is caused to oneself rather than to others. But one need not reject the legitimacy of criminal paternalism altogether to conclude that injuries caused to oneself are not as worrisome as injuries caused to others.

Finally, can the offence of drug possession plausibly be construed as an instance of criminal paternalism—designed to prevent the injury that drug users cause to themselves? If drug prohibitions were truly believed to be in the interests of offenders, the severity of the punishment would have to be less than the injury suffered by committing the offence. Otherwise, the 'cure' would be worse than the 'disease'. Perhaps *no* instance of criminal paternalism can pass this test, although I think it is best to remain agnostic about this empirical claim. Surely it is possible to *imagine* a drug that would be so injurious that users would be better off in prison than free to persist in their use. But it is highly unlikely that any existing drug satisfies this description.[84] Punishments are simply too severe to be in the interests of offenders.[85] For these several reasons, I will not further explore the possibility that the harm sought to be prevented by the offence of drug possession—harm X—is the injury done by drug users to themselves.

The more likely possibility, I think, is that the offence of drug possession is *non*-paternalistic; it is designed to prevent users from harming *others*. This alternative, however, encounters a major obstacle: Persons who possess a controlled substance need *not* harm anyone else. Unlike tokens of battery or theft, which invariably violate the interests of victims in physical well-being or economic security, many (if not most) cases of drug possession do *not* actually cause harm to others. To concede that some tokens of drug possession are harmless to others does not entail that the offence of drug possession cannot be construed as a victimizing offence. Indeed, many victimizing offences resemble the offence of drug possession in this respect. Consider the offences of attempt, conspiracy, and solicitation. These offences are typically called *inchoate, anticipatory*, or *non-consummate*. Not all tokens of these offences result in harm; many attempts, conspiracies, or acts of solicitation cause no actual harm to anyone. These offences are designed to prevent a substantial and unjustifiable *risk* of harm created by a culpable defendant. Although these three offences are the most familiar examples of inchoate offences, many other offences—such as drunk driving— are similarly designed to prevent conduct that creates a risk of harm. In what

---

[83] Consent is a defence to crimes that cause bodily injury that is not serious. See Model Penal Code, 2.11(2)(a).

[84] Of course, not everyone agrees with my empirical conjecture. Thomas Gleaton, Director of PRIDE, is reported to have said: 'If my child, my loved one, or my friend breaks the law by using illicit drugs, please arrest him or her'. See Trebach and Zeese (eds.) (1990), n. 2 above, p. 166.

[85] For further discussion, see Stephen Nathanson, 'Should Drug Crimes Be Punished?' in Steven Luper-Foy and Curtis Brown (eds.) *Drugs, Morality, and the Law* (New York: Garland Pub. Co., 1994), p. 153.

follows, I propose to construe the offence of drug possession as an inchoate offence—like attempt, conspiracy, and solicitation. These offences are prohibited because they create a substantial and unjustifiable risk of harm to others.

According to the von Hirsch and Jareborg analysis, two steps are required to measure the harmfulness of an inchoate offence. The first is to make a living-standard valuation of the completed harm; the second is to apply an appropriate discount for the degree of risk.[86] The first of these steps has already proved to create a major hurdle. The completed (or consummate) harm of most inchoate offences is easily identified. Attempt, conspiracy, and solicitation are designed to prevent the harms caused by the *object offence*—the crime attempted, the object of the conspiracy, or the offence solicited. Even in the case of drunk driving, which lacks an object offence included in the indictment, the harm to be prevented is clear: the conduct substantially and unjustifiably increases the probability of a crash. In the case of drug offences, however, a great deal of speculation and guess-work are needed to identify the interests that are violated if the risk created by the offence of drug possession were to materialize.[87] The completed harm or object offence of the inchoate crime of drug possession is nothing other than harm X.

What is the harm X that is risked by the inchoate offence of drug possession? For two reasons, I hope it is clear that the object offence to be prevented cannot be drug *use*. First, nothing can qualify as an object offence unless it is an offence itself, and drug use *per se* is not an offence in most jurisdictions. Secondly, drug *use*—even if proscribed—is no more a consummate harm than is drug possession. That is, drug use itself is (or would be) an inchoate offence; it is (or would be) proscribed because it increases the risk that the user will engage in further conduct that infringes the interests of potential victims.[88]

Why not suppose harm X to be death? To be sure, some cases of drug possession ultimately culminate in the death of non-users. Is the harm sought to be prevented by drug possession therefore analogous to that of homicide—appropriately discounted for the degree of risk? Certainly not. Generalizations from worst-case scenarios violate the sensible principle that the harm of a given offence should be derived from standard cases. The statistically average drug possessor does not cause death—or any other consummate harm that would make the offence especially serious.

But doesn't the use of standard cases to assess the harm to be prevented by an inchoate offence give rise to peculiar and unsatisfactory results—especially when a standard case is derived from a statistical average? The source of the problem is that the statistically average perpetrator of *many* inchoate offences causes no harm at all. Consider, once again, the offence of drunk driving. The standard

---

[86] Von Hirsch and Jareborg (1991), n. 12 above, p. 30.

[87] I describe inchoate offences that do not explicitly include an object offence as *simple* non-consummate offences in Douglas Husak, 'The Nature and Justifiability of Nonconsummate Offences', (1995) 37 *Arizona Law Review* 151, 169.

[88] I have already discredited the only plausible means to block this conclusion—to construe the offence of possession as an instance of paternalism, designed to prevent drug users from injuring themselves.

case of this offence does not result in a crash. Although estimates differ, the absolute risk of being involved in an accident while driving drunk is exceedingly small.[89] This fact indicates that the very concept of a standard case is problematic in the context of inchoate offences.

Still, something analogous to a standard case must be retained when trying to identify the completed harm of an inchoate offence such as drug possession. Judgments of the seriousness of an inchoate offence would be distorted if the focus were allowed to shift from typical cases to exceptional ones. In addition, reservations about generalizing from exceptional cases are exacerbated when the risk of causing the consummate harm is unevenly distributed throughout the population of offenders. Since the consummate harm X to be prevented by the offence of drug possession has not been identified, I cannot say whether the risk of causing this harm is distributed evenly or unevenly throughout the class of users. I suspect, however, that for any of the plausible candidates for X, it would be easy to show that the risk of causing this harm is distributed very *un*evenly throughout the population of offenders.

I am still no closer to identifying harm X. What general observations can be made about non-paternalistic rationales for drug proscriptions? Any plausible candidate for X is likely to suffer from a common defect: the punishment of drug possession is almost certain to be *overinclusive*. Consider, for example, the claim that drug possession is proscribed in order to reduce the risk that adolescents will use drugs.[90] This rationale makes redundant those several statutes that are explicitly designed to protect adolescents.[91] These statutes create a far less restrictive means to prevent harm X. A general proscription of possession seems *overbroad* if designed to prevent drug use by adolescents.

The same problem of overbreadth arises if the offence of drug possession is designed to reduce the risk that users will engage in various subsequent criminal activities. This candidate for harm X must be taken seriously, as the correlation between drug use and crime is beyond serious controversy.[92] Although the link between drugs and crime has stimulated an enormous literature that I could not hope to summarize here,[93] the strategy of proscribing drug possession altogether in order to reduce the risk that users will commit subsequent crimes is clearly overinclusive. Many criminals may be drug users, but few drug users are criminals.

[89] One commentator estimates that 'there is less than one fatality for every six hundred thousand impaired miles driven': H. Laurence Ross, *Confronting Drunk Driving* (New Haven: Yale University Press, 1992), p. 47.

[90] This rationale seems dubious; in perhaps no other context is a given kind of adult behaviour punished because adolescents would be more likely to engage in it unless it were proscribed altogether. See Franklin Zimring and Gordon Hawkins, *The Search for Rational Drug Control* (Cambridge: Cambridge University Press, 1992), pp. 115–36.

[91] See section 3 above.

[92] See Spencer (1995), n. 20 above, pp. 339–42.

[93] Among many other difficulties, the connection between drug use and criminal activity may be spurious rather than causal. For a defence of this position, see Helene White, 'The Drug-Use Delinquency Connection in Adolescents', in Ralph Weisheit (ed.), *Drugs, Crime, and the Criminal Justice System* (Cincinnati: Anderson Pub. Co., 1990), p. 224.

Why worry that non-paternalistic rationales for drug prohibitions are overbroad? In constitutional law, the relevance of overbreadth is typically associated with a demanding level of review known as 'strict scrutiny'. Constitutional challenges to drug offences, however, have consistently been upheld by applications of the less stringent 'rational basis test'.[94] I would think, however, that the justifiability of *any* offence that deprives persons of liberty—a fundamental right—should be subjected to the compelling State interest test that follows from applying strict scrutiny.[95] The State should not be allowed to imprison anyone in the absence of a compelling reason to do so. If so, the availability of less restrictive means to secure a legitimate statutory objective should *always* be relevant to the justifiability of a criminal offence.

Perhaps more progress can be made by moving to the second step in the process used to measure the harmfulness of an inchoate offence: to apply an appropriate *discount* for the degree to which the harm is risked. Without such a discount, the seriousness of an inchoate offence would be equivalent to the seriousness of its object offence. This result would be unacceptable; the seriousness of a crime that merely risks a harm should not be equated with the seriousness of a crime that directly and deliberately causes that very harm. A drunk driver who risks the lives of innocent victims does not commit an offence as serious as murder. Similarly, a person who possesses a drug and thereby risks causing harm X does not commit an offence as serious as that of a person who directly and deliberately causes X. The seriousness of drug possession cannot be equal to the seriousness of whatever object offence that crime is designed to prevent.

But what amount of discount is appropriate? Von Hirsch and Jareborg propose that the seriousness of crimes that 'only create a threat or risk to a given interest' should be discounted to the 'degree to which [the harm] is risked'.[96] They do not propose a formula to calculate the extent of this discount, preferring to leave the matter to 'further reflection'.[97] The simplest formula—to multiply the seriousness of the harm by the probability of its occurrence—is likely to provide too low a measure of the seriousness of inchoate offences.[98] Without pretending to offer a general solution to this problem, I propose a principle I hope to be non-controversial. No one, after all, believes that an inchoate crime can be *more* serious than its object offence.[99] In other words, the seriousness of the object crime places an upper limit on the seriousness of the inchoate offence. I will call this

[94] See, for example, *NORML v. Bell*, 488 F.Supp. 123 (1980).

[95] For further discussion, see Sherry Colb, 'Freedom from Incarceration: Why Is This Right Different from All Other Rights?' (1994) 69 *New York University Law Review* 781.

[96] Von Hirsch and Jareborg (1991), n. 12 above, p. 30.

[97] *Ibid*, p. 31.

[98] See the proposals in Paul Robinson, 'A Sentencing System for the 21st Century?' (1987) 66 *Texas Law Review* 1, 45.

[99] For a discussion of how the quantum of punishment for attempts relates to the severity of punishment for completed crimes, see Andrew Ashworth, 'Criminal Attempts and the Role of Resulting Harm Under the Code, and in the Common Law', (1988) 19 *Rutgers Law Journal* 725. If attempts and completed crimes were equally serious, von Hirsch would be wrong to regard harm as an important component of the seriousness of crime.

principle the **upper limit** principle. Apart from this principle, however, I am not optimistic about the prospects of measuring the discount in the harmfulness of an inchoate offence—especially in the absence of agreement about the nature of the consummate harm X.

In view of the foregoing difficulties, I propose to reconsider an earlier presupposition. Perhaps most drug offences—and the crime of possession in particular—should not be construed as victimizing. Suppose, then, that drug possession is a *non-victimizing* offence. According to this train of thought, drug possession is an inchoate offence designed to reduce the risk that the quality of life in a community will deteriorate.[100] As von Hirsch and Jareborg acknowledge, their living-standard analysis is inapplicable to non-victimizing offences. Some new criterion must be devised to gauge the harmfulness of such offences. Call this new test a **social-standard** analysis. Very roughly, a social-standard analysis would assess the magnitude of various non-victimizing offences by the degree to which they make the society a worse place to live. After all, a person's overall welfare might be adversely affected not only when he is directly victimized, but also when his community deteriorates. Can a social-standard analysis be developed to supplement a living-standard analysis? It is hard to know. In what follows, however, I will discuss three difficulties that plague any attempt to provide such an analysis.

First, entirely new conceptual tools would be needed to assess the seriousness of offences that lack victims. Offences gauged by a social-standard analysis might still be supposed to cause *harm*—as most defenders of drug prohibitions would continue to insist. But notice that the very *meaning* of harm must be altered to preserve this supposition. Von Hirsch decides whether a given offence is harmful by determining whether it wrongfully sets back the interests of victims. Harm, then, is a wrongful set-back to an interest—what Joel Feinberg has called the violation of a right.[101] If a crime lacks a victim, however, no interests of victims are set back, and no rights are violated. If a harm has been caused nonetheless, the concept of harm must be redefined as something other than a wrongful set-back to a victim's interest.

Of course, harm is not a technical term of legal art, and there is no reason to demand that the word be used only to describe wrongful set-backs to the interests of victims. The concept of harm might be construed more broadly, and equated with what is sometimes called disutility—any bad state of affairs. Drug possession causes disutility; therefore, it is harmful. Perhaps those theorists who endeavour to apply a social-standard analysis will conclude that society itself has rights and is capable of being harmed. This broader conception of harm, however, can only be adopted at a substantial price. If harm is to be equated with any bad state of affairs, theorists should be pressed for an explanation of why the disutility allegedly caused by drug possession should merit *criminal* sanctions. A wide range of behaviour causes social disutility—society would be better if it

---

[100] See James Q. Wilson, 'Against the Legalization of Drugs', (1990) 89 *Commentary* 21.
[101] See Joel Feinberg, *Harm to Others* (New York: OUP, 1984), p. 34.

weren't performed—but no one believes that *punishment* is the appropriate means to prevent that behaviour. Many of us fail to exercise enough; we do not eat as well as we might; we could work harder; our study habits are in need of improvement; and so on. All of these behaviours cause social disutility and—on the broader conception—harm. The criminal sanction is generally justified to prevent conduct that violates the rights of victims.[102] But the justifiability of criminal sanctions to prevent conduct that causes disutility but does not violate the rights of victims is quite another matter. Most of the point of the requirement that criminal offences be designed to prevent *harm* is lost if the concept of harm is stretched so broadly. Does *any* act that causes social disutility now become eligible for punishment?

Secondly, return to what I called the **upper limit** principle in attempts to discount the seriousness of inchoate offences. If drug offences are construed to lack victims, applications of this principle produce some very curious results. Suppose that the offence of drug possession is designed to reduce the risk that society will deteriorate. According to the upper limit principle, the offence of drug possession can be no more serious than the offence of directly and deliberately causing society to deteriorate. How serious, then, is drug possession? The obvious problem in answering this question is that there *is* no offence of causing social deterioration. The upper limit principle seemingly identifies the seriousness of drug possession as zero.

Perhaps a concrete example of this difficulty might be helpful. According to John Kaplan, drug use creates the risk of a specific kind of social deterioration. Drug users tend to lose motivation and to become lazy, and drug proscriptions are a legitimate means to help ensure that persons remain productive.[103] Although he acknowledges 'both practical and moral questions' in 'advocating the prohibition of [drugs] on the grounds that we must preserve the social productivity of the citizenry', and he concedes that 'we do not usually think that the government should require us to be productive', Kaplan purports to find no 'inconsistency between saying that a government should not punish laziness and saying that it may use its law to prevent access to things that make people lazy— or even aid in their being lazy'.[104] But how would Kaplan purport to measure the seriousness of drug possession? Since an act that directly and deliberately causes the state of affairs to be prevented by the offence of possession—a reduction in social productivity—is not (and presumably ought not to be) a crime at all, it is hard to see how an act that merely risks that state of affairs can be a crime, let alone a *serious* crime.

Finally, the problem that a living-standard analysis was created to solve—the problem of incommensurables—resurfaces if an entirely different standard is

---

[102] I do not mean to suggest that all rights are or ought to be protected by the criminal law. Some rights should be protected by the civil law. Drawing the line between tort and crime is tremendously difficult. For a recent discussion, see the Symposium on the tort/crime distinction in (1996) 76 *Boston University Law Review* 1–373.

[103] John Kaplan, *Heroin: The Hardest Drug* (Chicago: University of Chicago Press, 1983), p. 131.

[104] *Ibid*, pp. 131–2.

used to gauge the seriousness of non-victimizing offences. Theorists must struggle to juxtapose a social-standard analysis onto the common denominator provided by a living-standard analysis. In so doing, they will destroy the commonality of the denominator. Perhaps some new super-currency can be coined to express the seriousness of both victimizing and non-victimizing offences. Although this possibility cannot be excluded, I confess to pessimism about the prospects for success.

I have made very little progress in identifying the nature or degree of the harm X to be prevented by the offence of drug possession. The inquiry fails almost before it begins.

6. The Seriousness of Drug Offences: Culpability

Whatever the difficulties in assessing the harmfulness of drug offences, an analysis of the culpability component of the seriousness of these offences seems much more straightforward. Supreme Court precedent notwithstanding,[105] almost all jurisdictions[106] now define drug possessory offences—including the offence of possession with intent to distribute—to require the *mens rea* of knowledge.[107] Thus a defendant is not liable unless he knows that *what* he possesses is a controlled substance. Moreover, possession itself (in the criminal law) is usually defined to include knowledge; a defendant must 'knowingly procure or receive the thing possessed or [be] aware of his control thereof'.[108] As a result, the level of culpability of drug offenders seems high relative to what is required of most other offenders; the majority of non-drug crimes can be committed with mere recklessness. In this respect, at least, drug offences seem more serious than most other crimes.

Not all drug offences, however, require the *mens rea* of knowledge. Remarkably, the most serious drug offence in positive law—the strict liability for drug-related death statute[109]—requires no culpability with respect to death.[110] It is noteworthy, however, that the drug offence enforced most frequently but punished least severely—simple possession—requires a high degree of culpability. Even though the statute penalizes the peculiar state of *constructive* possession[111]— to be contrasted from actual possession—a *mens rea* of knowledge is needed. This requirement persists despite criticism from commentators, some of whom

---

[105] *U.S.* v. *Balint*, 258 U.S. 250 (1922), represents one of the first Supreme Court cases to uphold the constitutionality of strict criminal liability. The conviction was affirmed despite the fact that the indictment had failed to specify that the defendants *knew* they were selling prohibited drugs.

[106] Washington is an exception. See *State* v. *Cleppe*, 635 P. 2d 435 (Washington 1981). Even here, however, the absence of knowledge functions as an affirmative defence.

[107] See New Jersey Criminal Code, 2C:35–5 and 2C:35–10.

[108] Model Penal Code, 2.01(4).   [109] New Jersey Criminal Code, 2C:35–9.

[110] How can an offence with such a severe punishment be defined to dispense with culpability? In upholding this statute, the New Jersey Supreme Court relied heavily on an analogy to felony-murder, which also eliminates the requirement that a defendant be culpable for the death that is caused. See *State* v. *Moldonado*, 645 A.2d 1165 (N.J. 1994).

[111] Courts sometimes stretch the concept of constructive possession to include circumstances in

propose to take 'more stringent steps to wipe out the evil' by allowing drug possessors to be convicted in the absence of any culpability.[112] Thus, even the most basic drug offence seemingly qualifies as relatively serious. The analysis seems simple. Or is it? On closer inspection, the culpability of persons convicted of the offence of drug possession is far less clear than appearances suggest. In this Part, I will describe a number of fairly small reasons—and one very large reason—to be sceptical that the offence of drug possession requires a high degree of culpability.

Scepticism about the culpability of drug offenders emerges by examining the treatment afforded to persons charged with drug possession who *lack* the *mens rea* of knowledge. Most (but not all) of these cases involve *mistakes*. The practical significance of defining a possessory offence to include knowledge is to mandate the acquittal of defendants who are mistaken about whether they possess a controlled substance. Of course, many such defendants *are* acquitted. A defendant who receives a package, wholly unaware of its contents, neither is nor ought to be liable for possessing the drugs it contains.[113] In fact, however, the substantive law is far less generous to mistaken defendants than one might suppose.

In the first place, the very definition of knowledge is altered to allow persons who lack actual knowledge to be convicted of drug possession. Ordinarily, knowledge is defined as awareness.[114] This definition should preclude the conviction of a defendant who is not aware that he possesses a controlled substance. In many circumstances, however, actual awareness of drug possession is not a prerequisite to liability. These circumstances are called 'willful ignorance' (or 'willful blindness'). Consider those defendants sometimes called 'mules'. Suppose that a person does not inquire about the contents of a container he is paid to transport, typically across a border. Most of these defendants are not really *mistaken* about what they possess; they have no belief one way or the other. Yet such persons are routinely convicted of drug possession, despite their lack of actual knowledge.[115] In such cases, the definition of knowledge is revised from simple 'awareness' to 'awareness of a high probability'.[116] Many commentators have been critical of the use of this peculiar definition of knowledge in cases of willful ignorance.[117] Moreover, much of the judicial resistance to the harsh punishments for drug offenders has been expressed in the context of sentencing willfully ignorant mules, who play a relatively minor role in a scheme of drug distribution.[118]

which the defendant appears merely to be in the vicinity of a controlled substance. See, for example, *Earle* v. *U.S.*, 612 A.2d 1258 (D.C. App. 1992).

[112] See Arthur Goodhart, 'Possession of Drugs and Absolute Liability', (1968) 84 *Law Quarterly Review* 382, 385.

[113] See *State* v. *Richards*, 382 A.2d 407 (N.J. 1978).

[114] Model Penal Code, 2.02(2)(b)(i).   [115] See *U.S.* v. *Jewell*, 532 F.2d 697 (9th Cir. 1976).

[116] Model Penal Code, 2.02(8). The Commentaries indicate that this definition is designed to 'deal with' the problem of willful ignorance.

[117] See Douglas Husak and Craig Callender, 'Willful Ignorance, Knowledge, and the "Equal Culpability Thesis": A Study of the Deeper Significance of the Principle of Legality', (1994) *Wisconsin Law Review* 26.

[118] 'I can't continue to give out sentences that I feel in some instances are unconscionable', said U.S. District Judge J. Lawrence Irving. 'Every week, I get these cases of "mules"—most of them

But what of actual *mistakes*—cases in which a person believes what is false? Here again, the criminal law is less charitable than one might think. Recall that New Jersey (and most other states) treats possession of a controlled substance (or possession with intent to distribute) as a single offence, so that possession of heroin is the same offence as possession of marijuana. What is the significance of this fact? The answer is that widely accepted principles in the general part of the criminal law would apply very differently if defendants who possessed different substances committed different offences. If possession of heroin were a different and more serious offence than possession of marijuana, for example, a mistake about the nature of the substance could be a defence to the more serious charge. Suppose that Edwards possesses cocaine, reasonably believing it to be hashish.[119] One might suppose that Edwards' mistake about the nature of the drug she possesses would give rise to a defence to either charge, since it 'negatives the culpable mental state required to establish the offence'.[120] After all, Edwards *knows* neither that she possesses cocaine nor that she possesses hashish. Of course, this result is incorrect. Both the Model Penal Code and New Jersey Criminal Code provide: 'Although ignorance or mistake would otherwise afford a defense to the offense charged, the defense is not available if the defendant would be guilty of *another offence* had the situation been as he supposed. In such case, however, the ignorance or mistake of the defendant shall reduce the grade and degree of the offense of which he may be convicted to those of the offense of which he would be guilty had the situation been as he supposed'.[121] Thus, Edwards would appear to be guilty of the less serious offence of hashish possession, rather than the more serious offence of cocaine possession. This result, however, would be correct only on the (contrary to fact) assumption that possession of the two substances are different offences. In fact, Edwards is not guilty of '*another* offense had the situation been as she supposed'. She is still guilty of the original charge of possessing a controlled substance—notwithstanding her reasonable mistake.[122] What is true of possession is also true of distribution. Thus a defendant who sells crack, believing it to be cocaine, is subject to the enhanced penalties that apply to crack.[123]

Mistakes are also irrelevant for many of the elements of more serious drug

---

Hispanic—who drive drugs across the border. Ninety percent of the time they don't even know how much they're carrying—they met somebody in a bar who paid them $500. If it's a couple of kilos, you hit these mandatory minimums and it's unbelievable . . . You're talking 10, 15, 20 years in prison'. See Michael Isikoff and Tracy Thompson, 'Hitting a Small Nail With a Very Large Hammer', *Washington Post National Weekly Edition*, 10–16 December 1990, p. 25. After sentencing another first-time 'mule' to a mandatory 10-year prison term for his minor role in attempting to ship 681 grams of crack, Judge J. Spencer Letts denounced the sentence as 'worse than uncivilized—it is barbaric': see n. 3 above, p. B1.

[119] I include the supposition that the defendant's belief is reasonable, although this qualification should be irrelevant if the statute requires knowledge. Even an unreasonable mistake should suffice to undermine the *mens rea* of knowledge.

[120] See New Jersey Criminal Code, 2C:2–4(a)(1).

[121] *Ibid*, 2C:2–4(b) (emphasis added).

[122] See *State* v. *Edwards*, 607 A.2d 1312 (N.J. 1992).

[123] See *U.S.* v. *Collado-Gomez*, 834 F.2d 280 (2d Cir., 1987).

offences. For example, a reasonable mistake of fact about the proximity to a school zone is not a defence for persons who commit drug offences there.[124] Reasonable mistakes about the age of the person to whom drugs are distributed,[125] or about the age of the person employed in a drug distribution scheme,[126] are not defences. Liability is 'strict' for the crucial element on which conviction typically depends.

But my scepticism about the culpability of drug offenders is not derived solely from focusing on cases in which defendants are mistaken or willfully ignorant. The conclusion that drug offences require a high degree of culpability is misleading for a more fundamental reason. As I have indicated, drug possession is best construed as an inchoate offence.[127] That is, possession *per se* is not the consummate harm that this offence is designed to prevent. Instead, this offence is designed to prevent some other harm—harm X. But a defendant may be liable for the inchoate offence of drug possession even though he has no culpability whatever with respect to harm X. Unlike the fairly unusual situation in which a defendant is mistaken about what he possesses, a typical defendant probably lacks any culpability with respect to harm X. He neither has nor has good reason to have the slightest idea that his conduct will cause this harm. In other words, a defendant is *strictly liable* with respect to the consummate harm X.

Even when a defendant *has* reason to believe that harm X is more likely to occur because of his possessory offence, why suppose that he should be blamed for X? In von Hirsch's terminology, what is the rationale for *imputing* harm X to him?[128] Many of the candidates for harm X cited by commentators would not occur but for the intervening choice of another agent. William Bennett, for example, defends his strategy of targeting casual users in the war on drugs on the ground that such persons are 'much more willing and able to proselytize [their] drug use—by action or example—among [their] remaining non-user peers, friends, and acquaintances. A non-addict's drug use, in other words, is *highly contagious*'.[129] Suppose that Bennett is correct about the tendency of non-users to mimic the behaviour of users. What is missing from his analysis, however, is a reason to blame and punish the drug user for the fact that others voluntarily choose to imitate him.

None of the familiar inchoate offences suffer from the foregoing defects. Attempt, conspiracy, and solicitation all require that defendants have a very high degree of culpability with respect to the consummate harm or object offence sought to be prevented. Liability for most inchoate offences typically requires purpose—the highest degree of *mens rea*—with respect to the consummate harm. This result is achieved in either of two ways. Sometimes a purpose to cause

---

[124] New Jersey Criminal Code, 2C:35–7.   [125] *Ibid*, 2C:35–8.   [126] *Ibid*, 2C:35–6.

[127] See section 5 below.

[128] Andrew von Hirsch, ' "Remote" Harms and Fair Imputation', in Simester and Smith (eds.), (1996), n. 58 above, p. 259.

[129] William Bennett, *National Drug Control Strategy* (Washington D.C.: Government Printing Office, 1989), p. 11 (emphasis in original).

an ulterior harm is explicitly included as an element of the offence; the legislature proscribes the doing of one act with the intent (or purpose) to do another.[130] On other occasions, a purpose to cause the consummate harm is required by judicial interpretation.[131] Both of these devices ensure that defendants are not liable for an inchoate offence unless they act with the highest level of culpability with respect to the object offence or consummate harm.

The offence of drug possession, however, is an exception to this generalization. It imposes the functional equivalent of strict liability; a defendant can be liable for this inchoate offence even though he has no culpability at all with respect to the consummate harm X that the offence is designed to prevent. By neither including X as an element of the offence nor interpreting the statute to include a purpose to cause the consummate harm, the State effectively dispenses with a culpability requirement. The condition that defendants *knowingly* possess a controlled substance is relatively unimportant, since no culpability whatever is needed for the harm that this offence is *really* designed to prevent.

In fact, a defendant can be liable for possession even though his criminal act is consciously designed to *prevent* X. This conclusion can be reached for any of the plausible candidates that might be substituted for the variable X. Suppose that John Kaplan is correct that drug offences are designed partly to ensure that workers remain productive.[132] Imagine that Smith, who tends to be lazy, consumes methaqualone (speed) at his lunch break in order to remain more productive. Or suppose that James Wilson is correct that drug offences are designed partly to prevent persons from becoming bad neighbours.[133] Imagine that Jones begins to use marijuana in order to become better acquainted with persons who live across the street and smoke regularly. To complete these scenarios, suppose that Smith succeeds in increasing his productivity, and that Jones succeeds in becoming a lifelong friend with his neighbours. Needless to say, both Smith and Jones would be liable for the offence of drug possession, notwithstanding the fact that their criminal acts were calculated to prevent, and actually did prevent, the occurrence of the consummate harm X.

Do the foregoing considerations provide reason to conclude that the offence of drug possession is unjust? *Should* the State require that drug offenders be culpable with respect to whatever consummate harm X these offences are designed to prevent? After all, no one complains about a few other offences that resemble drug possession in this respect. Consider drunk driving, for example. This offence, of course, is designed to prevent the consummate harm of a crash. But a defendant who is sufficiently intoxicated need have no degree of culpability whatever with respect to this harm. He need not even be negligent that his drinking will increase the risk of an accident. Drunk driving is regarded as a fairly

---

[130] Burglary, for example, is defined as an entering of a building with the purpose to commit a crime therein: Model Penal Code, 221.1(1).

[131] For example, courts typically construe the offence of attempted murder to require an intent (or purpose) to kill.

[132] Kaplan (1983), n. 103 above.   [133] Wilson (1990), n. 100 above, p. 524.

serious offence.[134] Is the failure to require that drunk drivers be culpable with respect to the consummate harm of a crash an objectionable feature of this offence? If not, why protest this feature in the context of the offence of drug possession?

These questions are difficult.[135] I am inclined to believe that the offence of drunk driving would be less problematic if defendants *were* required to have some degree of culpability with respect to the consummate harm. Suppose that a defendant becomes intoxicated but is not even negligent with respect to the subsequent risk. Imagine, for example, that she had no reason to suspect that her punch had been 'spiked', or that she had no reason to think that she would be driving before becoming sober.[136] In such cases, the imposition of liability seems somewhat unfair. In any event, there is a crucial dissimilarity between drunk driving and the offence of drug possession. As a matter of fact, the vast majority of persons who drive while intoxicated *are* culpable with respect to the consummate harm; they are at least reckless about the risk of a crash. In the case of drug possession, however, the situation is otherwise. For any consummate harm substituted for X, many offenders—probably a majority—lack any degree of culpability with respect to that harm. Persons are punished in order to prevent an unnamed consummate harm that they need not actually cause, nor have reason to believe they are risking.

At the very least, these considerations reveal that the culpability of drug offenders is not nearly as clear and straightforward as appearances seemed to suggest. Despite the fact that the offence of drug possession is defined to require the *mens rea* of knowledge, there is room for considerable doubt that drug offenders are very culpable. Since the judgement that drug offences are serious requires both that defendants cause a great deal of harm *and* that they act with a high degree of culpability, I conclude that drug offences in general—and drug possession in particular—do not seem to qualify as serious.

7. IMPLICATIONS OF FAILURE

I have described the difficulties that arise in attempts to assess the seriousness of drug offences in general and drug possession in particular. The problems that result when desert theory and the principle of proportionality are applied to gauge the seriousness of these offences are overwhelming. They stem largely from the obscure nature of the harm that drug offences are designed to prevent, and the lack of culpability of offenders with respect to that harm.

---

[134] But see Douglas Husak, 'Is Drunk Driving a Serious Offence?' (1994) 23 *Philosophy & Public Affairs* 52.

[135] For further discussion, see Douglas Husak, 'Reasonable Risk-Creation and Overinclusive Legislation', *Buffalo Criminal Law Review* (forthcoming).

[136] See the discussion of these (and other) examples in James Jacobs, *Drunk Driving: An American Dilemma* (Chicago: University of Chicago Press, 1989) 75–6.

What conclusions should be drawn if the problems in applying the principle of proportionality to the offence of drug possession are as formidable as I have suggested? Only two alternatives are viable. When a general theory cannot be applied to a particular case, either the general theory is defective, or there is something peculiar about the particular case. A third possibility—to simply ignore the discrepancy and proceed as if no problem exists—is disingenuous in light of the sheer number of drug offenders who are punished within our criminal justice system. As I have indicated, drug offences are not unimportant anomalies that a theorist can afford to dismiss.

I will not disguise my own preference from the remaining two options. I am persuaded by desert theory and, like von Hirsch, am unwilling to compromise the principle of proportionality for the uncertain prospect of utilitarian gains. I will not *argue* for this position here; von Hirsch is more than able to speak for himself in defending a desert theory of punishment and sentencing.[137] I do not believe that the difficulties I have identified provide good reason to abandon desert theory; it is more highly corroborated than is the judgement that drug possession is a serious offence.

In any event, the foregoing problems do not arise simply from defects in von Hirsch's theory. I doubt that any competitive desert theory of punishment and sentencing would do much better in gauging the seriousness of drug offences.[138] Perhaps *no* respectable theory—desert or otherwise—can succeed here.[139] But I am uncertain, since almost no legal philosopher has bothered to make the effort. Remarkably, commentators have developed theories of punishment and

---

[137] See von Hirsch (1993), n. 6 above and (1985), n. 11 above.

[138] Alternative desert theories are equally problematic. **Unfair advantage** theories are frequently invoked to assess the seriousness of crime. Commentators who defend unfair advantage theories differ in their explication of the nature of the unfair advantage that criminals are alleged to gain. These accounts may *seem* to provide sensible insights into the seriousness of the offence of drug *distribution*. After all, quick and easy fortunes amassed by drug dealers seem unfair from the vantage point of persons who earn an honest living. But the same is true of *any* criminal who sells what the law prohibits. In any event, whatever may be the case with drug distribution, how might one measure the amount of unfair advantage gained by drug possession? The offence of drug possession (I have supposed) is a surrogate for the offence of drug use, and, to be sure, the illicit drug user engages in an activity from which law-abiding persons are forced to refrain. But I see no clear way to measure the extent of this advantage. Moreover, to the extent that drug offences are defended by a paternalistic rationale, possession and use would actually seem to confer a *dis*advantage on offenders.

[139] It may be tempting to believe that the source of the problem is desert theory itself. The difficulties I have raised might be resolved by a theory that attaches more significance to deterrence. Although this suggestion should be taken seriously, I do not believe it is likely to solve the present problems. According to a deterrence theory, perpetrators of one crime should be punished more severely than another not because they deserve harsher punishments, but because they are more important to deter. Why, though, is there more reason to deter one crime than another? The best reason to believe that one crime should be deterred more than another is because it is more serious. Thus a deterrence model, no less than a desert model, must provide criteria to gauge the seriousness of offences. In providing these criteria, the deterrence theorist will be forced to confront most of the problems I raised above. Perhaps there are reasons other than seriousness to punish one crime more severely than another. But on any plausible deterrence theory, the seriousness of an offence must play a major role in decisions about how much punishment should be imposed on offenders. Thus even a deterrence theory cannot disregard proportionality—although it may allow proportionality to be outweighed by considerations that desert theorists would exclude.

sentencing in (otherwise) impressive detail without so much as mentioning drug offences. The general unwillingness of legal philosophers to apply their theories of punishment and sentencing to drug offenders is perplexing. Imagine a theory of evolutionary biology that was applied to all animals other than mammals, or a theory of chemistry that was applied to all gasses other than hydrogen. Perhaps theorists say so little about drug offences because they are aware that their theory *cannot* make much sense of them.[140] But if this is their opinion, why do they not say so? If I am mistaken, and these commentators *are* able to support the judgement that drug offences are serious, I encourage them to make their reasoning explicit. At the very least, I hope to have succeeded in placing the burden of proof on those commentators who maintain that drug offences are serious.

What are the implications of failure? The more cautious conclusion is that drug possession is not a very serious offence. This conclusion supports the harm-reduction compromise, which I earlier described as an attractive position in the debate about drug policy.[141] If severe punishments such as imprisonment should be reserved for serious offenders, persons who merely possess a drug should not be imprisoned. Of course, this conclusion is at odds with current law.[142] To be sure, the harm-reduction compromise represents an enormous improvement over the status quo. Still, I am not wholly persuaded of it. In the remainder of this chapter, I propose to consider a more radical possibility.[143]

Von Hirsch and Jareborg have anticipated that their theory would not provide much assistance in identifying the seriousness of drug offences.[144] In the course of applying his general principles, von Hirsch claims: 'Matters admittedly become more complicated when one . . . goes on to crimes (such as drug offences) the wrongfulness of which is in dispute. Here, analysis is impeded by the lack of an adequate theory of criminalization'.[145] I think, however, that this claim is under-stated—even if we assume that drug prohibitions should not be categorized as victimizing offences. In fact, desert theory *does* contain some of the fundamental elements of a 'theory of criminalization'. If the seriousness of crime is dependent on harm and culpability, a criminal offence designed to prevent an obscure harm, and which involves little or no culpability, must have a degree of seriousness that approaches zero. It is hard to see how a person can deserve to be punished at all for such conduct. Applications of desert theory to drug offences are not simply 'more complicated'. If a person does not deserve to be punished for what he has

---

[140] Peter Alldridge may be correct to speculate that this 'is an enquiry best avoided for fear of what might be discovered'. See Alldridge (1996), n. 58 above, p. 239.

[141] See section 1 above.

[142] 64% of all persons convicted of simple drug possession in state courts were sentenced to jail or prison for an average period of over 4 years—and sometimes for life without parole. See U.S. Department of Justice, Bureau of Justice Statistics, *Drugs and Crime Facts* (1994), p. 20; and *Harmelin* v. *Michigan*, n. 53 above.

[143] I explore this alternative further in Douglas Husak, *Drugs and Rights* (New York: Cambridge University Press, 1992).

[144] They write: 'Since we do not feel [drug possession] should be criminalized, it is no wonder that we find it difficult to rate its seriousness'. See von Hirsch and Jareborg (1991), n. 12 above, p. 34, n. 51.

[145] Von Hirsch (1993), n. 6 above, p. 106.

done, his conduct should not have been criminalized in the first place. Despite my reluctance to contribute to the further polarization of the drug policy debate, a principled case in favour of the offence of drug possession has yet to be made.

Thus von Hirsch provides the basis for a potentially radical application of his theory—an application he has barely begun to explore. He typically restricts the scope of his inquiry about the seriousness of crime to 'conduct that has been pro-hibited already'.[146] But a desert theory can also help to decide whether an existing offence is a justifiable exercise of legislative authority. Although he aspired to defend a theory of deserved punishment, von Hirsch's work is immensely valu-able in helping to establish the moral limits of the criminal sanction. Connections between these two fields of inquiry are long overdue. Too many theories of pun-ishment and sentencing are divorced from the content of the substantive criminal law. Many philosophers have assumed that a theory of punishment need not refer to the nature of the crime for which the offender is punished. The criminal sanc-tion could be justified as long as the *system* of laws is basically just. Thus an entire generation of legal philosophers advanced sophisticated theories to justify pun-ishment while paying virtually no attention to the justifiability of particular offences.[147]

I have used desert theory and the principle of proportionality to suggest that the offence of drug possession might be an unwarranted use of the criminal sanc-tion. This conclusion is easily misinterpreted. I do not deny the legitimacy of drug proscriptions in special circumstances in which drug use is especially danger-ous.[148] Nor do I insist that makers of public policy must ignore the problems caused by the abuse of drugs. As I have indicated, conduct may create disutility even though it does not warrant the imposition of punishment. Not all social problems call for a criminal justice solution.[149] The better approach for dealing with these problems, however, lies outside the scope of criminal justice. Cautious critics of contemporary drug policy often refuse to raise the banner of decrim-inalization until they are given an alternative blueprint for coping with the social problems caused by drug abuse. Although this request may seem reasonable, in fact it demands too much. A philosopher of the criminal law should not be required to solve the 'drug problem' any more than to solve, say, the 'education problem'. I have not defended a new drug policy—a solution to 'the drug prob-lem'—but have challenged the justifiability of our punitive response.

---

[146] Von Hirsch, *ibid*, p. 4. However, this limitation derives from his realization that harm is not a *sufficient* condition for criminalization. For present purposes, I am concerned with whether harm is *necessary* to justify the criminal sanction.

[147] One recent example, Michael Davis writes that a theory of deserved punishment presupposes only a 'relatively just legal system' but 'leaves to theories of legislation the explanation of why the law should forbid certain acts and not others'. See his 'Method in Punishment Theory', (1996) 15 *Law and Philosophy* 309, 311.

[148] See, for example, the statutes proscribing drug offences that involve minors in nn. 35–7 above.

[149] Consider, again, the state of public education in both England and the USA. Almost no one believes that improvements in education cannot be made, or that educational policy is an inappro-priate matter for governmental intervention. But few commentators propose to remedy the problem within the penal system by punishing either bad teachers or bad students.

If my arguments are sound, the offence of drug possession is not at all serious, and may be an unjustified use of the criminal sanction. Although the route to this conclusion is somewhat novel, the conclusion itself is not new. Many commentators have denounced drug prohibitions as ineffective and counterproductive.[150] These consequentialist arguments supplement my own, although it is important to note that I have not relied on them. My argument has not cited cost/benefit considerations, or been motivated by frustration about the prospects of victory in the 'war on drugs'. My conclusion is supported on grounds of principle rather than policy.[151] Even if drug prohibitions could be made to *work*, and to do so without causing greater evils, the justifiability of these prohibitions is open to grave doubt.

[150] See Nadelmann (1989), n. 1 above.
[151] The distinction is developed in Ronald Dworkin, *Taking Rights Seriously* (Cambridge: Harvard University Press, 1977), pp. 22–8.

Part III

Relating Theory to Contemporary Punishment Practice

9

Doing Justice to Difference

BARBARA A. HUDSON

1. INTRODUCTION

During the 1980s sentencing reforms were enacted in the USA, Sweden, Canada, and Australia, and in England and Wales with the Criminal Justice Act 1991, which, broadly, followed the 'desert' or 'justice' model of penal policy. The reforms were designed to secure greater consistency of sentencing through adherence to the principle of proportionality of severity of punishment to seriousness of the current offence.[1] One of the most laudable features of the reforms was their stated aim of ensuring that sentencers did not discriminate among offenders on the basis of gender, race, or economic status. To this end, the American state sentencing guidelines which received most acclaim from advocates of the desert model for the distribution of punishment—the Minnesota Sentencing guidelines—opened with a statement that sentencing should not be influenced by race, gender, or economic status, a sentiment only faintly echoed in section 95 of the Criminal Justice Act 1991.

The purpose of this chapter is to examine some questions that have been raised by critics of penal policy and practice—before and since the reforms—concerning correlations between race, gender, economic factors, and sentencing outcomes. Key issues raised will be whether discrimination has increased, decreased, or remained stable; whether there have been any changes in forms of discrimination; whether desert is the penal rationale most likely to reduce or eliminate discrimination; what implications for discriminatory sentencing can be derived from current trends away from desert and towards a more incapacitative, risk-oriented penal strategy. The question of whether equality of penal treatment is, in fact, the most desirable goal, will also be addressed.

Discrimination can take one of two forms: direct or indirect. Direct discrimination occurs when a decision is made with inappropriate reference to race, skin colour, gender, age, employment status, or other characteristic not relevant to the decision to be made; indirect discrimination occurs when a rule or practice that is framed as general, in fact applies differentially to particular groups of persons. An example of direct discrimination in sentencing would be two defendants with

---

[1] A. Ashworth, 'Criminal Justice and Deserved Sentences', [1989] *Criminal Law Review* 242–51.

exactly the same criminal record, charged with the same offence, with the same job prospects and similar in all other relevant circumstances, receiving different sentences simply because one was black[2] and one white. Indirect discrimination could occur if, for example, there was to be a presumption against custodial sentences for employed persons, but employment rates were significantly and consistently higher for white than for black people. Both direct and indirect discrimination are prohibited by the Race Relations Act 1976, and although criminal justice does not come within the remit of the legislation, most of those who are concerned about discrimination in penal policy and practice are concerned with both its forms.[3]

Investigations of criminal justice discrimination have, in the main, concerned themselves with direct discrimination, and have frequently used differences in proportionate imposition of custodial sentences as the primary measure of discrimination.[4]

Although it has been notoriously difficult to establish clear-cut findings of direct race discrimination in sentencing,[5] there has been widespread acceptance among criminologists and others that this does exist, and that therefore its reduction was a valid reason (along with other reasons) for the restrictions on judicial discretion that were implied by the movement towards desert-based sentencing reforms. It is also widely, but not unequivocally, accepted that if discrimination against minority ethnic groups occurs, it is in the direction of greater severity of sentencing. Conversely, research on gender has more convincingly (though again, not unequivocally) demonstrated that males and females are treated differently in criminal justice processes, but there has been disagreement on whether females are recipients of greater severity or greater leniency.

2. Race and Gender: Malign or Benign Discrimination?

Race and gender pose empirical and policy problems that are both similar and different for the U.S. criminal justice system. They are similar in that blacks and women occupy subordinate social and economic positions in American life, and their interests are less likely to be represented in the justice system than are those of white men. They are different in that blacks are overrepresented in arrest statistics and jail and prison populations while

---

[2] Within this chapter, 'black' refers to Afro-Caribbeans when referring to the UK, African-Americans when referring to the USA, unless otherwise specified. This is because it is these minority groups who appear to be forming disproportionate percentages of prison populations. In the UK, the sentencing patterns of Asians appears to be very similar to that of white offenders.

[3] See N. Dholakia and M. Sumner, 'Research, Policy and Racial Justice', in D. Cook and B. Hudson (eds.), *Racism and Criminology* (1993) pp. 29–30.

[4] For a review of British data in relation to race, see R. Hood, *Race and Sentencing* (1992), Ch. 1; for American data, see J. Petersilia, 'Racial Disparities in the Criminal Justice System: A Summary', (1985) 31 *Crime and Delinquency* 15–34, reprinted in B. Hudson (ed.), *Race, Crime and Justice* (1996), pp. 15–38. For a review of data on gender, crime and sentencing see F. Heidensohn, 'Gender and Crime', in M. Maguire, R. Morgan, and R. Reiner (eds.), *The Oxford Handbook of Criminology* (1994), pp. 997–1039.

[5] R. Reiner, 'Race, crime and justice: models of interpretation' in L. Gelsthorpe, (ed.), *Minority Ethnic Groups in the Criminal Justice System* (1993), pp. 1–25.

women are underrepresented. If over- (or under-) representation is assumed to result from similar effects of bias and subordination, the two patterns are hard to explain.[6]

In June 1995, black Americans formed 12 per cent of the general American population, but 51 per cent of the prison population; women (of all racial and ethnic groups) made up 51 per cent of the general population, but 6 per cent of the prison population.[7] In England and Wales in June 1995, 10 per cent of the male prison population and 11 per cent of the female prison population was classified as 'black', compared with about 1 per cent of the general population; females, who as in the USA are around 51 per cent of the population, accounted for just under 4 per cent of the prison population.[8]

It could be, of course, that these statistics require no special explanation, that they are merely reflective of the crime rates of the respective groups. Certainly, as measured by arrests, prosecutions, and other official measures of crime, African-Americans and Hispanics in the USA and Afro-Caribbeans in the United Kingdom, have higher crime rates than white groups; females throughout the Western world have lower crime rates than males. These arrest and conviction figures are supported by other measures such as victim surveys.[9] Furthermore, arrest, prosecution, and conviction statistics show that proportionately more black than white suspects and offenders are apprehended or convicted for serious offences such as robbery, whilst proportionately fewer women than men are convicted of serious and/or violent offences. Whether or not arrest, prosecution, and conviction statistics do reflect crime rates reliably is a matter of much debate.[10] There is evidence that black citizens, especially young black citizens, are more often stopped by police than white citizens; that they are less likely than their white counterparts to be cautioned rather than prosecuted; and that they are less likely to benefit from plea bargaining. Studies of cautioning and prosecution of females, especially white females, on the other hand, show that they are more likely than males to be cautioned rather than prosecuted.

Whatever the real relationship between arrest and prosecution statistics and 'true crime', it is certainly the case that proportionately more black than white people, and proportionately more men than women, come before the courts, and that these disproportions are greatest for offences such as robbery and other violent crimes—the very sorts of crimes which are thought by the courts, by legislators, and by the public to warrant imprisonment. Differential imprisonment rates may well, therefore, reflect discrimination by police and/or by prosecutors, but, it then may be argued, sentencers can only pass judgment on cases that

[6] K. Daly and M. Tonry, 'Gender, Race and Sentencing', in M. Tonry (ed.), *Crime and Justice: A Review of Research*, Vol. 22 (1997), pp. 201–52, at p. 201.

[7] US Bureau of Justice statistics, quoted in Daly and Tonry, (1997), n. 6 above, p. 199.

[8] Home Office, *The Prison Population in 1995*, Statistical Bulletin 14/96, (1996).

[9] A. K. Bottomley and K. Pease, *Crime and Punishment: Interpreting the Data* (1986), at p. 28 on race and the reporting of crime; Home Office, *The 1996 British Crime Survey England and Wales*, Statistical Bulletin 19/96, at p. 32 on gender and violent crime.

[10] Bottomley and Pease, n. 9 above; Reiner, n. 5 above; B. Hudson 'Racism and Criminology: Concepts and Controversies' in D. Cook and B. Hudson (1993), n. 3 above, pp. 1–27.

appear before them, and so their imprisonment decisions will reflect earlier decisions to investigate, to arrest, and to prosecute.⟩

⟨This is the case made by the studies which have found no evidence of discrimination at the sentencing stage of criminal justice processing. For example, in England and Wales a much quoted study by McConville and Baldwin of sentencing in the Crown Courts found that 'defendants are treated equally' once they attain the status of convicted offenders⟩ a finding echoed in another study, which included cases dealt with by magistrates' courts, by Crow and Cove.[11] Robert Reiner, in a very measured review of the studies available at the end of the 1980s, concluded that none had established a 'clear finding of discrimination against blacks'.[12] In the USA, evidence of sentencing discrimination has been similarly scanty and equivocal. The most frequently cited work during the 1980s was Kleck's review of a large number of investigations, which concluded that there was no evidence of discrimination in the most frequent offences.[13] Other commentators, such as Wilbanks, in a book which aroused considerable controversy,[14] have come to the same conclusion about lack of discrimination in American courts, arguing that what the black community faces is a crime problem, not a criminal justice problem. In an exhaustive review of British studies, David Smith urges a similar conclusion, arguing that even allowing for findings of discrimination in proactive law enforcement strategies, in decisions to arrest and prosecute, and in some of the decisions made by courts (for example, remands on bail and remands in custody), high rates of black imprisonment derive largely from high rates of black offending:

A fair assessment of the limited evidence is that while substantial bias against black people has been demonstrated at several stages of the process, in large part the difference in rate of arrest and imprisonment between black and white people arises from a difference in the rate of offending.[15]

Kleck even suggested that there was statistical evidence of greater leniency in the sentencing of black offenders, especially in homicide cases. He said that whilst black perpetrators of violent assaults and murders of white victims were more likely than white perpetrators to be sentenced to death or to long terms of imprisonment, intra-racial (black-on-black) crime was sentenced more leniently. If there was discrimination, he argued, it was in regarding crimes against black people less seriously than crimes against white people. Kleck's finding that in some instances black offenders are sentenced more leniently than white, and that

[11] M. McConville and J. Baldwin, 'The Influence of Race on Sentencing in England', [1982] *Criminal Law Review* 652–8, at 658; I. Crow and J. Cove, 'Ethnic minorities and the courts', [1984] *Criminal Law Review* 413–17.

[12] R. Reiner, 'Race and Criminal Justice', (1989) 16 *New Community* 5–21, at 15.

[13] G. Kleck, 'Racial Discrimination in Criminal Sentencing: A Critical Evaluation of the Evidence with Additional Evidence on the Death Penalty', (1981) 46 *American Sociological Review* 783–805, reprinted in B. Hudson (1996), n. 4 above.

[14] W. Wilbanks, *The Myth of A Racist Criminal Justice System* (1987).

[15] D. Smith, 'Race, Crime and Criminal Justice', in M. Maguire, R. Morgan, and R. Reiner (1994), n. 4 above, 1041–117, at pp. 1089–90.

differences in severity and leniency can depend as much on the race of the victim as on that of the offender, have been supported in subsequent studies.[16]

More recent research on race differences in sentencing has been critical of the methodology and the definition of discrimination in these studies. Hood's study of sentencing in Crown Courts in the West Midlands[17] pointed out the statistical inadequacy of previous studies, which either do not include enough cases to generate a reasonable number of black offenders and thus allow for meaningful comparisons, or do not include sufficient variables to be sure that what might at first appear as discrimination cannot be 'explained away' by the circumstances of the offence, previous record, or some other factor. In discussing my own investigation of sentencing in North West London,[18] I questioned the narrow focus of most studies on rates of imprisonment. I did find some discrepancy in rates of custodial sentences given to black and white defendants, especially where the offence was a less serious assault or robbery case (actual bodily harm rather than grievous bodily harm; robbery but not armed robbery or robbery with violence). More significant, however, were sentences given in theft cases, where black offenders were more likely to receive sentences such as suspended imprisonment and community service where white offenders convicted of similar offences, with similar records, would be more likely to receive conditional discharges or other 'low tariff' sentences. This finding was consistent with other studies, such as David Moxon's survey of Crown Court sentencing, which found black offenders to be less likely to receive minimum-intervention sentences than their white counterparts.[19] It also fits with the results of the National Association for Care and Resettlement of Offenders (NACRO) survey of prison inmates, which finds Afro-Caribbean prisoners with fewer previous convictions than white inmates, having had fewer non-custodial disposals before receiving their first non-custodial sentence.[20]

Before the Criminal Justice Act 1991, it seemed that for offences that were not so serious that there was a very strong presumption of a custodial sentence, black offenders were receiving 'last chance' community sentences whilst white offenders were being given 'first rung, second rung, third rung on the penal ladder' sentences.[21]

At first glance, it would seem that there could be no doubt that women are treated more leniently by the criminal justice system than men are: that if there is criminal justice discrimination against females, it is benign. Not only are there disproportionately fewer females in the prison population than in the general population, but the proportion of women in the prison population

---

[16] For example, M. A. Myers and S. M. Talarico, 'The Social Contexts of Racial Discrimination in Sentencing', (1986) 33 *Social Problems* 236–51.

[17] R. Hood (1992), n. 4 above.

[18] B. Hudson, 'Discrimination and disparity: the influence of race on sentencing', (1989) 16(1) *New Community* 23–34.

[19] D. Moxon, *Sentencing Practice in the Crown Courts*, Home Office Research Study no. 103 (1988).

[20] National Association for the Care and Resettlement of Offenders, *Black People and the Criminal Justice System* (1986).

[21] B. Hudson, *Penal Policy and Social Justice* (1993).

(almost 4 per cent) is significantly smaller than the proportion of women in the overall population of offenders. Most importantly, the proportion of women prisoners is lower than the proportion of females involved in the more serious offences, i.e., in the offences most likely to result in imprisonment: during the 1980s, women's share of serious offences varied between 14 per cent and 18 per cent.[22] This apparent leniency in sentencing has been referred to as the result of chivalry—most judges and magistrates are men, and they do not like to be unkind to females. The same phenomenon of chivalry has been invoked to account for the higher percentages of female than male suspects who are cautioned, and female defendants who are acquitted in contested trials.

Some commentators, however, allege that this 'chivalry' is more a myth than a reality: 'when their crimes are compared, sentencing does not vary much between the sexes'.[23] Surveys of prison populations can be drawn upon to demonstrate that smaller percentages of the women are imprisoned for serious, violent offences than men, and higher percentages for property offences: in June 1994, 17 per cent of female sentenced prisoners had been convicted of violence against the person, compared with 22 per cent of male sentenced prisoners; 43 per cent of female sentenced prisoners had been convicted of theft, handling or fraud and forgery compared with 20 per cent of men. Furthermore, women are more likely than men to be imprisoned without previous convictions: in 1993, 39 per cent of adult female sentenced prisoners had no previous convictions, compared with 32 per cent of sentenced men.[24]

It is necessary to treat statistical comparisons of the sentencing of men and women with a very great deal of caution. The differences in the absolute numbers are such that a small increase in the actual numbers of women in prison (or, for that matter, in women apprehended for crimes) will have a much larger impact on imprisonment rates (or crime rates) than would a similar increase in the absolute number of male offenders or prisoners. Moreover, as Mike Hough suggests, the kinds of aggregated statistics generally used in research on gender discrimination 'do not tell us a great deal', because they do not account for the different 'mix' of crimes and criminal histories of men and women coming before the courts.[25]

What is needed, then, to assess whether there is discrimination in sentencing or not, is to know whether the proportions of women who are being given prison sentences for first offences, property offences, or any other offences, is the effect of the nature of the crimes involved, or of other influences, such as gender bias. Hough and his co-researcher at the Home Office, Carol Hedderman, have reviewed a number of studies, and he suggests that the most reasonable supposition to make on the basis of available data is that: 'on the face of it women are

[22] F. Heidensohn (1994), n. 4 above, at p. 1001.
[23] H. Kennedy, *Eve Was Framed: Women and British Justice* (1993), at p. 22.
[24] NACRO, *Women in Prison*, Briefing no. 33, (1995).
[25] M. Hough, 'Scotching a Fallacy: Are the courts tougher on women than men?', (1995) 19 *Criminal Justice Matters* (Spring) 22–3, at 22.

being treated leniently, but not as leniently as their less serious offending warrants'.[26] Available statistics, he concludes, 'suggest, but certainly don't prove', that female offenders may be the recipients of benign discrimination.

The same caveats about comparative statistical studies to isolate discriminatory sentencing of black offenders could be made: since the absolute numbers of white offenders are so much larger than those of black offenders, such methods are not likely to yield meaningful and reliable information. In England and Wales in 1995, 95 per cent of the general male population aged 15 to 64 was white; 87 per cent of the prison population was white[27]—such differences make comparisons extremely dubious. When one considers the differences in the age structure of the minority and majority ethnic groups, and considers differential arrest and prosecution statistics and the evidence of discrimination at those stages of the criminal justice process, again it is clear that the prison population, or even the sentenced or convicted population, would hardly provide a 'like-with-like' comparative population. If, further, it is desired to consider the combined effects of race and gender, the population of black female offenders is so small that quantitative techniques are doubly inappropriate. (The significance of the finding of 'no discrimination' against black female offenders in Hood's study is, therefore, undermined because the numbers of cases do not match his own methodological prescription of a large enough sample to give substantial numbers in each ethnic group.)[28]

The crucial research question is not the quantitative one of numbers of males and females imprisoned, but the qualitative one of whether the explanation of apparently anomalous sentencing can be found in the nature of the crimes involved, or in some other factors. Similarly, with race discrepancies, the research that needs to be done is first of all qualitative: are there differences in sentencing because of differences in crime patterns, or are other factors influencing sentencing decisions? Concern focuses on differential criminal justice outcomes that appear to be the result of the exercise of discretion by magistrates, judges, and other criminal justice professionals, rather than differential outcomes *per se*. Finding evidence of such use of discretion needs an examination of actual cases, avoiding the masking of specific features of cases that all too easily happens with aggregated statistical surveys.[29]

3. DISCRIMINATION AND DISCRETION

Like black offenders compared to white, female offenders appear less likely than men to receive the whole gamut of sentencing options. During the 1980s, when

---

[26] *Ibid*, at 22.   [27] Home Office (1996), n. 9 above, at p. 11.

[28] R. Hood, (1992), n. 4 above, Ch. 11.

[29] For a discussion of the need for qualitative study in relation to race and criminal justice, which suggests that quantitative methods should be used 'within a qualitative framework', see M. Fitzgerald, ' "Racism": establishing the phenomenon' in D. Cook and B. Hudson (1993), n. 3 above, at pp. 56–61.

dealing with offences which were neither so serious nor so trivial as to carry strong sentencing presumptions, many sentencers, especially magistrates, sentenced progressively—fine for a first offence, then probation, then community service, then custody for subsequent offences. Women and black offenders were both said to have 'shorter tariffs' than whites and males.[30] Whilst black offenders were less likely than whites to receive probation and conditional discharge, females were less likely than males to receive community service and fines.

These sentencing patterns reveal that Afro-Caribbeans tend to be seen very much as criminals, not likely to need or to benefit from help; women tend to be seen as weak, as dominated by criminal men, or as sick. Thus Afro-Caribbeans were less likely to receive sentences such as conditional discharge, which reflects little imputation of culpability, and probation, which reflects an assessment of the appropriateness of help or treatment rather than punishment. Females, on the contrary, if not imprisoned were likely to receive those disposals which imply low culpability or acknowledged need for help; they were also more likely than men to receive disposals such as hospital orders or probation orders with conditions of treatment, again reflecting imputations of sickness or inadequacy.[31] If women offenders were not seen as sick or addicted, their criminality was often linked to domination by a criminal man, or to a relationship with a violent man, either a husband or an abusive father.[32] These implications of sentencing statistics are borne out by qualitative research that has been carried out on decision-making, particularly content analysis of reports made to courts by probation officers, social workers, and other official 'experts'.

The first tranche of these qualitative studies, and so far the majority, have looked into decision-making about female offenders. Studies by feminist criminologists such as Susan Edwards, Mary Eaton, and Anne Worrall[33] of the way women offenders are discussed, and the criteria on which decisions about them are made, by solicitors and barristers, probation officers and magistrates, found a preoccupation with women's role as wives and mothers. Judgments were being made about the cleanliness of the home; whether women were single, married, or co-habiting; and whether they appeared loving and caring of their children. These detailed investigations of the language used by decision-makers fleshed out earlier findings that linked the imposition of custodial or non-custodial sentences with whether a female offender had children, whether she was caring for them herself, or whether they had been taken into local authority or other care.[34] These qualitative studies are also consistent with studies of women prisoners which found that many of them had children who were in care.

The implication of studies such as that of Farrington and Morris into the link

---

[30] D. Moxon (1988), n. 19 above.   [31] H. Allen, *Justice Unbalanced* (1987).

[32] P. Carlen, *Women, Crime and Poverty* (1988); K. Daly, *Gender, Crime and Punishment* (1994).

[33] S. Edwards, *Women On Trial* (1984); M. Eaton, *Justice for Women: Family, Court and Social Control* (1986); Anne Worrall, *Offending Women: Female Lawbreakers and the Criminal Justice System* (1990).

[34] D. Farrington and A. Morris, 'Sex, sentencing and reconviction', (1983) 23 *British Journal of Criminology* 229–48.

between gender factors and sentencing is not that women are treated *worse* than men but that, for both sexes, gender-role stereotypes influence outcomes. Thus responsibility for children is a factor influencing the sentencing of women, as employment record is for men. Employment for men and domestic responsibilities for women operate as constraints on imprisonment—magistrates and judges are reluctant to disrupt a man's career, and are reluctant to inflict the suffering of separation from the mother on a child, as well as being mindful of the extra costs to the State involved in imprisonment in such circumstances. It is in the way that these factors act as mitigating circumstances, however, that feminists and other critics have seen the courts as reinforcing stereotyped gender roles, and punishing those who do not live up to the stereotype of male 'breadwinner' or female 'mother'. This is the 'double jeopardy' of which feminists have complained: being punished not only as law-breakers, but as transgressors of role expectations.

These studies of the discourses constructed around female criminality have not restricted their criticism to the use of judgemental criteria concerning motherhood and wifedom. They also take issue with the way in which women are pathologized and infantilized. Women, it is claimed, are seen as incapable of being fully responsible for their actions, whether through innate (feminine) irrationality; through being slaves to their bodies and hormonal levels (the menopausal shoplifter), or through being dominated by a man (the prostitute controlled by her pimp). Models of justice constructed to explain the sentencing patterns of female offenders have thus been described as 'familial' (Eaton) and 'paternalistic' (Edwards).[35]

Studies of female offenders have consistently found that discussion of the actual offence becomes buried in discussion of these 'lifestyle' factors—sexuality, maternal/marital status, emotional problems, etc. In contrast, similar studies of black offenders have found concentration on the offence, to the exclusion of consideration of circumstances or factors which may be explanatory or mitigatory. Analyses of probation officers' reports have found that unemployment, loss and bereavement, breakdown of personal relationships, accommodation difficulties, and other circumstances which might be used as mitigation, or as reasons for the provision of help by probation officers rather than punishment through imprisonment, in the case of white offenders, are constructed as further indicators of 'trouble' in the case of black defendants.[36]

For white men and for females, in other words, family circumstances, involvement with criminal associates, and both work and its lack, blur the ascription of blame. For black offenders they are further sources of blame, interpreted either as showing (in the case of the employed black father or mother) that responsibilities are being neglected, or that family responsibilities have been rejected in the first place. As Kathleen Daly has put it, the line between being seen as a criminal

---

[35] See n. 33 above.

[36] B. Hudson, *Content analysis of social enquiry reports written in the borough of Haringey* (1988, unpublished report, Middlesex Area Probation Service); P. Whitehouse, 'Race, bias and social enquiry reports', (1983) 30 *Probation Journal* 43–9.

and as a victim is somewhat blurred for white women,[37] who are readily seen as victims of biology, of poverty, of addictions/mental illness, or of men. White men can, with the assistance of skilled and sympathetic solicitors and probation officers, be constructed to some extent as victims of economic and personal circumstances. For black females, the stereotypes of strong women, sexual promiscuity, and tolerance of a crime, drugs, and prostitution culture undermine the women-as-victim perception,[38] and for black men, there is almost no blurring of the boundary between offender and victim. (Indeed, any such blurring is in the direction of victim to offender: black people are far more readily stereotyped as 'suitable enemies' than as 'ideal victims'.)[39]

The problem posed by Daly and Tonry[40] in considering the differential sentencing patterns for women and minority ethnic groups is that if law takes the standpoint of the white, middle class, male (as is generally assumed within critical legal scholarship),[41] why does the exercise of discretion by the socially powerful group appear to disadvantage one socially subordinate group—black offenders—but advantage another socially subordinate group—white women? This reflection on the penal implications of race and gender demonstrates that what is important is the link between stereotypes of race and gender and criminal justice decision-making. Race stereotypes are being drawn on to produce differential patterns of sentencing of black and white offenders; differential patterns of sentencing of female and male offenders are such as to reinforce gender roles and stereotypes.

The feminist critique of sentencing discretion has been that if there is leniency (allowing for offending patterns), it comes at a heavy price. That price is the adoption by female offenders of an 'offender as victim' role, or an 'offender as sick role', or of a 'good mother struggling against the odds' role. It involves fitting oneself into the repertoire of roles and constructions of femininity afforded by a gender-divided and gender-stratified society. For women, their crimes are dissolved into their characteristics and lifestyles; for black offenders, their characteristics and lifestyles are dissolved into their crimes. With both groups, the more detailed, theoretically sophisticated studies have shown that criminal justice discretion is being used in a way which measures black offenders and female offenders against the 'norm' of the non-gendered, non-racialized, white male.

During the second half of the 1980s, critiques of discriminatory use of criminal justice discretion moved beyond radical criminologists and legal theorists, civil

---

[37] K. Daly, n. 32 above.

[38] In my content analysis of social enquiry reports (n. 35 above), I found that relationships between women, children, and men were discussed, in the case of white women, in terms of the present partner and the degree of support provided; in the case of black women, the paternity of children was discussed, especially whether or not children had different fathers, and little mention was made of present support.

[39] N. Christie, 'Suitable enemies', in H. Bianchi and R. Van Swaaningen (eds.), *Abolitionism—Towards a Non-Repressive Approach to Crime* (1986) and 'The Ideal Victim' in E. A. Fattah (ed.), *From Crime Policy to Victim Policy* (1986).

[40] K. Daly and M. Tonry (1997) n. 6 above, at p. 201.

[41] See, for example, V. Kerruish, *Jurisprudence as Ideology* (1991).

rights and prisoners' rights groups, and were taken up by more mainstream criminologists and legal scholars, and also, most importantly, by policy-makers and
by members of the legal profession itself. The Home Office's first statistical
breakdown of the racial composition of prison populations appeared in 1986,
using data from a prison census taken on 30 June 1985.[42] Criminal justice agencies began to be required to adopt policies of equal treatment, to introduce ethnic
monitoring procedures and other measures to reduce discrimination. At the same
time, agencies such as the probation service became more sensitive to equal treatment issues, for example the apparent over-representation of non-serious, first-
time female offenders on probation caseloads.

Increased official attention to possible criminal justice discrimination against
black people was undoubtedly fuelled by the urban disorders of 1980–81, and
especially by the Broadwater Farm events in October 1985. The resentment of
policing attitudes and methods revealed by the killing of PC Blakelock, and subsequent allegations about the treatment of black suspects and other participants
in the events, demonstrated a crisis in relationships between black communities
and the police and also between black communities and the magistracy and judiciary. Although the media and many police officers reacted with anger and hos-
tility against black 'thugs',[43] at more senior official levels there was much concern
at the apparent breakdown of police-community relationships, and of black dis-
trust in the criminal justice system.

Representatives of the Commission for Racial Equality, the Society of Black
Lawyers, and similar groups began to be listened to with much greater attention,
as did individual black lawyers, probation officers, and allied professionals who
confirmed some of the reported experiences of black suspects, defendants, and
witnesses. Research was commissioned; race-awareness training was introduced
for police officers, probation officers, magistrates and judges, and ethnic monitoring of criminal justice decision-making began, somewhat hesitantly at first.
Women offenders' groups were organized by probation services, who also insti-
tuted 'gate-keeping' schemes to try to keep first-time, non-serious female offenders off probation caseloads; regimes in women's prisons and other penal
institutions also came under scrutiny, with the suspicion that they were reinforcing stereotyped assumptions about female offenders. This burgeoning of official
concern with possible race and gender discrimination may have been prompted
by the threats to public order perceived to be posed by black communities; it certainly derived in great part from the growing influence of the women's movement, and the appointment of more women to the judiciary, to management
posts in the probation service, and to positions of influence in the Home Office. It
was, however, also part of a wider preoccupation with disparity in sentencing,
and with the perceived overall fairness or unfairness of criminal justice.

---

[42] Home Office, *The Ethnic Origins of Prisoners: the Prison Population on 30 June 1985 and Persons Received, July 1984–March 1985*, Statistical Bulletin 17/86, (1986).

[43] J. Solomos, 'Constructions of Black Criminality: Racialisation and Criminalisation in Perspective', in D. Cook and B. Hudson (1993), n. 3 above, at pp. 130–3.

By the 1980s, a generalized assault on professional discretion was part of the
popularism of the Thatcherite project which aimed over the heads of professionals and local governments to 'speak' directly to the people,[44] and one manifest-
ation of this was that decisions by judges and magistrates were more liable to
popular question and criticism than ever before. There was also a 'legitimacy crisis' in the State, as the powerful feared that mass unemployment and other circumstances would lead to even greater social unrest,[45] so that any suggestion of
unfairness in sentencing achieved greater political saliency than previously.
These concerns meshed with the growing influence of criticisms of disparities in
sentencing and other decisions that were being voiced by legal scholars, criminologists, radical criminal justice practitioners, and other advocates of due
process/desert model sentencing reforms.[46] We should now ask to what extent
restriction of discretion, introduced progressively through legislation, guideline
judgments and other 'transmission mechanisms' in the 1980s, culminating in the
Criminal Justice Act 1991, to promote greater consistency in sentencing, has
brought about greater equality in sentencing. Further, have any gains in equality
been gains in justice for black offenders, and for female offenders?

4. Punishing the Past or Predicting the Future

The constructions of black and female criminality referred to above, with their
implications for blaming, mitigating, punishing, and treating, have arisen in the
context of predictions of the likelihood of reoffending. Concern with whether or
not women offenders have children in their care and with whether they are
involved with supportive partners or are either unpartnered or unsuitably part-
nered is not just concern for their and their children's well-being, but is also
related to assessments of whether or not they have strong ties to the community,
ties which are likely to make them less likely to offend in future. Community ties
provide support for efforts to change from a criminal to a non-criminal lifestyle,
and also are important as sources of informal social control. The stereotypical
woman who shoplifts around the time that her children are becoming independent, the time of life at which she may feel she is becoming less sexually attractive—the woman who is perhaps the most likely to be treated sympathetically by
the courts—is assumed to be sufficiently deterred from future crime by the shame
she will suffer through family and neighbours finding out about her offending.
People with strong community ties are assessed as having much to lose by continuing criminality, and therefore not in need of punishment to supply a further
deterrent. In the social enquiry reports on black offenders studied by myself and
other researchers, unemployment records, fractured relationships, unstable

---

[44] A. Gamble, *The Free Economy and the Strong State: The Politics of Thatcherism* (1988).
[45] M. Cavadino and J. Dignan, *The Penal System: An Introduction* (1992).
[46] B. Hudson, *Justice through Punishment; A critique of the 'justice model' of corrections* (1987),
Ch. 1.

accommodation arrangements, and the like were used as evidence that probation or other community sentences would not provide structured enough control, in the absence of reinforcing community ties, to prevent future offending.

One striking anomaly in sentencing is that both black male and white female offenders are more likely than white men to have mention made in pre-sentence reports of mental disorder. It is well documented that women are more likely than men to be considered in a mental disorder framework and therefore to be referred for treatment rather than punishment,[47] but black offenders are also readily perceived as mentally disordered.[48] One might, therefore, expect to see a greater proportion of black offenders diverted to a health/welfare system and out of the punishment/prison system. My analysis of social enquiry reports certainly found the same ascriptions of mental disorder to black offenders reported by other researchers. Words like 'schizophrenic', 'personality disorder', as well as non-clinical judgemental terms such as 'aggressive' and 'neurotic' were used in reports about black offenders, and appeared to be the judgements of the report authors themselves, rather than being repetitions of clinical diagnoses. The outcome of these cases was generally, however, imprisonment rather than treatment either in hospital or in the community. Black females are doubly prone to labelling as mentally disordered, but they are less likely than white females to be diverted from the penal system to the health/welfare system. Ruth Chigwada has pointed out how many black women first come into official processes through mental health rather than criminal encounters:[49] these women, rather than being diverted from the penal system to the psychiatric system, are being diverted in the other direction.

Black women also live in communities with higher rates of unemployment than white communities, higher rates of poverty, and higher incidence of single-parent households. An analytic framework developed to theorize the interactions between race, gender, age, and crime suggests that the race difference in crime rates increases with age, and also suggests that differences in crime rates between majority and minority groups will be greater for women than for men, and will increase with age.[50] This is because older, white women are the group least likely to be involved with crime, whereas for black women, economic pressures that can lead to crime are more likely to persist through adulthood. Being a member of a minority ethnic group, it is hypothesized, brings the chances of men and women being involved in crime closer together. It is hardly surprising, therefore, to find a higher proportion of black offenders, both male and female, than white being assessed as facing more problems of sickness and of adverse personal-social circumstances; it would, therefore, be reasonable to expect that

[47] H. Allen (1987), n. 31 above.

[48] D. Browne, 'Race issues in research on psychiatry and criminology', in D. Cook and B. Hudson (eds.) (1993), n. 3 above.

[49] R. Chigwada, 'The policing of black women', in E. Cashmore and E. McLaughlin (eds.), *Out of Order? Policing Black People* (1991).

[50] J. Hagan, 'Toward a Structural Theory of Crime, Race, and Gender: The Canadian Case', (1985) 31 *Crime and Delinquency* 129–46.

black offenders, both male and female, would have higher rates of probation, with or without conditions of psychiatric treatment, and other disposals offering help or treatment rather than punishment, than would white offenders. This, however, as is well established by the research, is not the case, and it is awareness that assessments of the difficulties faced by black offenders seem to result in more punishment, and less help, that contributed to the critiques of the discriminatory potential of rehabilitative penal strategies in the 1970s and early 1980s.

The argument against the rehabilitative orientation of pre-1980s punishment strategies was that such assessments are used not to mitigate blameworthiness, but to judge that black offenders are highly likely to reoffend. With the odds so stacked against them, the pressures to reoffend would remain great, and therefore they would need more than contact with a probation officer, or attendance at a psychiatric clinic, to restrain them from further crime. If black unemployment rates are usually high, whereas white unemployment rates rise during recessions but fall during economic recoveries, then it is more plausible, so the argument goes, to see white offenders as committing crime because of temporary problems, which can be expected to be overcome with the passage of time and assistance to become more employable, whereas black offenders' life problems are intractable and therefore their likelihood of reoffending far greater.

Even with the eradication of racist stereotypes, it could confidently be argued that any consideration of potential future offending is likely to lead to more interventive punishment of black offenders generally, and of women without families compared to women with strong family involvement. The combination of objective circumstances and subjective bias could not, it would seem, lead to anything other than criminal justice disadvantages for black offenders and for non-familied women. A two-pronged strategy therefore emerged to make criminal justice less susceptible to the charge of discrimination: (i) reduction of direct bias through anti-racism and anti-sexism training and through restrictions of discretion; and (ii) promotion of sentencing objectives of fair punishment for the present offence rather than linking sentence to estimates of likelihood of future offending.

This seems an eminently reasonable strategy to have adopted in relation to race and sentencing. Attempts to devise predictors of the likelihood of reoffending consistently produce racially-correlated factors. David Farrington, in a detailed summary of 'prediction of future offending' studies, concludes that:

It seems clear that socio-economic deprivation is an important risk factor for offending and anti-social behaviour. However, low family income and large family size are better measures and produce more reliable results than low occupational prestige.[51]

Such factors are clearly racially-correlated. An American study which has been extremely influential in current policies of 'selective incapacitation'— long imprisonment for those classified as actual or potential persistent

---

[51] D. Farrington, 'Human development and criminal careers', in M. Maguire, R. Morgan, and R. Reiner (eds.) (1994) n. 4 above, at pp. 548–9.

offenders—suggests as indicators of likely recidivism the highly race-correlated factors of previous incarceration, juvenile criminal records, and unemployment records.[52] Consideration of these predictors and similar assessment tools demonstrates the difficulties of eradicating discrimination: even if 'ethnic origin' is not allowable as a predictive factor, indirect discrimination through racial correlation is much harder to avoid.

The development of predictive 'risk of reoffending' scales and similar devices has been, in part, a response to concern with direct discrimination arising from prejudiced use of discretion. Discrimination by individual criminal justice professionals has been much easier to acknowledge than systemic disadvantage. Hood's study highlights differences in outcome which are related to the sentencing culture of different courts, and different judges,[53] just as studies of race discrimination by police have concentrated on 'canteen culture' and 'bad apples'.[54] Discretion, and lack of clear policy on sentencing, was highlighted on both sides of the Atlantic as the problem before the sentencing reforms of the 1980s; could it be that the resultant policies themselves are responsible for disproportionate penalization of black offenders in the 1990s?[55]

Reduction of discretion by itself can, as in the case of 'risk of reoffending' assessment, merely displace discrimination from the direct to the indirect form. A probation officer, defence counsel, judge, or magistrate may no longer be allowed the freedom to make purely subjective judgements about a particular defendant, with his/her discretion unstructured by any rules or procedures, but may instead make the same judgments based on compliance with factor assessments which are race-, class-, or gender-correlated. As well as the 'risk of re-offending' scales used to assist sentencing, decisions about prosecution or caution, bail or custodial remand, may be made by checking factors such as family ties, residency, and employment; in other words, the same race- and gender-linked characteristics which recur at most criminal justice decision points. Reduction of discretion, therefore, does not in itself necessarily promote equality of treatment.

Analyses of the racial impact of restrictions on discretion at points earlier in the system have—not surprisingly—revealed a tendency to shift from direct to indirect discrimination (for example the use of 'ties to the community' criteria in bail assessment schemes, or 'risk of reoffending' scales for probation pre-sentence reports). It could be that the notions of seriousness of offences (the crucial factor for proportionate sentencing) incorporate the same sort of racial correlation, consciously or unconsciously. This argument has been put forward vigorously by Michael Tonry,[56] who argues that much of the recent increase in black incarceration rates can be attributed to policies of 'tough' sentencing of

[52] P. Greenwood and A. Abrahmse, *Selective Incapacitation* (1982).

[53] R. Hood (1992), n. 4 above.   [54] R. Reiner (1989), n. 12 above.

[55] A. Blumstein, 'Racial Disproportionality in the US Prison Population Revisited', (1993) 64 *University of Colorado Law Review* 743–60.

[56] M. Tonry, 'Racial Politics, Racial Disparities and the War on Crime', (1994) 40 *Crime and Delinquency* 475–94; and *Malign Neglect: Race, Crime and Punishment in America* (1995).

'serious' crimes. He points out that since the 1980s, incarceration rates among black Americans have tripled.

Desert-based policies have disadvantaged black and impoverished people not just by their lack of attention to the processes of differential charging, plea-bargaining, and conventions such as the sentencing 'discount' for pleading guilty, but also by the definitions of crime seriousness that have been incorporated into proportionate sentencing schemes. Tonry and others draw attention to the ways in which the 'injustices of just deserts'[57] have been magnified by the adoption of incapacitative 'war on drugs' policies, and the incorporation into sentencing practices of the politicized belief that it is the spread of drug use which has fuelled the rise in crime of the 1980s and 1990s. They demonstrate that different senten-cing severity has attached to the use of powder cocaine—a drug primarily and stereotypically associated with white and rich-black people—and crack cocaine, the drug associated with the black urban poor. In England, one could point to the harm-reduction, medical approach which is still taken to the use of heroin, trad-itionally a 'white' drug, and the criminalizing, penalizing approach which has emerged in response to crack cocaine. There are also the differences between offi-cial responses to alcohol and to marijuana. Alcohol, the recreational 'drug of choice' for the majority of white people in this country, is not criminal of itself. Whilst driving under the influence of drink, being drunk and disorderly, and committing assaults and other such acts whilst drunk are crimes, drinking alco-hol without other accompanying anti-social behaviour is not illegal. In contrast, possessing marijuana, the recreational 'drug of choice' for many Afro-Caribbean groups, is of itself illegal, whether or not accompanied by other anti-social acts.

Drug crimes in the USA, and the racially-correlated crime of 'mugging' in Eng-land and Wales, have been selected for 'get tough' campaigns, and it is these offence categories which are contributing most to rising black incarceration rates. Tonry argues that the race effects of these 'war on crime' strategies are perfectly pre-dictable, and any jurisdiction which cares about racial justice would avoid them.

Desert theorists might well have (and indeed have) responded that this rise in incarceration of black people—and the general move to increased punitiveness—is the result not of the move to proportionate sentencing, but of the 'hijacking' of desert sentencing schemes by the 'get tough' approaches to law and order that emerged during the 1980s.[58] Critics of desert could counter with the argument that estimates of the seriousness of crimes are made either by politicians, swayed by the law and order campaigns of the popular media, or by the senior judiciary, with its middle-aged, middle-class, white, male, viewpoint, and therefore cannot but select the crimes of the powerless, as the actions of those who are most 'Other', for those to be taken seriously and punished most severely.[59] Rather than

---

[57] M. Tonry, *Sentencing Matters* (1996) at p. 13.

[58] See, for example, D. Greenberg and D. Humphries, 'The Co-optation of Fixed Sentencing Reform', (1980) 26 *Crime and Delinquency* 206–25; A. von Hirsch, 'The Politics of Proportionality', in *Censure and Sanctions* (1993), pp. 88–102.

[59] B. Hudson (1987), n. 46 above; R. Paternoster and T. Pynum, 'The Justice Model as Ideology: a Critical Look at the Impetus for Sentencing Reform', (1982) 6 *Contemporary Crises* 7–24.

pursue these arguments, it seems more fruitful to ask which elements of the desert rationale are most effective in reducing discrimination, and which are problematic. Could there be any policy, which combined aspects of desert with other strategies, which might yield any approximation to 'justice' for economically and socially disadvantaged minorities?

5. JUSTICE AND DIFFERENCE

From the standpoint of avoiding injustice to the socially disadvantaged, the most significant virtue of desert is its principle that punishment should be limited to punishment for crimes already committed, and any strategy which departs from that is bound to be discriminatory in its effects. Indeed, it is during the period in which desert theory has been influential that concern with discrimination has been to the fore. Whilst research and policy might have been directed at ensuring non-discrimination in process rather than equality of outcomes, it is only under a desert model that discrimination is problematic; indeed, it is only under a 'justice as fairness' model that the idea of discrimination has any meaning. If the goal of penal policy is to reduce reoffending, or to protect the public from the dangerous, then more severe punishment of those whose personalities and circumstances make them more liable to reoffend, is not just legitimate, it is desirable. This effect of the embrace of a future-oriented policy is illustrated by Norval Morris's consideration of the link between race and violent crime:

Criminals X and Y had identical criminal records and had committed identical crimes, but X was not a school dropout, X had a job to which he could return if not sent to prison, and X had a supportive family who would take him back if allowed to do so, while the unfortunate Y was a school dropout, was unemployed, and lacked a supportive family. And let us suppose that past studies reveal that criminals with Y's criminal record and with his environmental circumstances have a base expectancy rate of 1 in 10 of being involved in a crime of personal violence. While no such calculations have been made for criminals like X, it is quite clear that they have a much lower base expectancy rate of future violent criminality. I suggest that Y should be held longer than X based on these predictions . . . As a matter of statistical likelihood, X is white and Y is black.[60]

Morris's theory of 'limited retributivism' argues for considerations of dangerousness to be allowed to override equality of punishment, but within wide presumptive sentence bands, where the maximum term even for an offender assessed as posing danger of reoffending, must remain within the allowable limits set by estimates of proportionality of penalty to current offence. He is urging a place for concerns of dangerousness and recidivism in a basically desert-oriented system. The mass incarceration of black Americans[61] has accelerated as penal strategies

[60] N. Morris, 'Dangerousness and Incapacitation', in R. A. Duff and D. Garland (eds.), *A Reader on Punishment* (1994), at p. 257.
[61] Tonry (1995) n. 56 above, at p. 4, reports that in 1991 in Washington DC, and Baltimore, 42 and 56%, respectively of black males aged 18 to 35 were under justice system control.

have shifted from the desert ideal of 'doing justice' to a risk-oriented 'new penology'[62] concerned with prevention of risk of reoffending, and with managing a 'dangerous' underclass of people who are assumed to be likely to become more rather than less criminal as they develop. Morris's allowance of departures from equal distribution of punishment because of considerations of dangerousness takes on a new import if the idea of proportionality, of 'justice as fairness', is abandoned.

Both rehabilitation and desert are based on ideas of the essential similarity of criminals and non-criminals. For rehabilitationists, the offender is presumed to have the normal range of motivations, and through help, treatment, or counselling can reform; for adherents of desert, the criminal is like the non-criminal in being possessed of rationality and will, so that he/she can make prudential choices about the likely benefits and pains of crime, and can receive the moral communication conveyed in the pronouncement of sentences.[63] Contemporary penal strategies based on ideas of dangerousness and persistence incorporate much of the thinking of social theorists such as Charles Murray, who suggest that criminals really *are* different, that they have a crime-tolerant way of life and are quite content to live on welfare benefits topped up by the proceeds of crime.[64] This shift towards a criminology and penology of dangerousness and difference is signalled in James Q. Wilson's book, *Thinking About Crime*, which in the 1990s has become the work which most influences policy-makers, to a large extent displacing the political influence of Andrew von Hirsch's *Doing Justice* in the 1980s.[65]

If there are advantages of principle and practice in seeing offenders and non-offenders as having a fundamental equality in their possession of rights and of 'normal' motivational structures, a disadvantage of desert lies in the way in which it has conceptualized the 'equality' of penal treatment which it sees as a prime virtue of criminal justice. In particular, there are deficiencies in the way in which the idea of penal equality has been operationalized in proportionate sentencing policy and practice. The critique of sentencing disparity which desert theorists mounted against rehabilitation-oriented sentencing in the 1970s targeted dissimilar punishment of 'similar offences by similarly situated offenders'. Proportionality's weakness has been in its failure to specify criteria for similarity and dissimilarity of offenders' situations. Whilst desert theorists have been— rightly—concerned that over-emphasis on dissimilarity can produce enhanced punishment for disadvantaged offenders in future-oriented systems, they have been less preoccupied with the injustice that can occur because of disregard of dissimilarity of situation in past-oriented systems.[66]

---

[62] M. Feeley and J. Simon, 'The new penology: notes on the emerging strategy of corrections and its implications', (1992) 30 *Criminology* 449–74, and 'Actuarial justice: the emerging new criminal law' in D. Nelken, (eds.) *The Futures of Criminology* (1994).

[63] A. von Hirsch, *Censure and Sanctions* (1993).

[64] C. Murray, *The Emerging British Underclass* (1990).

[65] J. Q. Wilson, *Thinking About Crime* (1975), 2nd edn. (1983); A. von Hirsch, *Doing Justice: the Choice of Punishments* (1976).

[66] B. Hudson, 'Beyond proportionate punishment: Difficult cases and the 1991 Criminal Justice Act', (1995) 22 *Crime, Law and Social Change* 59–78.

Not only does strict proportionality make it difficult for sentencers to take into account discrimination—direct or indirect—at earlier criminal justice stages, it also makes it difficult to consider differences in opportunities to refrain from crime. In other words, desert in practice has not given as much attention to calculations of culpability as to rankings of offence seriousness; the desert principle that punishment should be proportionate to the blameworthiness of the offender has been overly focused on just one of the elements of blameworthiness.

This neglect of offenders' situations has been accomplished by substituting the idea of procedural equality for the phenomenological inequality of actual offenders acting in actual circumstances. Law takes to itself the right to specify what criteria of sameness and difference are relevant to its decision-making. If differences of gender, race, class, and so forth are ruled irrelevant, the criterion that is ruled relevant is agency: we are all presumed equally possessed of free will; we can all choose to commit crime or to refrain from crime.[67] The appeal to common-sense notions of 'justice' and 'fairness' that gave desert reformers so much credibility when they pointed to the differences in sentences being served by people convicted of the same crime, is, however, also readily enlisted if we ask whether someone committing a crime 'for kicks' deserves the same punishment as someone committing 'the same' offence because of economic desperation. Although the action might be the same, the culpability of the actors in the two situations is surely different.

Michael Tonry[68] has questioned the inflexibility of proportionate sentencing, raising the issue of whether someone confronted with adverse social circumstances should be given credit for past restraint from crime. He sketches an example of a minority group offender, raised in a single-parent, welfare-dependent household, who has cured himself of drug addiction, who works whenever work is available, and who supports his children and their mother, and argues that such a person should be treated leniently, at least for a first offence; he should be given credit for his efforts to 'overcome the odds'. The difficulty with Tonry's suggestion is that it incorporates notions of the 'deserving' and 'undeserving' poor: what if he had not overcome his addiction; what if he had not managed to support his children? This selective, individual leniency is exactly the approach that the feminist research, quoted above, argues has disadvantaged those women who have not fulfilled conventional gender roles.

One possible solution might be to introduce some form of 'categorial leniency', such that offences which are characteristically associated with poverty are evaluated as being of lesser seriousness than more 'expressive' offences which are not correlated with economic circumstances. In effect, this would bring about a sentencing approach not unlike that envisaged in the Criminal Justice Act 1991, where offences of violence against the person were to be more severely punished

---

[67] Hudson (1995), n. 66 above; Kerruish (1991), n. 41 above.
[68] Tonry, M. 'Proportionality, parsimony, and interchangeability of punishments', in A. Duff, S. Marshall, R. E. Dobash, and R. P. Dobash (eds.), *Penal theory and practice: Tradition and innovation in criminal justice* (1994).

than property offences. Property crimes are the most clearly statistically correlated with poverty, violent crimes the least, so this would not offend against a harm standard of seriousness; the difference would be that the definition of seriousness would incorporate a reference to culpability as well as to harm.

Such an approach would be consistent with the penal 'decrementalism' advocated by Braithwaite and Pettit,[69] who urge progressive lowering of penalties for the most common offences, to the point at which there are demonstrable, causally related increases in crime. It would, moreover, reverse the situation currently found in most Western jurisdictions, which is, Braithwaite has argued,[70] that where desert is least, punishment is greatest. In making this statement, he is referring to the discrepancies between the punishment of 'white-collar crime', such as tax fraud, insider dealing, computer fraud, and the crimes of the poor such as burglary, minor robberies, and social security fraud. Braithwaite's view, which I certainly share, and which would also be acknowledged by other writers on the differences between penalization of 'suite crime' and 'street crime', is that both criminalization and penalization are inescapably class-correlated, and future reform efforts should be in the direction of reversing the present bias towards excessive punishment of the crimes of the poor.

Another way of allowing for consideration of differences in situation would be to widen the concept of 'fair opportunity to resist', which is recognized in the defences of duress and mental incapacity, to include economic incapacity. This concept is mentioned by Hart,[71] who allowed that the ascription of responsibility might be less for people who were in circumstances such that conformity with the law was more difficult than for most people.

The idea that economic circumstances might influence blameworthiness is considered by desert theorists. Von Hirsch, for example, in spelling out his theory of proportionate penalties acknowledged that:

the impoverished defendant poses a dilemma for our (retributive) theory. In principle, a case can be made that he is less culpable because his deprived status has left him with far fewer opportunities for an adequate livelihood within the law.[72]

Von Hirsch and other desert theorists decide against allowing for economic circumstances to have significant influence in sentencing decisions, however, partly because of the experience of the use of personal and social characteristics

---

[69] J. Braithwaite and P. Pettit, *Not Just Deserts* (1990); J. Braithwaite, 'Inequality and Republican Criminology', in J. Hagan and R. Peterson (eds.), *Crime and Inequality* (1995).

[70] J. Braithwaite, 'Retributivism, Punishment and Privilege', in W. Byrom Groves and Graeme Newman (eds.), *Punishment and Privilege* (1986).

[71] H. L. A. Hart, *Punishment and Responsibility: Essays in the Philosophy of Law* (1968), at pp. 190–1.

[72] A. von Hirsch (1976) n. 65 above, at p. 178. Von Hirsch's sustained commitment to a rational sentencing policy which respects the moral integrity and civil rights of offenders has produced a body of work which stands out as a powerful, principled challenge to the punitive politics of the harsh 'law and order' climate of the 1980s and 1990s. My differences from his position are very much those of a sociologist posing dilemmas of implementation and elaboration of his ideas in a class- race- and gender-stratified society, rather than disagreements with the general principles of his approach, and I am happy to acknowledge his influence on my own work.

to enhance penalties for disadvantaged offenders in forward-looking, rehabilitative, and incapacitative systems, and partly because of the difficulty in operationalizing a 'hardship' defence.[73] There is concern that admission of a hardship defence or mitigation, especially along the lines outlined by Tonry, would bring back the discrimination and disparity seen in future-oriented sentencing practices, and also that reducing penalties because of economic constraints might mean that sentencing is sometimes inadequate to reflect the suffering of victims. This latter point is the principal reason given by Morris in arguing for desert setting the lower as well as the upper limit to punishments. Whilst this is undoubtedly a difficulty, my own view is that it is not possible always to 'do justice' to both offenders and to victims in the same part of the criminal justice system: the seriousness of the harm could be stated by the judge, who would then explain the reasons for assessing culpability as lower than in a standard case, and recognition of the victim's suffering should be made effective through adequate statutory compensation. Punishment is inflicted on offenders and it must therefore, as desert theory itself argues, be linked to the blameworthiness of offenders rather than to any other consideration.

Another formidable obstacle to the admission of a hardship defence is the conception of choice and freedom of will in law. In discussing Hart's consideration of choice, volition, and fault, von Hirsch states that proportionality:

cannot be based on the idea of a fair opportunity to avoid the criminal law's impositions—since it concerns the quantum of punishment levied on persons who, in choosing to violate the law, have voluntarily exposed themselves to the consequences of criminal liability.[74]

It is this concept of choice that seems most crucial to the question of whether or not economic circumstances should be allowed to influence estimates of culpability. Are there circumstances or factors (poverty, gender, race, as well as addictions and physical duress) which deny or reduce freedom to choose one's actions?

Legal reasoning incorporates an either/or notion of choice and freedom of action: either one can choose or one cannot choose. It finds difficulty in accommodating the idea of choice as a matter of degree. In thinking about a mitigation or even a defence of restricted opportunity to conform, the question is whether one could first of all establish, and secondly operationalize, a concept of choice that envisaged degrees of freedom of action. Lack of income would not by itself signal lack of freedom of choice to comply with the demands of law. Someone might, for example, have a highly-paid job as a surgeon or company executive, but then give it up to pursue a career as an artist; a qualified computer analyst might take up an 'alternative' lifestyle. If the art career was unsuccessful, if the alternative lifestyle left the erstwhile computer analyst with his/her material wants unsatisfied, should this enable them to commit crimes without blame?

---

[73] A. von Hirsch, *Censure and Sanctions* (1993), at pp. 106–8.

[74] A. von Hirsch, 'Proportionality in the Philosophy of Punishment', in M. Tonry (ed.), *Crime and Justice: An Annual Review of Research*, 16 (1992), at p. 62.

Where poverty is a matter of choice, surely any resulting crime must also be a matter of choice?

Economic duress, if it is to be admissible at all as a 'relevant criterion' in establishing blameworthiness, must be allowable first and foremost in cases where the poverty which constrains choice to refrain from crime or not, is not itself out of choice. One attempt to defend an economic duress mitigation approaches the problem by considering life choices as structured. After arguing that although, in the sense used by existentialist philosophers, we are all free, Groves and Frank say that what matters is differences in life-chances: the millionaire and the ghetto-dweller might have the same number of choices available to them, but the millionaire's choices would be such as to enable them to achieve goods (money, shelter, social status, leisure activity) that are socially valued legitimately, whereas such opportunities would be severely restricted for the ghetto-dweller.[75] Freedom of socially meaningful choice, they conclude, is a matter of degree: only in law and existentialist philosophy is it an absolute.[76]

This absolutist conception of choice that is incorporated in law amounts to, as David Garland argues, a conflation of the ideas of *freedom* and *agency*:

The idea of agency refers to the capacity of an agent for action, its possession of the 'power to act', which is the capacity to originate such actions on the basis of calculations and decisions. Agency is a universal attribute of (socialized) human beings . . .

Freedom, on the other hand, generally refers to a capacity to choose one's actions without external constraint. Freedom (unlike agency) is necessarily a matter of degree—it is the configured range of unconstrained choice in which agency can operate.[77]

Groves and Frank propose that freedom of choice should be reconceptualized as a continuum with four main divisions—compulsion; coercion; causation; and freedom. Compulsion would be something like having a gun pointed at one's head and being ordered to commit a crime, or it might be an extreme state of mental disorder; coercion would mean very strong persuasion either by persons, or by external or personal circumstances, and in these two cases responsibility would either be absent (compulsion), or very much diminished (coercion). Causation— I would prefer the less determinist term motivation—could involve peer pressure, provocation, economic pressures, influence of drugs or alcohol, in situations where pressures were not so great as to amount to lack of choice, or where entering such states of economic or chemical influence had been voluntary. This 'caused' offence would be the 'standard case' where the desert penalty would be most clearly applicable. In such a case, the penalty would form part of the choice equation, tipping the balance of advantage and disadvantage against committing the crime,

---

[75] W. B. Groves and N. Frank, 'Punishment, Privilege and Structured Choice', in W. B. Groves and G. Newman (1986) n. 70 above, Ch. 5.

[76] I have used a similar argument, in *Penal Policy and Social Justice* (1993), Ch. 6; and in 'Punishing the poor: a critique of the dominance of legal reasoning in penal theory and practice', in A. Duff *et al* (eds.) (1994) n. 68 above, pp. 292–305.

[77] D. Garland, ' "Governmentality" and the problem of crime', (1997) 1, 2 *Theoretical Criminology* 173–214, at 196–7.

in situations where choices are clearly available, operating as a countervailing pressure to the pressures influencing the individual towards crime. This is the deterrent punishment scheme envisaged by adherents of rational choice theories of offending.[78] Complete freedom of choice would, say Groves and Frank, be relatively rare, and would be the situation of the anti-social actor who could gain socially valued goods as easily by legal as by criminal means. This person would be the most blameworthy, and culpability in such cases would be enhanced. In fact, rather than in the writings of Nietzsche or Dostoevsky, such a criminal would be the suite criminal more often than the street criminal.

There is still the difficulty of how to measure economic pressure of the sort that produces compulsion or coercion rather than merely motivation. Groves and Frank (writing of the USA) suggest that the criterion would be a combination of an annual income of $6,000 or less; being unemployed at the time of arrest; and having less than a high school education. In England and Wales at the present time, one can readily think of groups of people who have no legitimate income at all sufficient to supply basic material needs, or who have no access to their supposed income. Young people who are not eligible for welfare benefits under the present regulations might come into this category: the young homeless and those with chaotic lifestyles who cannot accommodate themselves to the rules of the jobseekers' allowance; women whose men withhold money, or only give them money if they engage in prostitution or other criminal activity; people leaving penal, psychiatric, or residential care institutions who receive benefits in arrears but who need to pay for food and shelter immediately, would seem to be candidates for a defence or mitigation of economic duress.

These suggestions are attempts to combine what is, in my view, the prime virtue of desert—that is, that people should only be punished for offences that they have already committed, not for crimes that they might (but might not) commit in the future—with the virtue of rehabilitative strategies—that is, sensitivity to offenders' situations. Such sensitivity, operationalized through social background enquiries, motivational interviewing, awareness of rates of unemployment, local climates of racism, etc., would not have the same deleterious impact if it is used in mitigating culpability rather than as a predictor of reoffending. This is the crucial point: knowledge about the offender should be used in assessments of culpability for crimes already committed, not for prognostications about crimes to come.

It could be argued that both these suggestions—defining crimes correlated with poverty as less serious than those with no such association, and establishing a defence or mitigation of economic duress—would introduce positive discrimination in favour of minority ethnic groups and women whose lives do not accord with standards of conventional femininity. If disproportionately more black than white offenders (male and female) are likely to be convicted of poverty-linked crimes and meet the conditions of economic duress, they would benefit

[78] D. Cornish and R. Clarke, *The Reasoning Criminal: Rational Choice Perspectives in Offending* (1986).

disproportionately from such initiatives. On the other hand, the numbers of white offenders are so much greater than those of black offenders, that substantial numbers of the majority group would also benefit. More than anything, the penal system is the system which deals with the wrong-doing of the poor.[79] The penal system is 'voluntary' only for people whose actions are unconstrained by poverty, addictions or other compelling circumstances; the involuntarily impoverished, especially those with no legitimate income at all, cannot be said to 'choose' to violate the law. By far the greatest actual number of beneficiaries of such an innovation would be white, male, impoverished, offenders, because these are by far the greatest number of offenders. Although there might be a slight disproportion of benefit in favour of black offenders, such a result could not really be called positive 'discrimination', if the group which provides the largest number of beneficiaries is the majority group.

Another important critique of desert/proportionality's espousal of equal penal treatment is that 'equality' tends to mean 'like men'. If treating women differently has meant, on average, treating them more leniently, equality as gender-blindness must be disadvantageous for female offenders. Kathleen Daly has demonstrated how the desert and determinate sentencing reforms introduced throughout America in the 1980s have increased the imprisonment of women.[80] She points out that most states have sought to equalize the sentencing of men and women, either by making the presumptive sentences in punishment schedules and guidelines approximate the average terms passed on men, or by adopting a 'split the difference' tactic. This latter practice has had little or no ameliorating impact on the sentencing of men (because there are so many more male than female offenders), but has increased penal severity towards females. Whilst advocates for black offenders might reasonably posit parity with white offenders as a desirable goal, it is suggested that parity with men would not seem so desirable for those advocating on behalf of women offenders.[81] This reasoning makes sense if 'parsimony' rather than 'equality' is seen as the most important penal aim, a position with which Tonry and Braithwaite are associated. Whilst parsimony as a general principle is something I would wholeheartedly support, special pleading on behalf of women seems uncomfortably close to the paternalism complained of by Edwards and some of the earlier critics of the treatment of women in the courts.[82]

This difficulty is resolved if 'equality' can be taken to mean punishment of equivalent severity or leniency, and of equivalent relevance to circumstances, for offences of *equal culpability given knowledge of circumstances*, rather than a simplified sameness, let alone a 'same as men' standard. To reject sameness is not to reject equality, but is to ask for a more complex formulation of equality. The confusion of equality and sameness is built into much of the scholarship on discrimination in sentencing, as well as being embedded in law:

[79] B. D. Headley, 'Crime, Justice and Powerless Racial Groups', (1989) 16 *Social Justice* 1–9; B. Hudson (1993), n. 21 above.

[80] K. Daly, (1994), n. 37 above.   [81] K. Daly and M. Tonry (1997), n. 6 above.

[82] S. Edwards (1984), n. 33 above.

to accept that 'justice' and 'equality' are to be achieved by parity of treatment is to collude in the acceptance of the inequalities which co-exist with such 'equal treatment'. To assume that justice for women means treating women like men is to ignore the very different existences which distinguish the lives of women from the lives of men of similar social status. Yet this attitude to 'justice' and 'equality' not only underlies legislative provision, it is also to be found in studies of the law and the criminal justice system.[83]

Many feminist legal theorists claim that the law 'is male', in that it incorporates an unreflexive male standpoint; it sees women only as men see them, and only in relation to men.[84] What is needed is that it should become 'gendered', not in the sense of reproducing and reinforcing stereotyped gender roles, but in being able to incorporate female as well as male world-views. Whilst progress is being made—recognition of the importance of domestic violence; some rethinking of the concept of 'provocation' to take into account the circumstances of abused wives—much is still to be accomplished.

This new thinking on provocation incorporates something like the notion of choice as structured by life circumstances, and as being a matter of degree, discussed above in relation to a defence or mitigation of economic duress. It also calls for recognition that choices are not structured just by economic circumstances, but also by race and gender. For example, from the male standpoint, the question usually asked about abused women is 'why didn't she leave?'; it has taken feminist psychologists and others to explain that although the choice to leave exists, battered women may lack perception of leaving as a real choice, because the abuse has shaken their confidence to such a degree that they no longer see themselves as active framers of their own destiny. Calculations of culpability should take into account the rich volume of research literature that is available showing the pressures which lead women towards crime in real-life situations.[85]

The call for different treatment then becomes not special pleading for leniency but for a 'woman-wise' penal strategy which does not increase female offenders' oppression *as women*. Such gendered criminal justice consciousness might very well lead to support for the abolition of imprisonment for women as a standard penalty. Abolition would not be because of special pleading, but because of the low numbers of women committing violent offences, and the even lower numbers of women who commit violent or serious offences because of consciously anti-social motives. Imprisonment would become an unusual response to an unusual crime, needing special justification.

In formulating her ideal of women-wise penology, Pat Carlen also demands that the punishment of men 'does not brutalize them and make them even more violently or ideologically oppressive towards women in the future'.[86] She

---

[83] M. Eaton, (1986) n. 33 above, at p. 11.

[84] C. A. MacKinnon, *Toward a Feminist Theory of the State* (1989); C. Smart, 'The Woman of Legal Discourse', (1992) 1 *Social and Legal Studies* 29.

[85] See, especially, the work of Pat Carlen, for example, (ed.) *Criminal Women*, (1985); *Women, Crime and Poverty* (1988); *Alternatives to Women's Imprisonment* (1990).

[86] P. Carlen, (1990) n. 85 above, at p. 114.

suggests that because of the small numbers of women committing serious, violent offences, as well as being an appropriate response to the numbers and patterns of female crime, abolition of women's imprisonment could be used as an experiment in developing effective and constructive responses to crime, which could then be extended to the punishment of men. This once more demonstrates that feminist criminologists and legal theorists are not asking for special-case leniency, but that they are challenging the present assumption that the male penal norm is generalizable. Given the association between masculinity and crime, there is far more sense in demanding that the penal treatment of men take into account women's view of the world, than for the penal treatment of women to be the same as that of men! Experience of sentencing patterns of female offenders in the USA since 1980 and in England since the 1991 Criminal Justice Act, however, shows that 'parity of treatment' in practice has meant more imprisonment of women, rather than more rehabilitative, non-custodial sentences for men.

6. Conclusion

For sentencing to achieve equal appropriateness rather than equality of injustice, law needs to become open not just to a female standpoint, but also to the standpoints of different minority ethnic groups. Criminal justice should be reflexively 'racialized' in the same way that it has been suggested it should become gendered.[87] Again, some progress has been made, for example the recognition of racial motivation as an aggravating factor in offences, but progress is slow and halting, and to an even greater extent than with the acknowledgement of a female standpoint, there remains much to be done.

In opening itself to multiple standpoints, law would be moving away from a simple rule-following logic towards the more relational *'ethic of care'* formulated by the feminist jurisprudence movement.[88] At the forefront of the proposals of these writers is that defendants should be considered in their relationships and circumstances, and that questions of blameworthiness and the choice of penalties should reflect such considerations. What this amounts to is appreciation that the subject being blamed is not the abstract 'reasonable person' of legal discourse, whose ascribed characteristics turn out to be those of the middle-aged, middle-class, white male; but a real, flesh and blood individual, an individual whose scope for action, whose perception of choices, whose life experiences, may be very different from those sitting in judgment.

These questions of desert, discrimination, and equality are difficult. It is too

---

[87] K. Daly, 'Criminal Law and Justice System Practices as Racist, White, and Racialized', (1994) 51 *Washington and Lee Law Review* 431–64.

[88] See K. T. Bartlett, 'Feminist Legal Methods', (1990) 103 *Harvard Law Review* 829–88; F. Heidensohn, 'Models of Justice: Portia or Persephone? Some Thoughts on Equality, Fairness and Gender in the Field of Criminal Justice', (1986) 14 *International Journal of the Sociology of Law* 287–98; B. Hudson, *Understanding Justice* (1996), pp. 145–9; C. Smart, *Law, Crime and Sexuality* (1995), Ch. 10.

easy to shift from direct to indirect discrimination and thereby to make unfairness more difficult to challenge; it is too easy to become over-pessimistic when faced with evidence of the disadvantaging use of personal-social factors in the past; it is too easy to become confused about whether or not to advocate equal/the same treatment. What is beyond doubt is that responding to difference is the most challenging of tasks for criminal justice: the ideal of finding a response to difference which neither represses it, as in the future-oriented strategies of old-style rehabilitation and new-style incapacitation, nor denies it, as in oversimplified and unsophisticated proportionality schemes. Whilst proportionality of penalty to harm is an important element of penal justice, and whilst fairness and equality of treatment are vitally important values of law, 'justice' involves more than questions of distribution; it involves moving beyond the 'distributive paradigm',[89] towards acknowledging the demands of alterity, that is to say, of developing sensitivity to the needs of the 'Other',[90] someone who is like oneself in essential humanity and in the possession of rights, but unlike in biography and perspective. 'Justice' is about recognizing the Other in her/his individuality and ensuring that what is delivered by law is appropriate to that individual. 'Justice' cannot be done unless difference is acknowledged, and given its due.

I am suggesting here that the most fruitful approach to issues of equality and discrimination would be one that combined the desert principles of only punishing already committed crimes, and acknowledging the offender's right to desert upper limits on punishment, with a sensitivity to difference throughout the entire process of criminalizing harms, assessing culpability, and deciding appropriate penalties. Punishment theory needs to continue to explore problems of differences in culpability of offenders, and needs to recognize that 'equality' is not necessarily 'sameness'. Legal thinking about questions of blame and punishment must open itself to the understandings of feminist and post-modernist critiques of law in general, and of proportionality theory and practice, in particular, if justice is ever to be done to difference.

[89] I. M. Young, *Justice and the Quality of Difference* (1990), Ch. 1.

[90] This perspective of 'justice-as-alterity' is being developed by post-structuralist writers on law and justice, such as Drucilla Cornell, *The Philosophy of the Limit* (1992). It draws on the philosophy of Levinas: E. Levinas, *Totality and Infinity* (1969); *Otherwise than Being or Beyond Essence* (1981) and the critiques of his theories of justice offered by Derrida: J. Derrida, 'Violence and Metaphysics: An Essay on the Thought of Emmanuel Levinas', in *Writing and Difference* (1978); 'The Force of Law: the Mystical Foundation of Authority', (1990) 11, 5–6 *Cardozo Law Review* 920–1045, and aims to develop a defence and elaboration of the ideal of justice whilst acknowledging deconstructionist and feminist critiques of law as an existing institution and set of practices.

10

Sentencing, Equal Treatment, and the Impact of Sanctions

ANDREW ASHWORTH AND ELAINE PLAYER

One distinguishing mark of Andrew von Hirsch's writings is that they narrow the gap between the philosophy of punishment and the justification of sentencing and penal practices. It is difficult enough to establish a convincing rationale (or set of justifications) for State punishment in principle. It is even more difficult to apply that rationale to actual sentencing systems, not merely in respect of the range of available sentences and the practices of courts at the sentencing stage but also in relation to the practices of 'penal agents' (e.g. prison officials, probation officers) in carrying out the sentences imposed by courts. And yet if justifications for State punishment are to be practical, they must be justifications which relate to the actual punishments to which convicted offenders are subjected. As Antony Duff and David Garland have argued:

a justification of state punishment must show not merely that punishment achieves some good, but that it is a proper task of the state to pursue that good by these means.[1]

Our concern in this chapter is principally with those last three words, 'by these means'. We recognize that the range and type of sentences available in any given jurisdiction are likely to be the product of various political and social forces, and also that the actual delivery of those sentences (whether in custody or in the community) may well diverge from their official descriptions and aims. Attempts to justify punishment should, in our view, take full account of these factors.

The chapter begins with some general reflections on the place of our topic within the range of questions about sentencing theory. We then focus on two questions about the impact of sanctions—whether sentences should be adjusted in response to the sensitivities of a particular offender, and whether sentences should be adjusted to reflect the varying conditions and requirements of nominally identical sentences.

---

[1] R. A. Duff and D. Garland, 'Introduction: Thinking about Punishment', in R. A. Duff and David Garland (eds.), *A Reader on Punishment* (OUP, 1994), p. 3.

1. PUNISHMENT THEORIES AND EQUAL TREATMENT

The first task is to locate our enquiry within the general field of sentencing theory. Those writers who support utilitarian or consequentialist rationales for sentencing tend to justify sentencing as a (general) deterrent: even though the infliction of pain on citizens is an evil, it can be justified if it produces more overall benefits than disbenefits.[2] This means that other ways of reducing crime should be tried first—education, crime prevention strategies, etc.—but that if it is still necessary to resort to State punishment and that promises a net social benefit, this may be done. Presumably the same applies to the types of sentence available: although in principle they should be such as to inflict as little pain (as few deprivations) as possible, they ought to impose sufficient punishment to achieve the required crime-preventive benefits. Since the emphasis of such theories is usually upon general deterrence, a crucial aspect of the sentencing system would be the beliefs of (potential) offenders about the hard treatment they would receive if they committed certain types of offence. Deterrence theories, then, tend to turn on what citizens believe about the punishment they are at risk of receiving; and it is possible that those beliefs do not accord with penal realities, since people may be so misinformed that they think prison (for example) is easier or harder than in fact it is.

Modern retributivist and desert-based writers have increasingly drawn a distinction between justifying the censure of wrong-doers and justifying the element of hard treatment that State punishment typically involves.[3] The justification for officially censuring an offender is that it is right to communicate authoritatively to the citizen that he or she has broken the law, to confront the citizen with that and to express disapproval. When it comes to justifying the further step of imposing 'hard treatment' on offenders, the tendency is to resort to a combination of deterrent and fairness rationales. Andrew von Hirsch and Uma Narayan argue for a more subtle combination of these rationales which preserves the respect for individual autonomy which underlies desert theory. They both recognize that general prevention is one of the justifications for hard treatment as part of the penal system: without it, law-breaking would be intolerably high and the element of control or order in society would be unacceptably low.[4] But they argue that the component of hard treatment in each sentence may be justified not on consequentialist grounds but as part of the meaning of censure—what Antony Duff, in his reconstruction of their arguments, refers to as a 'prudential supplement' to the moral element in the censure.[5] One implication of this approach is that the

---

[2] For selected readings, see A. von Hirsch and A. Ashworth (eds.), *Principled Sentencing*, 2nd edn. (forthcoming, 1998), Ch. 2.

[3] R. A. Duff, *Trials and Punishments* (Cambridge UP, 1986); A. von Hirsch, *Censure and Sanctions* (OUP, 1993), Chs. 2 and 9; U. Narayan, 'Appropriate Responses and Preventive Benefits: Justifying Censure and Hard Treatment in Legal Punishment', (1993) 13 *Oxford J.L.S.* 166.

[4] Von Hirsch (1993), n. 3 above, pp. 12–14, and Narayan (1993), n. 3 above.

[5] R. A. Duff, 'Penal Communications', (1996) 20 *Crime and Justice* 1, at 41–5. Duff himself lays

penal hard treatment must be proportionate to the seriousness of the crime, so as to reflect the appropriate degree of censure.

This is not the place to develop fuller arguments on these points. Suffice it to say that proportionality is not only regarded as a key principle by desert theorists but also accepted as a weak (limiting) principle by many consequentialist writers, such as Morris and Tonry,[6] Lacey,[7] and Braithwaite and Pettit.[8] Although their interpretations of the principle vary somewhat, they all accord some recognition to the autonomy principle and to the Kantian principle that no person should be used solely as a means to an end, even though none of them adopts what Michael Tonry terms 'the strong proportionality principle'[9] espoused by Andrew von Hirsch and others.

None of this is to suggest that only a small number of principles and justifications, stemming from utilitarian or retributivist theories, ought to have a bearing on sentencing. Account must also be taken of various principles of social justice. We would argue for a general principle of equal treatment, by which we mean that a sentencing system should strive to avoid its punishments having an unequal impact on different offenders or groups of offenders. It is a principle with similar roots to proportionality, in that it seeks to respect individuals by ensuring fair treatment.[10] One aspect of this would be the principle of non-discrimination expressed in Article 14 of the European Convention on Human Rights, which states that rights 'shall be secured without discrimination on any ground such as sex, race, colour, language, religion, political or other opinion'. To some extent this principle may appear to go hand in hand with the proportionality principle, since the latter should also ensure non-discrimination.[11] But when viewed on the wider social canvas, there may be a gap between the two. Any aspiration to equal punishments is doubtful because of the skewed population of people coming before the courts—for example, the over-representation of the underclass (a creation of the social system, not merely or even chiefly of the criminal justice system); the differential approach to female suspects and offenders;[12] the unequal system of criminal law, with far more offences aimed at the less well-off; and policing and prosecution policies, which are selective and ensure that those brought before courts are not necessarily those accused of the most

---

greater emphasis on communication and on penance, and his justification for hard treatment is developed in part IV of that paper.

[6] N. Morris and M. Tonry, *Between Prison and Probation* (OUP, 1990), p. 105; see further M. Tonry, 'Proportionality, Parsimony and Interchangeability of Punishments', in A. Duff, S. Marshall, R. E. Dobash, and R. P. Dobash (eds.), *Penal Theory and Practice* (Manchester UP, 1994), at pp. 80–2.

[7] N. Lacey, *State Punishment* (Routledge, 1988), pp. 193–5.

[8] J. Braithwaite and P. Pettit, *Not Just Deserts* (OUP, 1990), pp. 101–2, 126.

[9] Tonry (1994), n. 6 above.

[10] We recognize that there is an extensive literature, much of it written by feminist scholars, on the different strengths of equality-based and difference-based social policies in respect of men and women, especially in the context of discussions of discrimination. This chapter focuses on equality in the impact of sanctions, without tackling broader issues of social justice.

[11] For full discussion of this, see Barbara Hudson in Ch. 9 of this book, above.

[12] cf. C. Hedderman and L. Gelsthorpe (eds.), *Understanding the Sentencing of Women* (1997) with K. Daly, *Gender, Crime and Punishment* (1994).

serious crimes.[13] We recognize that these larger problems mean that equality of punishment can never be fully achieved in practice, but we believe that there are strong reasons for striving to achieve it where practicable.

There are other formidable barriers to equality of punishment which would exist even if those brought before the courts were indeed those accused of the most serious social wrongs. One such barrier results from the elements of tactical planning or negotiation at stages between the decision to prosecute and the sentencing decision. The most obvious area is plea negotiation: the prosecutor may agree to state the facts in a certain way in exchange for a plea of guilty, or to drop a higher charge in exchange for a guilty plea to a lesser charge, or to drop some charges in exchange for guilty pleas to others.[14] To some extent this may result in the court passing sentence on a basis that might not reflect the 'real' offence(s) committed. Other decisions, on the initial choice of charge and on mode of trial, may also have sentencing implications. A second barrier to equality of punishment stems from inconsistencies in the allocation of punishment, originating in local sentencing policies or in the idiosyncrasies of particular judges. This is not the place to examine the causes of these inconsistencies, of which there is considerable evidence.[15] Suffice it to say that any commitment of the judiciary and the magistracy to consistency of sentencing tends to be qualified by a strong insistence on judicial independence and an equally strong insistence that 'each case must be treated on its own facts' and that 'no two cases are alike'—phrases which sound persuasive only until they are analysed with care.[16]

However, both of these are to a large extent practical problems, to be solved at a legal-political level within the jurisdiction, rather than theoretical flaws in particular justifications for punishment. Even if we had a criminal justice system which could deliver consistent sentencing based on the real facts of offences, there are two further problems to be confronted, and they are the focus of this chapter. One arises from the variation in conditions and regimes in penal establishments to which offenders may be sent for imprisonment—a single sentence, but with variable content. The other stems from the varying reactions of individual offenders to similar punishments, or, more practically, from the fact that some offenders would experience distinctly more (or less) pain than most offenders when undergoing a particular form of sentence. We deal with these varying individual sensibilities first, and then turn to variations among penal establishments.

2. EQUAL IMPACT AND INDIVIDUAL SENSIBILITIES

It is not difficult to think of cases in which the impact of a given sentence will have a different impact on individual offenders. A pregnant woman who is imprisoned

---

[13] On this last point, see A. Ashworth, *The Criminal Process* (OUP, 1994), pp. 155–8.

[14] For further discussion, see *ibid*, Ch. 9.

[15] See A. Ashworth, *Sentencing and Criminal Justice*, 2nd edn. (Butterworths, 1995), Ch. 1.

[16] See A. Ashworth, E. Genders, G. Mansfield, J. Peay, and E. Player, *Sentencing in the Crown*

may suffer more greatly, as may a person who is pathologically claustrophobic or who is suffering from a major physical illness. Many mentally disordered offenders may find the experience of imprisonment significantly more painful than others. In relation to non-custodial sentences, there is an absolutely clear example of the problem: the differential impact of a fine on offenders with differing financial resources. Problems of this kind suggest that it is wrong to proceed as if each unit of punishment (i.e. each month's imprisonment, or each £10 of a fine) has an objectively quantified punitive impact. We would argue that fairness requires a recognition that the same sentence may have a disproportionately severe impact on certain offenders, and that only if one adopts a principle of equal impact can this problem be minimized.[17]

The range of factors which may affect the response of different individuals to a given sentence is immense. When Jeremy Bentham came to list what he termed 'circumstances influencing sensibility', he enumerated 32:

1. Health. 2. Strength. 3. Hardiness. 4. Bodily imperfections. 5. Quantity and quality of knowledge. 6. Strength of intellectual powers. 7. Firmness of mind. 8. Steadiness of mind. 9. Bent of inclination. 10. Moral sensibility. 11. Moral biases. 12. Religious sensibility. 13. Religious biases. 14. Sympathetic sensibility. 15. Sympathetic biases. 16. Antipathetic sensibility. 17. Antipathetic biases. 18. Insanity. 19. Habitual occupations. 20. Pecuniary circumstances. 21. Connexions in the way of sympathy. 22. Connexions in the way of antipathy. 23. Radical frame of body. 24. Radical frame of mind. 25. Sex. 26. Age. 27. Rank. 28. Education. 29. Climate. 30. Lineage. 31. Government. 32. Religious profession.[18]

This may be considered over-elaborate, but Bentham notes that individual sensibilities may render a sentence either more or less severe than normal. How ought a sentencing system to deal with these variations of response? Bentham's principle of equal impact was stated thus:

Rule 6. It is further to be observed, that owing to the different manners and degrees in which persons under different circumstances are affected by the same exciting cause, a punishment which is the same in name will not always either really produce, or even so much as appear to others to produce, in two different persons the same degree of pain: therefore

That the quantity actually inflicted on each individual offender may correspond to the quantity intended for similar offenders in general, the several circumstances influencing sensibility ought always to be taken into account.[19]

In view of the emphasis on *general* deterrence in Bentham's writings, it may be considered surprising that he set such store by detailed individual calculations of this kind. However, those theories which have some requirement of proportionality of sentence to the seriousness of the offence must surely concern themselves with this problem.

Court: report of an exploratory study (Oxford Centre for Criminological Research, 1984), pp. 20–4, 62–3.

[17] The principle is discussed by Ashworth (1995), n. 15 above, pp. 79–80 and 142–5.
[18] J. Bentham, *Principles of Morals and Legislation* (1789), Ch. VI, para. 6.
[19] *Ibid*, Ch. XIV, para. 14.

Equality of impact is widely accepted as a strong principle of fairness in the calculation of financial penalties. There has long been legislative recognition of the need for courts to take account of the means of the offender, in calculating the amount of fines, so as to ensure that they have an approximately equal impact on people with differing financial resources.[20] Indeed many other European countries operate systems of 'day fines', which take account of the seriousness of the offence and also link the amount of the fine to the offender's annual income.[21]

The same principle has, however, been less rigorously applied when calculating the length of custodial sentences. In the leading case of *Bernard* (1997)[22] the Court of Appeal reviewed several earlier decisions, and the judgment yields two general principles. First, a medical condition which might at some unspecified future date affect either life expectancy or the prison authorities' ability to treat the prisoner satisfactorily is not a reason for the Court of Appeal to interfere with an otherwise appropriate sentence, although it might be a matter for the Home Secretary to consider in relation to his powers of release. In this category falls the offender who is HIV positive. Secondly, a serious medical condition, even when it is difficult to treat in prison, does not automatically entitle an offender to a lesser sentence than would otherwise be appropriate, although it might enable a court, as an act of mercy in the exceptional circumstances of a particular case, to impose a lesser sentence than would otherwise be appropriate. The first principle seems to reflect the court's reluctance to alter sentences in response to uncertain predictions, whereas the second principle allows for the exceptional reduction of a sentence in response to a serious condition with a clear prognosis.

The second principle in *Bernard* may be illustrated by reference to the facts of *Green* (1992).[23] A man who pleaded guilty to supplying heroin was sentenced to 18 months' imprisonment, a relatively short sentence for this crime which took account of the offender's condition. From an early age he had suffered from sickle cell anaemia. The disease took a severe form with him, and he had required blood transfusions on many occasions. The Court of Appeal, which received evidence that management of his illness was seriously impaired by his imprisonment, and that there was a risk of deterioration leading to death if specialist facilities were not readily available, suspended his sentence with immediate effect. This is a somewhat extreme case. In *Bernard* the Court stated that a serious medical condition which is difficult to manage in prison does not automatically justify sentence reduction. In *Green* such a reduction was granted, not merely because the medical condition was difficult to manage, but because the impaired treatment he would receive if kept in prison would place him at greater risk, and would therefore reduce his life expectancy.

An example of the Court's less compromising view of offenders who are HIV

---

[20] See now Criminal Justice Act 1991, s. 18 (as substituted).

[21] For a brief history of the attempt to introduce such a system in England and Wales, see Ashworth (1995), n. 15 above, pp. 261–6.

[22] [1997] 1 Cr.App.R.(S) 135.   [23] (1992) 13 Cr.App.R.(S) 613.

positive is *Moore* (1993),[24] where the offender had been convicted of possessing heroin with intent to supply and sentenced to 5 years' imprisonment. He had been diagnosed as HIV positive, and on appeal it was argued that the sentence should be shortened to make allowance for his reduced life expectancy. The Court of Appeal held that courts should not 'manipulate the sentence so as to achieve a desirable social end',[25] and that the medical condition should be drawn to the attention of the prison authorities, who should raise with the Home Office the possible exercise of the Royal prerogative of mercy if the condition worsened significantly.[26] This is an example of the first *Bernard* principle, and of the courts' unwillingness to reduce sentences where there is considerable uncertainty: reduction is usually left to executive action when more facts are known.[27]

Medical conditions are not the only factors to be considered when seeking to apply the principle of equal impact to custodial sentencing. In *Parker* (1996)[28] the Court of Appeal examined the harsh treatment suffered by certain categories of prisoner who are segregated for their own protection. In this instance the offender had been convicted of robbery of two young girls. He was described as a socially isolated person, and was segregated under rule 43 after he had been assaulted by other prisoners. The Court of Appeal held that these were not reasons for reducing his sentence, and described as 'exceptional' the earlier case of *Holmes* (1979),[29] a mentally impaired offender, whose sentence had been suspended because of his treatment at the hands of other prisoners. One possible justification for the *Parker* approach is that the whole purpose of rule 43 segregation in prisons is to remove what might otherwise be a source of inequality of impact, by protecting vulnerable prisoners from mistreatment by other prisoners. Although conditions vary between prisons, it is by no means always true that prisoners on rule 43 suffer greater pains of imprisonment than other prisoners.

A further factor to be taken into account is where a woman is pregnant or has the responsibility of caring for young children. In cases where a court decides that the offence justifies a custodial sentence, what account should be taken of the fact that the offender is pregnant? Imprisonment is sure to bring extra hardship to a woman who is in the later stages of pregnancy. Moreover, although such prisoners are taken to ordinary hospitals to give birth, the intrusiveness of security for some such prisoners (including the use of chains) has in our view been inhuman and degrading. This points to the minimal use of imprisonment for defendants

---

[24] (1993) 15 Cr.App.R.(S) 97.

[25] Applying a ruling in *Stark* (1992) 13 Cr.App.R.(S) 548.

[26] The procedure is no longer the Royal Prerogative but the discretion of the Secretary of State to release a prisoner in 'exceptional circumstances' or on 'compassionate grounds': Criminal Justice Act 1991, s. 36.

[27] *Moore* made an application to the European Commission on Human Rights, citing in support the decisions in *Green* and also *Leatherbarrow* (1992) 13 Cr.App.R.(S) 632, where the Court of Appeal suspended part of a prison sentence, as an 'exceptionally merciful course', on account of his critical breathing difficulties stemming from chronic emphysema. See also *Varden* [1981] Crim.LR 272 and *Herasymenko* (1975), reported in D. A. Thomas (ed.), *Current Sentencing Practice* C5-2B01. The European Commission rejected the application.

[28] [1996] Crim.LR 445.   [29] (1979) 1 Cr.App.R.(S) 233.

who are pregnant.[30] However, we recognize that pregnancy cannot be regarded as an absolute bar to a prison sentence, even if it should in most cases lead courts to impose a different sentence. Once the child is born, and in other cases where a defendant has the responsibility of caring for a young child, there is the additional element of the damage which imprisonment can cause to a third party—notably, to a young child who is liable to be separated from the mother. There are some cases in which the Court of Appeal has quashed a custodial sentence on a mother when the father has also been imprisoned at the same time, in order to ensure that young children are not deprived of both parents,[31] and there are a few cases in which a custodial sentence imposed on a single parent has been quashed for this reason.[32] There are certainly some spectacular cases in which courts have been influenced by the effect of a custodial sentence on innocent third parties,[33] but in general courts have not taken account of what might be termed the 'ordinary' effect that imprisonment has upon that person's partner or children.[34] This is probably best regarded as an unavoidable concomitant of imprisonment, and supplies a good reason why custodial sentences should be reserved for serious offences.

The cases discussed above, whilst not representing the entire span of individual sensibilities listed by Bentham, serve to give some impression of the range of practical problems to which a sentencing system has to respond when applying the principle of equal impact. Clearly the English courts have accepted this principle as an element of fair treatment; yet they have been considerably more reluctant to tailor the length of a prison sentence to reflect the specific hardships than to adjust the level of a fine to match financial resources. In principle there can be no justification for adopting different standards of fairness in relation to the imposition of different types of penalties. Yet the previous examples have shown that, in practice, striving for equality in the impact of custodial sentences is a more complex process than it is in relation to fines. What are the central differences between the two, and how can they be accommodated?

The first distinction concerns the certainty and validity of the information upon which definitive judgements are made. Except in cases of pregnant women and those with young children, information about an offender's sensibilities to imprisonment is typically far less precise and certain, particularly at the time of sentencing, than information about his or her financial circumstances. As was evident in the cases discussed above, some medical conditions may require a

---

[30] See *Scott* (1990) 12 Cr.App.R.(S) 23, although there is no shortage of cases in which pregnant women have been sentenced to custody.

[31] *Vaughan* (1982) 4 Cr.App.R.(S) 83; *Whitehead* [1996] 1 Cr.App.R.(S) 111.

[32] e.g. *Franklyn* (1981) 3 Cr.App.R.(S) 65.

[33] e.g. *Olliver and Olliver* (1989) 11 Cr.App.R.(S) 10.

[34] A survey of 1,766 women prisoners in England and Wales in 1994 found that 61% of them were mothers of children under 18, with about one-third of the children being under 5 years old. Most of the children were placed with temporary carers, usually female relatives, during the mother's imprisonment. Many children were reported as having behavioural problems as a result of separation from their mothers. See D. Caddle and D. Crisp, *Mothers in Prison*, Home Office Research Findings No. 38 (1997).

prediction of the sentence's impact (how long will the HIV-positive prisoner live?) whereas an offender's present wealth or past income is more certain. This may help to justify the *Bernard* approach of reluctance to alter sentences on the basis of predictions and a preference for executive release if and when a medical condition becomes clear and severe in its effects. Indeed, there is an important time factor: in fixing the amount of a fine the court can expect to obtain information about an offender's financial position, whereas an offender's reaction to imprisonment will rarely be known at the time of sentence. In many of the cases discussed above, the point was raised as a ground of appeal which had arisen subsequent to the trial—hence the argument that it should be treated as a matter for the prison authorities, Parole Board, or Home Secretary. If a court is to consider it, the central question is what counts as sufficiently objective and certain evidence. It may be argued that where there are medical reports on an illness and on the typical response of patients to it, courts will have some objective basis on which to reach a judgment, as they do in pregnancy cases. A difficulty arises, however, when such evidence rests heavily upon professional opinion and when professional opinion is divided. How should courts assess such information? The approach adopted by the Court of Appeal appears to give credibility only to information that claims to be value-free and can be validated by scientific method. The difficulty with this approach is that it inevitably discriminates against the recognition of those types of human sensibilities that are currently difficult to define within those parameters, most notably those that require a prediction of future effects and those that concern the psychological state rather than the physical condition of the individual. To expect the courts to do otherwise, however, may call for complex judgements beyond the capabilities of sentencers.

A second issue concerns the causes of the offender's sensitivity to imprisonment. A distinction can be drawn between the effect of a medical condition on the experience of imprisonment, and the effect of imprisonment on the medical condition. Imprisonment may have many pains, in terms of deprivation of freedom of movement, heterosexual relations, employment and so on, and for a prisoner with a medical condition there may be extra pains. The justification for reducing the length of a custodial sentence because of an offender's medical state is arguably more compelling if, as in *Green*, there is evidence that imprisonment has a deleterious effect on that condition. This is the approach which ought to be adopted when sentencing pregnant women. It is the same approach as is routinely adopted by courts when considering community sentences and financial penalties. An elderly person with a heart condition would not be given strenuous work on a community service order. Similarly, a fine may be considered an inappropriate penalty for an offender who is already heavily in debt.

A third point, which argues strongly in favour of striving towards assessments of equal impact in custodial sentencing, distinguishes between the *nature and scale of the costs* or deprivations created by imprisonment and those that may arise from a financial penalty. The loss of freedom imposed upon a prisoner deprives him or her of a finite resource, namely time. The loss of financial resources need not be viewed in this way: an individual may be able to create opportunities to obtain more money. Death is a certainty for everyone, and it can therefore be argued that all prisoners must inevitably experience an irreplaceable loss of time. Yet for most people death is viewed as a distant prospect. In the case of an offender suffering from a life-threatening condition, however, the limits of life span are in view and, in consequence, the irremediable loss of time is felt more acutely. A related point is that for a prisoner to know that he is to die in custody is likely to be regarded as more painful and ignominious for him and for his family and friends. A logical implication of this is that elderly offenders are also likely to experience a heightened awareness of their mortality and should thus receive sentences which are reduced to take account of their shorter life expectancy. Paradoxically, this appears to be the approach of the English courts, despite their reluctance to modify sentences for the terminally ill.[35]

A fourth issue concerns equal impact and dulled sensibilities. It is quite fair that, when assessing the proper amount of a fine, courts should exact increased financial penalties from those who are wealthy, in an attempt to produce equal impact. But it does not follow that courts should impose longer prison sentences on those who are thought to have become hardened to the experience of imprisonment. Pragmatically, differences of impact should only be taken into account if they are likely to be significantly outside the normal range of responses to a given sentence. The type of sensitivity that could be legitimately considered should, in our view, include physical and psychological illness and significant physical and mental abuse from which the prison authorities fail to provide adequate protection. But what constitutes acceptable evidence of the effects of these problems? We argued earlier that standards of scientific validity were inappropriate when reviewing such evidence since all such assessments inevitably involve a level of judgement. However, the existence of illness or abuse can be factually determined and a degree of objectivity can be gained in the assessment of impact if the opinions of independent doctors and psychologists are sought. Extending the range of individual sensibilities beyond these factors seems to us to represent a dangerous path that leads to invidious value judgements and discrimination. This point is particularly relevant to the question whether sentences should be lengthened for those believed to be desensitized to imprisonment. It is not possible to determine with any degree of reliability which offenders are particularly robust in dealing with the pains of imprisonment, and such assessments would be vulnerable to stereotypical assumptions influenced by class, race, gender, and sexuality.

Our conclusion, then, is that the principle of equal impact is a principle of fairness which ought to be observed by the courts. Our argument has been that the

---

[35] One difficult case is *John Francis C* (1993) 14 Cr.App.R.(S) 562, where a man aged 79 was convicted of 13 serious sexual offences against young children. The Court of Appeal upheld the sentence of 8 years' imprisonment, on the basis that this was reduced from 12 years to reflect the offender's age and life expectancy, although the Court recognized that he 'may not be able to live any part of his life in the community again'.

main aim should be to avoid clear inequalities of impact, whether at the sentencing stage or in the 'execution of sanctions'. Bentham's list of 32 'circumstances influencing sensibility' and his 'rule 6' might be thought to import a spurious air of precision into the exercise, as Nigel Walker pointed out:

We might have quite complicated calculations, starting with the assumption that the normal sentence is appropriate for a man of, say, 25, and that the offender will live for three score years and ten (or indeed until the average age of death for an overweight heavy smoker, or whatever he is). A ready reckoner would then tell the sentencer how many months to deduct for a man of, say, 43. If this is regarded as *reductio ad absurdum*, why?[36]

It is unnecessary to go to these lengths because sentencing is not such a precise exercise. The justifications are strongest when the inequality of impact would be at its greatest, which is why we have focused on clear cases in our discussion. Such cases can be identified, and it is right for the courts and prison authorities to respond to them.[37]

3. Equal Treatment and Variable Penal Practices

A second kind of problem in achieving equality of treatment arises from variations in the delivery or execution of sentences. Courts may impose sentences which are nominally the same, but which are administered in such different ways as to have different impacts on similar offenders. Concern about variations in the form taken by non-custodial sentences led the Government to introduce 'national standards' for the various forms of community sentence: when a court imposes a sentence such as probation or community service, it is now clear what should follow from the making of that order (in terms of the obligations of probation officers and offenders, frequency of contact, reporting of breaches, etc.).[38] One result of introducing the national standards seems to be greater equality of treatment for those receiving a given form of sentence.

Our focus in this section, however, is on custodial sentences. It is widely recognized that conditions in English prisons vary considerably, and that the experience of serving a sentence can be considerably more onerous in one establishment than in another.[39] In view of the physical difficulties of ensuring similarity of conditions, the question arises of whether the actual conditions under which a sentence is served should lead to an alteration of its length. The reasoning would be that sentences are intended to be so calibrated as to inflict a certain amount of punishment and no more, that account should therefore be taken of variations in the degree of 'hard treatment' suffered in different conditions, and that an acceptable scale for converting these varying penal conditions

---

[36] N. Walker, *Punishment, Danger and Stigma* (Blackwell, 1980), p. 122.

[37] See also the discussion by Bottoms in Ch. 3 of this book, above, pp. 56–7.

[38] Home Office, *National Standards for the Supervision of Offenders in the Community*, 1st edn. (1992); 2nd edn. (1995).

[39] M. Leech, *The Prisoner's Handbook* (OUP, 1995).

into custodial time can be found. 'Penal calculations' of various kinds are not without historical precedent. In 1853, following the abolition of transportation, Joshua Jebb invented a new structure of penalties that translated years of transportation into years of penal servitude.[40] In 1982 the Lord Chief Justice, Lord Lane, suggested an approximate equivalence between hours of community service and months of imprisonment.[41] And there is a statutory scale which converts unpaid fines into short terms of imprisonment in default of payment.[42]

One difficulty of exchanging harsh conditions for shorter sentences, however, is that it assumes that their hard treatment elements are not only functionally equivalent but also equally valid means of inflicting State punishment. This suggests that the hard treatment element of imprisonment can legitimately extend beyond the loss of liberty to the imposition of conditions which are known to be unnecessarily detrimental to the body and mind of the prisoner. Yet this stands in fundamental contradiction to a widely-respected tenet of modern penology: the aphorism of Alexander Paterson that offenders are sent to prison '*as* a punishment and not *for* punishment'.[43] Lord Woolf, in his report on the prison disturbances in April 1990, repeatedly asserted this principle:

while a prisoner should be subjected to the stigma of imprisonment and should be confined to a prison, the prisoner is not to be subjected to inhumane or degrading treatment.[44]

This form of the argument can claim the authority of Article 3 of the European Convention on Human Rights, which declares that 'no one shall be subjected to torture or to inhuman or degrading treatment or punishment'. Thus the argument now has two distinct strands. First, prison conditions which fall below the minimum and which constitute inhuman or degrading treatment are simply not acceptable. Secondly, insofar as the conditions in prison establishments vary, over and above the minimum, there is the question of whether, and, if so, how, to take account of those variations when calculating sentence length.

(a) Minimum standards for prison conditions

In the English context, the first strand of the argument must be developed at a practical and a theoretical level. In practice poor conditions may be found in many prison establishments. No doubt it would be claimed by the Prison Service that the conditions which were criticized as inhuman and degrading by a team of European inspectors in 1990[45] have now been improved. Yet there has been a long series of reports from Her Majesty's Chief Inspector of Prisons which are critical

---

[40] See L. Radzinowicz and R. Hood, *The Emergence of Penal Policy in Victorian and Edwardian England* (OUP, 1990), pp. 498–502.

[41] In *Lawrence* (1982) 4 Cr.App.R.(S) 69, linking 9 months' imprisonment with a community service order of 190 hours.

[42] Criminal Justice Act 1991, s. 22 (as amended); cf. now Crime (Sentences) Act 1997, ss. 30–2, permitting courts to impose various community sentences on fine defaulters.

[43] See S. K. Ruck, *Paterson on Prisons* (1951).

[44] Woolf, *Prison Disturbance, April 1990: report of an Inquiry* (1991), para. 10.19.

[45] Committee for the Prevention of Torture and Inhuman and Degrading Treatment or

of the conditions in various prisons.[46] It would not be difficult to argue that the dilapidated and overcrowded conditions that afflict many local prisons, in particular, are still 'inhuman and degrading'.[47] Cold, damp and insanitary conditions are still to be found in a number of establishments, largely because the fabric of the buildings is worn out and because they were not designed (for example, in terms of sanitation) to cope with the numbers of prisoners they are now expected to house. This is not to ignore the existence of some modern prisons which have all the necessary facilities. Our point is that there are many older prisons, still in use, which arguably inflict inhuman and degrading treatment on their inmates. And, of course, it is not the prisons themselves that 'inflict' these conditions. Insofar as the Home Secretary and the Prison Service are aware that sub-standard conditions exist in certain establishments, and yet they continue to allocate prisoners to those establishments, it can be argued that those authorities are knowingly causing distress to prisoners and infringing their fundamental rights.

Two counter-arguments may be raised. The first is a 'practical' argument, of the kind deployed by the Government in its response to the recommendations in the Woolf report.[48] This is that it is building new prisons as fast as is practicable, but that such is the volume of serious crime that it is a simple matter of public necessity that some prisoners have to be housed in less-than-satisfactory conditions. The position will improve, it might be claimed, but for the present it must be accepted that the prison authorities are doing their best to cope with the problems. This reasoning is unconvincing. Every person's right not to be subjected to inhuman and degrading conditions is an absolute right: according to Article 15 of the European Convention on Human Rights, it is not even one of those basic rights that can be taken away 'in time of war or other public emergency threatening the life of the nation'. The Government does have a choice: it could pursue a penal policy less reliant on imprisonment. What could have been done, following the Woolf report, would have been to ensure that the prison estate was brought up to acceptable standards at a time when the prison population was fairly stable. Instead, in the years since 1993 there has been a sharp turn towards a more punitive sentencing policy without ensuring that the prison accommodation is in place in time to cope with the impact of that policy. The Government has chosen to breach the European Convention and to infringe the rights of many prisoners. Supporters of the policy would claim that improved protection of the public supplies the justification. Critics would argue that the evidence for that is lacking, that electoral advantage is the real reason, and that in any event the hope of

---

Punishment, *Report to the United Kingdom Government on the Visit to the United Kingdom from 29 July to 10 August 1990* (Strasbourg, 1990).

[46] See R. D. King and K. McDermott, 'British Prisons 1970–1987: the ever-deepening crisis', (1989) 29 *B.J.Crim.* 107; H.M.Chief Inspector of Prisons, *Annual Report for 1995–1996* (HMSO, 1996); H.M.Chief Inspector of Prisons, *Doing Time or Using Time: Report of a Review of Regimes in the Prison Service* (HMSO, 1993).

[47] See further the discussion by Kleinig in Ch. 11 of this book, below.

[48] Home Office, *Custody, Care and Justice: the Way Ahead for the Prison Service in England and Wales* (HMSO, 1991).

improved protection cannot amount to a justification for breaching such fundamental rights.

The Government might, alternatively, scrutinize the practical application of the concept of inhuman and degrading treatment. Mr Howard, as Home Secretary, made it clear that a degree of austerity in prison conditions is to be expected, although standards of decency are to be upheld.[49] However, he and his predecessors resisted the case for recognition of the European Standard Minimum Rules for the Treatment of Prisoners (1973) by English law or even in the Prison Rules. The courts, for their part, have held that the Prison Rules do not vest any special rights in prisoners, such as the right to minimum standards.[50] It seems likely that one reason for the previous Government's reluctance to recognize minimum standards was the knowledge that some English prisons do not, and probably cannot (because of their construction), attain them. This brings the argument back to the question of choice of penal policy. Since the Government knows of the shortcomings of many Prison Service establishments, it ought to ensure that prisoners are not allocated to those establishments until and unless they can be assured that their rights under Article 3 will be respected.

Our conclusion, on the first strand of the argument, is therefore that no prisoners should be subjected to conditions which violate Article 3 of the European Convention on Human Rights. The political and practical difficulties lie in concretization and in enforcement. Article 3 itself is couched in general terms, 'inhuman or degrading treatment or punishment', and the European Standard Minimum Rules fail to offer clear parameters on many issues.[51] Unless the general declaration in Article 3 can be concretized in such a way as to give guidance on the key issues that prisoners and prison authorities have to confront, the prospects for progress in this direction are slim. But one could imagine that many governments will not be anxious to see a code of specific minimum standards, if only because of the cost implications for their prison system. Moreover, enforcement of the standards would need to be ensured. The English courts have been reluctant to intervene in order to insist on any minimum standards, giving great weight to administrative arguments on behalf of the Prison Service.[52] Incorporation of the European Convention on Human Rights into English law might have some effect on this, insofar as the courts would have to respond to arguments based on Article 3. But it does not follow that the courts would have regard to the European Minimum Rules when interpreting Article 3, and it is not clear what the future of minimum standards might be at the European level.[53]

---

[49] This aspect of Mr Howard's speech to the Conservative Party conference in 1993 is analysed by R. Sparks, 'Penal Austerity: the Doctrine of Less Eligibility Reborn?', in R. Matthews and P. Francis (eds.), *Prisons 2000: an international perspective on the current state and future of imprisonment* (Macmillan, 1996).

[50] *Williams* v. *Home Office (No. 2)* [1982] 2 All ER 564.

[51] Casale comments that the European Rules consist of 'vague wording and qualified statements of principle [which] create loopholes and allow circumvention': S. Casale, 'Control and Prison Conditions', in E. Player and M. Jenkins (eds.), *Prisons after Woolf: Reform through Riot* (Routledge, 1994).

[52] cf. however *R.* v. *Deputy Governor of Parkhurst Prison, ex parte Hague* [1992] 1 AC 58.

[53] In their introduction to *Western European Prison Systems: a Critical Anatomy* (Sage, 1995),

Our argument is that prison conditions which fall below the standards implicit in Article 3 impose hard treatment without moral authority, and therefore lose their legitimacy as an element of State punishment. Where conditions do fall below these standards, there can be no question of adjusting the length of sentence in order to make allowances for the unusually harsh treatment. Such punishment is illegitimate, and ought not to take place at all. We recognize that in the recent past the British Government has not always been fastidious in its concern for the rights embodied in the European Convention on Human Rights. Although incorporation of the European Convention into English law might improve the position, there is a question which will need to be confronted for some years to come: if prisoners continue to be placed in conditions which fall clearly below the minimum standards, what should be the official response? The first response would be to ensure that all steps are taken to prevent the occurrence or recurrence of sub-standard treatment; but that, if such treatment does occur, consideration should be given to compensating prisoners financially for the violation of basic rights or making significant reductions in sentence-length. How this might be done will be discussed in section 4 below.

(b) Variations in prison conditions

The principal concern in this section is to examine variations in prison conditions, over and above the minimum conditions (assuming that they are attained), and to consider whether the variations are so considerable that they ought to be reflected in sentence-length. To prepare the ground, an outline of variations in prison conditions will be given, focusing on security classification and on regime activities.

Following their reception into prison all prisoners are given a **security classification**, to reflect the degree of security thought necessary for their containment. In England and Wales there are four categories for adult male prisoners, ranging from A (highest risk) to D (lowest risk).[54] Prison establishments are similarly classified, and prisoners are allocated to an establishment with the appropriate security classification.[55] Different security ratings lead to different conditions, in relation to such matters as perimeter security; inmates' freedom of movement between different parts of the prison; the degree of human or electronic surveillance; and the intrusions on privacy caused by routine searches of inmates' bodies and possessions. From this it might be thought to follow that, the greater the level of restriction imposed on inmates in a particular security category, the

Ruggiero, Ryan, and Sim speculate (p. 7) that, following the Maastricht Treaty, the liberalism of the Council of Europe 'could well be superseded by the European Union's more hard-line, formalized approach to criminal justice matters'.

[54] With the exception of those placed in category A, female prisoners and male young offenders are not subject to this schema at present. They are simply designated as being suitable for open or closed conditions.

[55] Some prisons may house inmates with different classifications, with certain units or parts of the establishment having a different security rating.

greater the level of hard treatment experienced—although, in practice, the position is complicated by some other, more liberal aspects of the regime within high security prisons or units.

Can these differences be justified? It can be argued that the prison population represents a range of security risks, not only in the threat some prisoners present to the maintenance of good order in each establishment, but also in terms of their propensity to escape from custody and the danger they would pose to the public if they were to escape. Thus it is justifiable for the prison authorities to operate a system of security classification, in order to fulfil their primary duty of providing conditions necessary to hold prisoners securely in custody. However, the security categorization actually imposed must be tied to the incapacitative purpose which justifies it. Thus, first, only those restrictions which are essential to contain prisoners of a certain kind should be permitted. For example, the present policy of dispersing category A prisoners among several prisons, rather than concentrating them in one or two, means that large numbers of category B prisoners in the dispersal prisons are subjected to the stricter security requirements designed for category A prisoners. In principle this is unjustifiable. Secondly, the determination of prisoners' security classifications should be based on relevant criteria which are consistently applied.

If it can be shown that the security level is not excessive and that allocation procedures are fair, the presumption is that the resulting hard treatment can be regarded as a legitimate component of State punishment. But, insofar as some groups do receive harder treatment, as a result of greater security measures, does this justify a reduction in sentence? A distinction should be drawn between those who are placed in conditions of security which are intended to be appropriate to the danger they represent, and those prisoners who are subjected to higher security than their classification warrants. An example of the former group is category A prisoners held in conditions of maximum security. Traditionally, the facilities within these prisons have tended to be relatively extensive and the regimes have afforded certain concessions to these long-term prisoners.[56] For example, inmates are likely to be allowed the privacy of their own cell and various opportunities to exercise autonomy over their lifestyle, such as being permitted to cook their own food. The rationale for these ameliorations of the prison environment seems to be that high security should be counterbalanced by conditions that limit the oppressive nature of security restrictions and minimize the degree of alienation and psychological deterioration of prisoners serving long sentences. We agree that this is the right approach, and we would therefore conclude that the length of an offender's sentence should affect the conditions under which it is served, but that the conditions should not affect the length.

However, the position is different where prisoners are subjected to conditions of greater security than their classification warrants—for example, category B

---

[56] We are assuming that, even if local prisons were brought up to the European Minimum Standards, prisoners held in conditions of high security would continue to have greater facilities than others.

prisoners held in dispersal prisons, designed to contain category A security risks. There is an argument that this harder than warranted treatment should be reflected in some reduction in sentence length, unless it can be maintained that some of the more liberal aspects of regimes in dispersal prisons amount to compensation for the higher security.

Many of the differences between prisons relate to variations in their **regime activities**. The number of hours a prisoner is allowed out of his cell each day is one basic indicator. Following from this, there is a range of activities in which inmates can selectively participate. Some will be unstructured pursuits, such as using the library or watching television; others will be more rigidly controlled or structured, such as participating in educational or training courses or therapeutic programmes. At one level they all represent ways of keeping prisoners occupied and minimizing the negative consequences that inactivity and boredom might have for good order in the prison. At another level they can be regarded as opportunities for inmates to minimize the deleterious effects of imprisonment and to 'address their offending behaviour' in ways that reduce their chances of reoffending after release.

The important point in the present context is that the regime in a given establishment may depend on a range of factors. Choices made by the present governor, or by previous governors, have a definite influence. Other prison staff, too, may play a role in shaping the regime of a particular prison. Even in decisions about priorities in spending, governors may make choices that have a considerable effect on the experience of imprisonment for the inmates. Other factors, such as the number of people committed to prison by the courts in a particular catchment area, may also affect or constrain regimes. In times of overcrowding, particularly in local prisons, activities which might otherwise be available may be suspended because of problems of staffing, space, or logistics, or the waiting lists may become so long that some prisoners are denied access.

Does this variation in regimes constitute an unfair allocation of hard treatment? In order to explore this issue, four questions need to be addressed. The first is whether non-identical regimes inevitably undermine the principle of equal treatment. One answer to this is that equal treatment is unlikely to be provided by homogeneous and monolithic regimes and programmes, and may be better served by equal access to a range of opportunities designed to respond to different individual needs. However, this falls short of justifying the present range of regimes in English prisons, which often vary according to influences unrelated to the needs of particular inmates. The second question is whether a particular variation in regime amounts to a breach of the contract between prisoners and the Prison Service. These contracts, introduced following the Woolf report,[57] are not intended to have any legal effect but are supposed to give rise to 'legitimate expectations' on both sides. Complaints about the Prison Service's failure to meet the contractual 'expectations' may be heard by the Prisons Ombudsman. If

---

[57] Woolf Report, paras. 12.120–12.129.

it is decided that there has been a breach of contract, we would argue that this may support an argument for financial recompense or for a compensatory reduction in sentence length.

A third question concerns prisoners who have been denied access to rehabilitative facilities relevant to their needs. The Prison Service's 'Statement of Purpose' proclaims that one of its key tasks is to look after those in custody in ways which will enable them to lead law-abiding and useful lives. Rule 1 of the Prison Rules is in similar terms, but it is almost certainly too vague to create a right enforceable through the courts. Thus where a prisoner has no access to rehabilitative schemes because there are insufficient resources, or because of the highly specialized needs of the individual prisoner, an action for judicial review is unlikely to succeed.[58] Nonetheless the inmate could be said to have suffered additional hard treatment that could be to his or her long-term, as well as immediate, detriment. A fourth question relates to those prisoners who do undergo certain rehabilitative programmes. Some therapeutic programmes are psychologically arduous and emotionally painful to undertake,[59] and it could be argued that participants receive a greater degree of hard treatment than other prisoners who acquire a vocational skill with far less effort. Should the former group receive some reduction in sentence-length? Assuming that it is not compulsory for prisoners to undertake the programme, either of two arguments could be maintained. One is that the choice to take the programme is one that might benefit the prisoner in the long-term (by increasing the chance of law-abidance), and so that benefit may be taken to counterbalance any short-term unpleasantness. On this view, no reduction would be called for. An alternative argument might be that some recognition should be given to the demands of certain therapeutic programmes, either because the pain of the rehabilitative endeavour is a legitimate form of hard treatment, or because it is in the public interest to offer an inducement to prisoners to participate in such programmes.

Variations in prison conditions for women raise a special set of problems. It has long been recognized that the small number of female establishments results in some women being held long distances from their homes, inhibiting contact with their families, and exacerbating the hard treatment in imprisonment. The size of the women's system also restricts the range of regimes and programmes available to female prisoners. Such systemic discrimination may be dealt with in the short term by the imposition of shorter sentences, but in the longer term a more radical reappraisal of the role and organization of imprisonment for women is called for.

In summary, then, our view is that the Prison Service should assume some overall responsibility for maintaining equality of the impact of imprisonment, in the context of reasonable security requirements. Where it falls significantly short of this goal, the main response is to attack this shortcoming on human rights

[58] G. Richardson, *Law, Process and Custody: Prisoners and Patients* (Weidenfeld, 1993), Ch. 6.
[59] cf. E. Genders and E. Player, *Grendon* (OUP, 1995), pp. 117–18, and Duff (1996), n. 5 above, pp. 52–3 on confrontational group work.

grounds. If the failure to achieve standards persists, the possibilities of financial compensation and sentence reduction should be examined.

4. TOWARDS EQUALITY OF TREATMENT

We have established that conditions vary considerably in the English prison system. We have also argued, in the first part of this chapter, that fairness in sentencing requires efforts to achieve equality in the impact of sanctions. However, where prison conditions fall below the minimum required by Article 3 of the European Convention, the proper response is to close that establishment or, at least, to reduce the number of inmates held to a level at which minimum standards can be maintained. We recognize that in the present political climate that is unlikely to happen. We therefore argue that, as a matter of principle, if custodial sentences have to be served in establishments that fall below minimum standards, either monetary compensation should be paid or sentence-lengths ought to be reduced significantly. If a prisoner's human rights are violated the discount ought surely to be substantial. Where the establishment satisfies the minimum conditions but there are unjustified hardships of another kind—for example, prisoners subjected to a higher security level than is warranted, prisoners not provided with the appropriate rehabilitative programmes—it might be appropriate to provide for lesser reductions. Arguments of this kind are neither novel nor academic. Some years ago Lord Lane CJ deployed similar reasoning in two Court of Appeal decisions:

Sentencing judges should appreciate that overcrowding in many of the penal establishments in this country is such that a prison sentence, however short, is a very unpleasant experience indeed for the inmates.[60]

It is no secret that our prisons at the moment are dangerously overcrowded. So much so that sentencing courts must be particularly careful to examine each case to ensure, if an immediate custodial sentence is necessary, that the sentence is as short as possible.[61]

At a time when overcrowding is again posing major problems for prisoners and the Prison Service, these judicial arguments are particularly apposite.

However, when the argument moves from the level of principle to that of practice, the matter becomes greatly complicated. One problem is how the conditions in each prison are to be rated, for the purposes of allowing reductions. This would need to be accomplished by an independent body, perhaps the Prisons Inspectorate. It would not be a question of giving each institution a percentage rating, but rather of rating it according to a certain checklist, where necessary in relation to particular prisoners. There might be three categories: below minimum standards, minimal regime, and full regime. A second problem concerns the allocation of prisoners to establishments. At present this is a Prison Service task, determined

---

[60] *Upton* (1980) 2 Cr.App.R.(S) 132, at 134.   [61] *Bibi* (1980) 2 Cr.App.R.(S) 177, at 178.

first by the security classification, and then by such matters as locality, sentence length, and the availability of places. This administrative decision can have a significant impact on the offender's experience of custody, as we have shown. The courts have recognized this, holding that a category A prisoner should have the right to be informed of any matter or fact or opinion relevant to his security classification (unless covered by public interest immunity) and to be given reasons for decisions in relation to security classification.[62] It is arguable that there should be a more accessible machinery for challenging security and allocation decisions. A third problem is that some prisoners might wish to be allocated to prisons falling below minimum standards, if their concern was merely to complete the sentence as quickly as possible. It certainly does not follow that challenges to allocation decisions would always be on the ground that they subjected the offender to unsatisfactory conditions: some offenders, faced with a choice between 12 months in a clean, new privately-run prison, and 6 or 8 months in a run-down and overcrowded local prison, might prefer the latter, especially if it were nearer to home and made it easier for visitors. A fourth problem is how any adjustments to the length of a prison sentence would be effected. This could not be done by the court at the time of sentencing, since it would not yet know what allocation decision was to be made.[63] Yet whilst it would be convenient if adjustments were made by the prison authorities, this might be thought to be an inappropriate tampering with a judicially imposed order. Only a court should be able to alter an order, although it would be a mechanical task since the court would be told of the prison to which the offender had been sent and its rating. A fifth practical problem would be that some offenders are transferred from prison to prison, often at very short notice, and this might require re-adjustment of the sentence each time.

The practical problems of implementing the principle are therefore considerable, and we will not go into further detail at this stage. We recognize that one objection to the system of 'honesty in sentencing', which would have empowered the Prison Service to allocate remission of sentence for co-operation and positive good behaviour, was that it would blur the line between the allocation of punishment and the administration of sentences, and would place some unreviewable power over sentence length in the hands of prison authorities. That scheme, set out in the Crime (Sentences) Act 1997, is not to be implemented by the present Government. Avoidance of the objections rightly raised against it would be a major part of operationalizing the principle of equal treatment for which we contend.

5. PROPORTIONALITY AND EQUAL TREATMENT

Earlier in this chapter we recognized that a principle of proportionality plays a part in most contemporary philosophies of punishment and, without arguing the

---

[62] *R. v. Secretary of State for Home Affairs, ex parte Duggan, The Times*, 9 December 1993.

[63] It is well established in English law that a court has no control over the prison or regime to which an offender is sent: for a recent discussion, see *Lancaster* (1995) 16 Cr.App.R.(S) 184.

point, we have assumed that it is right that it should do so. Andrew von Hirsch gives proportionality a central role, asserting that 'the principle calls for A and B to receive comparably severe punishments, if the gravity of their crimes is approximately the same'.[64]

We have sought to argue for a principle of equal treatment which would recognize that sentences may have a different impact, either because the individual offender has significantly different sensibilities or because certain sentences can impose significantly different burdens and restrictions on offenders as a result of administrative decision-making. We contend that attempts should be made to remove these differences of impact. Courts should reduce sentences to make allowance for distinct and serious medical conditions; if they only become known after sentence has been imposed, there should be the possibility of judicial determination of their relevance to sentence, even if executive discretion is the means of giving effect to them. At the stage of 'execution of sanctions', i.e. in the carrying out of court sentencing orders, efforts to equalize the impact should be made by authorities such as the Probation Service and the Prison Service. Insofar as these are unsuccessful, either financial compensation or even a sentence reduction should be considered.

We have been frank about the difficulties of implementing such a system—custodial regimes are likely to differ, for some good and other less good reasons; if financial compensation is used, the appropriate scale needs to be considered; and if sentence reduction is used, some parameters need to be established. There would be considerable problems in deciding on sentence reductions to reflect unsatisfactory conditions, not least in relation to early release provisions. Our main concern is less the details and more the point of principle that it is right to strive to avoid clear inequalities of impact, as a response to the practical realities of the English penal system—and, probably, many other contemporary penal systems. One fundamental question raised by the discussion is to whom sentences are addressed. Andrew von Hirsch argues that the element of censure in criminal sentences addresses the victim, the perpetrator, and the public at large.[65] He adds that 'the message expressed through the penalty about [the criminal conduct's] degree of wrongfulness ought to reflect how reprehensible the conduct indeed is'. It might therefore be argued that, persuasive as the principle of equal treatment might be, any attempt to adjust proportionate sentences is bound to send inappropriate messages to the addressees of State punishment. This need not be so, however. The assumption of sentencing theories based on censure or communication is that offenders are individuals with sufficient autonomy to be capable of responding to punishment. If that is so, they ought equally to be capable of appreciating why the sentences imposed on certain offenders are reduced in order to produce equality of treatment. If A and B commit similar crimes and have similar criminal records, A ought to be able to appreciate why a court gives B a lesser sentence if B suffers from a life-threatening illness or if the

---

[64] Von Hirsch (1993), n. 3 above, p. 75.   [65] *Ibid*, pp. 10–11.

prison conditions to which B is subjected are patently worse than those experienced by A.

Recent penal history tells that the communication of sentences to the general public is particularly problematic, largely because of the presentation of sentences by the media. The demise of the unit fine system, introduced in order to ensure equality of treatment for offenders with different financial resources, provides an object lesson in how a sound principle can be undermined by reporting which fails to explain the reasons behind the sentences imposed.[66] Perhaps these are arguments for relying more on executive discretion or financial compensation to deal with problems of unequal impact. But insofar as sentence reduction is used, one important step in implementing the principle for which we argue would be for a court to announce both the proportionate sentence and then the adjusted sentence in the particular case: if courts were less reticent about their sentence calculations, perhaps misunderstandings might be less frequent.

[66] See n. 21 above for references.

11

The Hardness of Hard Treatment

JOHN KLEINIG*

In February, 1996, Rosemary West was convicted of ten murders of young women, including a daughter and stepdaughter. The British public were shocked by the gruesome details as they gradually unfolded. West (whose co-defendant husband committed suicide in custody) was sentenced to life imprisonment on each count.[1] In a subsequent newspaper article, Stephen, Rosemary's eldest son, reportedly complained about the apparently comfortable life his mother had in prison. His mother was reading the classics, attending seminars, and working 40 hours a week making toys: 'She is happy and quite content and has found a lot of friends. This is disappointing, really. I wonder if you can call it punishment at all?'[2]

In the USA, Stephen West's concern has been expressed and acted upon for some time. Boot camps have grown in popularity; at least two states have re-introduced chain gangs;[3] several others have begun to remove inmate facilities such as gym equipment and television sets; and others have banned cigarettes, or scaled down telephone access, or food choice. Just how hard should the hard treatment of imprisonment be?

There are, of course, various motivations at work in such initiatives. Some are obvious and inherently reasonable, albeit at times improperly exploited[4]—such

---

* I have little doubt that this contribution would have been improved had Andrew von Hirsch been able to review it beforehand. Nevertheless, I am very grateful for comments on earlier versions by Derek Brookes, Tziporah Kasachkoff, Charles Lindner, Margaret Leland Smith, and Larry E. Sullivan.

[1] West subsequently appealed her conviction, but was unsuccessful. See *Rosemary Pauline West* [1996] 2 Cr.App.R. 374.

[2] *The Times*, 19 March 1996, p. 5.

[3] In one one those states—Alabama—the threat of a suit and international criticism has led to their discontinuance. However, the state retained the use of 'hitching posts'—something like a pillory, and only recently has a federal judge ruled against them. See Adam Nossiter, 'Judge Rules Against Alabama's Prison "Hitching Posts" ', *New York Times*, 31 January 1997, p. A14. In a variation, prisoners employed in 'chain' gangs are sometimes being kept under control by means of stun belts, which allow corrections officers to deliver an 8-second burst of 50,000 volts to the kidneys from up to 300 feet away. See Peter L. Kilborn, 'Revival of Chain Gangs Takes a Twist', *New York Times*, 11 March 1997, p. A18; William F. Schulz, 'Cruel and Unusual Punishment', *New York Review of Books*, 24 April 1997, pp. 51–2.

[4] I am mindful of Hugo Bedau's observation that 'along with patriotism, security—national security and prison security—is the last refuge of scoundrels': 'Prisoners' Rights', (1982) I, 1 *Criminal Justice Ethics* (Winter/Spring) 38.

as the need to maintain a secure and untroubled environment. Other reasons are blatantly politico-economic. Budgetary concerns are taxpayer and therefore voter concerns, as is crime, and in the lead-up to an election year American politicians found it useful to talk tough on crime. Although the huge investment in imprisonment is costing the American taxpayer plenty, it is made more palatable for many if prison life cannot be painted in glamorous terms.[5]

Though institutional and politico-economic concerns do much to drive change, they are supported by other, more ideological considerations. Some, such as Stephen West's, are retributive: a sense that proportionality between offence and punishment has been lost where imprisonment seems to lack a suitably reprobative and penitential dimension. Alternatively, it is argued that those who offend forfeit their claims to or become less eligible for the comforts of life, and cannot complain if their conditions are cheerless and hard. Others, however, argue that considerations of deterrence are of central importance: if prisoners find gaol too congenial, their incarcerative experience will fail to inhibit future criminality. And since, for many of the homeless, impoverished, and drug addicted, even the confinement of gaol is likely to provide better conditions than they are used to and can easily expect outside prison, these critics would argue that conditions should be spartan, if not hard.[6]

How hard may hard treatment be? What factors should determine or limit its hardness? In section 1 I review very briefly what I consider to be the major argument for prescribing the hard treatment that constitutes punishment. The standardization of (much of) that hard treatment as imprisonment is briefly recounted in section 2. In section 3 I consider several factors that might be appealed to in limiting the hardness of the hard treatment of imprisonment, claiming in particular that imprisonment must be neither inhumane nor degrading. In section 4 I suggest some positive, restorative directions that should be pursued when imposing hard treatment. Finally, in section 5 I relate the earlier discussion to some incarcerative practices—those concerning space and environment, work and activity, amenities, visitation and access, and opportunities.

I should make it clear at the outset that, because of the scale of the problems involved, I will generally confine myself to custodial sanctions, and to the hardness that may be associated with them—not primarily by virtue of their length, but with reference to the deprivations or additional impositions that may be associated with incarceration. Of course, length of sentence cannot be separated too sharply from the deprivations that are associated with it. In terms of proportion-

---

[5] In 1995, Richard Zimmer, then a New Jersey Representative, introduced what was termed the 'No Frills Act', designed to make a state's eligibility for prison construction money dependent on its commitment to removing weight-lifting equipment, in-cell coffee pots, and inmate access to computers, to ending the showing of R-rated movies, and to ensuring that prison food was no better than that served in the Army. See Mark Curriden, 'Hard Time', 1995, LXXXI *ABA Journal* (July) 73.

[6] In the USA the two are usually distinguished, gaols (jails) being locally run centres of detention/correction for misdemeanants, and prisons being state and federally run structures for felons; but I shall treat them as one here. My concerns apply most critically to prisons, though conditions in many gaols are woefully inadequate. Overcrowding has led to a mixing of the populations.

ality, a short hard sentence may be considered equivalent to a longer sentence without any added hardships. My main concern, however, will be with the conditions under which a prison term is served out rather than with its duration.

1. PUNISHMENT AS HARD TREATMENT

Punishment, it is said, is hard treatment.[7] That is, it involves not merely condemnation, rebuke, or censure, but some substantial imposition on a wrong-doer. Why *hard treatment*, as distinct from condemnation or censure, should be justified, has engaged the attention of philosophers from the very beginning. The classical theories of punishment—deontological and consequentialist—are largely attempts to answer such a question.

Here I do little more than rehearse what I believe to be the strongest considerations in favour of the practice of punishment.[8] Punishment is punishment *for* and, unlike mere penalization, which is a deliberate imposition for some rule infraction, punishment has a distinctively expressive character. It involves a stigmatizing condemnation of the punished. It does so, because the person punished has been judged to be guilty *inter alia* of some *moral wrong-doing*, that is, of violating basic conditions of our human engagement.[9] I leave aside the specific character of the wrong-doing and, for the present, the issue of a punisher's authority to punish.[10] It is sufficient at this point to note that what punishment is *for* is a breach of standards that are believed to be of fundamental significance in our human intercourse.[11]

We might, of course, respond to moral wrong-doing in a number of ways. We can criticize, censure, or rebuke the wrong-doer. And generally that would not be out of place. Were that all we did, however, it would be inadequate. Merely to rebuke or censure the wrong-doer would fail to register the seriousness of what was done. Some *proportionate* response is called for, as a simple matter of fairness or justice. Proportionality is not simply an optional add-on to the censure, but is

---

[7] I associate the phrase with Joel Feinberg, 'The Expressive Function of Punishment' (1968), reprinted in *Doing and Deserving* (Princeton: Princeton University Press, 1970), pp. 95–118.

[8] I have provided a fuller discussion in 'Punishment and Moral Seriousness', (1991) XXV, 3–4 *Israel Law Review* 401–21, and even earlier in *Punishment and Desert* (The Hague: Martinus Nijhoff, 1973).

[9] Here of course I make the controversial assumption that crimes are to be distinguished from mere administrative offences in part because an element of moral wrong-doing is involved. I have tried to say something in favour of this claim in *Punishment and Desert*, (1973), n. 8 above, Ch. 2, and in (1986) V, 1 'Criminally Harming Others', *Criminal Justice Ethics* (Winter/Spring) 3–10 (though see Joel Feinberg's response to the latter in the same issue).

[10] Any full theory of punishment—especially of institutionalized punishment—must address this issue. At this point I am concerned with what justifies the punishing of a person and not with what might justify *my* or *someone else's* being the one to punish the person.

[11] It is, I believe, the pre-eminence of moral considerations in human interaction that gives moral breaches the significance that punishment registers. Nevertheless, it is also my view that not every moral breach is appropriately punished by the State. The State has a limited function and some acts that are deserving of punishment are better left to others or, as some would sometimes put it, to God.

implicit in it. When we censure others for their wrong-doing, we mark them out as worthy of punishment. Where others have been harmed, endangered, or otherwise set back by the moral derelictions of another, some significant deprivation is signalled as appropriate.[12] Not only does the imposition serve to impress on the wrong-doer the character of what s/he has done, it also acknowledges the personhood of the victim and the seriousness of what was done to him. The complaint often heard, that some offenders are given no more than a slap on the wrist by the criminal justice system, registers the intuition that mere censure or disapprobation, detached from some proportionate response, is not enough.[13] *Ceteris paribus*, unless the disgraced person is also deprived, the offence is not given its due.

In saying that some proportionate response is *called for*, as a matter of fairness or justice, I should not be taken to imply that punishment should (all things considered) be inflicted or that punishment is all that we should pursue in our dealings with offenders. Other concerns may sometimes override those of retributive justice and some form of victim-offender reconciliation might also be sought. Nevertheless, in the absence of other considerations, wrong-doing normally provides sufficient reasons for punishment (albeit not legal punishment, for which other conditions may also be necessary).

2. Hard Treatment as Imprisonment

But even if we can grant that the hard treatment that punishment involves can be justified, further questions of hardness must be addressed. Here I want to distinguish two related issues.

There is, first of all, a question about *how much* punishment a wrong-doer should receive. This is what usually engages punishment theorists who have progressed beyond: 'Why punish at all?' As with the prior question, answers to: 'How much?' have retributive/consequentialist disputation as their traditional backdrop. Thus they have focused on issues of proportionality, commensurability, equality, and *lex talionis*, on the one hand, and incapacitation, deterrence, rehabilitation, and the maximization of utility, on the other. As with the prior question, I would answer the latter in retributive terms. The severity of punishment, I would argue, should be proportionate to the wrong-doing that has justified punishment in the first place. Unless it is so answered, at least in part, I believe that the retributive claims made in response to the prior question will be undermined.[14]

---

[12] Punishment is not 'hard-wired' to wrong-doing. The 'ought' of deservedness is 'ought, *ceteris paribus*' not 'ought, all things considered'.

[13] Those who find it difficult to see this connection might compare disapprobation and censure with gratitude. Gratitude may sometimes be shown by expressions such as 'thank you'. But 'thank you' is frequently insufficient as an expression of gratitude. A willingness to do something proportionate for the other is also called for. For the argument in connection with gratitude, see Terrance McConnell, *Gratitude* (Philadelphia: Temple University Press, 1993).

[14] This of course is subject to all sorts of refinements. The notion of proportionality needs to be explicated; the issue of fixing penalty scales has to be addressed; the relevance of prior record must be

A further question concerns *the form* that punishment will take. Although this question too can be approached via an engagement with retributive and consequentialist considerations, it does not do so quite as readily or exclusively. Here we might ask whether imprisonment, fines, community-based sanctions, confiscation, whipping and mutilation, demotions, and exclusions are appropriate ways of punishing or, since imprisonment is to be our focus, we might ask what what deprivations and impositions should be associated with it? Should those who are imprisoned also be required to perform hard labour, have their mail censored, be deprived of cigarettes, conjugal visits, access to the entertainment and news media, and so forth? It is with aspects of this latter question that I shall here be concerned.

(a) The birth of the prison

We need to remember that imprisonment, as a method of punishment as distinct from a method of detention, is relatively modern.[15] That is not to impugn it, though some who have reflected on the inadequacies of the prison system have seen its recency as evidence of its merely pragmatic value and its failure to have deep roots in moral consciousness. Certainly the speed with which imprisonment superseded other traditional forms of legal punishment, and has come to represent a largely unquestioned resource of the criminal justice system,[16] might give us pause and lead us to wonder whether it is not too convenient a device for dealing with the complexities of human failure. In the USA, with its massive problems of urban crime (despite recent declines), imprisonment has reached crisis proportions, and many communities no longer know how to cope with the demand for prison resources.[17]

However, rather than denigrating imprisonment as an overly convenient ('out of sight, out of mind') response to criminality, we can also view it as a more humane alternative to forms of punishment that prevailed until the nineteenth

---

dealt with. Andrew von Hirsch has grappled with some of these questions in *Past or Future Crimes: Deservedness and Dangerousness in the Sentencing of Criminals* (New Brunswick, NJ Rutgers University Press: 1985); *Censure and Sanctions* (Oxford: Clarendon Press, 1993); and 'Desert and Previous Convictions in Sentencing', (1981) LXV *Minnesota Law Review* 591–634.

[15] For a good overview, see Norval Morris and David J. Rothman (eds.), *The Oxford History of the Prison: The Practice of Punishment in Western Society* (New York: Oxford University Press, 1995).

[16] That is putting it too strongly. In parts of Europe there is a strong anti-incarcerative tradition. See, for example, the articles included in the section on 'Alternatives to Punishment' in (1991) XXV, 3–4 *Israel Law Review* (Summer-Autumn) 681–791.

[17] In 1995, there were nearly 1.6 million people in American federal, state, and local prisons, a figure of 600 for every 100,000 people—up from 455/100,000 in 1991 (see 'Prison and Jail Inmates', *Bulletin*, Bureau of Justice Statistics, NCJ-161132 (August, 1996)). The latter figure compared with 311 people in South Africa and 177 in Venezuela, the USA's closest rivals. In the USA, the rate for African-American and Hispanic males was 3,370/100,000, compared to 681/100,000 for black males in South Africa. In 1994, an additional 3.6 million people were under some form of correctional supervision (see 'Correctional Populations in the United States, 1994', *Executive Summary*, Bureau of Justice Statistics, NCJ-161559 (July, 1996)).

century. In his graphic account of 'the birth of the prison', Michel Foucault made much of the way in which the various corporal punishments of the eighteenth century sought to reproduce in the body of the condemned person the heinousness of the crimes s/he had committed. The procession of public torture was a 'penal liturgy' through which the convicted person confessed to, accepted the punishment for, repented of, and represented the crimes for which s/he had been found guilty.[18] The move to imprisonment coincided with and to some extent expressed a humanitarian turn in nineteenth century penology, a belief that reduction of rights rather than infliction of pain represented a more acceptable— 'civilized'—response to wrong-doing. Furthermore, according to Foucault, it represented a dramatic change in the ends of punishment—movement away from a retributive and socially educative focus to one that was consequentialist and individually reformative.[19] The prison, particularly in the view of some of its earlier advocates, was to be disciplinary rather than merely punitive. What had previously been inflicted in public was now to be imposed in private.

Early reformatively-oriented prisons were austere institutions, designed, according to their advocates, to instil in their inmates habits of discipline and virtue. The austerity of prison life freed the prisoner from worldly distractions and enabled him to reflect on his deeds and to respond penitentially to them. But in addition the disciplines of prison life—its routines, religious requirements, and labour—were meant to transform the presumed idleness and social irresponsibility of the prisoner into more constructive social dispositions and behaviour.

Reality, of course, rarely matched theory, and many prisons remained little more than warehouses for the socially unacceptable. In time, there would be more insistent and sometimes effective calls and demands for improved conditions and a questioning of the presumption of the humaneness of prison life.

As Foucault properly recognizes, one of the motivating factors behind the ideology of 'imprisonment as punishment' was its constitution as a humane alternative to the corporal assaults that had until then prevailed. The emerging egalitarianism of the enlightenment tradition acknowledged both the rights and the moral responsibility of the offender, and shifted the locus of punishment from body to soul. The offender was seen as rational, redeemable, and potentially useful, and the State was not to squander its human resources. The deprivation of liberty had penitential and social possibilities that the corporal tradition had too often ignored. Despite some of the capital penal legislation of the late eighteenth and early nineteenth century, only in the more serious of cases did the offender actually forfeit all future claims to human society.

---

[18] Michel Foucault, *Discipline & Punish: The Birth of the Prison* (NY: Vintage, 1977), p. 47.
[19] That change was itself connected with a move towards secularization—a loosening church/State nexus diminished the State's role as executor of God's retributive justice. The State came to have independent ends of its own.

(b) Prison reform

But what should determine the conditions under which the sentence is to be served? The imprisonment that presaged a more humanitarian approach to punishment did not deliver what it promised. Squalid conditions, solitariness or invasive and predatory behaviour, neglect, and abuse characterized many prisons of the eighteenth and early nineteenth centuries, and it was only through the diligent efforts of reformers such as John Howard in England and Elizabeth Fry in the USA that conditions began to improve. Not only were some of the more unsanitary and demoralizing features of prison life ameliorated, but constructive work and training programmes were introduced, prison personnel were gradually professionalized, and various health and legal services provided. Even so, the seclusion of prison life continued—and has continued—to make it possible for inmates to be housed under conditions that are frequently scandalous.

At the same time—at least in the USA, whose prison population is now over one and a half million, and in which illegal overcrowding of gaols and prisons is almost the norm—there are now insistent calls for the removal of many of the benefits that have been slowly exacted from a reluctant system. Imprisonment is expensive, and a crime-weary and tax-averse public has been responsive to calls to cut back on 'prison perks'.

At this point it is not my intention to deal with the specific exigencies of prison life, but to indicate some general considerations that might mediate decisions about the kinds of conditions under which a term of imprisonment is properly served. When I have outlined these, I will then turn to specific features of the prison experience.

3. LIMITING THE HARDNESS OF HARD TREATMENT

I begin with two side-constraints of long standing. Both the English Bill of Rights of 1689 and Eighth Amendment (1789) to the US Constitution eschew punishments that are 'cruel and unusual'.[20] Although these constraints have recently occasioned considerable debate in the USA, much of it has been directed to the question whether capital punishment should be considered cruel and unusual.[21]

---

[20] More recent documents, such as the Universal Declaration of Human Rights (1948) and the European Convention for the Protection of Human Rights and Fundamental Freedoms (1953) outlaw 'cruel, inhuman or degrading' and 'inhuman and degrading' punishment, respectively, and it is the latter that provide the focus for A. Ashworth and E. Player in Ch. 10 of this book, above. I shall later come close to this position by suggesting that the categories of 'inhumane' and 'degrading' best capture the constraints to be placed on punishment/imprisonment. But see n. 47 below.

[21] *Furman* v. *Georgia*, 408 US 239 (1972). See Margaret Jane Radin, 'The Jurisprudence of Death: Evolving Standards for the Cruel and Unusual Punishments Clause', (1978) CXXVI, 5 *University of Pennsylvania Law Review* (May) 989–1064; Hugo Adam Bedau, 'Thinking of the Death Penalty as a Cruel and Unusual Punishment', (1985) XVII *University of California, Davis, Law Review* 873–925.

I shall leave aside the issue of capital punishment's constitutional status. Here I ask the more general questions: What would make punishment, and the conditions of imprisonment in particular, cruel and unusual? And what would make for the unacceptability of such punishment? Although cruelty and unusualness have usually been considered together, and were possibly intended by their constitutional draughtsmen to be interpreted as a complex unity, I believe that somewhat different considerations are suggested by each, and so I shall first discuss them separately.[22]

(a) Cruelty

As its philological origins in the Latin *cruor* (gore, spilled blood) suggest, cruelty has paradigmatically involved 'the wilful inflicting of physical pain on a weaker being in order to cause anguish and fear'.[23] But the focus has now shifted from physical pain to include suffering in general, and remarks no less than blows may be deemed cruel. There is still the vexed question whether the cruelty of acts is a function (subjectively) of the motives, intentions, or state of mind of the cruel agent or (objectively) of the necessity of the suffering or the point of view or experience of or injury to his/her victims,[24] or, perhaps more likely, either one or the other, depending on the circumstances. Even though the central cases of cruelty concern suffering that has been deliberately inflicted, there is some reason to think that both individuals and institutions can operate cruelly from lack of sensitivity no less than from design.[25]

The wrongness of deliberate cruelty is almost foundational. That is, causing

---

[22] There has been a tendency in Eighth Amendment jurisprudence to see the phrase 'cruel and unusual' as something like the phrase 'null and void', a unitary and intensifying designation rather than as a dual disqualification. Thus, in relation to the contribution made by 'unusual', Justice Brennan remarked: 'The question, in any event, is of minor significance; this Court has never attempted to explicate the meaning of the Clause simply by parsing its words' (*Furman* v. *Georgia*, 408 US 238, at 276 n. 20 (1972)). See the discussion in Bedau, 'Thinking of the Death Penalty as a Cruel and Unusual Punishment', (1985), n. 21 above, pp. 880–3. However, Justice Scalia assumed a distinction between them when speaking for the Court in *Harmelin* v. *Michigan*, 111 S. Ct. 2680, 2686–87, 2701 (1991). And in the 1776 Maryland Bill of Rights, 1776 Constitution of North Carolina, and 1780 Massachusetts and 1784 New Hampshire Declarations of Rights, 'cruel' and 'unusual' are disjunctively rather than conjunctively related. For a listing of conjunctive and disjunctive references, see Peter Mathis Spett, 'Confounding the Gradations of Iniquity: An Analysis of Eighth Amendment Jurisprudence in Harmelin v. Michigan', (1992) XXIV, 1 *Columbia Human Rights Law Review* (Winter) 228–9 n. 126. I shall suggest later that different (albeit related) considerations might well be indicated by the two terms.

[23] Judith Shklar, *Ordinary Vices* (Cambridge, MA: Belknap Press of Harvard University Press, 1984), p. 8.

[24] Until recently, American courts expected serious injury to be involved as an objective indicator of cruelty. However, in a fairly recent decision it was held that cruelty could be established in the absence of 'significant' injury, at least as long as the other 'objective' elements were present—i.e. the need for the force, the degree of force in relation to the need, and the perceived threat to the officer at the time. See *Hudson* v. *McMillian*, 112 S.Ct. 995, at 999 (1992). In this case, it was allowed that where the force was applied 'maliciously and sadistically', the charge of cruelty could be sustained.

[25] I will suggest, however, that if we look at the wider category, inhumaneness, of which cruelty is a type, the notion of neglectful suffering is more easily accommodated.

suffering to another is an evil that stands in need of justifying reasons, and, when suffering is inflicted with a view to the hurt that is involved (whether or not pleasure is taken in inflicting it), justifying reasons are disavowed.[26] Infliction of suffering for the sake of proportionate good may be justified, but that is usually because such suffering is seen as part of an organic whole (as in retribution)[27] or as an unfortunate—though presumably necessary—means to some worthwhile end.

In jurisprudential discussion, objective approaches have led to the characterization of *excessive* or *disproportionate* punishments as cruel. Somewhat different ideas tend to be conveyed by each. Excessiveness looks to some end that is being pursued or sought. Disproportionality looks back to the offence for which the suffering is imposed. An excessive punishment will cause more suffering than is necessary to deter, rehabilitate, or achieve whatever other socially acceptable goals are being sought. A disproportionate penalty will be one that is out of keeping with the seriousness of the offence for which it is imposed.[28] So-called draconian penalties are disproportionate. I am inclined to give moral priority to disproportionateness in deciding whether to characterize a punishment as cruel rather than simply unnecessary. That is, a penalty that is more severe than is necessary to rehabilitate will not be cruel if it is not disproportionate to the offence for which it is inflicted, whereas a penalty that is disproportionate to the offence but not more severe than is necessary to rehabilitate or deter might well be considered cruel.[29]

Cruelty to a sentient being is bad enough. Cruelty to a rational sentient being is worse, because it is dehumanizing. As is also the case with coercion, one of the manifest effects of suffering—at least of certain types and degrees of suffering[30]— is to shift what moves us to act from a consideration of the merits of the case to whatever will relieve our situation. Such suffering tends to undermine that which constitutes our human distinctiveness, our capacity for appraisal.[31] Our

[26] The suffering sanctioned by retributive theory is for wrong-doing and intended to express reprobation rather than the desire to cause suffering. Nevertheless, Hugo Bedau seriously considers the possibility of justified cruelty if the stakes are high enough ('Thinking of the Death Penalty as Cruel and Unusual Punishment', (1985), n. 21 above, pp. 886–9).

[27] The idea of an organic whole goes back to Plato (presuming that the *Greater Hippias* is a Platonic dialogue), but is discussed at length by G. E. Moore in *Principia Ethica* (Cambridge University Press, 1903), pp. 27–36.

[28] In the legal discussion, the disproportionality condition can be violated even if the punishment is not particularly onerous. Thus it would violate the Eighth Amendment were a person to be sentenced to just one day in prison for the 'crime' of having a cold (*Robinson* v. *California*, 370 US 660, at 667 (1962)). Thus the legal and moral notions of what constitutes 'cruelty' may diverge.

[29] However, teleologically justified suffering *will* be characterizable as cruel if it is wilfully excessive: the dentist who drills without offering an anaesthetic.

[30] The qualification is important. Suffering may also 'bring us to our senses', a function which may have deep roots in the physiological value that pain has as a warning mechanism.

[31] I do not, of course, want to deny that (cruelly inflicted) suffering may provide a vehicle through which we may emerge ennobled. However it is precisely because suffering threatens our humanity that our ability to rise above it is ennobling. The latter possibility can hardly constitute a justification for inflicting it.

autonomy is expressed in our ability to reflect on options and to make choices based on a consideration of those options. Cruelty involves the infliction of a suffering that threatens to overwhelm our capacity to perform these basic operations. It tends to reduce us to the level of what we may characterize as animality—responsiveness primarily to the promptings of pleasure or pain. Actually, it may be worse than that, since both physical and mental cruelty often exacerbate suffering through an exploitation of the imaginative possibilities of our human consciousness.[32]

The potential for cruelty is endemic to prison society. The imbalance of power, and the environment of disgrace in which prisoners must live, create opportunities—even temptations—for the perpetration of cruelties both physical and mental. The potential for deprivations and requirements that cause suffering is enormous, and if deprivations and impositions are forced upon inmates simply or even primarily because of the suffering they will cause, or if they are disproportionate to the occasioning offence, some measure of cruelty will almost certainly be involved. Even more likely, deprivations that are imposed without regard to the suffering they will cause will likely be seen as cruel or at least inhumane. Unless there has been some conscious and conscientious trading off or balancing of suffering against some other essential and significant end (such as security or the demands of communal living) to be achieved at the cost of the deprivation or imposition, the charge of cruelty will be hard to defeat.

Cruelty in prisons may attach to the *kind* of additional deprivations involved, the *amount* of imprisonment, or the *procedures* that surround the ordering of prison experience. Extended periods of solitary confinement, unless they can be justified for security reasons, may well be cruel, since they deprive the individual of a basic human need, social engagement.[33] A legal provision such as the 'three strikes law' could also be considered cruel by virtue of its disproportionateness.[34] And strip search practices that have little regard for the sensitivities of inmates might also be thought cruel.[35]

The evil of cruelty in punishment should be calculated not only by reference to

---

[32] Physical torture is an almost exclusively human form of cruelty, especially in its more exquisite manifestations. Consider also the cases of a parent being forced to watch the torture of a child or of a prisoner who has a manuscript on which he has been labouring confiscated and burned before his eyes.

[33] In the court cases that have linked prison deprivations with Eighth Amendment interests, the denial of any or adequate medical treatment to prisoners has been seen as cruel, as has indifference to shocking prison conditions. See *Estelle* v. *Gamble*, 429 US 97, at 104 (1976); *Holt* v. *Sarver*, 309 F. Supp. 362, at 372–3 (E. D. Ark. 1970), *affirmed* 442 F.2d 304 (8th Cir. 1971).

[34] See, for example, Mark W. Owens, 'California's Three Strikes Law: Desperate Times Require Desperate Measures—But Will it Work?' (1995) XXVI, 3 *Pacific Law Journal* (April), 881–919. The California initiative was not novel. Similar penalties for recidivism had been previously imposed and upheld—see, for example, the Texas case, *Rummel* v. *Estelle*, 445 US 263 (1980).

[35] See Tracy McMath, 'Do Prison Inmates Retain Any Fourth Amendment Protection from Body Cavity Searches?' (1987) LVI *University of Cincinnati Law Review* 739–55. However, see *Payton* v. *Vaughn*, 798 F.2d 258, at 261–2 (E.D. Pa. 1992), where 'embarrassment' was held not to be sufficient to establish a claim to cruel and unusual treatment. See, further, *Jordan* v. *Gardner*, 986 F.2d 1521, at 1526–7 (9th Cir. 1993), where a cross-gender, clothed body search was held to be both 'unnecessary' for security and 'without penological justification'.

what it is for its victims, but should also have some regard to the effect that cruelty has on those who inflict it. Although some warped personalities will enjoy the infliction of suffering on others, most of those who act cruelly will need to anaesthetize themselves against the suffering they cause. And a society that fails to deal with cruelty will probably also need to develop mechanisms to desensitize itself to suffering. In so doing, it will diminish itself.[36]

(b) Unusualness

It may seem odd to reject punishment simply because it is 'unusual'. After all, what is unusual may be no more than what falls outside some statistical norm, and there is nothing normatively significant in that.[37] In the case of punishment, however, even statistical abnormality may be inherently problematic. For in cases in which impositions are novel, we are likely to lack assurance that what is done will not also constitute an affront to human dignity: 'frequency of use furnishes evidence of wide acceptability, and . . . the very fact of regular use diminishes the insult'.[38] That is not quite right, though it does gesture towards the US Supreme Court's claim that the constitutional proscription of cruel and unusual punishment 'must draw its meaning from the evolving standards of decency that mark the progress of a maturing society'.[39] As it turns out, what are characterized as unusual punishments tend to be not only statistically but also normatively abnormal. They generally distinguish in a way that humiliates. In the ongoing debate, such punishments have included bodily mutilation, branding, and certain forms of corporal punishment, and their effect has been not only to disgrace wrong-doers but also to bring them into contempt.[40]

[36] The jurisprudence of cruelty goes further than I do here. In *Robinson* v. *California*, a punishment was deemed to fail the Eighth Amendment test because it was prescribed for what the court deemed a 'chronic condition' or 'status' rather than some voluntary act (370 US 660, at 665–6 (1962)). Perhaps a kind of disproportionality is involved, though the failure seems more radical than that. Also, in the death penalty cases, punishment has been deemed cruel if the rationale for selecting those on whom it has been imposed is considered arbitrary and capricious. See *Furman* v. *Georgia*, 408 US 238 (1976).

[37] Thus, in *Trop* v. *Dulles*, Chief Justice Warren, speaking for the Court, stated that 'unusual' added nothing to the Eighth Amendment clause besides signifying 'something different from that which is generally done' (356 US 86, at 100–1 n. 32 (1958)).

[38] Laurence H. Tribe, *American Constitutional Law* (Mineola, NY: Foundation Press, 1978), p. 917.

[39] *Trop* v. *Dulles*, 356 US 86, at 101 (1958) (Warren CJ). In *Weems*, the unusualness, as well as the cruelty, of the *cadena temporal*, was a factor. It was noted that the punishment was 'unusual in its character',—that 'it has no fellow in American legislation' and 'comes under the condemnation of the bill of rights, both on account of [its] degree and kind' (*Weems* v. *US*, 217 US 349, at 377 (1910)). However, there is nothing conceptually to prevent the novelty of a punishment from being a peculiarly apt and restorative imposition.

[40] The issue of the 'surgical and chemical castration' of persistent sex offenders has proven more controversial. See William L. Baker, 'Castration of the Male Sex Offender: A Legally Impermissible Alternative', (1984) XXX, 2 *Loyola Law Review* (Spring) 37–399; Pamela K. Hicks, 'Castration of Sexual Offenders: Legal and Ethical Issues', (1993) XIV, 4 *Journal of Legal Medicine* (December) 641–67; Kenneth B. Fromson, 'Beyond an Eye for an Eye: Castration as an Alternative Sentencing

Avishai Margalit has recently argued that a decent society, one to which he believes we should aspire, is characterized by institutions that do not humiliate people.[41] On his account, humiliation has two dimensions—the rejection of a person from the human commonwealth and the loss of basic control. The former provides a sound reason for a person to consider his or her self-respect to be injured, and the latter is the effect of diminished self-respect. It is Margalit's task to show how certain social set-ups that reject the specific forms of life in which people express their humanity may effect such humiliation.

It is clear how a prison system may effect the humiliation of its inmates.[42] Even though prisoners are rightly disgraced by their imprisonment, and are prevented from exercising some of the rights of citizenship, they should still be permitted to retain the respect and dignity that is the due of every human being. Indeed, as Chief Justice Warren noted, 'the basic concept underlying the Eighth Amendment is nothing less than the dignity of man'.[43] A non-humiliating prison system will not reject prisoners from the human commonwealth by treating them as though they have forfeited the right of personhood—and thus may be exposed or presented in ways that would be expected to detract from their self-recognition as responsible and redeemable beings. Nor will it treat prisoners in ways that remove from them those elements of control that are fundamental to their standing as rational and sensitive beings. Such was part of the case against torture; but it could apply equally to punishments that have the effect of transforming a person's capabilities (as in mutilation) or of exposing a person to ongoing contempt (as with branding). We might want to say much the same about the use of chain gangs and certain kinds of prison garb, even though, unlike mutilation and branding, their effects need not be permanent. Chain gangs are often operated in public view, and the chaining together of prisoners, like beasts of burden, is designed to elicit contempt and create a sense of belittlement. Striped prison garb, too, has long associations that 'mark one out' as contemptible and wretched.[44]

Other features of prison life might also be seen as humiliating. In the early case of *Weems* v. *US*, a Philippine statute prescribing the penalty of *cadena temporal* was ruled unconstitutional in the case of an official who had made a false

---

Measure', (1994) XI, 2 *New York Law School Journal of Human Rights* (Spring) 311–37; Daniel L. Icenogle, 'Sentencing Male Sex Offenders to the Use of Biological Treatments: A Constitutional Analysis', (1994) XV, 2 *Journal of Legal Medicine* (June) 279–304.

[41] Avishai Margalit, *The Decent Society*, trans. Naomi Goldblum (Cambridge, MA: Harvard University Press, 1996). Margalit distinguishes this from a civilized society, in which *individual members* do not humiliate one another, and both from a *just* society.

[42] In the late 1960s, Chief Judge Henley spoke of imprisonment within the Arkansas Penitentiary as amounting to 'banishment from civilized society' (*Holt* v. *Sarver*, 309 F. Supp. 362, at 381 (E.D. Ark. 1970), *affirmed*, 442 F.2d 304 (8th Cir. 1971)). I am of course prescinding from the question whether imprisonment itself may involve humiliation. Although I sidestep the question, I do not want to dismiss it. See the concluding section 6 below.

[43] *Trop* v. *Dulles*, 356 U.S. 86, at 100 (1958).

[44] It is not the uniformity of garb as such, but the distinctiveness and associations of certain kinds of garb that is the problem here. Compare the yellow stars that Jews were required to wear in National Socialist Germany.

statement in a public record. Not only had he been sentenced to an inordinately long time in prison (15 years), but also under conditions that were seen as humiliating. The penalty required that he be chained from the wrist to the ankles, do 'hard and painful labor', receive no outside assistance, be under surveillance for life, be disqualified forever from public office, and lose various rights—'of parental authority, guardianship of person or property, participation in the family council, marital authority, the administration of property, . . . to dispose of his own property by acts *inter vivos*', to vote, and to receive retirement pay.[45] Stripped not only of liberty, the official was also stripped of the conditions of self-respect.

I have focused on cruel and unusual punishment because it provides a useful starting point for discussion of the limits to hard treatment. But the category—or categories—of cruel and unusual can be seen as specifying more general constraints that might be placed on hard treatment. Punishment that is cruel is more generally and appropriately characterized as *inhumane*.[46] And punishment that is unusual might be seen more generally as *degrading*. This is much closer to the terminology of contemporary statements of the side-constraints on the conditions of confinement.

(c) Inhumaneness

Generally we treat people inhumanely when we disregard their sensibilities as human beings.[47] More precisely, our inhumaneness is constituted by our failure to have an appropriate concern about the suffering that we cause them. If cruelty most often involves the deliberate infliction of suffering for the sake of the hurt involved, inhumanity toward others may just as often be registered by an indifference to suffering that is being caused. The inhumane may simply lack the empathy that enables them to see how the suffering that they cause to others is experienced by those others.[48]

The inhumane treatment of prisoners may be as much a matter of neglect as of deliberate policy. Overcrowded and vandalized prison facilities, an inadequate low calorie diet, lack of oversight that allows predatory behaviour to flourish,

---

[45] *Weems* v. *US*, 217 US 349, at 364–5 (1910).

[46] A child may be cruel without being inhumane, since its moral sensibilities have not yet been developed. Cruelty may be shown to animals, but inhumaneness is generally shown toward those with human feelings.

[47] It is the focus on sensibilities that distinguishes treatment that is inhumane from that which is inhuman: inhuman treatment is treatment that is not fit for or appropriate to human beings; there is no (explicit) implication about the way in which it affects the sensibilities of those on whom it is imposed. Clearly, though, the two notions are very close.

[48] Michael Davis has attempted to make inhumaneness a function of the *shock* that a particular treatment causes to our sensibilities, rather than the *disregard* for suffering that is shown by those who have caused it. For him no act is intrinsically inhumane, and judgements of inhumaneness will appropriately differ from society to society. This, I believe, confuses the *concept* of inhumaneness with a particular *conception* of inhumaneness. See his 'The Death Penalty, Civilization, and Inhumaneness', (1990) XVI, 2 *Social Theory and Practice* (Summer) 249–51.

unsanitary conditions that go unrectified, and an atmosphere of uncertainty and dread—all contribute to an environment that is properly describable as inhumane.

Humaneness, on the other hand, recognizes individuality and the varied ways in which people may suffer, and seeks to preserve them from suffering that is inappropriate to their situation.[49] Treating people humanely does not mean treating them softly or even subjecting them to conditions that are less than spartan. Hard treatment may be onerous, tiring, difficult, vigorous, austere, and rigorous without being inhumane. The athletics coach and military sergeant may both subject their charges to rigorous activity that aches and fatigues, but it is not thereby inhumane. It might be, of course, if the exercises are not carefully modulated and well suited to the essential ends of such activity—game- or battle-fitness.

The US Supreme Court debate is notable for the reluctance that the justices have shown to involve themselves in prison conditions. Historically, the Court took the view that it was not part of its task to supervise prison conditions. In part this reflected a belief in the separation of powers, the Courts' lack of expertise, and a policy of federalism.[50] But by the 1970s this had changed, and a range of prison conditions had been brought within the ambit of the Eighth and other Amendments.[51] However, it did not take too long for an increasingly conservative Court to rein in its involvement with the conditions of incarceration. A phrase used in *Estelle*—'deliberate indifference'—became the precondition for establishing an Eighth Amendment case where inhumane or otherwise degrading conditions were experienced by prisoners.[52] The inhumaneness of the conditions was not itself sufficient.[53]

---

[49] This might be a reason for concessions—particularly in regard to prison conditions—for those who are sickly or very old. See Nancy Neveloff Dubler, 'Depriving Prisoners of Medical Care: A "Cruel and Unusual" Punishment', (1979) *Hastings Center Report* (October) 7–10; Cristina J. Perierra, 'Do the Crime, Do the Time: Should Elderly Criminals Receive Proportionate Sentences?' (1995) XIX, 2 *Nova Law Review* (Winter) 793–819.

[50] See Note, 'Beyond the Ken of the Courts: A Critique of Judicial Refusal to Review the Complaints of Convicts', (1963) LXXII, 3 *Yale Law Journal* (January) 506–58. The courts took the view that the intention of the Eighth Amendment was to exclude certain kinds of penalties—torture, crucifixion, burial alive, burning at the stake, boiling in oil, live disembowelment, public dissection, and so on. See *Wilkerson* v. *Utah*, 99 US 130, at 136 (1879); *In re Kemmler*, 136 US 436, at 446–7 (1890). Once the Eighth Amendment was applied to the states during the years of the Warren Court, it was probably only a matter of time before it would be directed to prison conditions.

[51] See Michael S. Feldberg, Comment, 'Confronting the Conditions of Confinement: An Expanded Role for Courts in Prison Reform', (1977) XII, 2 *Harvard Civil Rights—Civil Liberties Law Review* (Spring) 367–404.

[52] *Estelle* v. *Gamble*, 429 US 97, at 105–6 (1976). An attempt to unpack the phrase 'deliberate indifference' was made in *Farmer* v. *Brennan*, 114 S. Ct. 1970 (1994), where Justice Souter, writing for the Court, interpreted it in the familiar criminal law terms of subjective recklessness (*ibid*, at 1979–80). The use of this subjective standard is criticized in Melvin Gutterman, 'The Contours of Eighth Amendment Prison Jurisprudence: Conditions of Confinement', (1995) XLVIII *SMU Law Review* 395–9.

[53] In cases in which actions are taken to restore order, a stronger subjective standard has been applied—whether, in causing suffering, prison officials acted 'maliciously and sadistically for the purpose of causing harm' (*Whitely* v. *Albers*, 475 US 312, at 321 (1986), quoting *Johnson* v. *Glick*, 481

(d) Degradingness

To degrade another is to detract from the other's dignity as a human being. Just as pornography is often said to degrade women by characterizing them in ways that detract from their rationality and autonomy, representationally reducing them to the status of sexual playthings,[54] what is sometimes done to prisoners is also said to be degrading insofar as it treats them as and reduces them to less than rational, autonomous beings. When the degradation of prisoners occurs, however, it is not simply representational, but actual. Prisoners who are degraded have been portrayed or forced to act in ways that are demeaning of their status as humans. What Kant demanded of capital punishment might be demanded of punishment generally, namely, that it be 'kept entirely free from any maltreatment that would make an abomination of the humanity residing in the person suffering it'.[55]

Although the notion of a universal human dignity probably has its origins in Stoic and Judaeo-Christian egalitarianism, in post-Enlightenment thought it has come to be ascribed to people in virtue of their capacities as rational beings. The capacity to frame for oneself the choices one makes, the paths one treads, and the goals one pursues is the foundation for human dignity. As well as something that one possesses as a result of one's standing as a human being, dignity may also be given behavioural expression as a kind of manifest bearing. Those who speak of 'dying with dignity' or of 'carrying oneself with dignity' have in mind not simply a standing but a manifest control over the terms of one's life (or death). Margalit speaks of such dignity as 'the external aspect of self-respect'.[56]

On the account of dignity just given, imprisonment may seem to be inherently undignified. For the choices of a prisoner are severely constrained, and prisoners manifestly lack control over the terms of their lives. But though I believe that the conditions of a person's confinement may well be undignifying, I doubt whether imprisonment as such can be seen in that way. The person who has committed a crime has chosen to risk the consequences of law-breaking, and thus the deprivation of some liberty. Moreover, though choices within a prison environment are constrained, they need not be so constrained that the prisoners are deprived of the kinds of choices that manifest their human standing and

---

F.2d 1028, at 1033 (2nd Cir.), *cert. denied*, 414 US 1033 (1973)). As noted above (n. 24 above), this latter standard has now been extended to other interpersonal encounters between prison officers and inmates. In *Hudson* v. *McMillian*, Justice Sandra Day O'Connor wrote that 'to deny, as the dissent does, the difference between punching a prisoner in the face and serving him unappetizing food is to ignore the "concepts of dignity, civilized standards, humanity, and decency" that animate the Eighth Amendment' (112 S. Ct. 995, at 1000 (1992)).

[54] I here prescind from a consideration of the accuracy of this claim. For critical discussion, see Alan Soble, 'Pornography: Defamation and the Endorsement of Degradation', (1985) XI, 1 *Social Theory and Practice* (Spring) 61–87.

[55] Kant, *The Metaphysical Elements of Justice* (1797), trans. John Ladd (Indianapolis: Bobbs-Merrill, 1965), p. 102.

[56] *The Decent Society* (1996), n. 41 above, p. 51.

self-respect. We can, indeed, distinguish prison conditions and demands that undermine dignity from those that do not. A prisoner who is expected to get up at a certain hour each morning is not deprived of dignity, whereas a prisoner who is expected to forgo the expression of his political opinions or religious observances in exchange for basic needs (for example, sanitary conditions or association with others) is being expected to sacrifice his dignity.

As part of their dignity, prisoners retain their human rights, albeit in a somewhat circumscribed form. They should be free to worship should they choose, they should be free to express their opinions on various matters, they should be free to have access to the courts, and so on. Their human rights do not evaporate on conviction—they are not 'forfeited'—though to a degree their exercise may be constrained.

A person who acts with dignity is one who possesses self-respect. The servile lack self-respect. Servility is undignified. Even though the servile may possess dignity by virtue of their status, they lack the dignity of manifest control over the way in which they deal with their circumstances. They deny in themselves the status that others should accord them. We acknowledge the dignity of others by according them respect. That is, we acknowledge them as centres of sensibility and rationality, with claims to autonomy that are to be recognized. When we treat others as ends and not merely as means to ends of our own, we show respect for them. When we avoid interfering with their non-invasive choices we show respect for them.

With the degradation of others, there often goes not only disrespect but also, on the part of those degraded, a lack of self-respect. The relation is causal rather than conceptual. To treat others as though they lack claims to our respect, to treat them as tools or playthings, may lead them to have a diminished sense of their own worth, dignity, and rights.

In distinguishing inhumaneness and degradingness as two general constraints on hard treatment, I have not wanted to suggest that they are unrelated. Treatment that is inhumane tends to be degrading, and that which degrades is often inhumane.

4. POSITIVE DIRECTIONS

If hard treatment ought to be bounded on the one side by negative constraints such as inhumaneness and degradingness, it ought also to be shaped on the other side by certain positive ends. Imprisonment is not just proportionate hard treatment, to be imposed without any consideration of what it may and ought to be seeking to accomplish.

We can appreciate the forward-looking dimension of punishment by recognizing that of any proposed punishment it is legitimate to ask: 'Who are *you* to punish?' For even if punishment is deserved and, moreover, ought to be inflicted, it does not follow that just anyone may inflict it. Some standing or authority to

punish needs to be established and, as with most authority, the authority to punish is partially justified in terms of ends that it is set up to achieve.[57]

In the case of imprisonment, we are concerned with *legal* punishment, with
those punishments that are mandated by the State. And thus we might reasonably
ask: What business does the State have in claiming for itself the authority to punish? More particularly, what business does the State have in employing *imprisonment* as a form of punishment? These are large questions, too large to be dealt
with at any length here, but they indicate a context within which questions about
the positive framing of hard treatment need to be discussed.

Put crudely, if the purposes of State power—and therefore the boundaries of
State authority—are essentially negative, if the State's mandate stretches no further than the protection of Lockean rights, then the positive function of punitive
hard treatment will be limited to just retaliation against those who have breached
those rights. Imprisonment as a particular form of hard treatment might have
additional preventive value in its incapacitation and deterrence of those who
have so offended. But if, on the other hand, State power is construed in more per-
fectionist terms, as a means through which a thick conception of the good is realized, then punitive hard treatment will have much more moralistic overtones.
The aim of imprisonment will be to educate, reform, and civilize. An acceptable
understanding probably lies somewhere between these extremes. A liberal State
will seek to sustain a plurality of goods by fostering a communally sensitive
autonomy in which individuality may flourish. Imprisonment will be individualized, and will attempt to establish or reinforce in the anti-social an appreciation
of the value of constraints in social life and the discipline and knowledge necessary to benefit from and contribute to it.[58]

This is not the place to argue for a particular role for State power. Were I to do
so, however, I would wish to defend a conception of State authority that func-
tioned to facilitate personal growth in a context of equal opportunity. In different societies this would manifest itself in different ways. In industrialized, and
primarily capitalist societies, it would be the function of the State not only to
encourage the development of individual enterprise, but to encourage it in such a
way that the gap between the successful and others did not become so great that
relations between the two became unconscionably exploitative, manipulative, or
oppressive.

It does not require too hard a look at the current prison population to see that
a vastly disproportionate number of prisoners come from the disadvantaged

---

[57] In this way, I seek to accommodate the consequentialist dimension of punishment. Although
(*pace* von Hirsch, *Censure and Sanctions*, (1993), n. 14 above, p. 12) I believe that retributive considerations are themselves sufficient to justify the hard treatment that is punishment, I claim that justifying the *authority* to impose that punishment may require recourse to consequentialist
considerations. See also *Desert and Punishment*, Ch. 4; 'Punishment and Moral Seriousness' (1991),
n. 8 above, Sect. VIII.

[58] cf.: 'Having chosen to use imprisonment as a form of punishment, a state must ensure that the
conditions of its prisons comport with the "contemporary standards of decency" required by the
Eighth Amendment' (*Wilson* v. *Seiter*, 501 US 294, at 311 (1991) (White J concurring)).

social and economic strata of society. Of course, various explanations for this are possible. Some will focus exclusively on individual deficiencies, others on social handicap. Probably neither is exclusively correct. We are neither independent of our environments nor mere expressions of them. A just social order will be concerned to moderate social disadvantage in ways that diminish the pressure exerted by an unfavourable background. Imprisonment, insofar as it is seen as an appropriate penalty for those who are convicted of crimes, ought to include among its initiatives programmes and services that will assist the incarcerated to live in a more social and personally productive manner. Even inmates who are never to be released might learn, from within the confines of their existence, to make something positively valuable of themselves, even to the extent of making a social contribution.[59]

5. Prison Practice

The foregoing discussion has of necessity been very general, and I will now attempt to indicate how the various factors I have been discussing might bear on some prison conditions.

Whatever else imprisonment involves, it involves a deprivation of 'liberty'. The liberty of which one is deprived is first and foremost freedom of movement. The prisoner is confined to a cell, cell block, or correctional facility for a relatively determinate period of time. But that is not all, for being imprisoned is not like being under house arrest. Prisons are institutions, and total institutions at that. Not only is freedom of movement controlled, but so too are many of the conditions of existence. What is available by way of amenities, what is permitted by way of daily routines, and what access to the larger social world is allowed, is under the control and to some extent subject to the discretion of prison authorities. Each of these dimensions of prison life may be scrutinized by reference to the considerations advanced in sections 3 and 4.[60]

---

[59] Though the incarcerated are denied the ability to move freely within the larger society, they have not thereby been cast out of the human commonwealth; nor need they be denied access to or intercourse with that larger society. There is much to be said for using prison time as an opportunity to create more productive bonds with society, whether this be through artistic and/or literary activity, or through socially useful commercial enterprises. Tragically, support for the latter is often the first thing to go when budgets get tight. It is as though hard time cannot also be productive time.

[60] In the USA, when the courts began intervening in state prisons they sought not only to remove conditions that were deemed cruel and unusual (or in other ways violative of constitutional protections), but also to impose certain minimum positive conditions that would ensure appropriate living conditions and provide particular educational, vocational, and recreational opportunities. For an early but detailed example, see *Pugh* v. *Locke*, 406 F. Supp. 318, at 332–4 (M.D. Ala 1976), *affirmed sub nom. Newman* v. *Alabama*, 559 F.2d 283 (5th Cir. 1977), *certiorari granted in part and reviewed in part sub nom. Alabama* v. *Pugh*, 438 US 781 (1978), *certiorari denied*, 438 US 915 (1978). For an informative review, see Ira P. Robbins and Michael B. Buser, 'Punitive Conditions of Prison Confinement: An Analysis of Pugh v. Locke and Federal Court Supervision of State Penal Administration Under the Eighth Amendment', (1977) XXIX *Stanford Law Review* 893–930 .

(a) Space and environment

Prison life is literally confined. Although—depending on the inmate's offence and demeanour—a prisoner may be allowed to leave his/her cell for a limited period each day, much of his/her life will be spent in a cell equipped with basic necessities—bed, toilet, wash basin, and maybe a few other amenities. But a cell may be too small, too exposed, too hazardous, and too uncomfortable to be humane. Although punishment properly justifies the (temporary) loss of civil rights, one does not thereby forfeit one's humanity, and so there ought to be sufficient space to allow certain basic activities to take place—standing up, walking round, sitting, lying down—and the cell environment should allow for at least a modicum of privacy (compatible with the need for security) and well-being.[61]

In recent times there has been a good deal of controversy over prison smoking policies. As those in the wider society have begun insisting upon smoke-free environments, it has been contended that uncontrolled smoking in prisons should be seen not only as (inescapably) unpleasant for some inmates, but also as unhealthy. It has even been successfully argued that the unwilling exposure to cigarette smoke constitutes cruel and unusual punishment.[62]

Another aggravation of the prison environment, though less seriously taken, is the level of noise that is permitted. The need for security encourages the development of prison space that not only permits the passage of noise from one area to another but, because of the materials used in its construction, ensures that a great deal of noise will be created. Should prisoners be subjected to a noise level that

---

[61] In *Rhodes* v. *Chapman*, the issue of double celling was considered. The Court took the view, expressed by Justice Powell, that there was no constitutional mandate for 'comfortable prisons', and, given other facts about the prison in question, held that double celling *per se* did not contravene the requirements of the Eighth Amendment (452 US 337, at 349 (1981)). However, Justice Brennan, in a dissenting opinion in which he argued that courts should examine the 'totality of conditions', recognizing their 'cumulative impact', stated that 'The court must examine the effect upon inmates of the condition of the physical plant (lighting, heat, plumbing, ventilation, living space, noise levels, recreation space); sanitation (control of vermin and insects, food preparation, medical facilities, lavatories and showers, clean places for eating, sleeping, and working); safety (protection from violent, deranged, or diseased inmates, fire protection, emergency evacuation); inmate needs and services (clothing, nutrition, bedding, medical, dental, and mental health care, visitation time, exercise and recreation, educational and rehabilitative programming); and staffing (trained and adequate guards and other staff, avoidance of placing inmates in positions of authority over other inmates)' (*ibid*, at 363). And Justice Marshall, also in dissent, noted that most of the prisoners were serving lengthy sentences and that double celling had a debilitating effect on prisoners (*ibid*, at 370). A decade later in *Wilson* v. *Seiter*, Justice Scalia, writing for the majority, argued that claims of a cumulative effect could be sustained only when the conditions 'have a mutually reinforcing effect . . . for example, a low cell temperature at night combined with a failure to issue blankets' (501 US 294, at 304 (1991)).

[62] In *Helling* v. *McKinney*, 113 S.Ct. 2475 (1993). See Lisa Gizzi, 'Smoking in the Cell Block: Cruel and Unusual Punishment?' (1994) XLIII, 3 *American University Law Review* (Spring) 1091–134; Lana H. Schwartzman, 'Constitutional Law—Eighth Amendment—Involuntary Exposure to Second-hand Smoke in Prison Supports a Valid Cruel and Unusual Punishment Claim if the Risk to One's Health is Unreasonable and Prison Officials are Indifferent to that Risk', (1994) XXV, 1 *Seton Hall Law Review* (Winter) 314–52. There is, however, some evidence of increased violence (from frustration) as prison environments change into non-smoking ones. See Matthew C. Leone, Patrick T. Kinkade, and Mark Covington, 'To Smoke or Not to Smoke: The Experience of a Nevada Jail', (1996) *American Jails* (January/February) 46–52.

most people on the outside would find intolerable? Or is there some reason to consider the noise level of many prisons intolerable, and in need of some moderation? Why should noise that would probably justify a complaint in an apartment house be treated with indifference in a prison setting?

Privacy and security will always be in tension within the prison setting. The value of privacy lies in its recognition of moral space, the need for people to define the terms of their self-presentation. But the recognition of privacy also creates opportunities for activities that will compromise prison security. It is necessary that invasions of inmate privacy be restricted to those for which a security justification can be *convincingly* provided, and that they be implemented in a manner that does not unnecessarily expose inmates to cruel or demeaning treatment. Strip (or even clothed) searches, a staple of prison life, should be conducted with the same constraint, professionalism, and detachment as a gynaecological or medical examination.[63]

One of the most serious problems currently confronting penal institutions in the USA and elsewhere is that of overcrowding. Although there exist (on paper) strict legal requirements regarding space allocations for each prisoner, a lack of coordination between the court and prison system, political intransigence, and reluctance to spend sufficient additional public monies on prison facilities (or alternatives thereto), have led to overcrowding in at least 50 per cent of American prisons. In some cases the overcrowding has reached crisis proportions, and along with this there have come a set of additional problems—severe discontent, an increase in prisoner-on-prisoner abuses, and the drying-up of already inadequate resources for vocational and rehabilitative programmes.

Because prisons are supported by public monies, it is only reasonable that citizens have some say in the way those monies are spent. However, a public that is supportive of increased use of imprisonment and unwilling to pay for the expansion of facilities to carry out its will must face a choice. There is a set of minimum conditions that must be met if prisons are not to be inhumane institutions, and there are facilities that must be provided if positive ends, such as rehabilitation and social reintegration, are to be pursued. Incapacitation and even deterrence are not enough, for the requirement of proportionality will not permit indeterminate or draconian penalties.

If the tax-paying public is not willing to support institutions of punishment that conform to these minima, then it should have to bear the consequences. Offenders should be released and not be cooped up under crowded, inhumane, and degrading conditions. A community makes rules, rules intended to preserve

---

[63] See *Jordan* v. *Gardner*, 986 F.2d 1521 (9th Cir. 1993); also David J. Stollman, 'Female Prisoners' Rights to be Free from Random, Cross-Gender Clothed Body Searches', (1994) LXII, 6 *Fordham Law Review* (April) 1877–1910. Strip and clothed body searches are justified by appeals to security and safety—the safety not only of prison officers but also of other prisoners, who might be assailed with contraband transported via body cavities. It is argued that such intimate searches are necessary, since inmates 'use our cultural sensitivity to touching each other in certain areas as a shield for their misconduct' (*Jordan*, at 1558 (Trott J dissenting)). The use of cross-gender searches is justified as a way of preserving the element of surprise (*ibid*, at 1554).

a certain quality of public and private life, and it should ensure that the rules are implemented in ways that conform to the moral norms that underlie them. It must therefore ensure that those for whom imprisonment is determined are not cast out of the human community as though they no longer qualify as beneficiaries of those norms.[64]

(b) Work and activity

Boredom is the psychic equivalent of lack of space. If it is inhumane to deny people adequate opportunities to exercise their bodies, it is degrading to deny them mental stimuli. Humans realize themselves through activity, and though that activity need not be work, productive work activity represents one of the major ways in which we break the bonds of solipsistic subjectivity and are able to influence the world beyond us. The enforced idleness of prison warehousing saps energy and breaks the spirit and does little to assist the reintegration of inmates into the wider community. Although some prisoners might expect to spend the rest of their days behind bars, most will be able to anticipate release, and if their prison experience does little to assist (or even impedes) their return to the wider community, recidivism should come as no surprise.[65]

Although some kinds of work and work conditions can themselves be dehumanizing, there is no reason why prison work should be of this kind. Work that is designed to serve the needs of the prison population itself—the provisions of food, maintenance, cleaning, and agricultural services—is inherently meaningful, and it is reasonable to expect that prisoners should contribute to the conditions of their well-being. Nor should there be any problem about the expectation that prisoners engage in other kinds of productive labour. Even though work assignments may need some individualization and, given the backgrounds of much of the prison population, training may also need to be provided, there is no reason not to require that those prisoners who can should work. Although some kinds of work will be inherently challenging and satisfying, some of the satisfaction of productive work will come from its recognition and valuing by others. Thus prisoners should not be expected to work without remuneration, or be treated as cheap or slave labour. Nevertheless, their remuneration might be discounted to take some account of the costs associated with their 'board and lodging'.[66]

---

[64] As the court in *Wolff* noted, 'there is no iron curtain drawn between the Constitution and the prisons of this country' (*Wolff* v. *McDonnell*, 418 US 539, at 555–6 (1974)).

[65] Even those who are imprisoned for life without the expectation of parole should be provided with meaningful work. To deny them that just because they will not be released back into the wider society, is to cast them out of the human commonwealth in Margalit's sense.

[66] There is a problem about what to do with the prisoner who refuses to work. Some prisons now expect their inmates to pay not only for 'board and lodging' but also for medical care. If the prisoner works, this may be deducted from their remuneration. If the prisoner refuses to work, then there may be an argument for garnisheeing future earnings. See Wesley P. Shields, 'Prisoner Health Care: Is it Proper to Charge Inmates for Health Services?' (1995) XXXII, 1 *Houston Law Review* (Summer) 271–302; Melody Petersen, 'Charging Inmates for Care Raises Issue of Risk to Their Health', *New York Times*, 23 November 1996, pp. B1, 6.

Although much prison work is likely to take the form of 'factory work', there is nothing inherently demeaning about hard labour. It can be made demeaning, as can all labour, when it is detached from significant social purposes, or when it is organized in the form of a chain gang (intended in part to humiliate). But strenuous labour can also constitute a valuable discipline. The same might also be said—though perhaps with reservations—about boot camps. Run along military lines, the latter subject their participants to intense discipline and physical training. As in the case of military training, they are designed to promote personal and interactive responsibility, increase self-confidence, and improve decision-making skills. As far as the success of such camps in combating recidivism goes, the evidence is mixed, and there is as well the ever-present danger that the power relationships involved will be inappropriately exploited.[67]

Apart from internal work assignments, most prisons do little to provide training and productive work activity. The rapid and huge expansion of the prison population in the USA, coupled with the trimming of prison budgets, has left few programmes in place.[68]

(c) Amenities

What kinds of creaturely comforts may prisoners expect to have? Should they expect colour TVs, cable access, videoplayers, movies of their choice, coffee-makers, libraries, and so on? Conservative critics of imprisonment often sneeringly refer to prisons as 'country clubs' (albeit ones that they are not in any hurry to join). To the extent that their complaints have had any substance, instances of excess are likely to be isolated (and it is sometimes forgotten that many of the amenities possessed by individual prisoners have been paid for out of their own pockets). Most prisons are poorly provided for, given their large inmate populations, and the weight of the argument should probably be for more amenities rather than fewer.

There are surely some basic amenities to which prisoners should have access—such as disease-free beds, a place to write, sanitary toilet and washing facilities, and access to current information about the world outside. And there is certainly an argument, given that many prisoners will be engaged in legal activity concerning their cases, for giving them reasonable access to essential legal materials.[69]

Among the service amenities to which prisoners should have access are medical and psychiatric care. In some places, attempts have been made to charge

---

[67] See Dale Sechrest, 'Prison "Boot Camps" Do Not Measure Up', (1989) LIII *Federal Probation* 15–20; Doris Layton Mackenzie, 'Boot Camp Prisons: Components, Evaluations, and Empirical Issues', (1990) LIV *Federal Probation* 44–52.

[68] Educational programmes must often be paid for by prisoners, something that they can usually ill afford to do.

[69] The latter has been the subject of a recent U.S. Supreme Court decision, *Lewis* v. *Casey*, U.S. Lexis 4220; 64 U.S.L.W. 4587 (1996), in which access has been limited.

prisoners for such amenities.[70] The purpose of this has been to reduce what is taken to be an abuse of such provisions: prisoners have sought medical assistance for frivolous reasons—or at least as a strategy for getting temporary relief from the confines of a cell. In principle, this may not be objectionable, though any implementation should take into account the prisoner's resources, as well as other prison conditions (lest prisoners need to use whatever resources they have to relieve other inadequacies in their prison environment).[71]

For some prisoners, the amenities of prison will be better than what they are used to. But this is no argument for not making such amenities available to them. It may mean only that what they are used to is not humanly tolerable.

Although we might reasonably expect prison life to be spartan, it should also provide amenities that enable inmates to develop a richer appreciation of the world in which they are expected to live and to which, in time, most of them will return. Given that there is a significant connection between indigence, social class, and criminal conviction, a prison regime should, despite its hardships, provide incentives and opportunities for people to surmount the obstacles of their situations. If they leave prison reduced in their capacity to value what is available to them in the outside world, their prison experience will have deprived them of goods to which they had a basic claim.

(d) Visitation and access

Among the most dramatic effects of imprisonment is severance—to a significant degree, at least—from valued social contacts. Inmates are generally permitted controlled and limited weekly visits, visits that may be frustrating and infrequent because of distance or bureaucratic routines. Their mail is often censored, and their ability to have phone access to others is constrained by limited phone availability.

For some of these restrictions security concerns will be cited. Yet such constraints can be devastating, because inmates' identities are often strongly bound up with those social involvements.[72] What is more, their capacity to stay out of trouble after spending time in prison is likely to be markedly affected by their capacity to sustain and benefit from such relationships.

To this we must add the impact of imprisonment on the other parties in such relationships. If the person who is imprisoned was significantly responsible for family income or family stability, incarceration will place great strains on those who remain outside. Although this may not count decisively against

---

[70] See Wesley P. Shields, Comment 'Prisoner Health Care: Is it Proper to Charge Inmates for Health Services?' (1995) XXXII *Houston Law Review* 271–302.

[71] If, for example, the prison diet is very low in calories, not only may this increase the likelihood of medical problems, but prisoners may seek to use their resources for purchases at the commisary.

[72] It is surely one of the great objections to solitary confinement, except as protection, that it isolates the individual from social contact and thus from one of the central sources of our human flourishing.

imprisonment, it may—especially in view of the need for future social reintegration—provide a reason for providing counselling services and for making access relatively easy and productive.

In responding to these concerns, we might ask whether private conjugal visits should be allowed and other intimate relationships be permitted to develop? One's initial response is affirmative: the sins of one should not (as far as possible) be visited upon innocent others. Every effort should be made to maintain those significant relationships that serve not only to sustain the inmate during his or her prison term, but also to provide a meaningful structure for re-establishing a life after the sentence has been served. Recidivism is not in the public interest.

But although these are strong reasons for trying to accommodate an ongoing conjugality, and also a reason for permitting someone who is incarcerated to marry someone outside the prison environment,[73] there are significant though not overriding security concerns that need to be addressed. What is passed between lovers in such situations may not be limited to bodily fluids.[74] Some balancing of risks and benefits needs to be undertaken. Furthermore, the question of pregnancy needs to be addressed, whether it is the woman who is imprisoned or the man. In the case of long-term imprisonment, does the State condone something which is fundamentally unfair to any child, should conception take place? If the man is imprisoned, does the State have some special responsibility for any child who is conceived in such circumstances?

Along with support for ongoing relationships, there is also an argument for establishing mechanisms that will enable victim-offender reconciliation to take place. Where such reconciliation can be achieved, non-recidivist attitudes and dispositions are also likely to be nurtured.[75]

(e) Opportunities

Although offenders are to be sentenced in a manner that is proportionate to their offence, most will eventually be released and will be expected to resume a place in the wider society. Imprisonment can increase the difficulties of the latter. Inmates are taken out of the everyday world, and their ability to negotiate its persistent and sometimes considerable demands may well be diminished by their lack of unregimented contact. If a person has been in prison for any significant

---

[73] Donatella Lorch, 'Bride Wore White, Groom Hopes for Parole: Prison Marriages Are on the Increase, Despite Daunting Rates of Failure', *New York Times*, 5 September 1996, B1, 7.

[74] A further problem is posed if the imprisoned party is HIV positive.

[75] Defenders of 'restorative justice' frequently argue that the existing 'punishment paradigm' attends to the violation of social norms, but overlooks the violation suffered by the individual victim of crime. Although the 'restorative paradigm' that is advanced is often seen as an alternative and essentially competing approach to crime management, I am here treating them as complementary. See, e.g., John Braithwaite, *Crime, Shame and Reintegration* (Cambridge University Press, 1989); H. Messmer and H.-U. Otto (eds.), *Restorative Justice on Trial: Pitfalls and Potentials of Victim-Offender Mediation—International Research Perspectives* (Netherlands: Kluwer, 1992).

period of time, s/he is likely to find social expectations difficult to fulfil. Added to this is likely to be the stigma of incarceration.

It is important, therefore, that prisons seek to address these matters, especially if we acknowledge that the State's authority to punish derives in part from the overall value that its punishment will have in maintaining a just and peaceable society. Recidivism is not just a failure of those who lapse again into crime; it also represents some kind of failure for the criminal justice system.

As mentioned earlier, a significant proportion of those who are incarcerated also lack knowledge and skills needed for productive employment; but this extends also to skills necessary for satisfactory social negotiation. And therefore we should expect that prisons will make efforts to provide for both the technical and social skilling of those who are as yet ill-equipped to take a productive place in the wider society. Unfortunately, in economically straitened times, it is just these progammes that are likely to be cut.

6. CONCLUSION

In the foregoing discussion I have offered a structure for assessing the appropriate hardness of hard treatment. In so doing, I have sought to extend penal theory beyond the classic debates between retributivism and consequentialism, and have endeavoured to provide a set of considerations that will operate much closer to the interface of theory and practice. In suggesting that imprisonment needs, on the one hand, to avoid practices that are inhumane and degrading and, on the other hand, to foster social goals that fall within the legitimate ambit of the State, I have attempted to provide a test for present practice. My strong impression is that current prison environments, particularly in the USA, commonly fail the test I have provided.

We stand, therefore, at a moral crossroads. We incarcerate those who disregard the norms that should govern our social intercourse, but then treat them in ways that compromise the human regard to which they are entitled. Some would want to argue that this is an inevitable accompaniment of imprisonment,[76] and that alternative ways of dealing with the perpetrators of criminality need to be found. With this I am in partial agreement: some of the problems we currently face are direct products of the huge numbers of those under intensive supervision. The resources being used to build and resource prisons might well be used to sponsor other initiatives that promise lower recidivism, especially on the part of those whose offences might well reflect social conditions and opportunities more than they do a predatory disposition. The Millian encouragement to engage in and foster 'experiments in living' might well be applied to our responses to those who have violated social norms and with whom, therefore, we must now deal.

[76] See, for example, Anthony O'Hear, 'Imprisonment', in A. Phillips Griffiths (ed.), *Philosophy and Practice* (1985) (Royal Institute of Philosophy Lecture Series, No. 18), pp. 203–20.

I am, of course, too late—myriad alternatives are being tried, from tent prisons in the desert, to boot camps, to family conferences. Even so, there seems to be increasing pressure on the existing prison system, and as a society we countenance institutional life that violates the basic standards to which we appeal in justifying imprisonment. Perhaps our paralysis reflects the unwillingness and political inability to deal with deeper social problems that find their expression in criminality. For that there is no easy solution.

Index